*To Sister Joan Gluth SSND
a great colleague during my
journey at NDP!*

I Never Really Left

Journey of a Priest, Missionary, and Lay Teacher Through 50 Years of Vatican II

Baltimore / May 2012

JOZEF J. GOETHALS

Otter Bay Books
BALTIMORE, MD 2012

*Cover photo: Saint Peters Basilica, Rome,
at the Opening of Vatican II (by the author)*

Copyright © 2012 by
Jozef J. Goethals
All rights reserved.

Permission to reproduce in any form
must be secured from the author.

Please direct all correspondence and book orders to:
Jozef J. Goethals
318 Rossiter Ave.
Baltimore, MD 21212

Library of Congress Control Number 2012935418
ISBN 978-0-9851566-0-2

Published for the author by
Otter Bay Books, LLC
3507 Newland Road
Baltimore, MD 21218-2513

www.otter-bay-books.com

Printed in the United States of America

This book is dedicated
To my parents August and Elza Goethals,
to *Felicitas,* my soul mate and inspiration,
and to my second family for 40 years:
Paul and Vicky(+) Braekmans
Andre and Bernice, Marc and Tracy Debels
Rene and Chris, Firmin and Yara Debrabander
Frank and Terri(+) Denys
Joseph(+) and Stephanie Hemelings
Hubert and Gabrielle Vereecke

Other books by the author

A Forgotten Family. The Flemish Roots of General George Washington Goethals(1858-1928)"Builder of the Panama Canal", Baltimore, MD: Gateway Press Inc. 2004.

Goethals-Tavernier-Vanmaele. The Ancestors of August Goethals (Torhout 1901-1978) and Elza Tavernier (Aarsele 1908-Torhout 1985), A Family History. Baltimore, MD: Gateway Press, Inc. 2006. (Published in English and Flemish)

Searching for Flemish (Belgian) Ancestors, Baltimore, MD: Genealogical Publishing Co. 2007.(In collaboration with Fr. Karel Denys, CICM)

Goethals 880-1900. The Story of the Goethals Story, Baltimore, MD:Gateway Press, Inc. 2009.

Contents

Foreword

Preface

Chapter One .... -1-
   Early Memories

Chapter Two .... -11-
   Pre-Vatican II High School Student 1950-1956

Chapter Three .... -33-
   Novice and "Philosopher" 1956-1959

Chapter Four .... -47-
   Roman Journey: Gregorian University and Vatican II 1959-1966

Chapter Five .... -73-
   Missionary: 806 Days in the Philippines

Chapter Six .... -101-
   Transition to the Laity

Chapter Seven .... -119-
   Lay Teacher: Notre Dame Preparatory School 1970-2001

Epilogue .... -153-

Appendices .... -165-
   A. Documents of Vatican II
   B. The Scheut Fathers- CICM
   C. Notre Dame Preparatory School Philosophies
   D. "Ungodly Rage"

Endnotes .... -179-

Foreword

Writing a short Foreword for a publication like the present one, I consider to be a special honor. The main reason for it is the simple yet very important fact that it deals with a theme which belongs to the very heart of most contemporary discussions on what religion should mean for us in the present age. How can the Christian churches be worthy messengers of the Gospel in a society like ours, open to where the Spirit is leading us, even if at times we might no longer clearly see in what direction this will lead us?

Introducing himself as a "Priest, Missionary, and Lay Teacher," the author Jozef J. Goethals describes in this book his personal journey in the search for a renewed Christian faith inspired by the Second Vatican Council, that epoch-making event that has characterized the more than fifty years of Christian history since. His purpose is not primarily to add another history of Vatican II to the existing literature on this subject. What he wants to offer to the readers' attention is five decades of his life "played out against the background of Vatican II" as he calls it. Yet it goes beyond that purpose. If he repeatedly refers to the Second Vatican Council, his ultimate goal remains the invitation he extends to all of us to join him on his life's journey, in the hope that the readers will themselves better understand their own journey of life, in whatever form their journey evolves.

No doubt the author is rightly convinced of the value of the ideas and concrete actions he defends as the enduring fruits of Vatican II. It is striking, however, -- at least in the view of the writer of this Foreword -- how Goethals stresses repeatedly how his experiences irreversibly created in his soul a deep sense of gratitude for all he received in his life, even if not a few less happy incidents have marked him thoroughly. After all, they kept in him Christian hope alive! In a word, this is a description of a concrete life journey of one who is certainly not afraid of looking forward as his life opens up new perspectives for a Church renewal radically embedded in Christian hope. It is indeed this hope which invites all people of faith to join in what our time might after all need most of all, a splendid variety of ways in living our Christian faith, at the right time and the right place. In this context, the author found his real vocation. Is this the New Pentecost?

This Foreword leads also to an appraisal of Goethals' work based upon reasons of a more personal nature. Almost sixty years ago Goethals and myself were both young students in a Catholic high school in the Flemish part of Belgium, becoming close friends. Our education, focusing upon a strong Catholic tradition, was enhanced by our membership in a youth organization called the "Catholic Student Action." These traditions were a sort of breeding ground for youth who wanted to put their lives at the service of the Church, and we both answered that call. Together with other Christian Action Movements which were popular in European postwar society, a plethora of new ideas and activities, rich in their diversity, put their stamp on Church and society. It should not be surprising at all that in such atmosphere gradually a tendency developed which made the Second Vatican Council possible, "opening the windows of the Church" as Pope John XXIII liked to say.

It might be understandable that a few observers of the religious scene of that time have deplored the steady growth of that diversity and pluralism in society, as well as in the church, as a token of lost unity. Others have judged the renewal trends to be a more positive current. To what group of thinking and acting Goethals belongs is clear. In the form of a concrete and honest testimony, the author describes in this book how the positive and negative aspects of a worldwide religious movement were part of his life's journey and keep playing a role to the present. Joining him in his odyssey can only be an enrichment. The journey goes on!

Fr. Jan Swyngedouw, CICM
Professor Emeritus - Nanzan University
Nagoya - JAPAN

Preface

The purpose of this book is not to be another history of Vatican II. More than 50 years after its closing, reams of commentaries are adorning libraries all over the world. The Second Vatican Council, however, was for me personally a life-changing event.

This book is an attempt to describe my personal journey from the pre-Vatican II student and seminarian through the post-Vatican II missionary, to the immigrant, married priest and educator in the last five decades. I am inviting the reader to join me on a journey from the blossoming of my priestly vocation in the 'old church' through the dawn of the 'new church' in the sixties and its journey of struggles, uncertainty, disappointments and successes in the ensuing decades.

During this journey you will meet the people who contributed to building my life and some who tried to destroy it, witness the highs and lows in my activities, and follow the process that led me to decide to return to the lay state. It will also provide the reader with some insights into the new spirit of the Vatican II Catholic Church, without attempting to make it a theological lecture.

Born from Catholic parents in war-torn Belgium, I grew up in what we call now the pre-Vatican II church. Education, social institutions and life in general were dominated by the church. That experience provided me with the idealism to go and "conquer the world for Christ." I decided that becoming a missionary was best way to do this. After a year of rigorous spiritual training, philosophy opened my mind to Thomism and existentialism. Studying theology in Rome revealed a new academic world and the universal church. Pope John XXIII then opened the windows of the church to let the "New Pentecost" blow in hope and renewal. As a missionary in the Philippines, I approached my duties with the firm belief that the church had already adopted the changes proposed during the council and that the hierarchy and my confreres were filled with the "spirit of Vatican II." Soon I found out that change is a very slow process in the Catholic Church and that pre-Vatican II structures and mentality were solidly imbedded in missionary activity. Unable to handle the pressures of the road I had chosen, I decided to leave the clerical state. The Second Vatican Council, however, had changed my life, and I remained a firm believer in the renewal of the church initiated by the council. During my thirty-one years of service to Catholic education in the USA, I attempted to make Vatican II a reality at Notre Dame Preparatory School in Baltimore, Maryland.

It is only by going through the process of writing this memoir that I have been able to make sense of the events I have briefly described above. I finally understood that the events in my life, the people I met, the struggles I endured, the defeats and the victories, were all part of a fabric through which a golden thread was woven. That golden thread was the presence of God who knew me, loved me, and never left me behind.

I did not create my life. I was called into being, was called to serve, called into an unknown future by this divine power who knew me. My life is a string of responses to God's calls. Sometimes I answered the call enthusiastically, sometimes hesitantly, sometimes after long soul-searching. I always, however, rediscovered the golden thread and knew that I was where I was meant to be. At times, I lost that thread, at times I completely ignored it, but I realized it was always there, even in my darkest moments.

It would be quite easy to dismiss my reflections above as the self-serving arguments of a "defrocked priest" who tries to justify the fact that he "left the priesthood and got married." If you would be inclined to think so, I invite you to be patient and join me on my journey and then judge my honesty at the end.

This journey is personal and by its very nature, limited. I am hoping, however, that my personal experiences, hopes, dreams and struggles will find an echo in the readers' experiences and make them better understand their own journeys. An additional limitation is the fact that the first two decades of my saga play themselves out in Belgium, the Netherlands, Italy and the Philippines. Although there are obvious parallels to be drawn between school and church life in the USA and those countries, their histories, mentalities and make-up reflect different social and cultural circumstances, making it necessary to go into some detail to explain the differences for the American reader.

My journey plays out against the background of the Second Vatican Council. The spirit of renewal of the council took hold of me from the very beginning. Gradually I realized that my whole outlook was dominated by "Vatican II thinking" and this outlook has stayed with me until today. Having stated before that this is not another history of Vatican II, I intend to familiarize the reader with some of the Vatican II documents. The documents which were directly relevant to my life will be described and quoted throughout the text. The appendix provides summaries of all sixteen Vatican II documents.

This year we are celebrating the fiftieth anniversary of the beginning of Vatican II. I am assuming that some of my readers have never experienced what we call the pre-Vatican II church. They are not aware of the changes the Council introduced in the liturgy because they have always attended liturgies in their own language and are used to seeing the celebrant facing them at the altar. Notre Dame Prep girls only know School Sisters of Notre Dame in their traditional habits from pictures in the cafeteria and Vatican II seems like an ancient historical event. It is estimated that of the almost 3,000 bishops who attended the council and voted for the sixteen documents, only a few are still alive. Furthermore, the church is divided over how much the 'Spirit of Vatican II' actually penetrated the life of the church in the last fifty years. The internal discussion over what kind of church we are or want to be, continues to this day.

I have been pondering for some time whether I would insert pictures in this memoir. After all, the text should describe succinctly enough how I felt throughout my experiences. Recognizing that my writing might not be sufficient to tell the entire story to a reader who does not know me, I decided to call on pictures to complement possible inadequacies. After all, pictures tell a story by themselves and may help to make it all more real. When friends of mine insisted, I got over my reluctance to have my face pasted over these pages. Now I leave it to the reader to make a judgement.

The end notes in this book are mainly explanatory and the Appendices may be helpful to put some things in context. In the *Epilogue*, I am reflecting on what I believe, on why I never left the Catholic Church I always loved, and of what kind of church I dream.

Acknowledgements

This book would never have seen the light without the assistance and the encouragement of a number of friends. Throughout the writing process, my wife Felicitas read chapter by chapter and always brought me back to reality when my memory failed me or led me off track. My former colleagues at Notre Dame Preparatory School, Sarah Myers and Lucy Strausbaugh encouraged me to start the project. Sarah's talent as a literary critic earned her the title of main editor. The theological and spiritual insights of both these friends have found their way into the final version of this memoir. I am indebted to Father James Finley and Paula Carroll for reading and correcting the manuscript and for their constructive comments. My former NDP student and friend, Yara Cheikh-Debrabander, provided a unique insight as an alumna of Notre Dame Preparatory School. I thank my friend and confrere Father Jan Swyngedouw CICM, who graciously accepted to write a Foreword and sent me comments on the manuscript. Finally, I gratefully acknowledge the talents of Ann Hughes and Kate Boyer of Otter Bay Books for completing a handsome volume.

CHAPTER ONE

Early Memories

I was born on 8 March 1937, three years before the onset on World War II, in Torhout, a town of 12,000 inhabitants, situated ten miles south of beautiful Brugge (Bruges) in the province of West-Flanders, Belgium. [1] I was the second of three children. My sister Cecile was born in 1934 and my brother Arthur followed in 1946. I sometimes kidded him that he was conceived during the D-Day celebrations. My father's barbershop and my mother's beauty salon were part of our house, situated between the old Saint Pieters church and the rectory. Recently, with some degree of sadness, I learned that the house where I was born had been leveled for a new apartment complex. This event, however, made local history, when archeologists discovered evidence of a settlement from the early third century Roman Empire right under our house. My home town, established in the seventh century around a monastic community, instantly became four hundred years older. I realized that I had been sleeping through my childhood and adolescence above remnants of the Roman Empire!

My father, August, was a third generation barber and my mother, Elza, a beautician, members of the hardworking "lower middle class" in town. August was well accepted in all social circles since he was always the life of the party and could tell a good story. He was member of the local music band, though he never studied music; secretary of the cycling club, though he never did one hour of exercise in his entire life; member of the Albertists, World War I veterans, though he was only seventeen when that war ended. The meetings and activities of these organizations, however, were always an opportunity for social interaction and a few (or a lot of) beers.

On 25 May 1940, the German Luftwaffe hit the town of Torhout with incendiary bombs. I was only three years old but I clearly recall running with my mother and sister to a shelter beneath the college of the Xaverian Brothers. The church, the Congregation Chapel and the rectory, all located near our house, were ablaze. Two days later the town was bombed again. On the twenty-eight of May the German troops entered Torhout and occupied the town until September 1944.

German soldiers were quartered in private homes. The Germans requisitioned one of our three bedrooms for two soldiers. We were lucky enough that our two "guests" were working at the army mess in the neighboring girls school. Hanz, a heavyset sergeant with a broad round face, had two children of the same ages as my sister and me, and was quite nice to us. He would take me to the army kitchen, and I often came home with sausages and other German army food supplies for my mother's kitchen. During the winter, my mother would sometimes offer fried herring to the soldiers and was rewarded with coal, which was difficult to obtain. Everything was rationed, meaning that one needed coupons for all the basic foods and necessities of life.

I remember my "collaboration" with the Germans. In their bedroom, the two quartered soldiers secretly kept a small black transistor radio, decorated with a silver eagle. (Strange how one remembers these details sixty years later.) Listening to the BBC of London was regarded as treason in the German army and punishable by death. Our soldiers "guests" would often listen to the BBC to learn how the war was really going for them and follow the advances of the allies. They would "hire" me as a lookout, ordered to warn them if any SS or Gestapo were approaching the house.

During the occupation, the Germans asked for volunteers to work in their ammunition factories. Many of the 500,000 jobless Belgians answered the call. After a while, however, this was seen as collaboration with the enemy. By 1942 the Germans were conscripting men between 20 and 50 to supply their work force. Many tried to leave the country or went underground. I clearly recall the day when two armed Gestapo soldiers came to the house to take my father as one of these laborers. My father

The author as soldiers' mascot 1939

was in bed with a serious stomach ulcer. Two wounded soldiers, who happened to be in the barbershop, intervened and convinced the Gestapo that my father was too sick to go and work in Germany.

The four years of occupation provided me with a string of memories. Day and night our lives were interrupted by the loud sirens of the air alert when allied planes passed by on their way to Germany. I still shudder today when the emergency system sirens sound at 1.00 P.M. in Baltimore! After continuously moving from our bedrooms to the cellar or the bomb shelter, my parents decided to use the cellar as sleeping quarters. Next to our beds each of us had a rucksack with some clothes and toiletries, ready to flee. My mother always had a small handbag with her. We later learned that in that handbag was a black silken pouch containing gold coins which diminished in number during the war: farmers were paid with gold coins for wheat, flour, eggs, butter and vegetables. Our parents were proud to be able to say that their children had never suffered hunger during the war. The famous pouch was empty at the end of the war!

At school, during air raids, we were trained to duck under our desks holding a wet towel over our mouth, or we would rush to the six feet deep trenches dug out in front of the school. I also remember helping to darken the house: every night sheets of plywood were placed over all the windows. If a single speck of light escaped we would hear fists hammering on the wood and a loud "Licht aus!" (lights out).

On 6 September 1944 the Germans left town. I watched a procession of tired soldiers in horse-drawn carriages, bicycles, push carts and even child carriages. A couple of hours later I was playing with some friends around the public pump near our house, when I saw a motorcycle with a soldier in a khaki uniform. I ran home and burst into my father's barbershop shouting, "The Americans are here! The Americans are here!" My father was shaving a German officer who immediately jumped up and dashed out of the shop.

In Torhout, as in many other cities in Belgium, the repression after the liberation was swift and violent. For me, that period was more fearful than the war years themselves. In the flush of victory collaborators were hunted and arrested. Many were members of the Flemish National Alliance (VNV), believed to be pro-German. Their militia volunteered to fight against bolshevism on the East front. They became known as the "Legion of Flanders" and were part of the Waffen SS, a branch of the Protective Squadron (SS) of the Nazi party. More than 10,000 Flemish men volunteered in the legion, also known as the "Black Brigade," and many died or came back wounded. A Belgian resistance group, known as the "White Brigade," hunted and arrested these volunteers as collaborators after the liberation. Believing that the Germans would win the war, many other people had worked with them in the hope of securing their future in the "new regime." Sadly however, some people took advantage of the liberation to settle old scores or enrich themselves. Scores were placed on a "black list," their houses or businesses were targeted and their belongings were thrown on the street by roving bands of White Brigaders.

Kindergarden with Sister Serafina 1942
(Author seated fifth from the right)

Young women who had been friendly with German soldiers were shaved bald and paraded through town. A great number were placed under arrest. I remember the day some of these "make-believe liberators" were passing in the street. Fearing that we would be a target, my parents had closed shop and we were placed in the cellar in "war-mode." It happened that two nephews of my father's sister-in-law had volunteered in the Legion of Flanders, went to the East front and were wounded. I remember them clearly from some of their visits in our house. One had lost an eye, the other his right arm. I liked them, because they were the ones who had prevented the Gestapo from taking my father to Germany as a forced laborer.

Another family situation placed us on the black list. One of my father's cousins, a teacher, was arrested for his "Flemish nationalist tendencies." The cousin's two sisters, who ran a bar in our neighborhood, were accused of being too friendly with the German officers. They were shaved bald, spat on and paraded through the streets of town. I recall my great uncle Remie, who had just witnessed his daughters paraded through town, smashing a kitchen chair in a dozen pieces in our living room. Fortunately, our house was spared from the angry crowds.

The next day, however, a neighbor came to warn us that we had better withdraw the Belgian flag from the house because someone did place us on the blacklist. This became obvious when our house was tarred with a series of 12 swastikas on walls and doors. We covered them with paint, but the next morning fresh ones appeared again. When an important member of the White Brigade challenged my father in his barbershop and wanted to know if he had accused him of painting the swastikas, my father calmly answered: "But sir, as a friend and a client of many years from whom I receive each year the first spring flowers from your garden, you would never do such a thing to me!" After this, no more swastikas were painted, but we were unfortunately branded as "blacks," -- the term used for collaborators. Later my father learned that another barber, who wanted to increase his clientele, was the culprit.

The only "collaboration" of my father was to have shaved and cut the hair of German soldiers, just as he did for the Canadians and British after the liberation. I can now imagine what a tightrope my father had to walk in his conversations with Germans and White Brigade members alike in his barbershop. Nobody was to be trusted: Germans would send you to prison if you talked against the war; others would brand you a collaborator if you talked in favor of it. My most vivid memory of those days was when I was walking with my aunt Alice in town, and a woman came up to us, spat in my aunt's face and shouted, "Black whore!" Not easy to forget!

Author's parents and sister in 1941

During the war, we children were oblivious to the dangers surrounding us. We felt safe in our family home and we got used to sleeping in our cellar and the bunker next door. We learned how to react to signs of danger and to duck when Allied planes were strafing the railroad from right above our house. The ruins of the church and the old burned-out movie house became our favorite playgrounds. We "played war," climbed on tanks, marched besides platoons of soldiers and collected empty gun shells. One day I came into my father's barbershop with an unexploded tank shell... Fortunately a German officer he was shaving defused it. That was the end of my shell collection days!

I grew up in the shadows of the imposing Romanesque St. Pieters church in my hometown. I have been wondering if the proximity of the church to my house played any role in my later choice to become a cleric. The church became a playground for my friends and me. We would play hide and seek behind the enormous columns and the statues of the saints until we were chased off by Charlie, the church caretaker. Charlie was a little cross-eyed man who considered the church his personal domain and protected St. Pieters from all "intruders" unless they came to pray. After learning Charlie's napping schedule, the church became our indoor playground.

Charlie kept a special eye on me since the time I had driven three dozen nails in the oak side door of the church. My uncle was a carpenter and I wanted to be one too. One day he had given me a hammer, a bunch of nails and a piece of wood and let me "work." Soon the piece of wood was "finished" and since I had some nails left, I decided that the church door needed some "repair." After a visit from the parish priest, my career as a carpenter ended for good.

During the Christmas season there was always a huge nativity scene in the church: lifelike figures of Mary and Joseph, flying angels and sheep, and a beautiful child Jesus with rosy cheeks. I just loved that little Jesus, and wanted to see it under our Christmas tree in the living room. One day I sneaked into the church during Charlie's nap and took Jesus out of his crib and exchanged him with my brown teddy bear, Rufus. I managed to hide little Jesus in my bedroom for almost the entire day until my mother found him and alerted the parish priest. The priest told my mother that Marie, nicknamed "the Prayer," a devout old lady who came to the church four times a day, almost got a heart attack when she noticed the teddy bear in the crib and scolded the parish priest for his joke in "bad taste"! I got a stern lecture about stealing church property and blasphemy, but I defended myself saying that I had just "borrowed" Jesus for a little time…For many years my parents retold the story with a smile on their faces, and I am sure that even Jesus smiled about it!

I can only try to imagine now what the war meant to my parents: martial law, rationing of everything, constant fear of being reported for criticism or expressing opinions about the occupation, food shortages and arrests in the middle of the night, complete loss of control over all the aspects of their lives. Real coffee or real butter were literally worth their weight in gold. Bread flour was hard to get: with his farmer-clients, my father sometimes bartered a hair cut or a shave for a sack of flour or a dozen eggs -- or he used his little stack of gold coins. I felt like a hero when I "smuggled" a few pounds of flour through town on my bike without being noticed by German soldiers. After the war I got to know the existence of some real luxuries in life, like chocolate and white bread. My first English was practiced on British soldiers, "Chicklets and chocolate please, sir,"--usually with satisfying results!

Although I was very young, I realize now that I learned some lifelong lessons from my war experiences. I learned that my parents were always going to be there to protect me, whatever the circumstances. I learned that people could really hate and were able to treat one another unjustly. I saw the emaciated skeletal bodies of my neighbors returning from German concentration camps. I saw the hatred of the crowds who paraded my relatives through town and threw people's belongings in the street. I felt the powerlessness and isolation of my family under the superiority of an occupying army.

I also witnessed the goodness of the German soldiers who provided food to my mother's kitchen and who prevented my father from being deported to Germany as a forced laborer. I saw the compassion of a neighbor who warned my parents that they were blacklisted after the liberation.

I learned that, in the end, goodness always prevails. The Germans left us and they lost the war; my family regained respect in the community. They persisted and never let evil or injustice triumph. After the war, I witnessed my family's compassion for German refugees, even encouraging me to go and help rebuild their devastated country.

Later in life, I remembered these lessons when I was feeling powerless and isolated, threatened by forces that seemingly were intending to destroy my intentions and activities. The war experience taught me that if you resist and persist, goodness triumphs--all the time!

First communion, 1945
St. Pieter Church, Torhout
With my parents, sister Cecile and brother
Arthur, 1947

CHAPTER TWO

Pre-Vatican II High School Student 1950-1956

Saint Rembert College, Torhout, Belgium

The apostles heard the invitation of Jesus,"Come and follow me!" Some saints have claimed hearing God's voice calling them out of their sinful lives into a lifelong dedication to the church. This is not what happened to me! During my early childhood I did show signs that the priesthood was attractive to me. At seven or eight, I secretly kept a chapel at home with an altar and all the paraphernalia to "say Mass." My mother, who certainly wanted to encourage my priestly tendencies, had sewn an alb and a chasuble from an old window curtain and gave me a toy mass set. Although I did not know Latin yet, I had memorized the "sacred words" and performed for an imaginary flock of communicants. At the age of seventeen, when I decided to become a priest and missionary, it was thanks to my parents who always taught me to care for and give to others; to the role models of priests and missionaries who crossed my path; to my active membership in Catholic youth organizations who inspired me with idealism and the desire to "conquer the world for Christ." The road to this decision and the first years of my clerical training unfolded through -- what we could call now -- the pre-Vatican II church.

In 1950 I started my Catholic high school education at Saint Rembert College in my hometown. High school in Belgium was called "college" or "humaniora" and ran over six years. In 1950 the school did not offer the many educational tracks that the students are able to choose today. The only choice we had was between the 'old humaniora or classical section' and the 'new humaniora or modern' section, the difference being the emphasis on classical languages (Latin and Greek) or modern languages (French, English and German) and the sciences. The classical direction was further divided into Latin-Greek, which I chose, and Latin-Mathematics. Once you had chosen, that was it for six years. Educational counseling still had to be invented and a number of priests-teachers were the only counselors we ever had for our spiritual, moral and educational needs.

Colleges in Flanders, like our St. Rembert College, were real bastions of Catholic thought and practices and were run and staffed mostly by priests and a few lay teachers. Most of the students were day students but the school also housed a number of boarders.

The classrooms were spartan: rows of desks, a blackboard, drab colors on the walls and no decorations except for pictures of the king and queen, Pope Pius XII and a crucifix. The classroom was the base for all subjects taught by a variety of teachers, with occasional trips to the laboratory for chemistry or biology. The study hall, where we spent three and a half hours a day, was equally boring: a large poorly lit hall with six rows of double desks dominated by a huge high "throne" where the "surveillant" could keep an eye on the 150 subjects. Each student was assigned to a desk where he kept his books and school materials.

All students were to report to the 7.30 Mass at the college chapel. I was fortunate enough to become an altar boy at the nearby nuns convent and although I had to serve Mass at 6.30 every day, it became a bonanza: my absence was not recorded when I missed a Mass. I was offered daily breakfast with Julie and Marie, two spinsters whose entire lives were dedicated to meeting visitors to the convent and who were ardently praying every day for my priestly vocation. I also had the privilege of "meeting" a group of female boarding students of the St. Vincentius Girls School who paraded to Mass every day. These meetings were limited to stolen glances, smiles and secret dreams. Later in life I learned that some of these girls always thought I would become a priest, but one of them confessed that she cried her heart out when she learned that I was entering the novitiate to become a missionary.

Classes started at 8.15 a.m. and ran until 12.05. As a day student, I had the privilege to go home for lunch and enjoy my mother's cooking. The smells which came from the boarding students dining room made me realize that being a day student was a blessing. By 1.30 p.m. we had to report to the study hall till 2.20 and classes resumed until 4.10. After an afternoon snack we reported again to study hall at 5.00 until 7.30. After supper at home, there was additional homework to finish and class work to prepare. Wednesday afternoon was scheduled for sports, which meant that everybody played soccer or volley ball. The daily schedule was set up in such a way that we did not have much time to "get in trouble." Extracurricular activities had to be performed during our scarce free time, weekends and vacations. As I was involved in many of those activities, my free time was filled to the brim. Saturdays were regular school days until 4.00 p.m.

On Sundays we were not allowed to completely get out of the control of the school. We reported to High Mass at 10 a.m. followed by a reading period. By 3 p.m. we were back in the chapel for sung Vespers. Later in the day the school often provided cultural events, concerts, movies, short plays, etc. A young assistant parish priest opened a youth center where on weekends we could enjoy American westerns and comics, play pool and ping pong, enjoy Belgian waffles and have a beer (yes, beer was allowed for teenagers in Belgium). Unfortunately the youth center was stag -- no girls allowed! Mixed company was reserved for the rare social action campaigns sponsored by Catholic Student Action.

The academic schedule was structured to fill our heads with as much information as possible, taught in lecture format. Textbooks were rare, so we became experts in note taking. In my six years of high school I cannot remember having *one* religion text book -- not even a complete bible. We had to rely completely on our class notes and compare them with 'good note takers.' Class discussions were taboo: who would dare question the knowledge of the 'master'? Tests and quizzes were geared toward regurgitating memorized information and semester exams were very demanding and comprehensive. These methods, however, seemed to have worked in miraculous ways: today I am still figuring out in my head how much seven times eighteen is, and I am doing it in Flemish. I am still able to recite the Greek alphabet and quote sections of Latin, Greek, French and English literary masterworks!

St. Rembert graduating class 1956
(Author seated second from the left)

The purpose of the six years of humaniora studies was to make us well-rounded humanists, versed in western languages, culture and history. After basic grammar and syntax training, they exposed us to the masterpieces of six languages: Latin, Dutch and French were taught for six years, Greek for five, German and English for four. Besides the languages there were six years of religion and algebra (a subject I hated and never really understood), geography and world history, five years of geometry, three years of physics and music, and two years of biology, trigonometry and chemistry. I can assure you that we were not always enthusiastic or motivated translating another section of the Iliad or the Aeneid or memorizing scenes from Moliere's *L'Avare*. The teachers, however, did not really care about how we felt about it. 'Self-esteem' was a word still to be invented. The only award was your grades; 'attention deficit' was not a disorder yet but it was "your problem." Performance deficiencies were not remedied by medication but by a red report card and parental punishment.

The majority of the staff of St. Rembert College were diocesan priests, particularly in the classic humanities section. The church hierarchy assumed that most vocations would be harvested from that section and statistics prove that they were right in that assumption. We were always surrounded and supervised by 'cassocks', which were seldom dry cleaned and smelled of books, sweat and cigar smoke. At St. Rembert the priests had their private rooms in the front building of the school. When called to a priest's room for 'spiritual guidance' or confessions, one could easily determine the social background of the priest by observing his furniture and room decorations. Some had spartan rooms with secondhand furniture and lawn chairs; others had oak desks, leather chairs, extensive libraries and original paintings on the wall, reflecting the financial status of their parents.

A large number of these priests must have lived quite a simple life. Their clerical salary, paid by the government, was not very high.[2] They supplemented it with Mass stipends, preaching and confessions in neighboring parishes or convents, and without doubt, regular checks from their families. Looking back at their lives, I realize now how dedicated most of these priests were and I often wonder how much impact they had on my growing desire to be "one of them." Their days were an unending chain of activities: they taught classes in a variety of subjects, took care of class administration, home works, tests and quizzes. They supervised us during study hall and recess and acted as counselors in spiritual and academic matters. They were overseers of dormitories and dining rooms, and chaplains of school organizations. They directed plays and conducted choirs. Furthermore, they still had to find time for their daily priestly duties of meditation, reciting their breviary and rosary and keeping up with spiritual reading. Their seminary training had certainly not prepared them for this.

The subjects they were teaching were not part of their training either: six years of philosophy and theology in the seminary did not prepare them to teach Latin, Greek or French. Their expertise in these subjects was usually acquired by personal study over many years and by practice in the trenches. Often a hobby or a line of interest became a sure path to a teaching assignment: you like Latin, you will teach it! You were a good soccer player, you'll become the soccer coach! You were a good actor in high school plays, you'll direct the play! Mathematics, sciences or modern languages usually were taught by lay teachers who had degrees in their subjects. Among the priests, only 6% had a proper degree in the subject they were teaching.

Years of personal study and dedication, however, produced many priest-teachers whose expertise and enthusiasm enlivened us with the orations of Cicero, the poetry of the Aeneid and the Iliad, the fables of La Fontaine, and the plays of Molière and Shakespeare. From these teachers I obtained a lifelong interest in the classics, a lifetime of listening to classical music and a passionate interest in art and history. Whatever their methods were, they worked! They may not have studied educational methodology or held degrees in the subjects they were teaching, but they gave us a rich humanistic education preparing us for university studies and providing us with skills and interests we took with us for the rest of our lives.

The weekly color-coded report cards, to be signed by our parents, were a reflection of our academic and behavioral progress: green was O.K.; red was so-so; yellow was bad; and white was 'criminal.' I remember developing an exquisite strategy when coming home with a yellow or white report. I would wait until early Monday morning, my father's day off from the barber shop, and have it signed while he slept late... Knowing that my father was partially color blind was an additional bonus!

Discipline was the all-encompassing reality at school. Every waking moment of our school day was subject to regulations and supervision: they made sure that they knew where we were and what we were doing *at all times*! The person who specialized in this was the prefect of discipline, feared by all students because of his reputation of being all-knowing, all-seeing and merciless. He saw to it that no infraction of rules went by unpunished. Students usually looked down on him as the 'not-smart-enough-to-teach-priest,' but they respected his street smarts. Punishments were varied: from writing a hundred times "I will not talk in class" to ten page essays on "The value of silence" or "The importance of behaving correctly." If I had collected these essays I could have published a book on the subjects! Real problem kids were handled by the prefect or home room priest and they sometimes ended up being suspended from the school. In all the years of my high school, I never heard of any cases of pedophilia or rumors of homosexuality. If there were any, it was certainly never talked about, as was any subject that had to do with sexuality.

From the nineteenth century until well into the twentieth, the reason for existence of Catholic colleges was not only to produce humanists but to produce lay people who were *Catholic* humanists and, most importantly, to foster vocations for the priesthood. Some colleges specializing in the latter were called *minor seminaries* or popularly 'priest factories' such as Roeselare, Hoogstraten, St. Niklaas and Mechelen. They were direct feeders to the major diocesan seminaries, religious congregations and traditional orders, such as the Jesuits or Dominicans. Obviously they were very successful: until the 1930s one half of their students chose the priesthood.³ Even the regular diocesan colleges, particularly the classical humaniora sections, were fertile ground for vocations.

It was therefore important that the students be morally trained and protected against the evils of the world. Above the every day practical rules were the *moral rules* incorporated in the axiom "everything was forbidden except those things that were obligatory." ⁴ Moral behavior was not so much about acting responsibly or following the dictates of one's conscience, but was rather about 'avoiding occasions of sin.' Our lives were thought of as minefields of temptation framed in a system of "minor and grave matter" and luring us into losing our "state of grace." Swearing, disobedience, cheating and lies were often minor matter, but anything to do with sex was 'grave matter.' This mother of all sins was hiding in all sorts of bad things: bad books, bad movies, bad girls, bad thoughts, bad actions (masturbation)... All of our natural curiosity about things sexual was turned into a life of guilt and negativity. A weekly quasi-obligatory confession on Saturdays, 'day of bath and confession,' became a listing of our sexual peccadillos. An old missionary, reputed for being stone-deaf, had the longest lines of weekly penitents. The yearly three day retreat, modeled after retreats for priests and monks, was a series of fire and brimstone talks by scary Redemptorist or Jesuit preachers. Every year we had to hear the same story about the boy who read a dirty book and "died the day after in a car accident in a state of mortal sin." The entire study hall felt guilty as charged and promptly went to confession that day, just to make sure!

Catholic Student Action

If there is anything during my high school years that inspired me with idealism, it was *Katholieke Studenten Aktie*, KSA (Catholic Student Action). As a typical Flemish institution, this movement warrants some explanation. At the onset of the Belgian State in 1830 all education in the country was in French. Priest educators were worried that the future pastors of the Flemish flock would not be able to speak the native language well and so they stimulated the development of the Flemish language. First they created study groups in the colleges where Flemish history and literature were discussed. Since most of the instructors were priests, they tried to preserve the Catholic character of these groups. By 1870 these groups had become bastions of Flemish nationalism who fought for "flamigantism" and in 1877 they organized the General Student Organization (*Algemeen Studentenverbond*) which would prepare its members to fight for recognition of Flanders in anti-Flemish Belgium. The Catholic hierarchy was very suspicious of the movement and was in constant conflict with the organization. The year 1903 saw the beginning of the General Catholic Flemish Student Association (*Algemeen Katholiek Vlaams Studentenverbond -- AKVS*). It was set up as an active church organization with a Flemish spirit, but gradually became the organ of Flemish nationalism (even anti-Belgianism) and was reported to be anticlerical because it reacted against clerical authoritarianism. The Flemish bishops moved against the association by introducing the KSA in the individual dioceses. In the 1920s, the Catholic hierarchy thought that in the AKVS 'Catholic action' had become secondary to their Flemish nationalism.

Catholic action was an re-christianizing movement propagated by Pope Pius XI (1922-1939). It's aim was to change the church into an army of "soldiers of Christ" who would "conquer the world for Christ" against the growing secularization of Western Europe. The laity was called to work under the direction of the clerics to "restore everything in Christ"(*Omnia Restaurare in Christo*).

The political situation in Belgium was another reason for action by the church hierarchy. In the early twenties Belgium approved the general voting rights and the Catholic parties experienced big losses. The hierarchy deemed it necessary to counter the growing secularization with

*Pilgrimage to Lourdes, France. In KSA uniform
with Bishop Emiel Desmedt of Bruges 1955.*

Catholic action. The KSA would do this in the colleges during the school year and in the parishes during summer vacations. The youth was mobilized to join that fight according to which social class they belonged, leading to the establishment of the Young Christian Workers (KAJ), [5] the Farmers Youth (BJB) and the Catholic Middle Class Youth (KBMJ). The students already had the AKVS, but since that was not "Catholic" enough, a new organization, the KSA would emanate from it.

The main purpose of the KSA was to be the breeding ground of future Catholic lay intellectuals and priestly vocations. It was in 1928 that the Reverend Karel Dubois, a West-Flemish priest-canon, founded the KSA by mandate of his bishop. It's motto became 'Restore Flanders in Christ' (*Vlaanderen hernieuwen in Christus*) From its initial emphasis on study groups, the organization developed into more of a youth movement with service to the people (*volksdienst*), creativity (*heemdienst*), sports and outdoor life. It became an organization with its own symbols, uniforms, songs, new themes and structures, often borrowed from the Boy Scouts and the German Youth Movement.

When I started my high school years in 1950, the KSA was already fully organized into a youth movement with summer and winter camps and outdoor activities. We participated in activities encouraging pride in being Flemish such as the yearly Flemish Song Festival and the Yzer Pilgrimage in Diksmuide;[6] we promoted campaigns for the expansion of the official Flemish language in daily life instead of using various dialects.[7] We took part in social charity campaigns and received leadership training. Our entire school and social lives were dominated by church-inspired activities on a continual basis.

My membership in the KSA was a fundamental element in my journey to a life of service. If high school life gave me academic and moral training, the KSA imparted idealism. The Catholic Student Action was much more than a place where we enjoyed good fellowship during camp trips, festivals and weekend outings. I was taught to live for something larger than myself, to live for an ideal of service to others while learning leadership. I discovered that if you want to change society, you have to commit yourself to the cause and fight if necessary. The idealism of "renewing Flanders for Christ" gradually became for me "renewing the world for Christ" and presented itself to me as an attractive life goal.

Aid to Eastern Priests (*Oostpriesterhulp*)
and the International Building Organization (*Bouworde*)

One of the people who certainly had a great influence on my vocation was a Norbertine monk from the abbey of Tongerlo, Werenfried Van Straaten. The meaning of Werenfried is "Warrior for Peace." Touched by the suffering of the fourteen million homeless Germans, among whom were six million Catholics, who were expelled from their homes in Eastern Europe and were living in bombed-out Germany, Van Straaten wrote an article in 1947 entitled *Peace on Earth? No Room at the Inn.* He pleaded the Belgians to be of assistance to these displaced people: not an easy appeal to be made to people whose war wounds were still raw and were mourning their loved ones killed by Germans. He believed that, "God is much better than we think and people too are much better than we think." At the end of a talk to a group of Flemish farmers' spouses, he suggested that they donate a large piece of bacon for the refugees. A subsequent talk to parishioners resulted in more than a ton of bacon and he was baptized with the name the *Bacon Priest*. Trucks of bacon soon began to deliver subsistence to scores of refugees.[8] A year later he collaborated with a German bishop, Mgr Kindermann, who had started a refugee organization and a seminary for refugee priests in Königstein near Frankfurt, Germany.

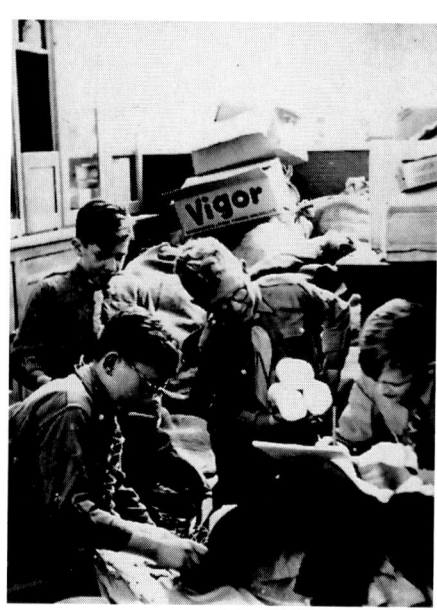

Gathering food for German refugees 1951

Priests were sent from Königstein all over Germany to provide material aid and pastoral care to the refugees. Werenfried organized a series of campaigns to support these "rucksack priests" and his organization *Aid to Eastern Priests* (Oostpriesterhulp) was born. Thousands of Flemish school pupils "adopted" a rucksack priest. Werenfried went on begging trips all over Flanders and the Netherlands to collect funds with his famous black begging hat to provide motorcycles and Volkswagen Beetles for the rucksack priests. In 1950 he financed the *Chapel Trucks*, remodeled secondhand buses serving as mobile churches and bringing the sacraments and material assistance to the refugees.

In the early fifties I got involved with the Chapel Truck Campaign. As KSA volunteers we would go door-to-door in the neighboring towns to collect money, clothes and canned goods. More often than not, we witnessed the resentment towards the former German occupiers and doors were slammed in our faces: I learned a whole new vocabulary not used in our household... We persisted and the charitable response gradually won over hatred: people were indeed "much better than we think." I spent some of my vacations sorting mountains of clothes and canned goods in the collection center in the abbey of Tongerlo. Aid to Eastern Priests became also a family affair: my aunt Maria served as secretary of the organization for West-Flanders. On many occasions I had to give up the use of my bed for the Bacon Priest who was in the area for one of his begging trips or for one of the East German rucksack priests. My aunt's house, with two unmarried spinsters, was deemed an "inappropriate" place to host priests.

In 1953, Werenfried responded to another refugee need: housing. The West German Government started a help program whereby refugees could obtain housing subsidies on condition they provided the bulk of the manual labor. The old, the sick and the weak were obviously unable to do this and Werenfried came to the rescue by organizing *building camps for volunteers.* The *Bouworde* (Building Organization) was born and Flemish and Dutch students, paying for their own travel expenses, spent their vacations providing manual labor in building houses, churches and dispensaries for the refugees in Germany.

During the summer of 1953, I travelled with seven of my friends in an old British army truck to the small village of Roigheim, north of Stuttgart, for my first building camp. For three weeks we prepared the foundations of a chapel and a few houses, teaching me much respect for the work of laborers. The small Catholic community prepared our meals and shared their rooms. My hosts were a Romanian family of four, the Salatskys. With the help of my basic German, I learned about their horrible war experiences and the plight of their refugee status. The year after, I participated in another building camp in Göppingen, east of Stuttgart. We returned to Roigheim for the blessing of the then finished St. Johannes chapel and for a visit with the Salatskys now occupying their new house. In 1954 more than 2,000 young men volunteered for the Bouworde in

Germany. To my great surprise, I found a picture of the Roigheim chapel on the internet...I wonder if the Salatsky grandchildren still live in Roigheim. Father Werenfried's organizations developed into international bodies, active in more than 140 countries. [9]

International Building Companion. The Saint Johannes chapel of Roigheim,

It is remarkable what Father Werenfried accomplished in the first decade of his dedication to refugees. Not only did he provide pastoral care and material help to thousands of refugees in war torn Europe, but he unleashed a storm of forgiveness and charitable giving in the people who were the war's victims. By 1956 Germany organized its own fundraising for Oostpriesterhulp and thus the receivers became generous givers themselves. Werenfried's two initiatives have blossomed into permanent international organizations and remain examples of Christian voluntarism and outreach to a world of poverty and discrimination. The Bacon Priest's life and my six years of participation in both his organizations became real building blocks for my vocation: they cultivated my desire to be of service to others to the point I wanted to do this for a living!

Thor Dance Group

On 11 July 1952, Heiko Kolt mesmerized the Flemish crowds who had gathered in Kortrijk to celebrate the 650 year anniversary of the Battle of the Golden Spurs.[10] Heiko Kolt was the son of an Estonian mother and Russian father, born in Warsaw in 1902, who had escaped from the Eastern block to the West. He became an accomplished ballet dancer, choreographer and director and invented an entirely new style of flag dancing by transforming the centuries-long tradition of flag twirling into dynamic and expressive flag dancing. Father Karel Vandewynckele, an enthusiastic priest of St. Rembert college, had witnessed the performance in Kortrijk. He recruited Heiko in 1955 to share his craft with fourteen young lads of St. Rembert ... and the dance group "Thor" was born. As lead dancer of the group, I was taught by Heiko Kolt that thoughts and feelings could be expressed in body movements, using a flag as the body's extension. Thor became an instant success and we performed in schools, parades and processions in Flanders. Some special performances were memorable to me: dancing at the birthday of Prince Alexander, the oldest son of King Leopold III at the royal palace in Laken near Brussels; and soloing before a crowd of 10,000 at the Golden Spurs celebration in Kortrijk. My most indelible memory was dancing for Pope Pius XII at his summer residence in Castel Gandolfo in 1956. When I stood in front of this almost ethereal figure with his piercing eyes, he told me, "This was a very fine performance. Thank you!" I knew I would never forget that moment. (see photo)

Later in the novitiate, the master of novices would remind me that this performance "might not have been very advantageous for my virtue of humility" ... O.K.! But how many people can say, "I danced for the pope!" My dancing experiences taught me never to be afraid to face large crowds in bringing a message you believe in, a talent my master of novices underestimated!

After I joined the missionary congregation, Thor performed all over Europe and even in the USA. Heiko Kolt shared his talent with many schools and youth groups in Flanders for years to come. At his death in 1977 he was recognized for his enormous contributions to Flanders' culture. His wish to be buried in Flanders, his adopted country, was granted.

Dancing for Pope Pius XII
Castel Gandolfo 1956

During the last trimester of high school there always was much curiosity and expectation about the direction the graduates would take the following year. Our choices were kept a secret because of the betting that was going on by the underclassmen about our life choices. The heaviest odds were on who would join the priesthood. We were only sixteen in the graduating class and three of us, Toon Ramon, Frans Deroo and myself chose the same missionary Congregation of the Immaculate Heart of Mary

(CICM) also known as the *Missionaries of Scheut* or the *Scheut Fathers*.[11] I don't think anybody was surprised that I was one of them. Somehow they had known for quite some time that I was made to be a priest.

I got to know a number of the Scheut Fathers who lived in a retirement home, located a few blocks from our house. The bearded retirees were faithful customers at my father's barber shop, the main reason being -- I later found out -- that he never charged them a penny! I befriended a young CICM brother with whom I was able to discuss anything under the sun. Fr. Lecluyse, a longtime family friend, became a sort of spiritual director guiding me in my nascent "vocation." During my regular visits to the retirement home I enjoyed listening to the tales of the old missionaries and gradually felt at home in their company. Their examples convinced me that I could live a meaningful life in that environment. My best friend Jan Swyngedouw had joined the Scheut novitiate in 1953 and my contacts with him during his vacations convinced me that Scheut was a happy place to be. Jan has been a missionary in Japan for 50 years. He became a professor at Nanzan University in Nagoya, Japan, and taught at CICM seminaries in Asia and Africa. He was active in inter-religious dialogue, especially with the Japanese Shinto tradition. He remains a lifelong true friend.

In the process of making the decision to join a missionary order, the idea of having to live a celibate life was never a major concern. Contact with girls as a teenager in the fifties was limited to occasional social projects with the VKSJ, sister organization of the KSA, and weekend visits with my friend Jan Swyngedouw, who had three beautiful sisters. (I had a terrible crush on one of them, and she became -- and still is -- a nun.). Boy-girl romantic relationship were customarily postponed until university years. Personally I enjoyed the company of women but thought that sacrificing this companionship was a given if you wanted to serve humankind. My experiences were limited to an occasional crush and superficial social contacts. I took it for granted that the absence of women in my life was not going to be a big deal. I would later realize that life without close companionship was probably something I could not handle.

Throughout my high school years, God's call to work in his vineyard came through the example of priests at the school. I was animated by the ideals of the KSA to be a "soldier of Christ" and conquer the world for him. Combined with the joy I experienced in helping people through Oostpriesterhulp and the Building Companions camps, the yearning to make "helping others" a lifelong task slowly matured into certainty.

My experience that even whole nations could forgive the atrocities of war and reach out to the needs of the defeated, made clear to me that "people were indeed much better than we think" as Father Werenfried had stated. The example of my parents, offering housing and food to the stream of Oostpriesterhulp priests and staff, brought this message home. God's call came through the people who surrounded me, not in a divine encounter.

If there ever was a moment in my teen years of a "divine encounter," it happened during the retreat of our graduating class at the Benedictine Abbey of Zevenkerke near Brugge. Walking by myself in the beautiful spring forest of the abbey, I suddenly became deeply aware of the absolute certainty that God really existed and that He would always play some role in my life. When later in life I struggled with my faith in God, the church and my vocation, I always remembered that moment even in the minute details of my surroundings. In a way, the experience created in me the belief -- even up to the present -- that wherever I would be, somehow He will be there.

Postscript: **Catholic Secondary Education and youth groups in Belgium today.**

In the seventh chapter you will witness the growth of a Catholic school --Notre Dame Preparatory in Baltimore -- into a Vatican II school, i.e. a school that adopts the renewal of Vatican II in its philosophy and daily activities. In this postscript I want to give the reader a glimpse into how Catholic schools and youth groups see themselves and are seen by society in Flanders today, compared to the description of fifty years ago which you have just read in this chapter.

If a student of the 1950s would visit Sint Rembert college today, he would still recognize many of the basic academics, even if the schools have been reorganized. Today secondary schools are divided into four types where the students gradually choose a direction depending on their skill and interests. *General Secondary Education* (40%) prepares them for higher education. *Technical Education* (30%) approaches their training in a more practical manner and prepares them for the job market. *Vocational Education* (30%) is job specific and concentrates on trade training. *Art Education* (2%) links general education to the performing and display arts.

The 1950 student would be amiss, however, in finding the evangelizing spirit of "conquering the world for Christ" of his old school, at least at first glance. As in many European countries, Belgium has been profoundly secularized in the last fifty years. Recently, the pedophilia scandals of the clergy only poured fuel on the fire and now even the few remaining practicing Catholics are disappointed and even angry at their church. Although Belgium is still seen as a Catholic country, less than 7% still attend Sunday mass. Church going is reduced to burials (61%) baptisms (57%) and weddings (27%). There is a widespread shortage of priests and nuns which results in priests serving several parishes, and lay people staffing the Catholic schools.

The dominating role that the church played in the past has been greatly diminished and this had its impact on the schools. Although schools are 70% Catholic, parents read the word 'Catholic' as 'quality' and don't choose a Catholic school because faith inspires their choice, but because it provides a good environment, has name recognition, grants a diploma which is a safe stepping stone to higher education, produces students who are professionally counseled and receive basic values. Being 'Catholic' appears only at the end of their list of reasons to chose the school.

A quick survey of a number of Catholic secondary schools shows that in their mission statements catholicity is no more shouted off the roofs, but is barely a whisper. 'Catholic' is replaced by 'Christian inspiration' and is almost an afterthought. My own alma mater Saint Joseph Institute frames its mission as follows: " SJI wants to be a school for life ... a humaniora where one becomes more human ... paying attention to the totality of the person. Therefore, in the many classes and activities there is attention for sports and culture, and as a Catholic school, we also want to give to the religious dimension its rightful place."[12] Its pastoral program "is striving for a Christian style of life ... in the imitation of Jesus Christ ... making students prepared and critical of the many false values they encounter."

Although all schools are supported by government subsidies, religion is a required subject. How religion is being taught has been a subject of contention and intense debate for several decades. The Belgian bishops developed a "Vision Program" [13] for religious instruction which became fully operational in 2004. The program makes a distinction between *catechesis* and *religious instruction*. Catechesis, intended to instruct and assist believers, is the responsibility of the parishes and other faith communities. The schools are not seen as communities of believers because they teach students who embrace a plurality of life philosophies. Although the majority of the students are baptized (96%), according to a recent study only 25% say they are believers, 38% don't believe, and 37% are doubting; 95% never or rarely read the Bible, 14% visit a church on a regular basis, and 68% never or rarely pray.[14] Since it is not direct catechesis, the Vision program presents to the students Christendom as a priority option next to others, inviting them to make a decision about their faith. Nothing in the program is written in stone but it is a framework that leaves much initiative to the teacher. As such the teacher has to be not only a witness of the faith, but a qualified instructor and a moderator of the communication process.

This approach has engendered a critique from conservative corners that the youngsters don't know enough about the Catholic religion. Archbishop Léonard recently announced in a newspaper interview of May 2010 that he wanted to "streamline religious instruction" because he opined that, "After all these years of this so-called religious education they know barely anything. Religion class is not religion class anymore...but nothing but sociology." [15] The statement produced a storm of reaction from teachers and academici defending the Vision program.

We might have to wait for the next generation to see whether the program is effective and produces new Catholic communities. The teachers seem to have a gigantic task presenting Christendom in an atmosphere of deep secularization and antagonism against the church herself. The school program itself is solid and there are many qualified and dedicated religion teachers in Flanders. There are concerns, however, that some of the young teachers have only seen their grandparents going to church and miss the 'living experience' of Catholicism. Others were hired because of an acute teacher shortage and might not be academically trained to teach religion. We also wonder how the parishes are able to provide the catechesis to young people if the youth remains absent from the church on Sundays and is not involved in parish activities.

The youngster of the 1950s would hardly recognize his Catholic Student Action (KSA) today where some fundamental changes took place during the last five decades. The "Renewing Flanders in Christ" clarion call of these early days, became "togetherness in play," a youth movement for a range of youngsters who play together to "detect their own possibilities and sharpen their talents" to become effective members of society. All of this is still claimed to happen against "a Christian background." Today, the parents who sent circa 40,000 youngsters to the weekend and summer activities, do not choose the organization because it's Catholic but because their kids can be active in a safe environment.

If the schools and the youth organizations were breeding grounds for priestly vocations in the fifties, today these institutions do not seem to produce the clergy for the future. Ordinations can be counted on one hand. In 2009 the Flemish dioceses had only one priestly ordination. A change in the celibacy rules could remedy this trend, but I don't see great improvement unless there is a reversal of the secularization process in the country.

*The seal of the CICM Scheut Missionaries.
"Cor Unum et Anima Una"
(One heart and one soul)*

CHAPTER THREE

Novice and "Philosopher" 1956-1959

On 9 September 1956, I arrived at the Novitiate of the Missionaries of Scheut in Zuun in Flemish Brabant, Belgium. A small suitcase stuffed with two black cassocks, toiletries, underwear and collarless shirts were all we needed for a year of "total separation from the world." It was a record year for new candidates: sixty-six fresh novices for the Flemish province at Zuun, and sixteen for the Walloon and Dutch provinces. Most of us came from large families; forty-eight of the sixty-six were products of the "old humaniora" and forty-six had been active in the KSA, a confirmation of how these institutions were breeding grounds for vocations. Father Hubert Peeters, the seasoned master of novices, thanked the parents for "providing replacements for the old missionaries and for giving their sons to Christ." He finally addressed the new recruits:"You have abandoned the world, not because the world is evil. No, the world is not evil, and you are a living proof of this. You are withdrawing yourself from the world because you know that the high ideal you dream cannot possibly be realized in the world. Today, a life of obedience, poverty and chastity begins in the service of God and the souls. The robe you are wearing is the symbol of this unequal promise." [16]

The novitiate in Zuun was located on a property with thirteenth century religious roots. In 1250 a group of Bernardine nuns established a priory, called *Klein Bijgaarden*, which survived until the French Revolution, when it ended up in private hands and was made into a residential "castle." The Scheut Fathers acquired the building in 1941 to house their novitiate. The quiet sprawling property with its walking paths, pond, woods and farm became an ideal playground for the young monks. For twenty-six years, Zuun housed an average of forty novices a year, mostly under the leadership of Father Hubert Peeters. The shrinking numbers of recruits changed the use of the property into a home for the order's retirees in 1968.

I still find it amazing how sixty-six warm-blooded teenagers so easily adapted to the daily rigors of prayer, reflection and manual work. Was it the discipline ingrained in us by our parents and/or the six years of stringent scheduling during our high school years? At any rate, the 365 days as novices were intended to teach us how to live in a religious community and to understand the consequences of the three religious vows of poverty, chastity and obedience. As many new orders founded in the nineteenth century, Scheut was a 'religious missionary congregation' which meant that its missionary ideal was imbedded in monastic spirituality and practices, including the three religious vows of poverty, chastity and obedience. At the end of our novitiate we would profess our first temporary vows and become official members of the congregation.

The regimen of daily prayers, reflection and indoctrination was geared to find out if we were fit for missionary life and the practice of the three vows. Complete isolation from the world was deemed necessary to test our vocation. For the entire year we had no idea what was happening in the outside world: newspapers and magazines were not permitted; television was still in its infancy, so we really did not miss it. Twice a week we went on two and a half hour walks in the surrounding towns, somehow reminding us that there was indeed an outside world with people without cassocks. Trips to the other Scheut study houses would give us a glimpse of Scheut life after the novitiate, but for the rest we were "imprisoned" in our idyllic surroundings. Incoming correspondence was monitored and outgoing mail passed through the magister in open envelopes. A limited number of family members could visit us twice a year. Whatever goodies they brought were consumed during their visit and the remainder was distributed to the community. These rare visits reminded us that we really did not belong to our families anymore but were part of the Scheut family.

One of the favorite members of my "new family" was Brother Willy Bonte. During my last high school years I knew Willy as "Bontje the toilet guy." His job was to make sure that the flush-less facilities at the school remained operable. He did this on a daily basis with a long iron plunger which he dragged noisily behind him. Bontje had decided to become a missionary brother. [17] His first assignment was to be chef in the novitiate kitchen. I kept visualizing "Bontje the toilet guy," but now donned with a chef's hat! For health reasons Brother Bonte never made it to the missions, but he faithfully served the Congregation for more than five decades in Belgium and was the honorary guest at the fifty year reunion of our novitiate in 2006. He represents the innumerable services the Scheut brothers have provided to the missions as architects, builders, mechanics, and teachers.

The practice of the religious vows during the novitiate was never a real problem. Attachment to material goods was no problem: we simply did not have any! The Congregation provided meals, we had a roof over our head and we did not have to handle money at all. Later in my religious life, the vow of poverty would prove to be the easiest to practice. The Congregation always provided for our material wellbeing. When we needed money, we went to the "economus" who served as purser and it was provided. The only requirement was asking permission to use it because we really did not own it! Later in the Philippines I would work with the poorest of the poor, while never really experiencing poverty myself. When I became a layman again, I did not have a dime to my name and for the first time I really understood what poverty was. I later learned that others who had chosen to leave the priesthood had quietly accumulated a sizable bank account in their personal name... Personally I thought that the training I had received from the congregation was a generous enough gift which I somehow had to reimburse. I did this by contributing to my former colleagues who stayed in the CICM, by organizing a pasta day at Notre Dame Prep, thus financing a nutrition program in the Philippines for the last twenty years, and by assigning a part of my estate to the congregation. When I returned to the "real world" I learned the value of money very fast, but it never became my god. I still credit a certain detachment from material stuff and money to my years of a poverty vow.

Much instruction was dedicated to explaining the vow of obedience. According to Canon Law the "evangelical counsel of obedience...requires a submission of the will to legitimate superiors, who stand in the place of God when they command according to the proper constitutions" (canon 601). Sacrificing your own independence and own will for the sake of God indicated a spirit of self-denial and mortification while you were mastering your passions. In the novitiate, the master of novices was really "the master" and disobedience was out of the question! As products of the fifties we were molded not to question any authority, be it parental, political, or educational. I cannot remember any crisis situation in which I would question the directions of my superiors in assigning me to further studies, parishes and teaching assignments. It would take a couple of decades before we requested a "dialogue" before we obeyed. I always had a problem, however, with the terminology used to describe the religious vows: they were the counsels of the "perfect state" in the church, suggesting a more elite class compared to the regular lay people. In a way, laypersons were seen as less perfect and second class.

The third vow of chastity was easy to practice in the novitiate, except for the demons in our head: there were no immediate temptations, no risqué movies, forbidden books or even smiles from Eve. In the conferences about the vows, chastity and celibacy were a given and were seldom discussed as a real possible problem in our futures. Throughout my training years I cannot remember discussions about the fact that celibate life could be a lonely one and that we would be working together with religious sisters, women catechists and mothers in the pastoral field. We were continuously warned against the dangers of "special friendships" embodied in the axiom *"numquam duo, semper tres"* (never two, always three). Somehow all friendships were deemed to be dangerous and might lead to sinful behavior. How human friendship could be a positive factor in our lives was never discussed. This approach to friendship was not only fodder in the novitiate, but was repeated in the spiritual training throughout our formative years.

The notion of "acculturation" and our integration into the cultures we would be facing -- including its women -- was still years away and never entered our curriculum. Adjusting to nonwestern cultures and relating to women seemed to be something we would have to learn on the job once we were in the missions. Many of us did so, but with varying success.

The master of novices was an old-hand in managing young lads and combined his experience with a great sense of humor. He was also a real fox who somehow knew everything that was going on in the minds of his novices. My biggest problem, he maintained, was my "lack of humility." During my high school years I had always been a leader in all the organizations I belonged: KSA leader, actor in plays, soloist in the boys choir, leading dancer in Thor, and even "mayor" when we tried a student government at school. Peeters, convinced that he had to bring me down a few pegs, voiced to me that I was "like a wild pony that always had to be reined in," thus preparing me for the vow of obedience. To subdue my pride, he suggested the use of the "discipline," a small leather whip with knots, intended to inflict corporeal punishment on ourselves. It was of no help because I never could bring myself to use it although I did hit my chair a few times just in case someone was listening. Fortunately this medieval practice was abandoned after our novitiate.

All in all, the novitiate was a happy year and a fertile ground for lifelong friendships. Surrounded by a group of nice guys who all were inspired by the same ideals, I felt that I was growing spiritually and became increasingly convinced that I was in the right place. Minor worries were the fear of a next "dry period" in my prayer life, whether the master of novices would think I made progress in my spiritual life, or spent enough time memorizing my Chinese characters. Not many things could get you in trouble, but I still managed to do it anyway. My manual labor job, with Herman Opgenhaffen as my assistant, was to give marine-style haircuts to my confreres (after all I was the son of a barber). One day we decided to give a mohawk cut to two unsuspecting confreres and since there were no mirrors in the barber shop, they were unaware of their transformation. When the two walked in chapel, it was mayhem! Father Peeters was not amused and we ended up with three weeks toilet duty and scrubbing detail of the palatial white marble steps, a remnant of the castle days of the convent.

The 66 novices of Scheut in 1956 with novice master Fr. Hubert Peeters (author seated, fourth from the left)

It was a given that not all sixty-six of us would persist; after all, novitiate was a boot camp for our vocation. Nine of the novices mysteriously disappeared during the year of our novitiate. We were only left with speculation about the reasons for their departure, and were just assuming that they had realized -- or were told -- that they "had no vocation."

After 1,186 hours of private and communal prayer, 364 hours of private meditation, 416 hours of religious instruction and 365 days of separation from the world, we were deemed ready to take the important step of first temporary vows of chastity, poverty and obedience. On 8 September 1957, fifty-seven of us professed our vows and officially joined the ranks of the Congregation. During the ensuing six years of study another fourteen decided they were not missionary material and fifteen left after ordination. Twenty-eight of the original sixty-six novices remained Scheut Fathers.

Today, more than fifty years after I entered the novitiate, the CICM has become a different congregation. In 1957 all the eighty-two novices were from Belgium and the Netherlands; today not a single one of the twenty-seven novices is from Europe and the same can be said of the one hundred men in training. The CICM membership in 1957 was 1,902; today they have 892 members of whom 452 originate from Belgium and the Netherlands and 388 are over seventy years of age. Of the thirteen provincial superiors, only three are from Belgium.[18] One could deplore the demise of missionary zeal in Belgium, but the absence of priest candidates follows the general pattern of lack of priestly vocations in the Belgian dioceses and all over Western Europe. On the other hand, the growth of candidates in the CICM mission territories shows that these missions have become missionary themselves, as Vatican II had wished in its church and missionary documents.

Philosophy in Nijmegen 1957-1959

Before we would be sent into the world to "convert souls for Christ," we would undergo six years of philosophical and theological training. Due to the large number of new "scholastics," our year was divided in three groups, assigned to three formation houses: twelve were sent to Nijmegen in the Netherlands to join eight Dutchmen; eight joined the six Walloons in Jambes; the remainder trekked to the Scheut headquarters in Anderlecht (Brussels). A widespread rumor had it that the "smart ones" were in Nijmegen, the "holy ones" in Jambes and the "rest" were in Scheut. I must admit that I felt special being among the Nijmegen exiled crowd to study philosophy "abroad" -- be it only just north of the Belgian border. The experiment was an initial step of the internationalization of the study houses a few years later.

The Bishop Hamer House, built in 1923 to house the novices and students of the Dutch CICM Province, was named after Bishop Ferdinand Hamer, martyred during the Chinese Boxer Rebellion in 1900. [19] Above the entrance of the spacious building, adorned with a Chinese pagoda on the roof, was a Chinese dragon attacking the cross with the motto "The light of the cross is the death of the dragon." (*Splendor crucis, draconis mors.*) Two decades after the inauguration of the Hamer House the Chinese communist dragon had expelled more than 150 Scheut

Bishop Hamer House
Nijmegen, The Netherlands

missionaries from China (1948-1955), but the device reminded us to keep our missionary spirit alive.

The nineteen hours a week of academic instruction were a welcome change from the spiritual teaching of the novitiate. We had no idea that the "love of wisdom" would be restricted to Thomism. In 1893, Pope Leo XIII had made the doctrines of St. Thomas Aquinas normative for the church and requested that they be taught in all Catholic institutions.[20] Philosophy was not to be a science in its own right, but "if rightly made use of by the wise, in a certain way [philosophy] tends to smooth and fortify the road to true faith ... and prepares the souls for the reception of revelation." [21] It belonged to philosophy to "religiously defend the truths divinely delivered and resist those who oppose them" (ibid.7). Therefore, "It is the glory of philosophy to be esteemed as the bulwark of faith and the strong defense of religion"(ibid). The pope urged teachers to "endeavor to implant the doctrine of Thomas Aquinas in the minds of students and set forth clearly his solidity and excellence over others"(ibid 31) and "use (his philosophy) for the refutation of prevailing errors"(ibid). The traditional church view that philosophy was the "handmaiden of theology" (*Philosophia Ancilla Theologiae*) was reconfirmed, with Thomas Aquinas as the obligatory master.

This authoritarian and defensive approach of Thomism led to the production of neo-scholastic manuals used in the seminaries until the era of the Second Vatican Council. Fr. Carolus Boyer's S.J. manual "*Cursus Philosophiae ad usum Seminariorum*" [22] was our neo-thomistic introduction to wisdom. The manual was an assemblage of unending distinctions, definitions and syllogisms, setting up philosophical structures that answered all the questions and questioned any answer that dared to be different from the proven structures. Not exactly a method inviting creativity or leading to real insights! Thus we started our quest for answers to life questions: *What is the soul? How do we know? What is the truth? What is good? How do we prove God's existence with our reason? What is being?* etc. Answers to these questions were neatly packaged in Aristotelian and Thomistic terminology and construction: matter and form, essence and existence, potency and act, substance and accident. We soon adopted these terms with increasing dexterity in constructing sure answers to questions humanity had struggled with for centuries. We learned to identify and analyze all the different "-isms" philosophers had come up with over the ages: atomism, monism, idealism, realism, determinism, hedonism, utilitarianism, dualism and nihilism and many others, usually making sure we could refute them and prove them wrong. "Our" philosophy was always able to get to the real truth and the ultimate "essence" of things, assuring us that we understood the real "existence"!

The ancient philosopher Heraclitus would have smiled at our efforts and reminded us that, "The untrained mind shivers with excitement at everything it hears." We were not shivering, however, sitting through the monotonous delivery of Father Egbert Kraeykamp, CICM, who practically recited to us the manuals of logic, epistemology, history and cosmology. After having dutifully taken class notes, we produced mimeographed study guides in Dutch to make sense of the Latin manuals. The ten hours of philosophy were complemented by scripture, biology, missiology, experimental psychology and Thsiluba, an African Bantu language I had to take up because of a possible future assignment to the Congo.

The spark that ignited my enthusiasm for philosophy came from our second year philosophy professor Father Jeff Wemaere, CICM. Only five years our senior, he introduced us to the phenomenology and existentialism of Husserl, Merleau-Ponty, Heidegger, Sartre, Jaspers and others, but in particular of his favorite French philosopher-author Gabriel Marcel. Wemaere's unbridled enthusiasm and ability to explain things in plain language took us into entirely new paradigms. Husserl had told us that we needed to return to the 'things in themselves' (*Zu den Sachen selbst*) instead of holding on to some theory or system instructing us how they must be. Nietzsche claimed that traditional philosophy turned away from the real world and pointed to the world of ideas: "Do not listen to those who offer you supernatural expectation." The existential situation became the point of departure for all enquiry. It was from my own existence that I would define myself and the world around me. My nature was not fixed in advance: I must create it by living. "The world of explanation and reasons is not the world of existence," said Sartre.

With enthusiasm we absorbed a whole new vocabulary which seemed to contradict whatever we had learned in our first year neo-scholastic classes: problem and mystery, nothingness and non-being, alienation, angst and despair, being and existence, demythologizing and objectifying... We devoured Gabriel Marcel's *Homo Viator, Être et Avoir,* and *Le Mystère de l'Être* with gusto and began to think that "reality cannot be summed up" and "existence transcends objective enquiry, and is thus a mystery." Now we were sure that "existence precedes essence" and we are free to create our own essence... "Man is nothing else but what he makes of himself," opined Jean-Paul Sartre.

I must admit that the experience of being trained in two opposing approaches to philosophical thinking was healthy: we were learning to question things that had been presented as absolute truth. Questioning is, after all, the purpose of philosophy. I subscribed to Socrates' opinion that, "The unexamined life is not worth living" and it became a habit for the rest of my life. Later, in my years in Rome and the Philippines, this questioning would get me in trouble. I was in good company, however, because Socrates himself paid dearly for his examination of the so-called obvious!

After enthusiastically being immersed in existentialism, I began to question its own claims to truth. Did existentialism leave us without any foundations to rely on? If we "are what we decide to be," can we still speak of a 'human nature' or do we end up with 'human natures' dependent upon the decision maker's opinions or imagination? Would this lead us to complete relativism making it impossible to distinguish between good and evil, right and wrong, true and false? Was Leibnitz possibly right when he stated in 1670 that "a distinction must be made between true and false ideas"? Was Martin Buber on the right track when he opined that "values must be discovered, not invented"?

To this day, I tend to lean towards the general belief that there are absolutes in philosophy, ethics and theology. Relativism appears to me as a poor excuse for solid thinking. Our insights into the absolutes (and dogmas), however, should be continuously examined and can be changed, deepened and reinterpreted over time. The exposure to radical alterations in the philosophical landscape prepared us for the theological revolution that would be generated by the Second Vatican Council. That council would tell us that there were other ways to look at the church and that the "examined church" was well worth living for.

The two years in Hamer House were memorable and enjoyable. We thought it was a privilege to live in a small community and we enjoyed the pleasant environment, the spacious rooms and decent food. We did not mind being referred to as "the intellectuals" by our confreres in Scheut. Little did we know that by the beginning of our second year, 28 October 1958 would mark the beginning of fundamental changes in the worldwide Catholic church: Cardinal Roncalli was elected as Pope John XXIII. Three months later this new pope announced at the Basilica of Saint Paul Outside the Walls his intention to convoke an ecumenical council. John XXIII's decision was going to fundamentally change the rest of my life.

Before the end of the second semester, the rector called me to his office and told me that the superiors had decided to send Jacques Clijsters, Toon Ramon and me to the Gregorian University in Rome for theological studies: would that be O.K.? The prospect of studying at the center of the church during an ecumenical council filled me with joy and unbridled expectations. For my parents it meant having me at home only once a year, but I later learned how proud they were. My father's customers in the barbershop were all informed about it, musing that "the Jeff was on his way to become a bishop." It had been a long tradition in Scheut to send students to the universities in Rome and Leuven for 'higher studies' to staff the Congregation's seminaries and formation houses with homegrown professors.

More than ever I was convinced that I was on the right track in my life's journey. I felt at home in the Scheut Congregation. Three years of prayer and spiritual life convinced me that God wanted me there. Two years of philosophy had taught me not to take any ideas for granted. I was ready and eager to be immersed in theology by the Jesuits at the Gregorian University, while the church was examining herself to find how she could speak to the world in a new voice.

Saint Peters Basilica
The Gregorian University
Study houses of the Scheut Fathers

CHAPTER FOUR

Roman Journey: Gregorian University and Vatican II 1959-1966

In September 1959 I arrived in Rome after a twenty-six hour train ride from Brussels. I had not been in Rome since 1956 when our Thor dance group danced for Pope Pius XII in Castel Gandolfo. From the first day I felt at home in this city; for some reason I always felt a close connection to Rome and everything Italian. Four decades later I learned that my very early ancestors originated from Rome in the ninth century. [23]

The Congregation's study house in Via San Francesco di Sales, where I would spend the next six years of my life, was a four story villa on the slope of the Janiculus hill in Trastevere. From my window I could see the entire city of Rome basking in the evening sun. Saint Peter's Basilica was only a fifteen minute walk. Below the house was the Regina Caeli Penitentiary and all night we could hear the shouted messages of inmate relatives from the Janiculus to the prisoners below -- a source of many Italian words not listed in a dictionary. A winding path climbing the sloped garden led to a vineyard-covered walkway overseeing Rome's panorama

-- an ideal place to recite our rosary and breviary. The dozen rooms limited the house to a small community and always provided a feeling of intimacy.

Father Hubert Standaert, a former missionary in the Philippines, was our rector and served as procurator general for the Congregation to the Vatican. This goodhearted and deeply spiritual man from Brussels acted like a father to the young scholars under his care. He loved to go shopping for our provisions in his fancy Alfa Romeo, drink espresso and smoke Tuscan cigars, was a fanatic canasta player and collected Vatican stamps as a real investment. Our small community of fourteen was served by the cook, Vincenzo, and our factotum, Luciano, who sampled the table wines once too often. From them I learned some Roman dialect and a secret recipe for pasta sauce which later would be made "famous" in the Philippines.

Every day we crossed the Ponte Mazzini in our black cassocks and walked through the center of Rome to Piazza della Pilotta for our classes at the Gregoriana, or the Pontifical Gregorian University. This institution, with the largest theology department in the world, was founded by Saint Ignatius of Loyola in 1551 as the *Collegio Romano*. Gregory XIII housed the university in a new building in 1584 and gave it his name. In 1930 the Jesuits opened a neoclassical new building on the Piazza della Pilotta, facing the Biblical Institute. During its 450 years the Gregoriana produced sixteen popes, twenty-three saints and fifty-one beatified. Today, its alumni represent 32% of the college of cardinals and almost a quarter of the world's bishops.

When I began my theology in 1959 the university numbered 2,687 clerics of which 1,712 were in the theology department. The classes, taught in Latin, were reserved for seminarians and the university did not provide anything but academics. In the last five decades the "Greg" has completely modernized and introduced medical, social and pastoral services for its changing student population: 16.5% of the circa 2,800 students are women, 9.25% are lay men, and classes are taught in Italian, French and English.

*The CICM study house in Rome, in front of
The Regina Caeli prison.*

Entering the Gregorian was like joining the United Nations. The circa 1,700 theology students coming from more than 125 nations were dressed in a Technicolor of cassocks. The German-Hungarian College, administered by cardinals at their foundation in 1552, wore red cassocks. One tradition has it that cardinal's red was chosen because of the uproarish behavior of the German seminarians; another tradition claims that the red would easily be recognized at the houses of ill repute in Rome... At any rate, *gamberi cotti* (boiled lobsters) was their favorite nickname. The Greeks donned blue cassocks and red sashes; Americans, double-breasted cassocks with crimson sashes; others had red buttons, purple or red piping which made them look like wannabe bishops. This special cassock fashion was in vogue until the seventies although a few kept their customary attire after that.

Wearing cassocks in Rome, however, was not a matter of choice. Early 1960 the Roman Diocese held its first synod in 500 years. While the synod of 1461 imposed penalties on priests for gambling, sorcery, blasphemy and fortune telling, and ruled against "fancy hairdos" for priests, the new synod listed a host of new rules for all priests residing in

Rome. The new diocesan constitution, which Roman Catholic bishops everywhere were urged to follow in their own dioceses, reflected the mentality of the Rome diocese just two years before the beginning of Vatican II. All priests had to wear cassocks and round-brimmed hats; they were forbidden to smoke in public, attend movies, sports events or any public spectacles except those approved by the church; priests and nuns were not to buy or use cars without special permission and not to travel in a car with only one member of the opposite sex, even members of the immediate family. Members of the clergy were only to write for Catholic publications. The Church claimed its right to advise laymen how to vote in elections and laymen should not argue religion in public with non-Catholics. Finally, women were advised to avoid temptations of "false emancipation." Pope John XXIII advised his priests in Rome during one of his addresses to the Synod that he was "grieved that some people should talk about the possibility, or even the convenience, of the Catholic church giving up what has been for centuries, and still remains, one of the noblest and purest glories of her priesthood- i.e. celibacy." Fortunately, Father Standaert never imposed on us the brimmed hat rule, but I noticed that he donned his own hat when he was going to the Vatican for his business dealings.

Classes at the Gregorian were all held in the universal language of the church: Latin. I was grateful for the six years of classical education at St. Rembert because Latin now became a living language for me. Most textbooks were in Latin, but some professors published their courses in their native tongues, Italian, Spanish or French. It was often a real pleasure to hear some professors explain the intricacies of a moral problem or a theological thesis with such Ciceronian ease, be it then with a French or American accent. Some students from the North American College, who were not that well versed in the classical languages, had real problems with Latin and were assisted by a number of tutors at their college. There were rumors that some were punished for trying to sell review questions and English translations of courses on the black market. Good old Yankee

After classes at the Gregoriana (The author and Peter Knecht, SVD)

business sense! After seven years of classes, textbooks and exams in Latin, it took me years to avoid Latin theological terminology when discussing an issue with friends, but I still enjoy reading the Latin Vulgate version of the bible.

Classes were held in a large Greek-theatre-like lecture hall, where the Jesuit professors lectured to about two hundred seminarians. Contact between professors and students was limited to the oral exams at the end of the year and was reserved for doctoral candidates whose dissertations the professors were guiding. On occasion a professor would have a 'question box' where students could deposit thorny moral questions. The moral theology professor, Father Francis Furlong loved the practice but he sometimes got very unusual objects in the box. He once stated that he was not going to demonstrate the use of the condom someone had placed in the question box... On another occasion he produced a plastic handgun which revealed to me its Latin translation, "*Habeo sclopetum*" (I have a handgun).

In between classes we had a chance to cultivate "international relations" and practice foreign languages. I practiced Italian with an Italian missionary, and German with Peter Knecht, a member of the Society of the Divine Word (SVD) who later became professor of anthropology at Nanzan University in Japan and is editor of *Asian Folklore Studies*. My English tutor was Gerry Sullivan from Butte, Montana, who introduced me to Thanksgiving, barbecue, American football and Broadway shows, produced every year at the American College. I will never forget my introduction to *My Fair Lady*: it took me some time to learn that the star of the show was Lisa Doolittle and not "John," but nobody would have ever guessed that the ladies with the fancy hats at the horse races were seminarians -- and some future American bishops. Thanks to Gerry Sullivan I lost my British accent for an American (Flemish) accent.

Extracurricular activities at the university were quite limited. *Vita Nostra*, the student organization, organized some activities for the students since we did not have access to public spectacles. There were regular movie projections, a soccer league and volunteer work in Roman parishes. When I learned that the International Building Companions had a building project on Monte Mario in Rome, my former experience and enthusiasm for the aid organization prompted me to organize the participation of a group of Vita Nostra members. During our first workday on site, we were interviewed by a reporter of the *Osservatore della Domenica*, a weekly magazine of the *Osservatore Romano*, which published an article on the "seminarians at work on a building project." Unfortunately, the article had compared us to the "working priests" of France -- a movement which had been partly suppressed by Pius XII in the early fifties. Our rector Father Standaert received a phone call from the Vatican requesting information about me, mentioned in the article. Father Joseph Fuchs S.J., who was advisor to Vita Nostra, called me to his room at the Gregorian and told me that he had been "advised by people at the Holy Office" to abandon the project. [24] Our building camp experience ended after one weekend! I still wear my "brush with the Holy Office" as a badge of honor from my days in Rome, but I also realized how closely the Vatican was watching "dangerous elements" in the church.

One of my favorite free time duties was serving as a tourist guide for groups of Belgian students, the yearly pilgrimage of the Belgian Military, vacationing CICM colleagues on stopovers in Rome, and some of the CICM bishops who attended Vatican II. Being a tourist guide was a gift to my passion for Roman antiquity and the centuries of treasures Rome had to offer. It provided also the added bonus of being "paid" with Belgian chocolate and cigarettes. Father Standaert initiated a tradition that any visiting confrere who had "seen the pope," had to treat the community with a bottle of Spumante. Christmas and Easter vacations gave us the chance to explore the Castelli Romani and take trips to Assisi, Florence and Naples, resulting in my lifelong love affair with Italy and everything Italian.

For decades theology teaching at the Gregoriana had been dominated by Jesuit luminaries like Timoteo Zapelena, the Dutchman Sebastianus Tromp and the Spanish moralist Marcellino Zalba. Tromp became professor of Fundamental Theology at the Gregorian in 1929 and taught the subject for 30 years. His favorite topic was *Corpus Christi Mysticum* (The Mystical Body of Christ). He is credited as the author of Pope Pius XII's encyclical *Mystici Corporis* of 1943. Pope John XXIII appointed him as secretary of the Preparatory Theological Commission of Vatican II. The schema (or draft) on the church he prepared was rejected and was replaced by a draft which later developed into the Constitution on the Church, *Lumen Gentium*.

The "*nouvelle théologie*" (new theology) movement which originated in France in the 1940s, was anathema to Tromp and other Gregoriana luminaries. The new theology's ideas, however, were here to stay and would be the root of the Second Vatican Council. This new theology attempted to go beyond neo-scholasticism and the rigidity of the manuals by returning to biblical, patristic and medieval theological sources, integrating pastoral experience into the theological studies and promoting the development of dogma. Notwithstanding the efforts of Pope Pius XII's encyclical *Humani Generis (Unitas)* (On the Unity of the Human Race) of August 1950, to end the movement, the *nouvelle théologie* remained an essential preparation of Vatican II and many of its ideas were adopted in the council documents. Some of the movement's leaders, Henri de Lubac, Jean Danielou and Hans Küng among others, became *periti* (experts) appointed by John XXIII to the Second Vatican Council.

In 1959, when I started my theology in Rome, I did not realize that most of my professors were already of a new breed of theologians who were carefully introducing novel approaches. Father René Latourelle S.J., who just had replaced Sebastianus Tromp as professor of fundamental theology, initiated a new way of thinking about the subject by moving away from the classical Apologetics. On occasion Tromp appeared for a few minutes at the side door of the great lecture hall where Latourelle was teaching, listened in, shook his head and left, to the great amusement of the seminarians. Latourelle served later as counselor to de Lubac and Danielou during the Vatican Council. In 1963 he published his *Théologie de la Révélation* (Theology of Revelation) which was translated into six languages and saw thirty editions over the years. It became a standard work on the subject.

Father Francis Sullivan S.J. was our professor of ecclesiology (theology of the church). For a few years he had co-taught with Timothy Zapelena, but in 1958 he took responsibility for the subject and taught ecclesiology and other courses until 1992. We studied a mimeographed copy of his *De Ecclesia* (About the Church) [25] which he would later publish in 1962. Although his course was mainly based on *Mystici Corporis* (The Mystical Body), Vatican II would soon realign ecclesiology in the Dogmatic Constitution on the Church and the Modern World,

*Moments in the life
of a Roman seminarian*

Gaudium et Spes (Joy and Hope) and *Lumen Gentium* (The Light of the Nations) and Sullivan's ideas on charisms became a part of the new teaching. He taught at the Gregorian until 1992 and at Boston College until 2009. He is regarded as a world expert on revelation, inspiration, tradition and the magisterium.

My most famous professor was the Canadian-born Father Bernard Lonergan, S.J.. I must admit that his courses on the Trinity and Incarnated Word (*De Deo Trino, De Verbo Incarnato, De Conceptione Analogica Trinitatis*) (About the triune God, About the incarnated word, About the analogical concept of the Trinity) were the most complicated courses I ever attended. His monotonous Latin with a heavy American accent and his interminable 'sub-distinctions' did not help. I never read his *Insight: A Study of Human Understanding* - Lonergan's most famous work among a plethora of publications. [26] The one idea I picked up from him, however, was his interest in the development of doctrine: he was convinced that our understanding of the revealed mysteries was an ongoing process, gradually leading to deeper understanding. During Vatican II his idea was confirmed in the Constitution on Divine Revelation which stated that there was a dynamic development of dogma.

When I was unlucky enough to draw Lonergan for my final third year oral exam, I knew I was doomed. Answering one of his questions with "*puto quod*" (I think that), Lonergan listened uninterrupted to my extended answer. In the end he said, "*Putasne?*" (Do you really think so?) and he failed me! Afterwards I realized that my answers were on the wrong track, but Lonergan just let me talk. This very humbling (and first) experience resulted in a shortened summer vacation and a second -- and successful -- oral exam in September. I still look back at this failure as a "claim to fame." Being failed by Lonergan, regarded by many as one of the most important Catholic thinkers of the twentieth century, was no small feat. No less than 250 doctrinal dissertations have been written on different aspects of his work.

Our moral theology courses were limited to the casuistic and legalistic approach of the manuals. Our manual was Marcellino Zalba's *Theologia*

Moralis Compendiun I & II. The book was no more than a training manual for future priests who hear confessions and provided interminable dissections of the subtle differences between mortal and venial sins. I always thought that we were taught how far we could go before a venial sin became a mortal one! Father Francis Furlong, S.J. taught us this catalogue of sins with gusto in American-accented Latin. Father Joseph Fuchs S.J. taught us a course in human sexuality and had to tread carefully in the area of academic freedom: the Holy Office was always watching. Fuchs was aware that a new approach to moral theology had reached Rome in the person of Bernard Häring, a German Redemptorist teaching at the *Accademia Alfonsiana* (1950-1986). Fuchs himself (with Karl Rahner) was the promotor of the idea of *fundamental option* [27] and adopted a new approach centering on the totality of Christian life and not on confession. The groundbreaking approach of Bernard Häring integrated the Bible, Christology and even the liturgy in moral discussions. I obtained a Flemish translation of Häring's *The Law of Christ* (1954) published in 1959 [28] and made it my favorite handbook for moral theology issues. The work revealed to me that there were more meaningful alternatives to the classical manuals.

Häring believed strongly in the church's need for reform and renewal and was praised by John XXIII for his ideas at the onset of Vatican II. He participated in several pre-conciliar and conciliar commissions and served later as secretary of the committee that drafted one of the most important documents of Vatican II, the Pastoral Constitution on the Church and the Modern World. Cardinal Cento referred to him as the "quasi-father of *Gaudium et Spes*." Between 1975 and 1979, Häring's publications were investigated by the Sacred Congregation for the Doctrine of the Faith [29] but he was never charged with any offenses. After reaffirming Paul VI's *Humanae Vitae* in his encyclical *Veritatis Splendor* (The Splendor of the Truth, 1993), Pope John Paul II labeled Häring's "fundamental option" as an illegitimate theology, because the pope opined that it undermined the Catholic distinction between mortal and venial sins. There is no doubt that Häring influenced Vatican II and was, in turn, influenced by the Council throughout his life. Both Fuchs and Häring had a deep impact on my own views on moral theology as being more than a catalogue of sins and rules of canon law.

The four years of theology at the Gregorian University, although often traditional in content and approach, gave me a solid training. Five semesters of biblical studies indicated that the Gregorian was aware of the importance of scriptural studies. The dogmatic theology was rounded off by courses in patristic, Protestant, ascetic and Eastern theology, church history, canon law, liturgy and even Hebrew and biblical Greek. It was a real privilege to have professors who were using novel approaches in their disciplines and who later championed the ideas and renovations of the Second Vatican Council in their teachings and publications all over the world.[30]

I heartily disagree with people who dismiss or look down at the theological training at Roman universities with the saying "*Doctor Romanus, asinus Lovaniensis*" (a doctor from Rome is still an ass in Louvain). One day, when I was vacationing in our study house in Leuven, I attended a class in ecclesiology. The CICM professor, who probably noticed my presence, explained how advanced and up-to-date his course was in comparison to the "traditional stuff taught in Rome." As the class progressed I noticed echoes of familiar arguments and language used by Father Sullivan in his course *De Ecclesia*. A closer inspection revealed that the professor's Flemish class notes were a literal translation of Sullivan's course! Now who was the *Asinus Lovaniensis*?

After I obtained my licentiate in theology, [31] the superiors assigned me to take on a second licentiate in missiology. Three more years in Rome and a year of work on my dissertation in Leuven extended my formal clerical "training" to ten years. By that time, I was tired of the books and was eager to "go to the missions."

Witness to Aggiornamento

As I stated in my introduction, it is not my intention to write another history of the Second Vatican Council. I do, however, want to take you with me to Rome during the council and share the excitement of witnessing the renewal of the church as I experienced it. Pope John XXIII had used the term *aggiornamento*, literally "bringing up to date," to indicate his intentions for reform. It became a familiar term during and after the council. From the very beginning we felt that John XXIII had started something special when stating that he wanted to "open the windows to let some fresh air in."

The first phase of preparation of Vatican II was well underway when I had arrived in Rome in September 1959. The council was going to be an integral part of my Roman experience for the next six years. Letters had been sent to bishops and universities all over the world requesting suggestions for discussion. In the ensuing two years, preparatory commissions prepared fifteen volumes and almost 10,000 pages with the advice and proposals of bishops, prelates, religious orders, the Curia and Catholic universities. The Roman Curia [32] had seen to it that the eleven preparatory commissions, under the leadership of Cardinal Ottaviani, were stacked with Rome-based theologians and experts, resulting in a quite traditional agenda. When seven of the schemata (or document drafts) were sent to dioceses all over the world, only the draft on the liturgy was approved for further discussion.

During the preparation stage, we already noticed signs that this council was going to be different. John XXIII had set up the *Secretariat for Promoting Christian Unity* under the leadership of Cardinal Bea and expressed his desire to invite non-Catholics to the council. On 2 December 1960, the Anglican Archbishop Geoffrey Fisher visited John XXIII, -- a first in Catholic-Anglican relations. Another hopeful sign was the establishment of a Vatican II press bureau. When Mgr Pericle Felici, Secretary General of the Preparatory Commission, announced this new bureau, he warned reporters, "Don't get involved in matters which are closed or forbidden to you!" Cardinal König of Vienna, however, thought that, "The Council is the business of the entire church -- which means all the faithful ... If you have something to say about the council, do not wait for word of your bishop, nor for news from Rome." The press followed König's advice and reporters, informed by their secret sources inside the council, told the entire world what was going on in Saint Peter's Basilica.

On 11 October 1962 Pope John XXIII opened 'his' Second Vatican Council. It was quite a sight when after the solemn opening session 2,908 "Council Fathers" (a name given to the voting participants in the Council) exited Saint Peter's Basilica. For the first time in history the attendants were a multicultural crowd representing all races and nations, a real sign that the church was a world church. I was wondering what these 3,000 bishops would come up with in the coming months. When John XXIII was carried out on his *sedia gestatoria* into the piazza, the crowd burst out in a spontaneous applause. It was thrilling and unforgettable to be present at Saint Peters Plaza on such a historical day.

The next day we read John XXIII's keynote address and realized that the pope wanted a pastoral council with a different tone, "...*We must disagree with the prophets of gloom, who are forecasting disaster, as though the end of the world is at hand...*" He emphasized that the Council Fathers had to look at the modern world and learn from it and he stated, "*The church...should never depart from the sacred patrimony of truth received...but she must ever look to the present, to the new conditions and the new forms of life introduced into the modern world...The substance of the ancient doctrine of the deposit of faith is one thing, and the way in which it is presented is another...The Spouse of Christ prefers to make use of the medicine of mercy rather than that of severity...demonstrating the validity of her teaching, rather than condemnation.*"[33]

While my main task was to attend classes and study, Vatican II was a continued subject of interest and I would absorb as much information as possible about the proceedings. On occasion, snippets of information would come from the two council fathers who were part of our small community at Via San Francesco di Sales. We took advantage of the public conferences given by the council's *periti* (experts) like Karl Rahner, de Lubac and Hans Küng. On occasion, I even tried to sneak into the Vatican Press Bureau to obtain press releases about the council activities. The new ideas of Vatican II came to us piecemeal and gave us a feeling of being an intimate witness to the church's "New Pentecost."

On October 13, 1962, the first real signs of this Pentecost appeared: Cardinals Liétart and Frings, both presidents of the Conciliar Commissions, rejected the proposed members of the commissions and requested that the Council Fathers themselves chose new members. The entire standing executive committee of cardinals approved their move and the power of the Curia was partly shattered. The council had expressed its desire for a genuine dialogue and had taken the first step. Three days later 160 new commission members were elected, now representing every continent. A message from the Council Fathers called for a "servant church ... peace among the nations and social justice," suggesting a new direction in council documents.

During the remainder of the first session, the liturgy schema was extensively discussed and finally approved on December 7. The first draft on the Sources of Revelation created so much contention that Pope John XXIII himself terminated the debate and assigned a revision of the document. The Council Fathers also debated the documents on the Mass Media and the Eastern Catholic Churches. Towards the end of the session the bishops made some decisions that guided the council into a fundamentally new direction. Against the wishes of Cardinal Ottaviani, head of the Holy Office (later the Congregation for the Doctrine of the Faith) they first placed the schema On the Church (*De Ecclesia*) on the agenda, criticizing it for its lack of ecumenical spirit and biblical grounding and being too juridical. Ottaviani and the Gregorian Jesuit Sebastianus Tromp were the architects of the church schema. In a speech on December 1, Bishop Emiel Desmedt of Bruges, Belgium, criticized the elitist attitude of the church making relations with other Christians and other religions impossible. He denounced the church's preoccupation with laws and the dominating role of the clergy which placed the laity in a passive role. "Shouldn't this schema be purged of its triumphalism, its clericalism, its juridicism?" Bishop Desmedt said, inviting the loudest applause of the council's history. Convinced that the church document should be the center of future deliberations, Cardinals Lercaro, Suenens of Belgium and Montini of Milan (the later Paul VI) set up an overall program converging everything on the Church document. By 3 December, the seventy-two preparatory schemata had been condensed to about twenty and the pope assigned a coordinating commission to integrate the work of the council. It was obvious that the quite conservative preparatory work had met with the new conciliar spirit of open dialogue, grounded in an ecumenical spirit and biblical sources. By the end of the first session, no official documents had been approved. Pope John kept expressing his wish that Vatican II be a pastoral council, should look further than the internal problems of the church, and be a council for all of humanity. On 3 June 1963, Pope John XXIII died and the Second Vatican Council was legally interrupted.

By the time I returned to Rome from my vacation in Belgium in September 1963, Paul VI was the new pontiff. Before his coronation the new pope stated that, "The continuation of the Second Vatican Council will be the focus of all our efforts." In his coronation message he indicated that the council "must...rejuvenate its forms and bring it up-to-date to meet the demands of the age." Just before the opening of the second session Paul VI announced that the Curia would be simplified and decentralized.

Everything pointed to the hope that the initiative of John XXIII would be continued and brought to a conclusion by the new Pope Paul VI. The church was hopeful. Three more sessions would be needed to finish the sixteen documents of Vatican II.

A special moment with Pope Paul VI

Like everything else in life, Vatican II became routine for us at the Scheut community. As much as we could we followed the news about the debates between the "progressives" and "traditionalists" in Saint Peters basilica, battling with each other to formulate the conciliar documents. Our main activity, however, was attending our classes and study. All kinds of events and news tidbits revealed to us that something unique was going on and that John XXIII's "New Pentecost" was taking shape under the leadership of the new pope. Paul VI took serious ecumenical steps towards union with the Eastern churches by meeting Patriarch Athenagoras in 1964.[34] In the spirit of the council, Paul VI publicly stated that "mutual respect will reduce the distance that separates us." Lay people, including women, were invited as auditors to the council. He established a commission to change Canon Law in line with the conciliar decisions and announced the establishment of the *Secretariat for Dialogue with Non-Christian Religions.* He donated his triple-crown tiara, centuries-long symbol of spiritual and temporal power of the papacy, as a gift to the poor.

Afraid that collegiality would limit the power of the papacy, Pope Paul VI unfortunately gave in to a conservative minority and added a note to the Constitution on the Church (*nota praevia*) stating that the pope "as supreme pastor of the Church, may exercise his power at any time, as he sees fit, by reason of the demands of his office." On the basis of this power, reclaiming the Petrine principle,[35] he later removed two issues from the Council's agenda: birth control and priestly celibacy, opining that the Council was not ready to discuss them. These two issues later led to a crisis of authority in the church and were ultimately decided in two encyclicals: *Humanae Vitae* (1968) and *Sacerdotalis Caelibatus* (Priestly Celibacy) (1967). I keep wondering what would have happened if Vatican II had the chance to openly discuss these two issues: Would we have a married priesthood today? Would the ripple effect of the rejection of *Humanae Vitae* in other areas of church life have been mitigated? Would this open discussion of sex and celibacy have created more accountability in the recent pedophilia cases? We will never know.

At the end of the second session we finally were able to read the first important official documents: the *Constitution on the Sacred Liturgy* and the *Decree on the Media of Social Communications*, promulgated on 4 December 1963. After each promulgation the *Osservatore Romano* printed a Latin version of the new document making it available to the public. It would take until March 1965 before the reforms in the liturgy would take effect: the promotion and use of the vernacular in the liturgy; the new form of the Mass and administration of the sacraments. I had welcomed the liturgical renewal which brought me closer to the people, using a language the faithful understood, involving them directly in the celebrations and facing the people in the Eucharist. Liturgy was no more an exclusive affair of the clergy who could speak the magical words and who thought that following rubrics to the letter was good liturgy. What was important about the liturgical renewal was that the faithful could experience the reality of the *aggiornamento* for the first time. They were not passive bystanders any longer. Many church members were not aware of the new theological insights adopted in the halls of Saint Peters Basilica, but the liturgical changes could be experienced in their Eucharistic celebrations and the sacraments, and that was something immediate and existential.

The promulgation of the *Dogmatic Constitution on the Church (Lumen Gentium)* in November 1964 at the end of the third session, was the highlight of the Council. Avery Dulles S.J. believes that this constitution "because of its central importance and its wealth of doctrine, probably deserves to be called the most imposing achievement of Vatican II." [36] The decrees on Ecumenism and on Eastern Catholic Churches were also approved. These three documents introduced novel ideas about the church and its relationship with other Christian churches. From a church seen as a spiritual super-state with the pope as absolute monarch and a clergy imbued with power over the passive followers, we come to a church which was now seen as a mystery, as the "People of God" where all the baptized stand next to each other sharing in the priesthood of Christ. Lay people are no more asked to obediently participate in the work of the hierarchy, but by reason of their baptism they are recognized as fully responsible members of the church. The paradigm of "accept [or pay] and obey" is changed: the lay person is a coworker. Belonging to the hierarchy and clergy now means service and not domination, and pope and bishops have a common collegial responsibility for the whole church. The Body of Christ is larger than just the Catholic Church and that church is in need of continuous renewal and reform (*ecclesia semper reformanda*). For the remainder of the documents we would have to wait until the closing of the council in December 1965.

The longest document of Vatican II, the *Pastoral Constitution on the Church in the Modern World (Gaudium et Spes)* is remarkable for its tone of optimism and the absence of condemnatory statements. The initial inspiration of the document came from Cardinal Leo-Joseph Suenens of Belgium who, at the beginning of the council had proposed that the church should not only look at itself (*ad intra*) but also ask how it conceives its relationship with the entire world (*ad extra*). Inspired also by the social encyclicals *Mater et Magistra* (Mother and Teacher) and *Pacem in Terris* (Peace on Earth) of John XXIII, the document put the church consciously in the service of humanity. From a church that was trying to dominate all fields of human endeavor, even to the point of hostility, we see emerging a church that recognizes the progress that humanity has made and is sent to be of service to the world. "Christ entered the world to give witness to the truth, to rescue and not to sit in judgment, to serve and not to be served."(3) Not only is the church conscious of what it can contribute to humanity but it is willing to learn from history and the accomplishments of humanity. It is therefore willing to enter into a dialogue with the modern world. It requires within the church to "foster...mutual esteem, reverence, and harmony, through the full recognition of lawful diversity"(92) and it quotes Pope John XXIII's famous words "Let there be unity in what is necessary, freedom in what is unsettled, and charity in any case." (92) The document further details some problems "of special urgency": marriage and family, development of culture, economic and social life, life of the political community, and the promotion of peace in the world. I often wonder if some of today's bishops are aware of what their brother bishops signed fifty years ago when one thinks about statements like "recognition of lawful diversity" and "freedom in what is unsettled."

The *Constitution on Divine Revelation (Dei Verbum)* placed the Bible at the center of the life of the faithful. Before Vatican II, the Bible played only a secondary role in the life of the Catholic faithful. The Catechism was the center of church life by which doctrine was transmitted. There were restrictions on scientific bible study and the scriptures were only secondary in seminary training and worship. Now the document places God's word at the center of everything. God's Word it is primary to all tradition. The magisterium is not above God's Word and has to serve God's Word, not itself. Bible study should be the base of theological training in the seminaries and God's Word should be the primary source of preaching. The document even confirmed one of my favorite insights, i.e. there is a dynamic development of dogma.

As a missiologist, the *Decree on the Church's Missionary Activity of the Church (Ad Gentes)* (To the Nations) was of special interest to me. This decree turned out to be the third longest of Vatican II (after *Lumen Gentium* and *Gaudium et Spes*). In November 1964 Pope Paul VI himself initiated an open debate on a draft of the mission schema but the council members called for a new draft. A year later another draft was rejected because it lacked a theological/biblical basis for the justification of the missions and was not in line with the decrees on ecumenism and on non-Christian religions. Furthermore, missionary activity was not seen as a task for the "people of God" as a whole. Changes were made and on 30 November 1965 they cast 2,162 yes-votes and only eighteen no-votes. The doctrinal principles of the document (chapter 1), providing biblical and patristic justification for the existence of missionary activity, are rooted in the constitutions on the Church and the Church in the Modern World. Although missionary activity is focused on bringing the Gospel to non-Christians by missionaries, the "whole church is missionary" and "everyone should play a part in missionary work among non-Christians." The focus today is less on territorial expansion -- virtually achieved in the nineteenth and early twentieth centuries -- but more on "making the

*The CICM bishops at the Vatican council
and the CICM community.*

Church an active presence within and native to the diverse and developing non-Christian cultures in which they exist."[37] The remainder of the decree covers missionary work itself: the enculturation of the missionary, the formation Christian communities and their growth into particular churches who are imbedded into their own customs and traditions; the essential role of lay people and catechists and the training of missionaries; the need for dialogue with other religions and cooperation with other Christian denominations.

For missionaries, next to the Decree of Missionary Activity, the *Decree of Ecumenism (Unitatis Redintegratio)* and the *Declaration on the Relationship of the Church to Non-Christian Religions (Nostra Aetate)* were opening new approaches and possibilities. While missions in the past took a negative stand against world religions (adherents were only to be converted), the activity of God in all religions was recognized. Other religions deserve understanding and esteem, and we are invited to have a serious dialogue with them. Other Christian churches are no longer seen as "dangerous" elements to be proven false and deficient. The church invites us to make an effort to understand them and make ourselves understandable to them, in an open and respectful dialogue. I was not sure yet how the reforms of religious life, clergy and seminaries would develop, but Vatican II suggested strongly that they adapt to the needs of the contemporary world and that the clergy is here to serve and not to be a clerical super-boss.

On 8 December 1965 the Second Vatican Council ceremonially closed. In three years and two months, the council had promulgated sixteen documents. Many were hoping that these documents would launch a fundamental renewal of the Catholic church. Pope Paul VI expressed his wish that we would "meet the whole human family in a spirit of brotherhood." Fifty years after its conclusion, the Catholic church has certainly implemented part of its renewal agenda. Unfortunately, the "New Pentecost" has not affected everyone in the hierarchy and the faithful.

During my last year in Rome, I worked with Father Steven Lindemans, CICM on a cross-reference guide of the Decree on the Church's Missionary Activity, connecting it with passages in the other fifteen documents of Vatican II. The work on my doctoral dissertation, however, prevented me from publishing the guide, but it permitted me to study all the conciliar documents in depth. That last year was spent in the Congregation's newly built home, the *Collegio Missionario Internazionale* outside Rome. Beginning in the mid-fifties the CICM opened novitiates in the Philippines, the Congo and the United States. A century after its foundation over 90% of the Scheut members were Belgian or Dutch. By the mid sixties the congregation had become more international and in 1967 they moved their General Administration from Brussels to Rome, to a new building next to the new Collegio Missionario, where we lived with about twenty-five students and priests from Belgium, the Philippines and the Congo. This was a conscious effort to internationalize the Congregation. I always thought that this new grandiose building was an expression of the "triumphalism" criticized by Bishop Desmedt during the Council. Some even called it the Taj Mahal. The CICM website claims that, "The spirit and aftermath of Vatican II led to further changes in the Rome setup and the idea of having a large international group of young members in Rome was given up." [38] In 1973 the Collegio was sold together with the adjoining General Headquarters and the General Administration moved into a rented building. The internationalization, however, progressed.

After completing the courses required for my doctorate in missiology, I was sent to Leuven to work on my doctoral dissertation. My seven year stay in Rome came to an end. Unfortunately, during that year I grew weary of books and research and expressed my desire to my superiors to go to the missions. Almost eleven years of training should have prepared me enough to join my friends in the mission field. Convinced that the Gregorian University had given me a solid training in theology and missiology and energized by the experience of the church's aggiornamento, I felt up to the task. My superiors agreed and assigned me

Acolyte at the bishop's consecration of Mgr Cardijn. 12 February 1965

Celebrating Mass at St. Priscilla catacombs

to the Philippines, probably with the intention to prepare me for a teaching job in one of our Philippine formation houses, which were teeming with candidates. I never finished my doctrinal dissertation and remain, as my wife calls me, a "doctor not yet."

My years in Rome and the experience of Vatican II changed my understanding of the church forever and I was eager to see how the new ideas would be implemented "in the field." I was ready to be an active participant in that implementation. I left Rome filled with gratitude: grateful for the privilege of my theology training; grateful for the fellowship of my confreres at Via San Francesco di Sales; grateful for the opportunity to witness Vatican II which gave us a church full of promise. I was inspired by the example and good humor of Pope John XXIII and enriched by the cultural treasures of this incredible city and country and the acquisition of its language.

At the same time, I also had become apprehensive about the incredible clerical power of Rome, manifested in the size of the miters and the amount of purple and red in the omnipresent cassocks. I was always asking myself: could it not be a little simpler? On a deeper level, I had witnessed the careerism, authoritarianism and legalism of Rome and its hunger for centralization and control. This was like a sleeping giant, only partially put asleep during the Council, who would be reawakened in the coming decades, supported by a new brand of bishops and the popes themselves. Although some welcomed the renewal, others were cautious and afraid of losing their clerical power and the security of centuries of tradition. Still others were plainly convinced that the reforms went too far and decided to do everything in their power to bring back the "true and orthodox church" they knew before Vatican II.

I almost physically felt that power of the sleeping giant when I was selected by our rector Father Standaert to read the Gospel to the Council Fathers during a liturgy which usually preceded their work sessions. To be an active participant, be it only for a few fleeting moments, in this history-altering event, addressing 2,500 bishops in this incredible setting, was a real privilege. It also made me realize that the bishops who were listening to the Gospel were not going to let go of their power that easily. I was wondering if the Council Fathers, who were seriously discussing the future of the church in this collegial setting, were going to hang on to the markings of triumphalism, clericalism and juridicism, so clearly denounced by Bishop Desmedt at the beginning of the Council.

I cannot leave my Rome experiences without describing an event at Saint Peter's Basilica etched in my memory. A few months after my ordination I was guiding a group of Flemish pilgrims around Rome and they had scheduled a Mass in the crypt under the floor of the basilica in the Clementine Chapel, also called the Chapel of Saint Peter. This chapel is named after Pope Clement VIII who modified it in 1592. Behind the altar are the remains of the *Memoria Petri* (Memory of Peter), the monument built by Emperor Constantine in the fourth century to protect the mortal remains of the apostle Peter. Pope Gregory XVI gave permission to celebrate Mass at this altar at any time in honor of St. Peter in 1836. During my years in Rome I had been to the basilica numerous times, but that morning I was the first person to enter, without another soul present. In this enormous and magnificent space, built by Michelangelo, Bernini, Maderno, Bramante and Raphael, I could feel the power, history and endurance of the church. At the same time, I felt a sense of belonging and being a part of this unique enterprise. As I celebrated Mass nearby the burial site of Saint Peter the apostle, I felt the closest I ever felt to the beginning of the church I was serving. It was an unforgettable moment.

My enthusiasm for the renewal coming out of Vatican II was going to be seriously challenged during my missionary days in the Philippines and later, as a religion teacher in Baltimore at Notre Dame Preparatory School. When I left Rome, I had been a priest for five years and it fit me like a glove. I was a happy priest and could not imagine doing anything else. [39]

CHAPTER FIVE

806 Days in the Philippines

In 1521 Ferdinand Magellan named the Philippines after Philip II of Spain. Spanish colonists and missionaries followed soon thereafter and Spanish culture infiltrated this Malayan-Polynesian culture for almost four centuries. Traces of this colonization can still be observed in Filipino religion, folklore, languages and cuisine. This country of 7,107 islands and 175 languages grew into a population of 101 million today (sixty-million in 1967) with a 94% literacy rate, and 90% Christian of which 80% are Roman Catholic. After the Spanish-American War the Philippines became American territory and finally gained independence in 1946.

After the Philippine Revolution of 1898, all Spanish missionaries were expelled and American bishops took over the missions. Bishop Dougherty of Nueva Segovia requested the Belgian Missionaries of Scheut to send priests and in 1907 the first eight Scheut fathers and a brother began the evangelization of the Mountain Province and the revitalization of lowland parishes. What these missionaries accomplished in the next hundred years can be called an unmatched success. More than two-thirds of the Mountain Province natives became Christians and numbers of them became priests under the leadership of native bishops. More than 150 Filipinos joined the CICM of which more than half work in missions all over the world. Next to the spiritual care they served the physical and social needs of the people. Bishop William Brasseur of the Mountain Province diocese, for example, established farmers' cooperatives, and erected eight rural hospitals and twenty dispensaries. Education was at the center of the missionaries' efforts and they established a Catholic school system. In the city of Baguio, the one-room Saint Louis School of 1911 became Saint Louis University with, at the present, a student population of more than 27,000. In addition, the CICM runs three colleges in Bayombong, La Union and Tuguegarao, and two seminaries.

*Departure to the Philippines
Rotterdam 10 August 1967*

Surrounded by my parents, my brother Arthur and sister Cecile, and close friends, I embarked for the Philippines on a Dutch cargo ship, the Sloterkerk, in Rotterdam on 10 August 1967. The Sloterkerk was going to be my home for thirty-six days. After ten years of training and study, I was finally on my way to "the missions," ready to conquer the world for Christ! Two steel trunks contained my worldly possessions of clothing and books. A British businessman with a thirteen-year-old daughter and an elderly American lady would be my fellow-passengers until we reached Hong Kong. The Sloterkerk, carrying cargo for Hong Kong, Singapore and Manila, needed to sail around the Cape of Good Hope in South Africa because Egypt had blockaded the Suez Canal after the Arab-Israeli war of 1967.

Being at sea for such an extended time was a first for me. Life on a cargo ship as a passenger is quite an experience. Treated as honored guests, we had easy access to the entire ship, and really had nothing to do except enjoy the vistas, read and enjoy the fabulous food at the captain's table. Ocean sunsets, flying fish and playful dolphins, and the power of the ocean in rough weather created unforgettable memories.

In Hong Kong, my classmate Jos Nijssen showed me around his mission. It was my first experience of the masses of people one observes in Asia. We visited some of his parishioners in the honeycomb high rises, where families of up to twelve people shared a one-room apartment. In Singapore Bishop Van Melckebeke, whom I had befriended during guided tours in Rome during the council, treated me like a VIP and personally came to fetch me from the ship to show me Singapore.

On 15 September we reached the Philippines, my new home for the next five years, or so I thought. Twenty-six months later I would be on my way to the USA after petitioning a leave of absence. The Congregation's plan was to give me some real field experience in mission posts before a teaching assignment in one of the formation houses. At the Inter-church Language School in Manila I studied Ilokano, one of the main languages of the Philippines used in most of the Mountain Province. I always loved languages, but this was a true challenge. There is no real comparison to make with European vocabularies, grammar or syntax. Ilokano is based on word roots altered by prefixes, infixes, suffixes and duplications of syllables. The daily regimen of six to seven hours of classes and study slowly got me into a completely new way of Malayan language thinking.

On weekends I was able to observe Filipino Catholicism, doing pastoral work in some of the CICM Manila parishes. The parish of Paco was founded by CICM Father Raymond Esquenet in 1908. Under Scheut management the parish grew into a mega-parish. It established a school which now serves more than 7,700 students. Several Masses were celebrated on Sundays for packed churches. During weekends, one could spend hours in the confessional. The first time I went to Paco, the parish priest asked me to hear confessions and when I objected that I did not know Tagalog, he told me not to worry and to just give the sinners absolution. Meaningful pastoral advice in the confessional did not seem to matter.

One of my most eye-opening experiences was assisting in the blessing of graves of the departed on All Souls Day in the town of Paranaque. On that day, the entire Filipino family, following an old tradition, gathers around the tombs of its relatives, praying and celebrating all day and sharing food and stories. Our task was blessing the tombs, with the instructions from the parish priest to charge different amounts for a series of services: five pesos for recited prayers; ten pesos for partially sung prayers; fifteen pesos for solemnly sung prayers. Concluding that the relatives of the poor people were as dead as the rich ones, I enthusiastically sang the fifteen pesos ritual for all, charging only five pesos. When the parish priest got wind of my socially just initiative, he furiously scolded me. I learned that it was not healthy for my reputation to rock the boat. I did, however, make many poor Filipinos -- and their dead relatives -- happy that day.

After four months at the language school, I was assigned as assistant priest in Salegseg in Kalinga-Apayao in Mountain Province. The entire province had been entrusted to the Scheut missionaries in 1907. In 1925 Father Francisco Billiet, CICM established the first mission among the Kalinga in Lubuagan. Salegseg followed in 1939. If there was any place where one could feel like a real old-fashioned missionary, it would be

Salegseg. Located at 2,000 feet on a mountain slope in the middle of the Cordiliera Mountains, the village was surrounded by rice terraces and dense forest in mountains reaching up to 6,500 feet. The town could be reached through a couple of dirt "roads" which only permitted jeeps to pass at five miles an hour. Each day, a diesel generator provided a few hours of electricity to the mission. Contact with the outside world was limited and we had to rely on telephone contact in Lubuagan, another town several miles south of us. (In 1967 no cell phones yet!). The Salegseg mission had a church, rectory, high school building and a twenty bed hospital staffed by two young doctors of St. Thomas University, Jaime Morales and Doctora Tidang. My pastor was Fr. Emiliano Madangeng, who in 1971 became auxiliary bishop of Mountain Province and in 1981 succeeded Bishop William Brasseur as the first native Ifugao bishop of the diocese.

My task as assistant priest was visiting the surrounding barrios, administering the sacraments, helping to teach at the high school, assisting the pastor as chaplain of the hospital and driving the reliable Chrysler Jeep which drank gasoline like an old sailor. When barrios could be reached by jeep, Dr. Morales would accompany me, and as a team we took care of the medical and spiritual needs of the Kalingas. In the process I learned about medicines and nursing! I never could bring myself to tell my mother about some of these jeep trips in the mountains. On a regular basis we experienced typhoons (called hurricanes in the USA) which usually washed out the narrow mountain roads. One day we were stranded in a remote barrio and needed to get back to the mission before a second announced typhoon hit us. With the help of the locals we restored the road with rocks and gravel and, with the driver's door open and ready to jump out, we inched the jeep to safety, never forgetting the 2,500 feet deep gorge next to us. I learned another thing during these trips: Filipinos can fix anything with just a piece of wire and plastic tape!

Typhoons were not the only natural events we had to reckon with. On the morning of 2 August 1968 at 4.20 a.m., the rectory started shaking, my books tumbled from their shelves, and frightened shouts came from the

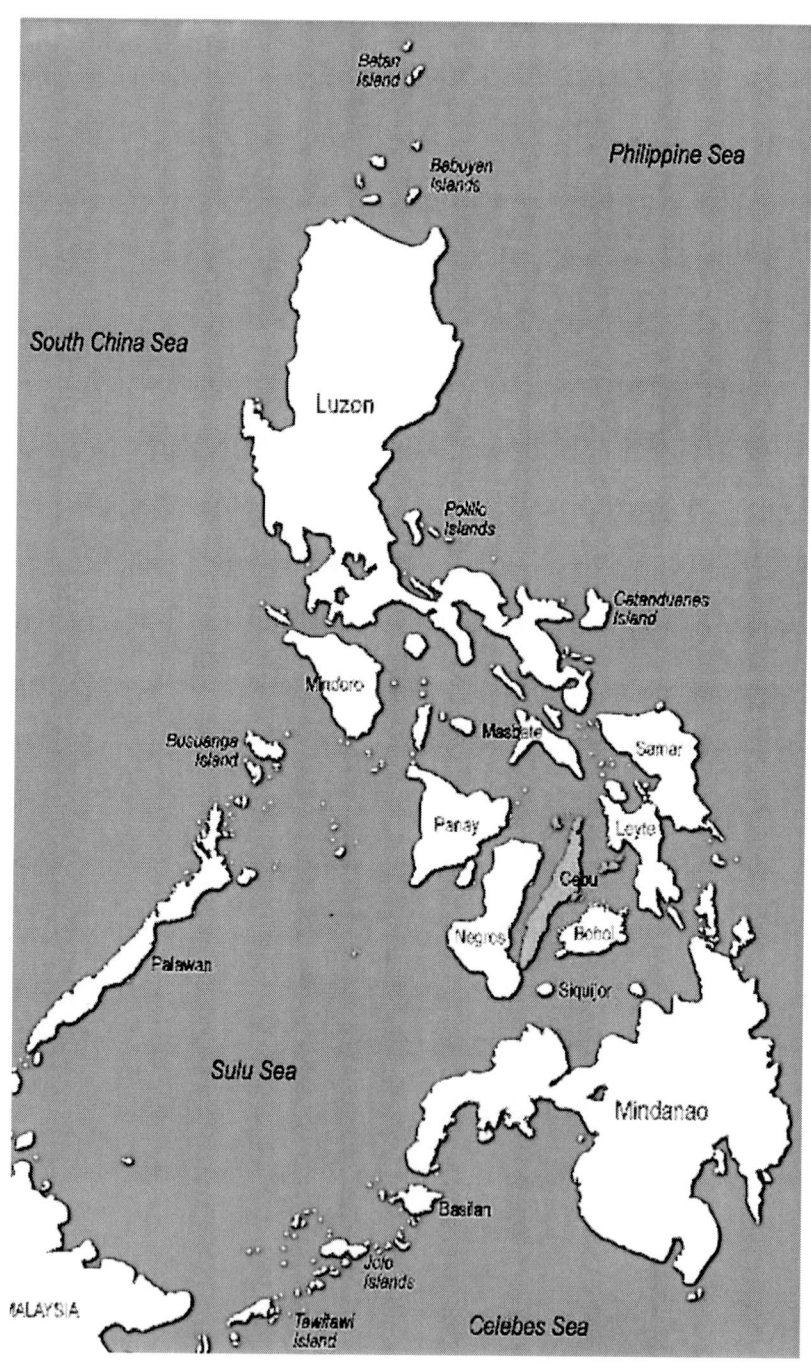

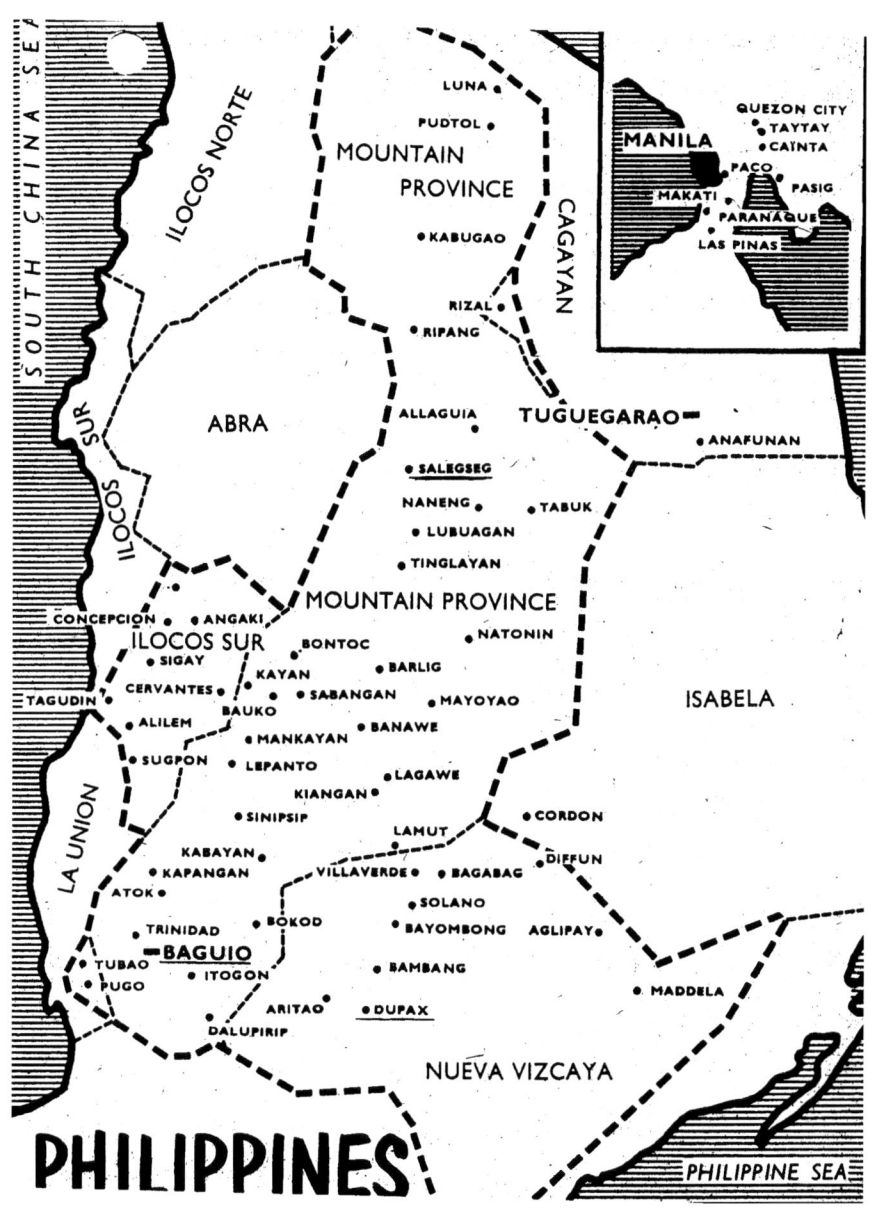

Mountain Province in Northern Luzon, Philippines

girls' dormitory. We had just been hit by a 7.3 earthquake. The wooden structures of the Salegseg mission withstood the event. In Manila, however, an apartment building, the Ruby Tower, had collapsed and buried 228 Filipinos. Since that day, I always sensed some kind of premonition for earthquakes and aftershocks.

Most barrios could only be reached on foot and barrio visits could take up to a week to ten days. Filipino catechists taught the children in the barrios and gathered the faithful for services. During my visits, I celebrated Mass, baptized newborns, validated marriages, heard confessions and on occasion assisted the dying. I was always accompanied by a "mission boy" who was familiar with the mountain trails and possible tribal hostilities. When there was no chapel in the hamlet, we were the guests of the Kalinga, known for their great hospitality. They offered us meals, usually boiled chicken and rice -- a real luxury for most -- and it took me some time to get used to the custom of having to eat first by myself, before the men and then the women and children joined the meal. On occasion I was not so sure that the meal was chicken because in the Mountain Province *aso* (dog) was a real delicacy. At night, I was assigned my own space and a woven screw pine (*pandan*) mat to sleep. Most single-room Kalinga dwellings are raised above the ground on posts and have floors of split bamboo. Adaptation to local customs sometimes turns out to be quite interesting. Since the forest was designated as toilet facility, I used to select the early morning hours to go into the woods, when one morning, a women's voice from a nearby bush greeted me with, "Good morning Father!"

Although administering the sacraments on these barrio trips was deeply satisfying to me, I learned soon that the participation in Christian rituals did not mean that the Kalingas had discarded their pagan customs and beliefs. I observed that after a Christian burial, for example, some families still practiced their Kalinga mourning custom of exhibiting the corpse in a high bamboo chair for several days. They wanted to make sure that the deceased could witness that all rituals were done properly.

The name Kalinga means "headhunters." For centuries headhunting was a noble custom and was considered a sign of male bravery and initiation into tribal life. Tattoos on the bodies of older men in the village were witness of recent headhunting and were admired by the women. Over the years, the Kalingas had instituted a unique system of peace pacts (*bodong*) to minimize headhunting and tribal wars. Although the practice was outlawed by American colonialism and the work of missionaries, headhunting still occurred on occasion. The peace pact system, however, was omnipresent in Kalinga-Apayao. I witnessed this when two of my high school students got into a fist fight one day. One of them got a bloody nose and in an instant the classroom divided into several groups according to their village: the nose bleeding had broken a peace pact! We had to suspend classes, the elders of the two villages gathered, a water buffalo was slaughtered and the *bodong* was reinstated.

Being an avid student of cultural anthropology I got into the study of the religious world of the Kalinga and realized how deeply their religious beliefs were ingrained into their daily lives. All their misfortunes, diseases, crop failures, accidents, and even death were believed to be caused by the

The mission of Salegseg

activities of malevolent spirits, known as *anitos*, or by breaking taboos. These spirits had to be appeased by the sacrifice of chickens, pigs, and on occasion, even water buffalos. The propitiation of the spirits was particularly evident in their burial ceremonies where spirits were believed to observe that all the rituals were done properly. If they were not, then their roving souls would inflict disease and other troubles upon the lives of the survivors. It is not difficult to see how a Christian burial ritual could be an additional assurance to the spirits. One night, I was called to administer the last sacraments to a parishioner in an outlying barrio. When that same night the parishioner died, his son assured me that his anitos "would be very happy with my priestly assistance."

During my trips to the barrios, I learned about the *podayan*, small shelters housing sacred stones, erected at the entrance of a village. I was warned not to disturb these "spirit houses" and respect the stones. Edward Dozier, in his wonderful study of the Kalinga [40] relates an anecdote, worth mentioning, about a Roman Catholic priest resident of the municipality of Salegseg. [41] *"The veneration accorded to the guardian stones in the podayan so infuriated the priest that on one occasion he kicked and scattered the stones of the shrine. He purposely defiled the sacred stones to show the Kalinga that no evil consequences are likely to ensue from such an act. Soon afterward, the priest became very ill, so ill indeed that he was unable to prevent a ceremony performed for his recovery by the Kalinga of the region who had an affectionate regard for him. The medium chanted her songs, sacrificed a chicken and performed her rites despite the priest's weak protestations to stop the rites. The priest recovered and while he attempted to convince the Kalinga that his illness had no connection to his defilement of the sacred shrine, the Kalinga felt otherwise. No doubt the priest, who was also extremely fond of the Kalinga, accepted the ceremony as a sincere expression of their affection for him."* [42]

I recall a similar experience when one of my mission boys got very ill with malaria. Doctor Morales could not improve his condition and we brought the boy to a hospital in Baguio, with similar negative results. We even started a novena in the parish, but the boy did not make progress. In desperation we finally agreed with the family to let the Salegseg medium arrange a chicken sacrifice and perform her rituals. Two days later the boy was back in the mission without malaria. Don't ask me to explain it, but I knew that the score was: Kalinga medium: one; modern medicine and Catholic prayers: zero!

*With the first communicants
Of Salegseg*

Salegseg was quite a lonely place. Beautiful with its mountains, forests and rice terraces, it was separated from the "civilized" world. Living in Salegseg was a continuous challenge. Notwithstanding some of the joys of missionary life "in the boondocks," I started to question what I was doing there. Being a product of the "clerical world," I was far removed from the "real world" of the people I was serving. Clerical as I was, I thought that the center of people's life was their relationship with God. What I did not understand was that their first concern was their survival, their need for education and medicines. They wanted the byproducts of Christianity, while their spiritual world was filled with spirits and cultural customs which they had practiced for centuries. I began realizing that Christianity was just a sort of a veneer in the Kalinga religious world. They accepted some practices of Catholicism as a necessary condition to obtain things that would alleviate their poor life condition. Christian rituals were seen as a "you-never-know" addition to their religious practices. Sometimes I wished I were an expert in agriculture, able to break their seemingly repeated habit of running out of their staple food, rice; or an economist who could teach them budgeting to save for a rainy day.

Administering the sacraments and celebrating Mass became increasingly an exercise devoid of meaning for me. Praying turned into an arduous task. After years of being used to living in close-knit communities, I found in this remote area no one to share my frustrations and doubts, or even having a stimulating conversation. My attempts to speak with my pastor usually ended in an uncomfortable silence. My faith in God was shaken and my outlook on life became dark. For the first time in my life, I had to deal with bouts of depression which I tried to ward off with too much alcohol.

My occasional trips over the treacherous mountain roads to Baguio City were a welcome break. In Salegseg I had to rely on cooking skills I had developed during my teenage years and my stay in Rome. My visits to Baguio allowed me to replenish my supply of canned goods and pastas. These compensated for the rather limited culinary talents of our mission cook, whose Filipino custom of not warning me when supplies will run out -- ("*awanen*, Father, there is no more) -- became a repeated refrain. When typhoons blocked all roads to the mission for days, I learned to create pastas and canned corned beef in a dozen different ways. In Baguio City, I was always welcome at Saint Louis University, where I could unwind with old friends and discuss philosophy and theology, share some of my troubles and a scotch or two. The residence of Bishop William Brasseur, who never failed to show his generosity to the Salegseg mission, became a regular stopover.

Towards the end of my stay in Salegseg, a couple of events further exasperated my situation. I was invited to give a lecture in Manila on the Vatican II mission document *Ad Gentes* to more than a hundred sisters belonging to different religious orders. Days later, I learned that some of my Scheut confreres were not as appreciative as the sisters by spreading comments like, "What does he know about the missions after a few months here?" Since the only goal of my visit was to describe the main principles of the document and show how it had developed during the council, I was surprised and disappointed by the criticism of my confreres. I never claimed to know better than experienced missionaries who were in the Philippines for years. Their criticism dampened my declining enthusiasm for my work in Salegseg and my growing uncertainty about the meaning of my vocation.

My personal problems culminated after some people in the mission had reported to the bishop that I had some kind of romantic relationship with the female doctor at our Salegseg hospital. The rumors started after I had a conversation with her, one evening, sitting on a bench outside the hospital, listening to her medical work problems. Although in plain view, that event became the fodder of gossip, shared, as I learned later, with a couple of my confreres. The whisper campaign became so oppressive that I requested the bishop for a transfer to another parish, and it was granted. The Sunday before I left Salegseg, I confronted the faithful in my homily about their gossip and the hurt it had caused me and others. There were a number of bent heads in the church.

Thank God, my superiors assigned me as prefect of discipline, dean of studies and professor at the CICM Maryhurst Seminary in Baguio City, replacing my classmate Walter Oorts. Since Walter was told to finish the school year at Maryhurst, the provincial superior gave me a temporary assignment as assistant priest in Dupax, Nueva Vizcaya until March 1969.

Arriving in Dupax, I hoped that my new assignment would give renewed enthusiasm to my faith and vocation. Dupax, historically a settlement of the Tsinay tribes, meant "a place to lie down in complete

*San Vincente Ferrer Church
Dupax, Nueva Viscaya*

relaxation" after they hunted in the surrounding mountains. This was not going to apply to me... The parish, San Vincente Ferrer, was founded by the Dominican Friars in 1726. They built the baroque church and rectory in 1773. Dupax was part of the Prelature of Bayombong under Rev. Albert Van Overbeke, CICM, a jovial, good hearted man who loved the Philippines and had done a lot for catechist training. He just loved being bishop and wearing the purple that went with it, giving him the nick name of Red Riding Hood.

My parish priest was Joop Van de Zande, a gregarious and popular Dutchman. We lived in the ancient Spanish fort-like rectory with its three foot thick walls and ramparts at the back which had protected the mission against surrounding tribes two and a half centuries ago. The story went around that the ramparts had also protected a parish assistant who was a little too close to a village official's spouse...

As assistant priest I served the surrounding barrios, supervised the catechists and occasionally taught at St. Mary's High School. Father Joop claimed to be a good friend of First Lady Imelda Marcos and on occasion journeyed to Manila in an air-conditioned limousine, leaving the parish in my care. One time, he stayed away longer than anticipated and did not leave enough funds for me to make the payroll of the high school teachers. Since we had a substantial stock of rice in our cellar, I decided to sell the rice and pay the teachers on time. This made the teachers happy. Upon his return, my parish priest exhibited a sampling of Dutch fury and added another item to my record as a troublemaker. A few years later Joop left the Scheut Fathers and in 1986 I learned that he had died at the age of fifty-three.

Before long, the doubts I had about my faith and vocation intensified while I was in Dupax. I started to have real problems praying and often asked myself if I still believed in what I was doing during the celebration of the Eucharist or when I baptized children. On occasional trips to Manila, I shared my problems with the director and founder of *Asian Social Institute for Graduate Studies* (ASI), Father Senden, CICM, who was known to many of the confreres as a gentle, good listener and trustworthy confidant. At the Institute, Father Senden introduced me to some students, among whom was Felicitas Pattawi. About a year earlier, I had met Felicitas, visiting my language teacher in Tuguegarao, Cagayan, on my way from Salegseg. Among her friends Felicitas seemed to have a knack to perk up her companions. She impressed me as a person who really cared for the poor. As the oldest of nine, she grew up with her large poor family in Tuguegarao. Although she had personally experienced poverty, she always believed that giving was preferable to taking or receiving.

When I met her at Asian Social Institute, she was a research worker at the Institute's Research Department and was taking up her master's degree in Sociology. Before she came to ASI, Felicitas had worked for eleven years in the barrios as a Presidential Community Development Worker, acting as a liaison officer between municipal government agencies, conducting adult education classes and supervising youth groups in agricultural community projects. After high school, she had earned an Associate of Arts degree at the Cagayan Teachers College, majoring in prelaw, and a B.S. in Agricultural Education at Central Luzon University. Because of her experience as a community development worker, Father Senden moved her from research worker to social worker at the Manila-Makati Rotary Club, which was helping slum dwellers in Guadelupe Viejo, Bel Air and the Makati area.

    The day after Christmas, I decided to go to Tuguegarao for a few days of relaxation and to talk to a couple of CICM friends for advice about my problems. Arriving in Tuguegarao, I was dangerously close to a complete nervous breakdown. I had assumed that I could be a guest at the small Spanish San Jacinto church,-- also called "The Ermita" -- but the CICM pastor, for some reason, considered me a "persona non grata." He let me know that there was no place in the inn and that I was not welcome at his rectory. I was surprised, confused and heartbroken. Rudy Pattawi, Felicitas' brother who served at San Jacinto, had overheard the pastor, and invited me to his parents' home. The Pattawi family, having themselves a priest and other clerics in the family, offered their home for the duration of my stay. I then shared with them my fears and frustrations and revealed that I had decided not to accept my new assignment at Maryhurst and that I was thinking of giving it all up and going home to Belgium. The entire family, including uncles, aunts and cousins, listened to me and somehow persuaded me to give it another chance. The Pattawi family had saved me that day. By the time I returned to Dupax after New Year, I had decided to make a final effort to reignite my enthusiasm at Maryhurst Seminary.

    Back in Dupax, I received a letter from Felicitas stating that her family as a whole had adopted me as another son. She described how she felt saddened when she had witnessed my Mass celebration at the Ermita and saw that I "looked like a callous and cold priest who did not feel and believe what he was doing." She said that she prayed that God would clear up my doubts. "Doubting," she wrote, "is searching, and searching is faith. I pray that you have a lasting peace of mind. Flight is never a solution to a problem. Life is a mystery and doubt is an integral part of it...God himself is a mystery but he can be found in all things: in the netted veins of a leaf, the intertwined branches of a tree, the rolling hills, the setting sun, a singing bird, a little flower hidden from view, a mossy wall, the silence of an empty church, the smile of a child, the kindness of a gesture, the compassion to a beggar. God is present in all of these...Try to find God there. Think of other people and do not concentrate on yourself: it will only lead you to feel cheated by your faith. Be the best of yourself. I do have faith in your perseverance!"

The Pattawi family and Felicitas

Her words revealed a person with a deep and simple faith to be envied. I still had to rediscover God and my vocation. I was struggling with the existence of two people in me: the popular, seemingly happy assistant priest, and the other priest who barely believed in the words and the gestures during Mass. It felt that I was just pretending and playing a role in a continuous comedy.

At the end of February, the rector of Maryhurst came to Dupax to talk to me and persuaded me to accept the assignment to the seminary. He believed that I belonged in an educational setting and that the community at Maryhurst would be my necessary support. The group of ASI friends surprised me at the Dupax church on 8 March with cakes and other food to celebrate my birthday and giving me moral support.

When I left Dupax at the end of March, a large group of people came to say good bye. I remember feeling horrible because I was the only one who knew how I was torn apart inside. I wrote Felicitas, "Maryhurst will be the place where I will rediscover myself and find God again. I am afraid to go, but there is a chance I'll make it there!" With a partly uplifted spirit, I left my second mission parish. I felt I was ready for Maryhurst.

Maryhurst Seminary

Baguio City, known as the Summer Capital of the Philippines, is situated 255 miles north of Manila in the Cordiliera Mountains, 5,000 feet above sea level. Its average temperature is fifteen degrees cooler that the rest of the islands. In 1953, the CICM built Maryhurst Seminary, a sprawling wooden building in the midst of a luscious flower garden, planned and tended by Brother Armand Lammineur. The seminary was built to respond to the growing number of Filipino aspirants joining the Congregation. When I arrived there by the end of March 1969, it housed ninety-eight "juniors"(minor seminarians) and fifteen philosophy students. My job description was to be dean of studies, prefect of the juniors and professor. From the very beginning I felt at ease working with these Filipino youngsters who were full of missionary enthusiasm and eager to get an education. I was hoping that their education would reflect the renewal and spirit of Vatican II, particularly the Decree on Priestly Formation *(Optatam Totius)* and the Decree on the Appropriate Renewal

As Junior Prefect at Maryhurst Seminary, Baguio City

of the Religious Life *(Perfectae Caritatis)*. It was my ardent desire to attempt to implement the ideas of these two documents at Maryhurst Seminary. It is therefore necessary to go into some detail about their content. In the end, my attempts proved to be futile and became a battleground, resulting in a shorter stay at Maryhurst than I had hoped.

The document on priestly formation was seen as an extension of the Constitutions on the Church and the Church in the Modern World Today. To be in the world was the nature of the church, to live in the world and be an instrument of Christ was the nature of the priest. The synod therefore called for adaptation and reform. The priest's training had to be doctrinal *and* pastoral. The need for decentralization emphasized the importance of the local church where pastoral preparation must take unto account "the specific environment in which the young priest will begin his ministry."(1,1)

From the very beginning, the document calls for decentralization and asks the local dioceses to "adapt the universal laws...to the special circumstances of time and place, so that the priestly formation will always answer the pastoral needs of the area in which the ministry is to be exercised."(1) The decree does not provide detailed plans but lists certain directives, advice and suggestions: after general advice to program major seminaries towards pastoral life, the bishops request a deepening of spiritual formation based on the Gospel values. What is special to this section is that, "Seminaries...are called not to domination or to honors, but to give themselves over entirely to God's service and pastoral ministry."(9) They insist that "no hardship of the priestly life should go unmentioned," (ibid) something I had not learned in my own seminary days.

The discipline advice was very different from what I had experienced in my own training, "...there should be developed in seminarians a due degree of human maturity, attested chiefly by a certain emotional stability to make considered decisions and by a right manner of passing judgement on events and people."(11) The program should provide "self-mastery, to foster solid maturity of personality."(ibid) The rules of discipline should be age-appropriate "so that they can gradually learn to govern themselves, to make wise use of their freedom, to act on their own initiative and energetically, and can know how to work along with their confreres and lay people as well."(ibid) They even suggested opportunities to interrupt studies to arrange for suitable pastoral apprenticeships in order to improve the selection of priestly candidates. Here was an entirely new language compared to what we heard during our own training, which was dominated by will power, avoiding dangers, blindly following rules and warnings about a dangerous world. They had also told us that prayer was the only way to solve all problems.

The section of the document treating minor seminaries seemed particularly applicable to the situation in Maryhurst. The document suggested that students "lead a life which is suited to the age, mentality, and developmental stage of young men, and which fully conforms to the laws of a healthy psychology. The students should be suitably involved in normal human activities and have frequent contact with their own families."(3) Applying these principles would prove to be a difficult task in Maryhurst, as the rest of my Maryhurst story will show.

Since we were training not only future priests but also future members of a religious congregation, the decree on the *Renewal of Religious Life* was as important as the Decree on Priestly Formation. The Fathers of Vatican II directed the religious orders to rethink their particular mission according to the spirit of the council: reflect on how the Gospel would be the center in their mission to a continuously changing world. They therefore laid out general principles which "must underlie an appropriate renewal of the life and rules of religious communities." This appropriate renewal involves two simultaneous processes. First, a continuous return to the sources of Christian life and the spirit of the founders; and second, an adjustment of the community to the changed conditions of the times. I thought there was one paragraph which particularly applied to us as a missionary congregation: "The manner of living, praying, and working should be suitably adapted to the physical and psychological conditions of today's religious and also, to the extent required by the nature of each community, to the needs of the apostolate, the requirements of a given culture, the social and economic circumstances any where, but especially in missionary territories." (3) It was important that our Filipino seminarians not only understood their own Filipino values and communities, but also that they were trained to face the cultural dynamics of other cultures where they would be sent as missionaries.

It would, of course, take years before individual orders and congregations would suitably revise and bring their constitutions, rules and working strategies into harmony with the documents of Vatican II. Not everybody was ready and eager to jump on the bandwagon of renewal and reform. Here was, however, a blueprint and a strong invitation to make changes. Were they ready to practice authority "in a spirit of service to their brethren, not their 'subjects'? Were they ready to "aim at giving a kind of corporate witness to their poverty"? My own limited experience in the Philippines had taught me that most Filipinos looked at the church as the place "where the money was." Most probably we could not help to stand out in this impoverished society as a wealthy institution, but were we giving corporate witness of the poverty we claimed to practice? Were our superiors ready to "listen willingly and encourage us to make a personal contribution to the welfare of the community?"

Armed with the desire for renewal and determined to give my vocation another chance, I arrived at Maryhurst in March 1969. Fathers Charles Foubert and Conrado Aquino, [43] two study companions from my Roman days, soon joined me. We formed a team intending to bring some changes to the seminary according to the wishes of the Vatican II documents. Before long we would find out that other members of the staff and some provincial council members were not as enthusiastic about changing the status quo. A meaningful dialogue became a challenge.

Convinced that priestly formation was more than academics, we understood that Vatican II proposed that personal development towards maturity and pastoral leadership training were central agenda of the "new seminary." We were looking for ways how this agenda could be initiated at Maryhurst. The attitude of some of the staff towards the students, however, reminded me of my own high school years in Belgium, when we were watched at all times to make sure we did not do anything wrong. There was no contact with the outside world, as if these students were already novices in training. Every minute activity needed a permission and initiatives or proposals by the students were summarily dismissed as "stupid." In addition, on more than one occasion, I heard some of the staff saying that, "You can't trust Filipino boys," expressing a mentality which was very questionable to me.

*Junior Maryhurst students
Agricultural community project
Marcela*

Fathers Charles, Conrado and I wanted to open a dialogue on a series of proposals: fostering more immersion of the staff with the scholastics and even the juniors, thereby creating a more flexible community; making an effort at adding Filipinos to the staff; involving the students in apostolic activities and social action adapted to their ages and schedules. We also wanted to engage in a dialogue with the other educational institutions of the CICM in Baguio City which would foster possible cooperation in academic life and personality development of the seminarians. [44]

It did not take long before rumors started to abound in Baguio and among some CICM confreres that we "wanted to abolish the seminary," that we "intended to move the whole seminary to Saint Louis University." Stories circulated that we "systematically were spreading among the students an atmosphere of unrest" and that we "did not like the seminary because there were only boys...!"

Some of these rumors seemed to be reactions to some of the changes we already had initiated at the seminary. We had prepared a new academic curriculum for Maryhurst and proposed it to the Bureau of Education of the Philippines for approval. Saint Louis University allowed our students to do research at the university library without being enrolled. It was true that we had sometimes sided with student proposals which had been promptly turned down by the rest of the faculty. It was also true that we had argued in favor of internationalization of the congregation against confreres who opined that we did not need to train Filipino CICM. It was known that we believed that in Maryhurst there was too much of a greenhouse mentality in which boys, who had been active leaders in their schools, were now being deprived of apostolic and pastoral activities. Finally, some looked with growing suspicion on a policy of trust we had initiated, emphasizing the seminarians' personal responsibility in their daily activities.

The mistrust and the gossip of my confreres began eating away my enthusiasm and my decision to make this last effort at Maryhurst -- a promise I had made to myself and to the family of Felicitas. On occasion I shared my frustrations with Father Senden at Asian Social Institute and with Felicitas, who kept listening and encouraging me to hold on. She stated, "You can only change a society or a group if you are a part of it and change it from within! Pick up your breviary and turn back to God for guidance. He is testing your humility!" When I confided in the rector of Maryhurst about my feeling that I was playing a comedy, he disagreed because I had asked to teach cultural anthropology and Filipino culture and not to teach religion -- afraid I would have to talk about things I hardly believed any longer. I buried myself in work. I reorganized the old Maryhurst library classifying system; published a course on cultural anthropology; developed a new academic curriculum for the Bureau of Education of the Philippines; organized a music combo for the juniors by buying guitars and amplifiers from a nightclub in Baguio; directed a production of *Twelve Angry Men*; tried to lay the groundwork of cooperation between Saint Louis College and Maryhurst.

An invitation by the Columban Sisters in Manila to give a seminar on Vatican II and missionary training became again fodder for criticism by some of my confreres who commented that this was just self-promotion. Others suggested that I certainly would be visiting Asian Social Institute. Nobody, however, ever had the heart to confront me directly if he had any doubts about my intentions.

In September, Fr. Charles Foubert and I organized a seminar about community development possibilities in Baguio for our juniors and invited students from local high schools to Maryhurst. When some confreres learned that the juniors had invited some girls to the event, they reported it to "the CICM authorities" stating that we were not satisfied with having only boys in the seminary.

The following month, Charles and I redacted a written report with our ideas for reform of Maryhurst which would serve as a basis for discussion in the next faculty meeting. That report was summarily ignored when we met. The rector told me that I had to forget my ideas about reform and that he intended to keep the status quo at the seminary for the foreseeable future. He added that all the problems I had with seminary training were nothing but a reflection of my personal problems. He had also asked Charles Foubert if he would be able to manage Maryhurst all by himself. Realizing that the reform was not going anywhere and that I had become a *persona non grata* I started to make plans to resign from Maryhurst before the beginning of the next semester. I knew that staying in the Philippines was not going to be helpful. My friendship with Felicitas and her friends at ASI was deemed questionable by some in the CICM community. I decided that leaving the Philippines and trying to forget Felicitas all together, would stop all suspicion.

I asked my superiors if I could go and study a year in the United States as a member of the Philippine CICM province. To my surprise, they said, "Yes," probably pleased to liberate Maryhurst from a troublemaker. On 28 October I wrote the provincial superior of the American Province about my new "assignment" and my plans to arrive in the United States in January. I asked him information about the New School for Social Research and Columbia University in New York and about the possibilities of staying in a parish while studying.

My last days in the Philippines had been emotionally draining. I felt guilty after witnessing the deep disappointment of my juniors at Maryhurst when I announced my new study plans. During a heart-wrenching farewell party, my students gave me a bound set of letters they had written for my departure. I was surprised to read some of their comments, revealing that my short stay at Maryhurst had not been fruitless. Their recurring comment was that they had begun to understand personal responsibility as a result of the policy of freedom we had introduced. Some thanked me for my "love of Filipinos and the Philippines." Some were grateful they had "learned that responsibility comes from within." One said that, "The Maryhurst you found when you arrived is not the same Maryhurst that you will be leaving."

The most cherished comment came from Conrado de la Cruz, whose life as a CICM missionary was cut short and ended in martyrdom in Guatemala in 1980. He wrote me, "Despite the misunderstandings of your policies, I know that that you'll be going with the conviction that you have done your best!" To this day, this is the most precious document I cherish from my stay in the Philippines. On 1 May 1980 Conrado and his companion Herlindo Castillo were abducted by secret police in Guatemala and were never heard from again.[45]

While gathering my worldly possessions for my trip to the United States, I reflected, with a sense of great gratitude, on the positive yet intangible things that I had accumulated in my short stay in this country. I admired the tenacity of my confreres who, devotedly and alone, stayed for years in remote mission posts without a complaint -- something I obviously was not able to do. I met many of them who loved Filipinos. Unfortunately, there were others who spoke about them with some kind of colonial disdain. I witnessed the enthusiastic hope of some confreres, sisters and lay people who embraced the renewal spirit of Vatican II and others who were suspicious and even critical of the New Pentecost. Except for some changes in the liturgy, the theology and spirit of the council had not taken root and was largely unknown. On a personal level, I realized that I enjoyed teaching and administration, that rumors could kill one's spirit, and that living a celibate life was a greater challenge than I had anticipated during my years of training. From the enthusiasm of my juniors at Maryhurst, I sensed that there was hope for the church in the Philippines and Asia in general. This hope has materialized in the last few decades of incredible growth and dynamism of churches in Asia.

I learned to appreciate aspects of a culture which were very different from my western ones. We westerners tend to be so impatient and have to do everything on time. From Filipinos I learned that time is not an absolute value. Once I asked my mission helper what time it was and her answer was, "It's exactly around four o'clock, Father." During one of my mountain trips, I inquired what time the next bus was coming through and the answer was: today! I was always wondering if this was the reason why Filipinos do not seem to age fast.

Above all, I learned to love the Filipino people as one of the most hospitable people I had ever met. They give the best they have to their guests though they are very poor. I also learned to admire other elements in their culture that makes them special. Family ties are very strong and they will make enormous sacrifices for the sake of their families. Their respect for elders is remarkable and permeates all interpersonal relationships. Filipinos will almost never directly disagree with you because they feel it is being disrespectful (*walang hiya,* literally "without shame"). This attitude often clashes with our Western habit of open discussion and 'telling it as it is.' This Filipino *kahihiyan,* or 'feeling of shame' always prevents someone to put family, friends or elders in an awkward position. The negative side of this cultural trait is that you might not know what the other is really thinking. A Filipino will almost never directly confront another person when they disagree. This can lead to procrastination and can prevent things from being done. "I am ashamed to ask, I am ashamed to correct you..." Westerners have the tendency to interpret this as dishonesty, but it is not: it is the feeling of being hesitant to openly request or verbalize something for fear of being embarrassed. Another trait is *utang na loob,* literally 'debt from within,' a feeling that you owe gratitude forever for an act of kindness. Generally, Filipinos are happy people and they seem not to be affected too much by adversity, probably because they believe that what happens to them is the result of fate, *bahala na,*("well,---let it be"). At the same time they love life and love to celebrate. The many religious and ethnic festivals are testimony of this.

After 806 days in the Philippines, I left the country at the end of November and flew to Rome to talk about my future with the Superior General of my religious order and pick up my credentials from the Gregorian University. I was still hoping that leaving the Philippines and studying in America might finally clarify what direction my life would take. I did not know that in the next four months I would start a new life chapter.

CHAPTER SIX

Transition to the Laity

In the summer before the opening of Vatican II, I was ordained a priest by Bishop Daem of Antwerp on 5 August 1962 in the church of the Scheut headquarters in Anderlecht near Brussels. Obedient to pre-Vatican II customs we had previously received the "minor orders" of lector, exorcist and acolyte and the "major orders" of sub-deacon and deacon in Rome. After the council the diaconate was restored to an independent order and Paul VI abolished the minor orders in 1972.

As one of the thirty-eight candidates prostrated on the cold church floor I remember thinking, "This is it!" For years I had looked forward to this day, but in a fleeting moment, I was wondering if I would have the strength to be steadfast in my chosen vocation. Only an act of faith brushed away my last doubts.

My first Mass in my home parish in Torhout was a special event. The local fanfare band accompanied me from my house to the church, the parish priest and mayor gave speeches and family and friends filled the church. Celebrating Mass in the convent where I had served as an altar boy for six years was particularly memorable. Seeing people kneel and ask for a blessing encouraged me to feel "special and chosen." Standing out in a crowd because of my cassock and roman collar was now enhanced by the title "Father." I saw and felt the pride of my parents and relatives in seeing me being celebrated by the community as the first priest in the family.

Ordination picture/ Blessing friends at first Mass/ Ordination memorial card ("Do this in memory of me")photo:Toon Ramon.

Now seven years after these celebrations, I would start the process that would return me to the lay state and, eventually, marriage. I understood that I was going to disappoint many of the people who had knelt down to receive my first blessing in my home town just after my ordination.

Resigning from the priesthood and leaving a religious order which has been one's family for fourteen years is not as easy as many might think. The "big exodus" of many priests in the early seventies is often seen as acts of selfishness, disloyalty to the church or even as just plain lust, while it represents histories of individual dramas played out over a long time. Like me, many struggled for years before they reluctantly left a life and a community they deeply loved. From talking to friends who joined the exodus in the seventies, I learned that there are many reasons why they resigned. Some gave up because they lost their faith in God or church altogether. Some were impatient with the lack of reform in the church; some could not bear living as a celibate priest any longer; others blamed their parents, the church, the society at large, or the time in which they grew up for "making a wrong decision" after being "brainwashed."

I also know priests who wanted to leave but decided to stay because they were afraid to face the secular world or lose the protection of the Congregation. Some stayed because they feared hurting their families. Forgiven of their peccadillos, some remained despite having fathered children and have grandchildren secretly supported by the Congregation. In the end, they all represent individual battles of conscience and they all live with the decisions they made. I do hope that the story of my own journey towards that final step of laicization I took in March 1970, creates some understanding and compassion for resigned priests who were often misjudged, rebuked or abandoned.

In early December 1969 I arrived in Rome with the plan to go study for a year in the United States as a member of the Philippine CICM province. I was surprised when the Superior General, Wim Goossens, suggested that I take a leave of absence. This was an official permission to remain for one year outside the religious houses of the CICM. The document stated that I was "dismissed of all duties and rights towards mentioned congregation except for the obligation to the religious priestly celibacy," in other words, to live like a celibate lay person. They agreed to pay my travel to the USA and gave $750 to provide for my immediate needs until I found a job. This little twist in the original plans gave me the subtle impression that the congregation had already decided that I was not going to remain one of their members. I accepted their suggestion and obtained the leave of absence on 13 December 1969.

Only years later did I learn from my archival files that the headquarters in Rome was informed by some of my Filipino confreres that I "was giving up as a priest and a member of the congregation." Headquarters also opined that I "did not seem to be ashamed to stay in CICM houses in Belgium, while others of his type would rather be embarrassed to do so." I also learned that a CICM confrere had visited my parents before my arrival in Belgium from Rome, informing them that I was giving up the priesthood and the Scheut Fathers and was going to study in the States. My parents had responded to him that they "were trying to understand but were very worried that I would not make it because I had never worked for a living and did not know the value of money..." In my home town, some people had spread the rumor that they knew "from very reliable sources" that I was leaving the priesthood and that "a woman was involved."

Upon my arrival in Belgium I had the painful duty to talk to my parents and siblings about my leave of absence. I was fully aware that I was going to disappoint them. I had witnessed their pride and joy when I chose to be a missionary, when I was assigned to study in Rome and when they were present at my ordination and first Mass. I dreaded breaking the news to them. How would they digest the reaction of the good Christians of my hometown where the news would soon spread as wild fire?

I shared some of the problems I had endured in the Philippines and told them about my doubts regarding my vocation. I explained how I needed the leave of absence to think about my future. I do not recall at all that they ever mentioned the visit of the CICM who informed them about my leave before my arrival in Belgium. They accepted my decisions and pledged their support but expressed their worries that I was going to live in another country by myself without ever having worked for a living.

The Christmas days that year were plain misery. The parish sacristan removed my picture from the town's pictorial display of missionaries in the rear part of the church. People who had known me for years, barely greeted me in the street. Others, however, came forward as loyal friends and treated me with some compassion. Priest-friends and some of the local CICM community kept visiting my parents and putting in a good word or two. One anonymous woman gave my mother an envelop with $850 to "assist me in the difficult road ahead." To this day, I am still sorry I never could personally thank this woman who gave me some hope that not everyone would condemn me.

When I learned that the costs of studying in New York were prohibitive and that a student visa prevented me from having a job, I changed my plans and applied for a tourist visa in the hope I could later change it to a permanent resident card. Crossing my fingers that things would work out in America, I left Belgium for the USA on 18 January 1970, leaving behind a family which was scared to death that I would never make it.

The situation could indeed have been disastrous without the support of Father Leo Zonneveld, the Provincial Superior of the American CICM Province, who had been requested to assist me. Not only did he welcome me at Missionhurst, the CICM headquarters in Arlington, Virginia, but he told me, against the objections of some of his confreres, that I could stay there as a guest as long as necessary. Father Leo called on his friends to assist me getting my green card, tried to get me a teaching job at the CICM high school in Philadelphia (which was denied), recommended me for a job at the Peace Corps, and arranged for a job interview with the CEO of the American Finance Company, where I ultimately got my first employment.

The two months I spent at Missionhurst became my last "retreat." From the looks and comments of some of my confreres, I knew that my presence was, at best, tolerated and some considered me already an outsider. I had the time to look back at my struggles with my faith in God and vocation, and at my attempts to give myself another chance. I was psychologically exhausted and tired of fighting. My lifelong desire to do good for others had been fulfilled in becoming a priest and a missionary. Now I realized that the clerical environment where I had chased that ideal had become a battleground. I had lost all my battles. My faith was shattered. My hopes for church renewal were crushed in Maryhurst. I had become deeply dubious that I could live the lonely life of a celibate. I had been wounded by the mistrust, gossip and suspicion of my confreres. My superiors seemed to have already decided that I was no longer one of them and it also seemed that they wanted to get rid of "the problem." In the end, I was tired of engaging in new battles. I had to decide to find a new environment in which I could still hang on to my ever enduring wish to do good to others.

Missionhurst
Arlington, Virginia

My ongoing correspondence with Felicitas and her friends at ASI revealed that, after I left the Philippines, she had been confronted by some Scheut fathers, who accused her of being the cause of my leaving the country and my leave of absence. Even her family, who had welcomed me and adopted me as a son, had been questioned. I started to believe that, if I was going to write a new chapter in my life, I would invite her to be a part of it. Gradually I came to the conclusion that taking the next step and asking for laicization was the only possible solution. On 2 March, I talked with Fr. Leo about all the above, and he advised me not to wait any longer and start the process of laicization.

On 5 March 1970, I wrote a letter to Pope Paul VI for "dispensation from all the obligations of the priesthood, including celibacy, so that I may be able to marry according to the rites of the Catholic Church." As reasons for my request, I focused on my "growing inability to live a celibate life of loneliness" and stated that my mission work had only reinforced this conviction. I explained that I intended to marry and live a good Christian life.

I was fully aware that part of the blame for my situation had to be placed on myself. Had I prayed enough as it had been urged during my training? Had I been too impatient with the lack of renewal in the church? Was it true that I had been "too easy in my relationship with women," as it had been reported by some of my Filipino confreres? On the other hand, there was the unwarranted criticism of confreres about me as a "troublemaker" and "know-it-all," the gossip about illicit affairs and the intention to "destroy the seminary of Maryhurst." The lack of exploring the real consequences of a celibate life and of working with women in pastoral life had proved to be a real oversight in our seminary training. Reverend Dries Coussement, who was my teacher in high school and became a trusted priest-friend, wrote me later when he heard I was leaving:*"For too long we have not seen the priest as a human being. For too long people thought that a priest, just because he was a priest, had to be able to face all his problems by himself. They thought that he had no need to express his pain and his needs to another human being. What the church had advised in its centuries-long practice, it denied to its own servants!"* His letter reminded me that from the first days of our novitiate we were warned against the dangers of "special friendships" and friendship was never discussed as a positive dimension of our humanity.

After submitting my petition for laicization to Rome, I left Missionhurst for Baltimore where I was welcomed by my friends Rene and Chris Debrabander. I knew Rene when he was a CICM philosophy professor in the Philippines at Saint Louis University in Baguio City. After a couple of weeks, I could write my anxious parents in Belgium that I obtained my own studio apartment and that I had secured a temporary job with American Finance Corporation. Fr. Leo Zonneveld had arranged a personal interview with a good friend of his who was the CEO of the company.

Stepping from the clerical world into the lay world became quite a cultural shock. As a cleric, one takes it for granted that people almost automatically show some kind of respect and call you "father" because of your Roman collar, intended to make you stand out in a crowd. Once a lay person, you somehow disappear into the crowd. My job at American Finance provided me with a quick dose of reality. Relying on my old study habits, I studied the manuals of loan approval and soon knew almost as much as the manager. He was convinced that I was a spy from headquarters after the CEO of the company had visited the office and called me by my first name. My "reputation" followed me from office to office of American Finance, and I let them believe that I was a spy.

Part of my job at the loan company was to help manage the accounts of poor people who made "household loans" of a couple of hundred dollars at almost 30% interest. When they were late in paying their bills, I had to call them. There I was, with my degrees in philosophy and theology and some years of working with and for the poor in the Philippines, giving poor people in America a hard time in their financial misery. I hated every minute of it and my Flemish accent was no big help either! I had to do it to survive. Rent, car insurance, groceries, and utilities were words which had never been items in my vocabulary. When I was a cleric, I always had a place to live and the congregation took care of all my material needs. My newly discovered poverty made me realize that never before did I live the vow of poverty.

While I was working at American Finance, the Baltimore Diocesan Office of Catholic Education arranged an interview at the all girls Notre Dame Preparatory School for a job as religion teacher. I don't know what prompted the School Sisters of Notre Dame, Ellis Denny and Helen Marie Duffy, to hire me on the spot as their first full-time male lay religion teacher at this all girls school. It was certainly an act of courage to hire a resigned priest to teach religion in a Catholic school. Were they impressed by my Roman degrees and pastoral experience, or was it just my Flemish accent?

Notre Dame would become my home for the next 31 years, where I could teach philosophy, religion and languages, could get involved in liturgical, pastoral and social justice initiatives, and was able to help develop and frame the Notre Dame school philosophy inspired by the principles of Vatican II.

My petition for laicization, only months after a leave of absence, surprised the CICM headquarters. They suggested that a more detailed explanation of my "growing inability to live a celibate life" was warranted and that testimony of a psychiatrist would accelerate my request. I answered them that before my ordination no psychiatrist had ever been hired to examine my ability to live a celibate life. Their suggestion was well intended but, in my opinion, could only strengthen the Vatican's contention that the massive exodus of priests during that time was mainly due to psychiatric problems of the applicants. On April 24 my petition was submitted to the Vatican and it would take until March the following year before laicization was granted.

After I had submitted my request, I felt at peace for the first time in a long time. Now that I had finally decided to leave the clerical state, there was nothing to prevent me from asking Felicitas to be a part of my life, a life I knew I could not face by myself any longer. I needed someone, but not just anyone. Knowing how religiously pious Felicitas and her family were, I was wondering how to announce my intentions to them. I finally took the courage to write her my first love letter, telling her that my deep friendship with her had evolved into love and that I invited her join me in the United States. This started a correspondence that could be described as "international dating by way of the post office." In her replies, Felicitas offered all kinds of excuses why joining me in Baltimore would be problematic. She stressed that she wanted to finish her master's degree. She had financial obligations relating to her scholarship at Asian Social Institute and she felt that she had responsibilities as the eldest of nine children to take care of her family. She thought that leaving the Philippines would make her abandon her desire to help the poor. She was struggling with her own feelings trying to figure out if she felt the same way about me as I did about her. She confessed that she was scared, not understanding why I would choose a dark-complexioned "ugly duckling" -- as her grade school teacher, a St. Paul sister, often called her -- to share a future with her. I was scared too, but only that she would not make up her mind.

In April, I wrote a long letter to my parents informing them about my final step, describing how it had been a heart-wrenching decision to turn my back on a priesthood I loved and a congregation that was a brotherhood for fourteen years. I knew I was going to hurt my family, but I also knew that I had to turn a leaf, lest I fall completely apart. I also informed them that I intended to invite Felicitas to be a part of my life and that I would ask her to join me in America.

Having known friends whose leaving the priesthood resulted in complete rejection by their family, followed by years of gnawing guilt about their choice, I realized how blessed I was when I received my mother's answer, "*We had a lot to digest these last months and although we did not understand everything, we accepted it because we understood how you were in pain and how it pained you to bring these matters to us. If we had known that you struggled for so many years in your profession, we would have personally called you home... In all honesty, you have done your job and made many people spiritually and materially happy in doing your best, and that is enough for us... You come from a family who needs to share with someone when things go well, and when things go wrong we equally feel that need. Not being able to do that would have destroyed you. We are grateful that the church has foreseen dispensation in such cases... We bless you and Felicitas in your future together and we know that you will do much good together to people who cross your path. Never be ashamed of your past life and now just live for the future!"*

After I became a permanent resident of the United States, I decided to call Felicitas and finally propose to her. When her mother answered the overseas call, I expressed my feelings for her daughter and, following Philippine customs, asked her permission to marry Felicitas. She told me she had no problem with it, but I would have to propose to Felicitas myself. When she came to the phone, I proposed. (This "international phone call proposal" would be recounted for years after we were married.) To my consternation, Felicitas told me that she wanted to finish her graduate studies first and that, in the meantime, I should "collect and select," -- her expression of telling me that I should date others to find out if I was really sure of my intentions. She asked me to call her back in six months, and if she was still my chosen one, she would marry me. I was dumbfounded and disheartened.

In the next couple of months, I urged Felicitas that she not postpone her trip any longer. I was afraid that her departure would become impossible because of the political situation and social unrest in the Philippines. It was the period of street protests against the Marcos regime and I had learned that Felicitas had been a regular participant in antigovernment activities. As an additional incentive, I requested even my own parents to write her. In a moving letter, they welcomed Felicitas as a daughter into the family and thanked her and her family for supporting me when I was in dire need. My mother wrote, "God is good and he finds a way for everybody. He will not leave you alone when the two of you do good things for others."

Being at the edge of hopelessness, I called on the assistance of my trusted CICM friend Fr. Herman Gadeyne in Manila, who knew my story and who recently had visited my parents in Belgium. I suggested to him that Felicitas travel to Belgium, where we could marry under the law. The civil marriage would make her automatically a Belgian citizen and make it easier for her to obtain a green card and immigrate to the United States. Father Herman promised to speak with her, obtain a Belgian tourist visa, and take care of all her travel arrangements.

Felicitas' family had suggested a possible wedding in the Philippines. I had to persuade them that this was financially impossible for me and that the Belgium-USA plan was the most practical one. In the meantime, Father Herman consulted Father Senden at Asian Social Institute about Felicitas' academic status and scholarship obligations. Senden agreed to award her master's degree because she finished all the required courses. Since her scholarship contract included employment at ASI, Father Herman agreed to have me reimburse the whole scholarship fee in case Felicitas terminated her job responsibilities at the institute.

Tenth wedding anniversary 1981

Herman had to meet her surreptitiously as "Josephina Reyes" to keep the gossip machine in the CICM corridors in the dark. He told her that I was sincere in my intentions to marry her and that, through Missionhurst, I had sent him the funds to reimburse her scholarship obligations, her visa and ticket and other needs. (The anonymous donation of the mystery woman in Belgium had come in handy, but my bank account was bare.) Father Herman finally told Felicitas that I would be waiting for her in Belgium on 28 December. Twenty-four hours later, Felicitas wrote Fr.

Herman a long letter in which she explained how she realized that she had learned to love me, enough to leave her family and country and join me in the United States. Fr. Herman went ahead with all the agreed upon travel arrangements.

During my Christmas vacation I flew to Belgium hoping for her arrival, but not knowing for sure that she would come. On the last day of the year Felicitas arrived. At the airport, in my excitement I forgot to give her the bouquet of roses I had prepared for the occasion. Years later, my father, unable to judge the age of Filipino women, revealed to us his first impression of Felicitas, "My God, what did he bring home; she looks like a sixteen-year-old girl!"

In Belgium it is the law that a civil wedding is officiated prior to a church wedding. With my brother Arthur and sister-in-law Rita and a few faithful friends present at the ceremony, Felicitas and I were married under the law at City Hall in my home town Torhout on 4 January 1971. My mother gave her own diamond engagement ring to Felicitas as a sign of my parents' blessing. My aunts, who previously had taken me out of their last will and later reinstated me, paid for our wedding bands. Felicitas got her Belgian passport that same day, and the next day we applied for her US immigration at the American consulate in Antwerp. The gossip in my home town, however, was in high gear but my parents showed much courage: they invited Felicitas and me to join them to Sunday Mass showing their approval and support for us to the parish community.

Just a few days after our wedding I had to return to my teaching job at Notre Dame Preparatory School in the Baltimore. To lessen the pressures on my family, Felicitas was a guest at the Beguinage rest home of Diksmuide while she was waiting for her travel visa to the USA. My brother and his wife, my aunts and two cousins took turns graciously hosting Felicitas during her stay, thus mitigating the cultural shock she had to endure. Never before had she left her country and family. Their kindness and generosity was a blessing and helped her prepare for her future in yet another continent.

The name Felicitas means "happiness." On Valentine's Day 1971, my happiness finally arrived in Baltimore and Felicitas and I could start our simple life together. We were anxiously waiting for my laicization papers from Rome so that we could get married in the Catholic church.

My laicization process, however, went through a little history of its own. In October 1970 Cardinal Shehan of Baltimore had received notice from the Sacred Congregation of the Doctrine of the Faith (SCDF) about my petition. The Baltimore chancery requested a new petition and an interview. They questioned me and a group of people who had known me before and after my priestly ordination. I was afraid this was going to delay the process forever.

My petition was expedited, however, by a decree of the SCDF on 13 January 1971, allowing religious superiors to handle dispensations of their own members. It was granted on 5 March 1971, a year to the date of my petition, and sent to CICM headquarters in Rome. Thinking that the Baltimore chancery had received a copy and had informed me, Scheut headquarters filed my dispensation papers as a closed case. Fr. Leo Zonneveld, on a visit to Rome, detected the error and finally forwarded the papers to me, offering his help in obtaining the necessary permits from the diocese of Virginia to marry us in the church.

On 11 September 1971, with no witnesses around, our Catholic marriage took place in Missionhurst, officiated by Fr. Leo Zonneveld. The diocese of Richmond had requested that the marriage take place "without witnesses and without any other form of publicity." Instead of being received as a couple in the Catholic community with open arms by receiving the sacrament of marriage, we were asked to be married secretly. In God's name: why?

Honestly, the secrecy was no surprise for me. One of the most important requests in the questionnaires was to make sure that no "scandal among the faithful" would ensue from granting my petition. The laicization document itself is testimony of this mentality which, in my opinion, found it's latest expression in the priestly pedophile cases in

America and elsewhere. The document, redacted in Latin, did not say, "Well, we know you are leaving, for whatever reasons, but in any case, we thank you for your years of service!" It rather felt as though a scarlet sign was hung around my neck with "Dangerous Person!" First, the authorities ordered that a laicized priest, especially a married one, was away from places where his priestly status was known. If no scandal was foreseen, the local bishop could dispense with this request. For a canonical celebration of a marriage, all pomp and circumstance had to be avoided. The local authority could determine if the wedding had to be performed in secret. Except for hearing confessions in case of death, the petitioner could not perform any priestly functions; where his condition is known, he cannot take part in any liturgical celebrations for the people of God and can never give a homily; he cannot be a director of a catholic school or teach religion. The local authority can decide that he can teach religion in a public school, or, with permission, in a Catholic one, on condition no scandal or wonderment will be given. All this seemed to be saying: we'd rather not see you acting as an active Catholic lay person, using your God-given talents and years of training for the benefit of the People of God!

When I first read this document, I already had been recommended by the Catholic Education Office of the Baltimore diocese, I was teaching religion in a Catholic school and distributing communion in the liturgies, and I was a cantor and lector in an inner city parish in Baltimore. I had continued my life as a Christian layperson and shared my faith and charity with my community, all without any "scandal to the faithful."

The relationship between the Missionaries of Scheut and its former members is varied. I was not always treated with fairness, and the criticism and gossip of some individuals pushed me deeper into my frustration. There are others who left the congregation and, for whatever reasons, do not want any further contact. A few years back, the pictures of all who left the congregation were removed from the portrait gallery at Scheut Headquarters in Brussels. Recently, they returned them to the gallery, recognizing the resigned confreres for the years they had served in the mission fields. Former members are now even mentioned in their published list of deceased members. I for one, cannot imagine my life without the support I received from some of my former confreres who have treated me decently. Every time I visit one of the Scheut communities, I still feel as "one of them" and for many in the Congregation, the feeling seems to be mutual.

Four of these former Scheut fathers got together on New Year's Eve of 1972 to celebrate the new year. The hosts showed up wearing slippers and the rest followed suit, resulting in naming our new social club the "Savatten Club" (Flemish for slipper) or in Latin the "Ordo Savattensis."

We vowed to meet every last Saturday of the month and we have done so for the last 41 years. Each family takes turns to prepare a gourmet dinner at which we all enjoy discussions and old Flemish songs. As the years passed, we welcomed other married ex-CICM friends who wanted to join and we included a former member of the Missionaries of Africa, also known as the White Fathers, and his Trinidad spouse.

Although each one of us has his and her own story, we all immigrated to the USA. We served the church in Africa, Asia, the USA, and Europe for an aggregate period of 215 years of our lives. We married Belgian, Irish, Taiwanese and Filipino women, some of them nuns. As immigrants, we all had to start a new life in an unfamiliar non-clerical world, but we supported one another in finding jobs and housing, swapping used furniture and even old worn out rugs, and we did everything new immigrant families do to survive, eventually becoming American citizens.

Missionhurst in Arlington soon referred to us as "the Baltimore Province," and called on us every time another CICM had decided to leave the Congregation. For years they let us use the Congregation's summer house on the Potomac River at Riverside, Maryland, for a yearly "retreat." Missionhurst assisted some of us with loans when we desperately needed financial help and we felt welcome and respected when we visited their headquarters. In return we welcomed a stream of visiting active Scheut Fathers, who usually left with checks in support of their apostolic activities. The Ordo Savattensis has been a blessing to all of us; an oasis of bonding families who had no family in this country, together in respect and charity. It is to the original members of the Savatten Club that I dedicate this memoir.

Members of the "Ordo Savattensis" (Slipper Club) and friends

CHAPTER SEVEN

Lay Teacher: Notre Dame Preparatory School 1970-2001

In September 1970 I started my new career as a lay high school teacher at Notre Dame Preparatory School (NDP) in Towson, Maryland. The school, sponsored by the School Sisters of Notre Dame (SSND), sits in a green oasis of sixty-eight acres in this well-to-do suburb of Baltimore. The low buildings, constructed in 1960 of field stone and limestone, rise among vast soccer fields, tennis courts and parking lots. Upon entering the school I was surrounded by about 650 smiling girls in blue uniforms and saddle shoes, belonging to grades one to twelve. Sister Ellis Denny, SSND, a no-nonsense tall Irish woman of strong faith and years of educational experience, was the principal. She was assisted by Sister Helen Marie Duffy, SSND, who had been connected with NDP since she professed her final vows in 1938. These two visionary women would assist Notre Dame in incarnating the renewal spirit of Vatican II into the school's mission and philosophy during the thirty-one years of my service to the school. In the process we would become close friends, although we did not always agree on everything.

This chapter will tell the story of the gradual infusion of Vatican II principles into the mission and life of Notre Dame Prep. An analysis of the NDP school philosophies of several decades will show how the spirit and ideas of Vatican II were taken seriously and progressively became the framework of the school philosophy and mission statements. This process did not evolve without the necessary intramural birth pains, and even a frontal attack on Notre Dame in 1995 by outside anti-Vatican II sources. The renewal story at Notre Dame as a "miniature church" mirrors in a certain way what happened in the Catholic Church at large where Vatican II changes were not always enthusiastically welcomed. My story will reveal, how in a particular way, the Vatican II documents on the Church, the Liturgy, Education and the Laity found their way into the fabric of Notre Dame Preparatory School, forging it into a Vatican II school.

When I arrived at NDP, the days of my struggles to leave the clerical life seemed almost a far memory. I was at peace with my decisions and myself. My family had courageously supported me and had accepted Felicitas as a future daughter. They were happy that I had been offered a job at a Catholic school and began to believe that I would make it in America.

The six months of work in the business world had taught me that I belonged in the education world. I felt that God had not abandoned me by giving me a chance to work in a Catholic environment in which I felt at home. I was wondering how this new chapter in my life was going to be written, but I started with new hope and a dose of enthusiasm. I was at peace and happy.

Only a few people at Notre Dame knew my background. Students and teachers only knew me as the new "foreign religion teacher" with the heavy Flemish accent. My clerical instincts still feared that some parents would find out that some "defrocked priest" was teaching religion to their daughters and that this would jeopardize my newly found happiness at NDP. I had learned, however, not to be too worried about problems until they really show up. So I was determined to make the best of it and to share with my colleagues and students the experiences I had gained and to spread the message of Vatican II.

The School Sisters of Notre Dame had already responded to the renewal call of the Second Vatican Council. During their thirteenth General Chapter in 1968, they had revised their constitution in accordance to the document on the Renewal of the Religious Life and the charism of their founder, Mother Theresa. They focused on decentralization and consensus in government and were looking for new areas of apostolic activity as part of their education efforts. In 1970, they produced a new constitution,"You are Sent," which was inspired by the Vatican II documents on the Church, the Missions, the Church and the Modern World and the Renewal of Religious Life. The renewal covered more than just the changes in their appearance by shedding their traditional habits for veils and uniform suits.[46] The liturgical renewal was apparent in the celebrations at Notre Dame Prep. I was personally encouraged by an administration showing openness for renewal just by having hired a resigned priest as a religion teacher. On the other hand, the school reminded me of my own high school years where priests were running the place, only to be replaced by sisters. Although there were a few lay teachers among the large group of SSNDs, departments and administration were under the direction of sisters. After all, it was a SSND school.

The School Sisters of Notre Dame opened the *Notre Dame of Maryland Collegiate Institute for Young Ladies* in 1873 on Charles Street in Baltimore. Forty years earlier, Caroline Gerhardinger of Bavaria, Germany, had founded a religious community of women to assist poor girls in small towns and villages in Bavaria. In 1847 Mother Theresa of

Jesus (Gerhardinger's religious name) set out to America with five companion sisters to help German emigrants in Pennsylvania. Since no bishop had invited them, they were advised to return home, but the sisters decided to remain in the USA. Through the intervention of Father John Neumann, now Saint John Neumann, they took over three Redemptorist parish schools in Baltimore and established their first school for girls, the *Institute of Notre Dame (IND)*. When that school became overcrowded, the order established *Notre Dame of Maryland* in 1873 on Charles Street in Northern Baltimore, on the campus where later in 1896 the *College of Notre Dame* received its charter.

In the fifties, the success of the college and high school made classroom space such a premium that accrediting agencies recommended a split of the two. The SSND decided on a new campus on Hampton Lane in Baltimore County and in 1960 Notre Dame Preparatory School moved to the brand new buildings.

The 1958 and 1962 admission booklets reflect Notre Dame's educational philosophy just before the onset of Vatican II. As a creation of God, the young lady's "ultimate goal is the possession of eternal happiness with Him in heaven; her proximate goal is the full living of the high, noble life of a Christian woman." These goals would be realized by imparting knowledge and forming their character. The school would see to it that "her will would be trained, her mind enriched, and her ideals heightened" so that she, as a truly Christian woman, can influence others and thus obtain her own happiness. They made it clear, however, that the school was "college preparatory" and therefore they aimed for students who "by their native ability, or by the opportunities they enjoy in virtue of their family positions, are potential leaders, and who will continue their education through four years of college." (1958) In 1962 this rather elitist aim was changed into "give maximal preparatory training to students who will continue their education through four years of college."

Religion was a required course, earning two credits over the four years, and considered to be the "fulcrum of the curriculum." All religion classes were taught by the residing chaplain. Other subjects were taught by twenty SSNDs and eight laywomen. The religion curriculum covered "Old and New Testament studies" in the framework of the Trinity, Mariology and--believe it or not -- Apologetics.[47]

Although the primary goal of NDP has always been the education of young women, the concrete manner in which this education was imparted was subject to changes. Over the last three decades the goals of this education have taken on different focus. New structures and methodologies were developed. From the early seventies, we observed a slow but growing adoption of the ideas promoted in the Second Vatican Council. The emphasis on an individualistic faith in the 1972 philosophy develops into a faithful that comes together, celebrates and reaches out to others.

My first year at the Prep was partly dedicated to the self-evaluation for its upcoming Middle States Evaluation.[48] I was chair of the school philosophy-writing committee. It was a time when educational psychology and methodology were the leading fields in education. Although we stated in our preparatory report that the new philosophy was inspired by the Vatican II's document on Education, there was not much evidence of it in the new philosophy. Except for mentioning that the school was "a Catholic private school for girls" and "fostered spiritual values," the remainder could have been the philosophy of any secular educational institution. For some reason we failed to include terms like Church, Gospel, Christ, faith. The document is rich in psychological jargon like "searching for meaning, share creativity, discovering values together, self-directed learning..."

Even the General Objectives of the Religion Department lack terminology that would suggest a Catholic school. We do mention "understanding religious principles," "personally meaningful insights," "clarifying their own values."

I have been trying to recall and understand why we were so hesitant in incorporating terms as God, Gospel, Christ, faith, etc., into the philosophy and why ideas of Vatican II were missing in the statement. If my memory serves me rightly, we had a certain reluctance to emphasize "Catholic" terminology for fear that this would prevent certain people from sending their daughters to Notre Dame. Political correctness was not yet invented, but it was certainly present.

Furthermore, the end of Vatican II was not so far away. Although liturgical changes were taking place and were slowly accepted by the faithful, the "masses" were not yet educated about the new spirit of the Council. It was a time of confusion and of a "where-is-this-all-going?" mentality. The educational establishment was drenched in psychology and methodology and Notre Dame subscribed to these trends. Faculty meetings and recollections were dominated by psychology Ph.Ds and method-experts who often made faculty members participate in public confessions -- with unpredictable traumatic results. On the other hand, I do not remember a single meeting in which the new theology of Vatican II or a conciliar text was explained or discussed. On the ground level, however, NDP was certainly an incipient 'Vatican II school' where the liturgical innovations were practiced and where novel approaches in church life were promoted in the classroom.

In 1972 we renamed the Religion Department the "Department of Religious Studies," making a serious effort to give the curriculum a more intellectual content. While searching for a solid program, we made errors in the process. We reduced the "Study of Old Testament Literature" to one class a week for Freshmen. The bulk of their time was dedicated to "informal consultation with the priest counselor or preparation for liturgies." The Sophomores covered only "New Testament Studies" in the second semester. The first semester was dedicated to "religion and the meaning of life." I am sure that class room text such as *J.P. Sartre on Atheism* and Peter Berger's *Possibilities of Sacredness* were well over the heads of most Sophomores.

In the spirit of the early seventies -- giving students more of what they wanted rather than what they needed -- we offered to the Juniors and Seniors a variety of courses from which the students could select according to their own needs and interests. Looking back at those offerings, I noticed that we were opening up new areas of high school teaching, like world religions and ecumenism, but we failed to cover the sacraments, liturgy, church history, scripture study and Christian morality. Notre Dame became one of the first high schools in the area to offer world religions. Some parents, at times, expressed their fear that we would "convert" their daughter to another religion or "make them Protestant." These offerings, however, were a response to the ecumenical spirit of Vatican II and its respect for non-Christian religions. In hindsight, other offerings, like *The Choice Called Atheism, Psychology of Religion*, and *Value Clarification* were rather a response to the fads of the seventies than an attempt to expand the program. We also began offering classes in *Love and Human Sexuality* which would eventually lead to a full course across all four grades.

    I was particularly pleased that Sister Ellis approved my offer to teach an Introduction to Philosophy elective course for seniors. To date, this offering has survived for forty years and has prepared many NDP graduates for their required philosophy classes in college.

    We were aware that students would not take religion classes seriously unless a real academic value were attached to them, i.e. academic quality points. Student response to the course material was varied. While the material did appeal to those students who were interested in their own personal development or who were interested in pursuing religious studies in college, some students conceived of religion as something totally subjective, without a body of knowledge to be studied. In the past, most students were taught religion as an 'extra' subject, and this made it somehow difficult to consider it a serious academic subject. The work which students did in this department was not counted towards class rank or grade-point-average.

    It was our belief that the curriculum had to offer serious content to be taken seriously as an academic subject. Class discussions by students who are not informed end up to be sessions of shared ignorance. To teach that content, however, we needed teachers who possessed the required knowledge and training. The department had an average of seven members (of whom two were full-time). The part-time teachers were SSNDs who did not have degrees in theology. It had been a custom in many Catholic schools to assign sisters to religion classes just because they were sisters. Not many lay people were taking up theology or related fields. Without belittling in any way the dedication and excellence of many of these part-time religion teachers -- lay and religious -- it does say something about the way we looked at religion teaching: it was not on the same level as another academic subject. In comparison, nobody would hire an art major for math or an English major for a history course!

The NDP administration was aware of these problems and decided to assign quality points to all religion classes. They gradually hired teachers who had theology training, resulting in more academic respect for religion classes. By the nineties, most religion department members had degrees in theology or a related field. It was also no coincidence that the religion program was always listed first in all Open House materials offered by the school, keeping an SSND tradition that religion was the "fulcrum of the curriculum."

The evaluation visiting committee commended Notre Dame for "keeping up with the renovations suggested by Vatican II and the efforts to bring a more intellectual approach to the study of God, His revelation to man, and His place in the daily lives of students." They recommended that, "The entire staff be made aware of the need to cooperate in creating a religious community." In the decade following the 1972 Evaluation, the Religion Department would be instrumental in shaping a new philosophy at Notre Dame that put the Vatican II theology in practice.

The 1982 NDP Philosophy

During the decade following the 1972 Evaluation, Notre Dame took steps that would shape its mission for years to come. The 1982 school philosophy, with its three pillars of *academic excellence, spiritual growth, social consciousness,* was inspired by the way the Religion Department was reorganized into three collegial branches: academic instruction, pastoral life and social service, as inspired by the theology of Vatican II.

Developments in the three areas abounded. The elective curriculum of the early seventies was consolidated into a core curriculum of required courses which were developmental in nature. The freshmen studied *Jewish Scriptures*; the sophomore year was dedicated to *Christian Scriptures*; junior year studied *Church History* and *World Religions*; and the seniors discussed *Ethical and Social Issues* and *Personal Relationships.* A course on sexuality and personal development was introduced within the four years of the religion curriculum. Next to their required course, the seniors could still elect the *Introduction to Philosophy* elective. The program covered the basic aspects of scripture and theology and was given full academic credit. At meetings for area Catholic schools, the program was praised and inspired imitation.

A happy NDP teacher!

Pastoral life expanded by introducing retreat days for freshmen, sophomores and mothers of students, an Advent and Lent program, Liturgy club, peer ministry, and faculty retreats. All these activities developed into a Campus Ministry office in the eighties.

If today Notre Dame's mission emphasizes social justice as an essential calling, it is thanks to the vision of Sister Ellis Denny SSND. She was convinced that NDP had to do more than just expose its students to social issues in its religion classes. In 1975 she hired the first full-time social issues teacher, Mrs Mary Coffey, whose task it was to hold formal classes in social issues and to organize volunteer service for the students. Notre Dame was the first girls school in Baltimore and the entire state of Maryland to address critical human rights issues with actions rather than words and inspired other area schools to follow suite.

Sister Ellis' initiative has developed today into a full-fledged service program with a host of service activities beginning at Middle Level and running through the Upper Level. In-house and off-campus activities are developmentally appropriate, providing a lifelong attitude towards service.

Following Vatican II's theology, all three areas were seen as complementary to one another and were coordinated into one Religion Department. "Catechetical instruction leads to knowing and active participation in the liturgical mystery, and inspires apostolic action" (Education document 4). This framework inspired the new 1982 school philosophy. The triptych of *academic excellence, spiritual growth and social consciousness* became the basis of the Notre Dame philosophy until the present. The language used in the document becomes a clear expression of Christian principles. It becomes an "education based on the Gospel." The "moral and intellectual values" of the 1972 philosophy becomes "religious and ethical principles inherent in the exercise of Christian faith: a faith which is genuine when it practices love and justice."

1993 NDP Philosophy

The 1993 philosophy shows clearly that the school understands what it means to be a Catholic school. The document is rich in religious terms: faith, Christ, Church, Gospel, God. Notre Dame is seen as a living community, sustained by faith, attempting to realize God internally and focusing on being an agent of change in the outside world. That mission is based on Gospel values compelling the students to "shape our world."

The administration and faculty were commended for their support of the religion department and social service program and stated that the "NDP community endeavors to help each student to take her rightful place in today's society in light of Christian values." [49]

In the interim period after 1982 some important social service initiatives had seen the light and became NDP traditions. During *Stone Soup Day* the entire school community comes together for a meal of soup and bread. Stone soup is inspired by the story of a poor woman who had no food and started boiling a stone in water. Passersby felt sorry for her and began adding vegetables to her boiling stone, resulting in a hearty soup. The students at NDP create the components for the soup and pay for their meal. The proceeds go to a selected charity.

Every year students, faculty, parents and administrators host a *Dinner for the Elderly*. More than two hundred guests from senior housing facilities and parishes in Baltimore arrive on campus for an afternoon of dining and entertainment by student musicians. In 1985, Edward Donnelan, a longtime director of Social Services, started *Camp Umoja* (Swahili for 'unity'), a four week academic and recreational summer camp for children of public housing in Baltimore, managed by NDP girls and boys from the Jesuit high school, Loyola Blakefield. A number of grocery stores and fast-food restaurants provide supplies for the kids, thus involving the broader community in this project.

When Sister Ellis Denny visited El Salvador in 1989 and saw the children of war refugees of the village of *Ignacio Ellucuria* sitting under a tree that was their school, an idea was born. Upon her return to Notre Dame she created a school-to-school relationship. Since 1991 NDP delegations of students and faculty have visited Ignacio Ellucuria, initially just visiting and supporting the poor students. The project has developed into high school scholarships and finally a school building. Recently, some of the high school graduates were sent to the University of San Salvador to learn to be doctors and engineers who will then return to the community. The sister-school in El Salvador is supported by yearly fundraisers at Notre Dame.

During our visit to the Philippines in 1992, we met Fr. James Desmet, a CICM classmate who just started a nutrition program at Saint Louis School in Tuguegarao. He was offering a hearty lunch to about eighty-five middle and high school kids and hearing impaired who came from poor families and did not have a lunch during the school day. We promised Father James that we would do something to help him. At Notre Dame, I proposed a pasta fundraising event. Sisters Ellis and Helen Marie readily approved and *Pasta for the Philippines* was born. With the support of the Social Service Department, CCAP (Christian Community Action Plan), teachers and staff, the *Pasta for the Philippines* has raised more than $41,000 in the last twenty years to fund 355,000 school lunches for the kids. As it often happens at Notre Dame, the project Felicitas and I started became a real Notre Dame tradition!

One cannot underestimate the value of the Social Service Program on campus for the individual students and the school as a whole. Not only do these projects benefit the marginalized locally and internationally, but the students themselves are changed and enriched by their experiences. They never see the world the same way again! What is especially remarkable, however, is that the motivation of their outreach is not some sense of secular responsibility for the global community -- as we notice in the public school programs -- but it comes from a deep spirituality. As baptized members of a Christian faith community, they have the duty to reach out to others in need and become "the saving leaven of the human family."(Document on Education, 8) Many graduates carry that mentality into their college years where we see them involved in volunteer work and social service projects. Some who have made social outreach their life's work, credit Notre Dame's social service as the birthplace of their commitment and dedication.

Finally, a new aspect of the 1993 NDP philosophy was the emphasis on Notre Dame's commitment to the "education of young women in the tradition of the School Sisters of Notre Dame." The charism of the SSND became more emphatically a part of the philosophy. The dwindling number of vocations to the order made it necessary to explicitly preserve the SSND charisma for the future, when increasingly laypeople are joining the teaching and administrative staff. Just as the Jesuits are infusing the spirituality of Ignatius of Loyola into their educational institutions, it is important that the spirit of the School Sisters of Notre Dame, who have served education of young women for 160 years, be infused into Notre Dame Preparatory School.

The 2002 and 2012 Mission Statements of Notre Dame show that the school has remained faithful to the basic principles developed over the last fifty years: a Catholic school, infused with the spirit of the School Sisters of Notre Dame and rooted in the teachings of the Catholic Church, expressed in the triptych of academic excellence, spiritual growth, and the practice of justice. The NDP community strives to answer God's call "...to act justly, to love tenderly, and to walk humbly with God." (Micah 6:8)

The 2012 Notre Dame mission is presented in three documents: *Mission Statement, Belief Statements* and *Graduate Profile*. (See Appendix C) The document states specifically what academic excellence, spiritual growth and practice of justice mean for the NDP student. The statements also reveal how Notre Dame Prep has adopted the main themes of the Second Vatican Council and is practicing its spirit, thus making Notre Dame a true Vatican II school.

A final note about the Notre Dame Prep motto. For three decades I have maintained that the translation of *"Veritatem prosequimur"* as "We Follow the Truth" was incorrect. The deponent Latin verb *'prosequi'* has a second meaning next to 'follow,' that makes more sense: to pursue, to go after, to search. The motto should read *"We Pursue Truth."* To my great joy, Notre Dame has adopted this more meaningful translation.

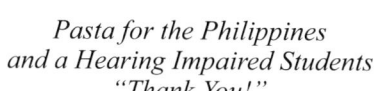

*Pasta for the Philippines
and a Hearing Impaired Students
"Thank You!"*

A Frontal Assault on Notre Dame

In the beginning of this chapter, I referred to Notre Dame as "a miniature church where the renewal of Vatican II was not always welcomed with open arms." In 1995, however, we could say that the school had already adopted Vatican II theology in its spirituality, liturgy and philosophical framework. What we did not expect was a frontal assault by outside sources on the very essence of Notre Dame as a Catholic school. We were tried in the press and over the airwaves and indicted by anonymous sources who spread half-truths, distortions and even plain lies. It was hard not to feel powerless in the face of this evil. In the end, Notre Dame prevailed. The episode mirrors that this still goes on in the Catholic church today, where Catholics, motivated by increasing discontent and considering themselves orthodox, will do anything to stop the renewal. Unfortunately, this movement seemed to be sanctioned by some actions of the late Pope John Paul II and the present Pope Benedict XVI in their attempts to "reform the reform."

A couple of years before the onset of the assault, there were some signs of what was to come. Parents of students had requested that the school bring in speakers on pro-life issues, but the school deemed them to be educationally inappropriate. Some parents had questioned religion faculty at the 1994 Open House, indicating doubts about the orthodoxy of the religion program. The religion chair and the principal received letters from prospective parents alleging that the religion curriculum was not consistent with Catholic doctrine.

In early February 1995, a parent of a former student met with the principal and religion chair to discuss some of her concerns. The parent seemed satisfied with the responses and the meeting ended amicably. Through my years as head of the religion department, I was present in similar meetings with parents who had concerns. Sometimes their worries were unwarranted, like the parents who thought that I was trying to convert their daughters to Islam after I had introduced a course on the subject. Others were belligerent, like the judge who wanted to explain to me how to run the religion department. When the no-nonsense Sister Ellis reminded him that he was an expert in judicial matters but I had theology degrees from a pontifical university in Rome, the conversation quickly took a different turn. I always felt that the school was ready to give parents a patient hearing but would support its faculty.

On 20 February 1995, a group of "concerned parents" sent an unsigned letter to all NDP parents postulating the "deteriorating support of the school for traditional strong moral and Christian values." They invited their fellow parents to report to a spokesperson if they had any experiences which would raise questions about "the direction of Notre Dame as regards its teachings on faith and morals." This letter was the beginning of a campaign by a group of self-described "traditional Catholics" against Notre Dame, which would rock the school and the archdiocese of Baltimore for several months. The chancellor of the archdiocese, Monsignor Malooly, stated that the unknown group was not acting with the consent or direction of anyone from the Cardinal's staff.

Two days after the letter was sent, anonymous callers began a telephone campaign to parents, former parents, and alumnae, presenting serious and unsubstantiated allegations about Notre Dame and some faculty members. They claimed that one teacher had demonstrated to the girls how to masturbate, and that another showed an abortion. Some parents hung up when callers would not identify themselves. The center of the group's concern was a video *Not a Love Story*, shown to seniors, with parental approval, for the last ten years at an evening workshop.[50] The video, which contains sensitive material, was used in discussions against pornography and violence against women.

A few days after the letter was sent to the parents, representatives of the group were invited by Sister Christine Mulcahy, provincial superior of the School Sisters of Notre Dame, to meet with the NDP board and administration. They refused the offer unless the administration, the NDP lawyer and any member of the religion department would be excluded from the meeting.

The group then took their concerns to the media. On 16 March 1995, *The Wanderer*, a weekly newspaper "providing readers with news and commentary from an orthodox Catholic perspective since 1867," published its first article on Notre Dame Prep under the title "Does Baltimore's Best Girls School Corrupt Students?" The video *Not a Love Story* became a stepping stone to launch a myriad of accusations about "serious breaches in Catholic Faith, morals, and liturgy at Notre Dame" and the paper listed a number of alleged scandalous incidents at Notre Dame Prep: faculty members involved in lesbian relationships; sex education programs which familiarize the students with various forms of birth control devices; the debunking of the Bible and assaults on Catholic doctrine in religion classes; student-faculty 'liturgies' which feature pumpkin bread, muffins, or some other kind of illicit bread; the celebration of liturgies by teams of nuns; an anti-priest mentality among faculty (which includes ex-priests and ex-nuns) and the administration; refusal of the school administration to host pro-life speakers; an abnormally high incidence of student abortions; teaching students not to believe in the Real Presence of Christ in the Eucharist in their religion classes.

As a member of the religion department for twenty-one years and its chair for six years, the only thing I could agree with was that there were ex-priests on the faculty...The remainder of the accusations looked like they were from another school somewhere. It did, however, give me a flashback to my days at Maryhurst Seminary in the Philippines where I was accused of similar unsubstantiated "crimes." I had witnessed the forces of "orthodoxy" at work during the Second Vatican Council fighting to prevent renewal in the church. I retreated from Maryhurst seminary after the same kind of forces accused me of trying to destroy the seminary. I was hoping that Sister Ellis and Sister Helen Marie were not going to give in to these forces. At first, I recall seeing fear in their eyes. This changed soon into a determination to fight for the integrity and the survival of their school. Being in the religion department, I was part of the target in the assault and was aware of the tactics of destruction I recognized right from the outset. I was not going to allow them to destroy what we had fought for the last twenty-one years. I knew that, in the end, the truth would prevail.

The core group of "concerned parents" told *The Wanderer* that they had reported abuses at Notre Dame four years earlier to Cardinal Keeler, but were denied a meeting. Unidentified parents are quoted saying that the cardinal had been aware for three years that there were serious problems at Notre Dame, but that "he'll do anything to avoid the orthodox people." They also revealed that they were pursuing leads in the way church teachings were presented, the intimidation of students, and possible child abuse. At no time, however -- they stated to *The Wanderer* -- "did we want to push ourselves. We wanted to be sure that we were not slandering anyone...and that we did not cause scandal." On the other hand, they also stated that the goal of the group was "to get rid of the administration and the religion department."

On 21 March *Defend Life* [51] mailed to Notre Dame constituencies a copy of *The Wanderer*'s article and a leaflet with the results of their own "investigation." The same group passed out a flyer at the Annual Catholic Schools' Fair at Camden Yards and at Sunday Masses at Cathedral, Immaculate Conception and St. Joseph's Texas parishes. The leaflet was a diatribe against Lucy Strausbaugh, head of the religion department. It questioned if she should teach at a Catholic school because she conducted workshops on the Enneagram [52] which "avant-garde nuns, priests, and laypeople use as a replacement for spiritual formation sessions and retreat houses ... and is an important part of the New Age movement." [53] They also claimed that Notre Dame used a sex education textbook that "subverts Catholic sex morality as regards to contraception, abortion, and homosexuality." For *Defend Life*, the "most alarming is the link between liberation theology, with its anti-Christian teachings, and NDP's involvement of its students in Central America," i.e. Sister Ellis' project of a sister-school in El Salvador!

In a series of articles in late March 1995, the *Baltimore Sun* brought the video controversy to a wider public. Frank Sommerville, the religion reporter for the *Sun,* stated that the video "contained hard-core pornography," and reported that Cardinal Keeler, according to his official spokesperson William Blaul, was not aware of the showing of the film and "was distressed" that sexually explicit materials had been used to teach teenagers at Notre Dame. The cardinal let it be known that the "appalling" and "inappropriate" video would no longer be used at NDP. Blaul described the video as "disgusting."

Cardinal Keeler's announcement, made before he ever talked or consulted with Notre Dame's administration, helped stir the media excitement. On talk radio, anonymous accusers described sex horror stories over the airwaves and denounced sex education programs at Notre Dame and other Catholic schools in the archdiocese. NDP students who called in to refute some of the rumors were treated as "puppets of the Notre Dame sisters."

It is hard to describe the atmosphere inside Notre Dame during those March days. Students were visibly upset about the things they heard and read about "their school." They did not recognize the school that was described in the accusations. The response of the NDP students to these attacks was very telling. To show their support for the administration and the religion department, they put together a liturgy for the entire school and invited Lucy Strausbaugh to be the "mother" at the liturgy and to light a candle. Many parents and alumnae, even some who had been participants in the anti-pornography video workshop, wrote letters to the newspapers, expressing their support for the school and belief in the religion department.

After a conversation with Sister Christine Mulcahy, SSND, Cardinal Keeler's office released a statement on 21 March, "The cardinal finds the video, 'Not a Love Story,' and its use in a Catholic girls high school to be appalling. He told Sister Christine that such inappropriate materials cannot be used in any Catholic school. To do so is not consistent with Catholic morals nor with the learning environment parents expect in a Catholic school. Sister Christine accepted the cardinal's directive that the use of this video must be immediately stopped."

It was also announced that Notre Dame had invited an assessment by the archdiocesan Division of Catholic Education to determine if the teaching content at the school was consistent with Catholic religious and moral values. On 28 March 1995, a group of the Department of Catholic Education Ministries came to the school to perform this task and assess the religion department. The team consisted of Dr. Donald J. Valenti, Secretary of Catholic Education Ministries/Superintendent of Catholic Schools; Mr. James J. DeBoy, Director of Religious Education; Sister Judith Schaum, SSND, Assistant Superintendent of Catholic Schools; Mr. Mark Pacione, Director of the Office of Youth Ministry; Mrs. Carol Pacione, Director of the Office of Family Life; and Ms. Joanne Cahoon, Coordinator of Adolescent Catechesis. Previously, one hundred parents, twenty-five from each grade, had been selected to respond to a survey. During the visit, the team interviewed the administration, the religion department, students and faculty. They reviewed the video *Not a Love Story* and participated in the workshop which had been given to students for several years.

The final report on the visitation came back on 5 May 1995. In a letter to the school that accompanied the final report, Cardinal Keeler stated:"In the course of the assessment, it became clear that many statements were based on inaccurate information and, sadly, took the form of innuendo and in some cases deliberate distortion... A great disservice has been done to dedicated educators by tactics of gossip and slander contrary to the gospel way that Jesus teaches and that gives guidance to the law of the church."

The report stated, "It was apparent that both administrators were fully aware and exercised their responsibility to ensure that the fidelity to Church teachings permeates all aspects of school life. Through their leadership young women have experienced the true and faithful spirit of

Vatican II. These students are encouraged to participate in Church life. This was demonstrated by the school's own religious activities, as well as outreach programs...The students reported that they felt that they were being prepared to live in our society with Christian/Catholic values....They seem well prepared to face the challenges of contemporary society without a jaded view, but rather with a sense of hope and a willingness to work for justice reflective of the gospel message." [54]

The team found that Notre Dame's curriculum was mainline in its topics presented and student text utilized. They stated, "It is our assessment that the religion teachers at Notre Dame Prep carry out their role with great sensitivity, competence, love for their students and great respect and loyalty to the Church... It is our belief that the allegations (against the teachers) are the result of some misinterpretations, gross distortions or blatant untruths." In the Executive Summary the assessment team concluded, among other things, "The administration and faculty have established a clear and pointed philosophy of Catholic education consistent with the teachings of the Church and the charisma of the School Sisters of Notre Dame; the religion curriculum is not inconsistent with the newly published *Catechism of the Catholic Church*; the treatment of human sexuality is patterned according to the archdiocesan document, *Catechesis for Human Sexuality*; the religious life of the school is marked by prayer, worship, and service; there is no apparent ambiguity between the teachings of the Church and what is practiced at Notre Dame. Based on observation, interviews, and surveys, it is the judgement of the team that the allegations levied against Notre Dame Prep are unsubstantiated and without basis." [55]

I personally had a problem with two statements in the Executive Summary,"The religion curriculum is *not inconsistent* with the newly published Catechism..." and " there is *no apparent ambiguity* between the teachings of the church and what is practiced at Notre Dame." (emphasis is mine) The first statement contradicted the recommendation of the team that "catechetical materials selected for use in the religion curriculum *continue* to reflect the teaching of the official church documents, particularly the Catechism of the Catholic Church." A clear indication that the curriculum was "consistent" instead of "not inconsistent." The second statement's adjective "no *apparent* ambiguity" seemed to suggest that there were perhaps "out of view, undetected, concealed" ambiguities. This contradicts the team's commendation that NDP be commended for the "praiseworthy effort they are making to prepare young women to identify, analyze and critique, *from a clearly Catholic perspective,* the issues and concerns they will encounter..." Furthermore, the team's commentary on the teachers in the religion department stated, " The need to *present church teaching in a manner that is clear, authentic,* and offered in a way that is understandable with the accompanying need to be sensitive to pressures, tensions and challenges of high school students in a very delicate and demanding responsibility. It is our assessment that the religion teachers at Notre Dame Prep carry out this role *with great sensitivity, competence, love for their students and great respect and loyalty to the Church."* (p.7 of the report; emphasis is mine) No ambiguity here at all!

Cardinal Keeler, Notre Dame, and the assessment team agreed to keep the results of the visit confidential until the *Catholic Review* could publish them on May 17. The day before, however, Frank Sommerville, informed by the cardinal's spokesperson, wrote an unbalanced story in the *Baltimore Sun* on the assessment under the title "Teaching found 'generally' Catholic." The article gave the impression that there had been problems to be corrected and that NDP had been placed under some kind of constant supervision by the archdiocese. The video was still referred to a 'pornographic.' After the report was published, Cardinal Keeler was invited to celebrate Mass with the Notre Dame community. He accepted the invitation but requested that the event not be publicized.

The Wanderer continued to publish articles on the matter in the ensuing couple of months. They also published information from a twelve page letter sent to NDP parents, under the heading "St. John Neumann Council of the Concerned Parents of Notre Dame Preparatory School." This unsigned swan-song of the group repeated the previously made charges and called the archdiocese's report "a whitewash." They even repeated the charge that members of the religion department "were hauling boxes of books and papers out of their offices and the school library" on the eve before the arrival of the assessment group.[56]

Notwithstanding the validation by the archdiocese, the personal attacks in the media continued until a teacher pursued legal action against some of the parents. The case was resolved in the teacher's favor.

If the "concerned parents" were really concerned finding the truth about the way Notre Dame was teaching their daughters, why did they adopt anonymity and subversive tactics? Or did they, from the outset, have in mind to "get rid of the administration and the religion department," believing that Notre Dame had been taken over by Catholic feminists? The fact that they characterized the results of the archdiocesan assessment as a "whitewash" shows their belief that the entire American church was corrupt, including the Department of Catholic Education.

One could charitably assume that some parents had real concerns about the way their daughters were being educated. The sad thing is that they allowed themselves to be kidnapped by *The Wanderer* and *Defend Life*, who obviously had their own agendas. Add to this the press and talk radio, who could not be happier to have a chance to unload on a "preppy rich school." From the reporting in the press, it became obvious that some of the parents relied, unfortunately, on a few inside sources at the school, who for whatever reason, were feeding information to the media.

As a Christian school, we should be motivated by charity and forgiveness in trying to bring the people who did the school wrong back into the fold. I was surprised to meet recently a couple of the "concerned parents" at a thank-you dinner for school benefactors. I can only hope and pray that readmitting them to the list of contributors to the school was prompted by confession, remorse and forgiveness. It is understandable, however, that the school discontinued an endowed "excellence in teaching award" established by the spokesperson of the "concerned parents" and refunded the gift.

The positive validation of the school by the archdiocese revealed that NDP's religion program and activities were well within the teaching of the post-Vatican II Catholic church -- a fact that some of the "concerned parents" probably will never accept. The experience was a blessing in disguise for the administration, faculty, staff, parents, alumnae and students. We learned that many alumnae, students and parents supported the school with all their heart with their many messages to local papers and the personal letters to the administration. The fundraising programs of the school did not suffer but became more successful. The school honed its policies of openness with the parents, particularly on the religion curriculum and the student texts used in the class room.

If Notre Dame keeps living by its motto "We pursue Truth" and remains faithful to its Vatican II inspired philosophy, I am sure that Notre Dame Preparatory will always remain a Vatican II school. Pursuing the truth requires continuous prudence and vigilance in examining our faithfulness to the truth. We cannot succumb to the "structures of deceit" growing on the inside or coming from the outside, lest we place ourselves on the path to self-destruction. What happened to the miniature church of Notre Dame in 1995, has happened and is happening still in the universal church.

"Ungodly Rage" -- a Postscript

Being present at the visitation of the archdiocese as a member of the religion department, I kept wondering why the Baltimore diocese did not assess the accusers of Notre Dame. What was *their* agenda? Why were they thinking they were representing the "authentic faith?" Where did they get their inspiration and modus operandi? Would the truth not have been better served by showing the other side of the coin to the public?

At a meeting of Evergreens for Life at Loyola College on 3 November 1995 sponsored by Defend Life, Donna Steichen, author of *Ungodly Rage:*

the Hidden Face of Catholic Feminism, was the guest speaker.[57] The event was advertised in *Defend Life's Newsletter*, "Donna will explain how numerous female religious orders, such as the SSND's and Mercy's, have been taken over by radical feminists. She will explain what we can and must do to effectively counteract the evils penetrated daily by such religious orders (i.e. The Notre Dame Prep abomination last spring, where hard core pornography was shown to NDP girls in the name of enlightenment)."[58] Some of the members of the "concerned parents" were strong supporters of Steichen's ideas and were present at the presentation. After hearing Steichen at Loyola, I read *Ungodly Rage* and recognized the language and the tactics which the accusers had used against Notre Dame.

Steichen opines that a substantial part of the American Catholic church is taken over by the ideology of Catholic feminism which is "inimical to most essential Christian beliefs." She believes that Vatican II has been catastrophic for the church and that female theologians and nuns were instrumental to the "misapplication of the spirit of Vatican II." She calls for a restoration of the authentic faith. The Catholic schools no longer teach the Catholic Faith and many institutions are "corrupt and systematically corrupting." She suggests that the lay people have to act against this corruption by exposing the "revolutionaries." (See more details in Appendix D)

My teaching position at Notre Dame gave me a chance to make a decent living for 31 years. In the early seventies, Felicitas and I had to make the best of it with small salaries. A teacher's salary at a Catholic school was barely enough to make ends meet. Notre Dame came to the rescue by giving Felicitas a job as a science teacher. She soon found out that working with teenagers was rather difficult for her. The following year, she was hired as activity director and social worker at Manor Care nursing home. This became a stepping stone for being hired by the Baltimore Housing Authority, where she would serve as a social worker and public housing manager until her retirement in 2000. During her employment, she went back to school to obtain a Social Service license and an associate degree in Gerontology. She felt at home working with the poor in the inner city of Baltimore and her bubbly personality made them tell her "you should run for mayor!"

Soon we found out that our income did not allow any extras and that, to visit our relatives in Belgium and the Philippines, would require a "second job" to cover expenses. For six years I taught summer courses in the theology department at Loyola College, painted friends' houses and classrooms at Notre Dame. In 1976 I got a chance to teach Italian to the opera singers at Peabody Conservatory of Johns Hopkins University and to chair the Humanities Department. My nine and a half hour workdays for eight years were worth every minute!

When in 1980 we bought our second house and moved close to Pennsylvania, I took courses to obtain a real estate license and tried to sell farms. I should have stuck to theology and languages. Business was never my forte. We thanked God we made a decent living and we thanked America for the chances given to us as immigrants. We felt this country was our real home and we both became American citizens. I will never forget the day we both went voting for the first time!

When Felicitas and I found out that we never would have children, we tried to adopt a child. The financial burden of the legal process was unsurmountable and made us give up this dream. We had also been told that adopting would be a problem because we were "a mixed couple." We then decided to help our eighteen nieces and nephews in the Philippines, whose parents could not afford college tuition. With the assistance of some of our friends of the Savatten Club and my brother Arthur and his spouse, we set up a tuition scholarship project. To date, fifteen of them have earned bachelors' degrees in nursing, architecture, business, engineering, philosophy, and computer science. A worthwhile investment in education!

Notre Dame was not only a place to work, it became my second home with real close friends and chances to grow and develop my God-given talents. The school gave me a chance to display my culinary talents and to develop some of my favorite hobbies. During my high school and seminary days, I grabbed every chance to act in plays and musicals. When Notre Dame invited me to play Tevye in *Fiddler on the Roof*, a dream came through. Now I could finally sing on the stage "If I Were A Rich Man," a song I had practiced for years in the shower. My role as Mr. MacAfee in *Bye Bye Birdie* was more challenging, but everyone forgave my Flemish accent in "Kids."

I will always be proud having reintroduced Latin in the NDP curriculum. Teaching languages became an avocation. During a two year hiatus from the religion department, I taught Latin, Greek, French and Italian. My students were always asking in what language I was thinking. When I told them that I was thinking in the language I was speaking, they reacted, "How is that possible?" Well, I don't really know, but it works for me. The students also asked me not to lose my Flemish accent and I never did. My relatives in Belgium, however, tell me now that I speak Flemish with an English accent.

During the administration of sisters Ellis and Helen Marie, the faculty was the focus of concern. Their mantra was "build a good faculty and you build a good school." Not only did they expand the lay faculty, increased salaries and benefits, but they kept an "open door policy" for new initiatives and solving disagreements. The closeness of the faculty was cemented by numerous social events like the Friday "wine and cheese gatherings" and created a fellowship that went beyond school matters.

After almost thirty years of full-time teaching, I began thinking of retirement. I was not ready yet to leave Notre Dame. In September 1999, Sister Christine Mulcahay, who had followed Sister Helen Marie as headmistress, accepted me as part-time teacher for Latin and Italian. This was going to keep me at Notre Dame, provide a partial income, and still give me a chance to substitute as a religion teacher and stay involved in the school's social justice activities. At the same time, it would allow me to give more time to a hobby which was gradually becoming a new calling: genealogy. This new passion was going to become a different area of my "searching for truth," and as such a part of my story. Eventually it would help bring me to the decision to write this memoir.

A chance meeting during one of my visits as a member of a Middle States Evaluation team in 1985 in Bethesda, Maryland, launched twenty years of genealogical research and publications. The school student roster showed Anthony and Henry Goethals, who identified themselves as great-grandsons of General George Washington Goethals. Several years earlier, in 1971, as new immigrant to the United States, I had crossed the George Washington Goethals Memorial Bridge in New Jersey, and was greatly surprised to see a bridge in the New York area named in honor of a man bearing my surname. A meeting with the two Goethals boys led to a meeting with their father, Henry W. Goethals and later with their uncle, Thomas R. Goethals. By then I had learned that their grandfather George had been the chief engineer of the Panama Canal and first governor of the Panama Canal Zone.

My genealogical curiosity took root when Thomas Goethals asked me to translate some letters in Flemish, written by Jan Baptist Goethals, the father of General George Goethals, who had emigrated from Belgium in 1849, to his relatives in Flanders. My knowledge of Flemish, French and Latin helped me in discovering several generations of George's family in Belgium, ultimately allowing me to reconstruct his ancestry to the middle of the fifteenth century. In my search, I found that the Goethals nobility branches in Belgium had, over the last 200 years, carefully "constructed" an extensive genealogical record back to the ninth century in Italy. [59]

Somehow they ignored the branch of George's ancestors. To set the record straight, I published my findings in *A Forgotten Family. The Flemish Roots of General George Washington Goethals in 2004*.[60]

Now badly affected by the genealogy bug, I set out to find my own roots. After a couple of visits to Flemish archives in Belgium and 127 microfilms from the Family History Library[61] in Salt Lake City, Utah, I had retraced fifteen generations of my family back to the end of the fifteenth century.[62] There were no academics, nobility or rich people among the 894 relatives I identified: only simple, hardworking people who overcame military occupations and the ravages of political and religious wars, and persisted through continuous setbacks. It was a revelation to me that, in my branch of the Goethals family, I was the first one who graduated from college and the only cleric in fifteen generations.

In my search for George Washington Goethals, I had explored the history of the Goethals branches in Belgium extensively. I was able to show, with discovered evidence, that the published genealogies of the two previous centuries had stretched the truth to prove uninterrupted lines of descent. My desire to "search for the truth" prompted me to publish my findings and corrections in a new book which had been fifteen years in the making, *Goethals 880-1900. The Story of the Goethals Story*.[63] Publishing it in English would also offer a wider public access to sources written mainly in Flemish, French and Latin. When some of the Goethals nobility read the book, they mainly ignored the corrections, holding on to their centuries-long claims. It taught me again that it was not only in the church that people would evade evidence to protect their institutional traditions.

The centuries-long genealogies of the Goethals would never have been written were it not for the desire of the nobility to prove their "noble" ancestry or of well-to-do citizens who could pay for such services. My namesakes displayed a long list of knights, magistrates, judges and lawyers, diplomats and clerics, theologians and philosophers. It was particularly satisfying to me to meet a host of religious men and women who over the centuries had faithfully served the Catholic church as priests, bishops and abbots, Dominicans and Jesuits, in times of peace and in times

Henry of Ghent (1217-1293); Bishop Goethals S.J. Calcutta; General George Washington Goethals, 1858-1928, builder of Panama Canal; Rev. Jacob Goethals, Abbot of Drongen d.1647; the Goethals Chapel, St. Bavo, Ghent; the Goethals family crest

and the 'Spirit of Vatican II' have taken root in their lives. In return, Notre Dame has provided me with more than just a living. She gave me lifelong friends, matured me in my faith, and supported me in my continued mission of working in the Lord's vineyard.

On the occasion of the fifty years celebration of Notre Dame on Hampton Lane, Fr. James McAndrews, S.J., delivered a homily, "The Spirit of Wisdom." He referred to the seven pillars which adorn the entrance of the school, symbolizing the Seven Pillars of Wisdom: Prudence, Knowledge, Discretion, Counsel, Judgment, Understanding and Power. Inviting the graduates to make the Seven Pillars the guiding posts of their lives, he stated,"Your yes to Wisdom's call can change your lives, your yes can change the lives of others, your yes can change the world... We have heard from one source or another that *there is a Spirit about this place.* Now we know what that Spirit is. It is the Spirit of Wisdom. It is the Spirit of Notre Dame." [65]

EPILOGUE
"I Never Really Left"

In the foregoing pages you have met the people who had an impact on my journey. Their example, encouragement and love inspired me to respond to God's call. You were also witness to the activities and events that cemented the course I was taking. I hope that I was clear enough in exposing my own inadequacy and failures. I trust that I have been compassionate to the people whose gossip and criticism I had to face. I have forgiven them a long time ago.

Recalling the happy and even unhappy days in that journey was not difficult. They are etched in my memory. Reconstructing my thoughts, feelings, doubts and motivations during the years of my "transition" was a more complicated task. Fortunately, I kept the correspondence with my parents and close friends Which we exchanged during that period. Furthermore, Felicitas surprised me one day with all the letters I wrote to her and her family up to the time I decided to request laicization. The letters allowed me to retrace and elucidate my state of mind in greater detail.

It is with a sense of deep gratitude that I look back on all the people who contributed to my journey: my parents, who from a very young age, imbued in me their desire to help others; the priests in my high school years who inspired me to reach for things that were bigger than myself. I am indebted to the Scheut Fathers who gave me an outstanding spiritual, philosophical and theological training and continued their friendship even after I left the Congregation. In times when I needed them most, my brother Arthur, my sister-in-law Rita, and some close friends showed their loyalty. Notre Dame Prep and the School Sisters of Notre Dame allowed me to continue my teaching ministry within the framework of the Catholic Church. The married priest members and their spouses of our "Savatten club" were my second and adopted family. Finally, my soulmate Felicitas, kept me sane and always encouraged in me the desire to see the needs of others over forty-one years of a happy life of simplicity.

I therefore sing with Edith Piaf "*Non, je ne regrette rien, rien de rien.*" (No, I don't regret anything, nothing of nothing.) I don't regret the years of spiritual and academic training which enriched me personally. I don't regret having been ordained a priest. I recall with a certain joy the times I shared the Eucharist with people in parishes, monasteries, prisons, and in remote mission posts in the Philippines. I think back to the happiness of parents whose children I was allowed to baptize. I remember the relief of penitents after an absolution and the peace on faces of people receiving the last sacraments. I don't regret training catechists in the barrios and future priests in the seminary. I will never forget the fervor and hope I saw in the faces of sisters with whom I shared my enthusiasm about Vatican II.

I don't regret having become a layperson again. When I left the clerical state and my religious order, I knew that I was always going to be a priest. The sacrament of holy orders "confers an indelible spiritual character upon the person being ordained."(*Catechism of the Catholic Church,* 1548.) Although I was discharged of my priestly obligations and functions, I could never be "un-ordained," just as a Christian cannot "undo" his baptism, even if he ceases to practice his faith.

During all the years I was teaching religion at Notre Dame Prep and Loyola College, I felt that I was continuing my priestly ministry of spreading the Good News. Acting as a Eucharistic minister, giving homilies at school liturgies or being a reader and cantor at St. Bernardine parish in Baltimore, participating in social service projects at NDP, gave me a chance to serve in a different way. That my students or the faithful in the pews were not aware that I was a priest, did not really matter. I knew it! Often I caught myself silently reciting the words of the consecration, "This is my body," as if I were concelebrating with the priest. *I Never Really Left* seemed to me the right title for this memoir.

My contacts with my former confreres of the Scheut Fathers, make me often feel that I "never really left" them either. The close friendship and our continued respect and support for their mission activities are testimony to this.

There are only a couple of occasions during which I officially acted as a priest in the last forty years. The day before Sister Helen Marie, SSND, headmistress of Notre Dame, died, I visited her at the School Sisters' Maria Assumpta Center. I remembered how many times she told me how great it would be if I could serve as a chaplain at the school. Although she apparently was unconscious, I knew she could hear me when I prayed with her, gave her my priestly blessing and told her that God was going to welcome her for what she had done for Notre Dame and "her girls."

When the spouse of my good friend and editor of my books, Henry W. Goethals was dying of cancer, she requested that I hear her confession and give her a final blessing. I could not refuse the request of a dying friend. The next day, she passed away and I presided over her funeral at Martha's Vineyard, MA.

Perhaps I am one of those resigned priests who would have loved, given a chance, to continue service to the church as a married priest. I know others who resigned who will not have anything to do with the Catholic Church any longer, who consider their years in the ministry as a waste of time, or who have lost their faith altogether. The shortage of priests today could be partially remedied if the Roman hierarchy accepted resigned married priests back into the fold and active ministry. Perhaps this will happen under future popes John Paul III or Benedict XVII...

When Pope Benedict XVI in 2009 created the Personal Ordinariates for Anglicans who wanted to become Catholic (Anglicanorum Coetibus), he did not seem to have problems with married priests serving the flock. Recently, Fr. Steenson, the Anglican bishop of Rio Grande, who was ordained a Catholic priest in 2009, and who was married with three children, became head of the new Ordinariate of St. Peter, Houston, Texas. Although he cannot be ordained a bishop because he is married, he will function as bishop and be a voting member of the US Conference of Catholic Bishops. I am wondering, should I become an "orthodox" Anglican, and apply for a spot in a new ordinariate? Some months ago, the *Catholic Review* in Baltimore had extensive coverage of the ordination of an Anglican priest who became a Catholic priest. I found it odd that not a single line in the coverage mentioned the fact that he was married. Not a very hopeful sign of things to come. I hope that, in my lifetime, I see the day when the Roman Catholic Church welcomes resigned married priests, ordains married men, women deacons and even women priests.

Throughout my journey, my faith went through stormy weather, but with God's grace I never abandoned the Catholic Church. I remain in the church because I need the Eucharist and need to hear the word of God. I respect and support my former confreres and the sisters I worked with, who on a daily basis perform great works of charity, social service and education which have always been a hallmark of the Catholic church. I remain in my church notwithstanding its obsession with power and sex, its uncanny feeling of superiority and unwillingness to listen. I recognize that my church is human and therefore has lived through conflict, scandal and corruption throughout its long history. The church has also shown that she is able to reform and renew when necessary. I will not allow that the human failings and even destructive activities of some of the church's membership and leadership deprive me of a community to which I have given the best of my days. Notwithstanding all its failings, the church is an essential extension of personal faith: faith and church belong together.

FAITH AND CHURCH [66]

Many Catholics today, shocked by the church's handling of the pedophile crisis or by statements of the hierarchy on other matters, are professing that they want to believe, but without a church. "Faith, yes; church, no!" Or even "Christ, yes; church, no!"

Faith in God, however, creates a bond with others who believe in him and is therefore relational and communal in essence. Faith engenders a community of the faithful who are invited to proclaim to others what they believe. They are inspired to celebrate together and to love everyone as God loves everyone. These are the four pillars, the basic duties and tasks of the faith community: form a community, proclaim the message, celebrate together, and show charity to all.

This is "being Church" with a capital letter. This Church has a vertical dimension because the faithful is God's people, they proclaim God's word, they celebrate God's mystery, and it is God's love of humanity which finds a mirror in the love for others.

This being *Church* however has also a horizontal dimension because faith takes place in space and time, in the historical framework of human history: an institution or *church* with a lower case letter c. The **C**hurch does not operate in a vacuum. It needed a **c**hurch, an institution, within which the faithful could respond to the call of the four central tasks.

The Gospel message of today would never have been possible without a church, without a community of believers. Without the church, the gospels could have been nothing but beautiful literature of the first century. It was the church that, generation after generation, continued to proclaim the Gospel and spread the Good News. This proclamation was not always faithful to the message, but it kept happening and came to us that way.

In the Acts of the Apostles we see a steady growth and a rapid expansion of followers. In a short time there was a need for a certain structure and order. The early church was a conglomeration of local communities of believers reflected in the letters of St. Paul. It was Paul who was the first church builder of communities who had a certain structure adapted to the local context (without a creed yet). Today these communities ares still local, but the structure has taken on universal uniformity. This uniform structure has grown historically to respond to the needs for order and organization, trying to remain faithful to the goal of being Church and to guide the four pillars of faith towards greater efficiency.

We cannot say, "We believe" while dismissing the history of "faith-in-church." It is an illusion that we can return to the sources of our faith by trying to connect to the Jesus of the first century while dismissing 2000 years of history rich in tradition. You cannot take off tradition as you take off a coat; we have to recognize what is good and bad in that tradition.

The link between faith and institution (church) is not as essential as the link between faith and Church. The big error is that today many believe that the link between faith and the institution is at the same level as the link between faith and the four central pillars of the Church. Obedience to the institution is important, but proclaiming the Gospel, celebrating the Eucharist, practicing charity and forming a community cannot be reduced to obedience to the institution.

On the other hand, the church (institution) has had a positive influence on each of the four central domains of being-Church, and that influence continues today. The church has created a framework within which we were able to celebrate the Eucharist on a weekly basis as a community of believers. Churches were built, leaders were selected to lead the celebrations, the church invested in art to make celebrations more beautiful and memorable. The church has shown an incredible dedication to education and charity: just remember the cathedral schools, the monasteries, the care for the indigent throughout church history and in all its aspects, the development of its social doctrine in encyclicals, its hospitals and charitable organizations. The church has continuously proclaimed the Gospel through evangelization in all its forms: preachers, text-copying monks, art and literature, Catholic lay movements, and the incredible work of the missionaries. Finally, the church has always been praying as a community and sharing as a community. Men and women adopted these tasks as a way of life in the religious orders and congregations. Even today, prayer groups and Bible study group flourish.

The church is necessary to realize the Church as God's project with humanity. As a community of believers we need organization, structure and order, and the church has provided this. It should therefore not be seen as a necessary evil, but as an organ necessary to support the journey of the faithful to the realization of the Church. We therefore should love the "one, holy, Catholic and apostolic church" as we proclaim it in the creed.

In time, the church has imbedded the four central tasks in rules, regulations, norms and organs, commandments and thou-shall-nots. The unfortunate result was that the structure gradually came to dominate the purpose, and we ended up with clericalism instead of a community of the faithful. The clergy is still seen as standing separate from, and higher than the faithful. The higher the clerical status, the more this is pronounced. The final responsibility always seems to be concentrated in the clergy, because all things have to be decided there. This *clero-centrism* is seen as an unchangeable given. The responsibility and power is still reserved for the people who are ordained (see the entire Canon Law book).

As a result of this clero-centrism, the laity is being undervalued. In many church organizations, parishes, and dioceses laypeople still depend on the goodwill of the clergy. Recently, this situation seems to be reemphasized by the actions of the leadership in the universal church. John Paul II warned against the "clericalization of the laity and the laicization of the clergy." Recent liturgical rules are making sure that lay ministers know their proper and subservient place around the altar.

Writing this memoir has gradually distilled for me the ensuing statements of belief and the kind of church I would love to see in the future. The statements of belief -- I now understand -- are the result of five decades of a mixture of hope and despair, joy and depression, good and bad, faith and darkness. Somewhere at the onset of these decades, I made a fundamental option for God, an option primarily devoted to the love of God and the service of others. This fundamental option was sometimes clouded by acts of impatience, selfishness, weakness, doubt and lack of charity, and was hidden under moments of complete self-love and self-service. In resisting my inner self-love and the outer forces of injustice, hypocrisy, and clericalism, I persisted searching for my fundamental option in the new challenges that life was offering me. In the end, I understood that my fundamental option had remained intact throughout and I was serving God and others in a new vocation. There is always hope, if there is faith and charity.

I BELIEVE

I believe that someone, who is more than human, has created everything that is alive. I believe that I can relate to this someone, just because he is *someone, not something.* Call that someone God, Father, Supreme Being, or any other term humanity has invented over the ages. I believe he will remain a mystery until he reveals himself fully when I die.

I believe that God has revealed himself in the humanity of Jesus Christ expressed in the Gospel message. Therefore, I call myself a Christian.

I believe that, as a believer, I form a bond with other believers in a community. That community is required to celebrate, share the message with others, and love everyone who crosses its path. Community, message, celebration and charity are the four pillars of faith and Church. They are God's project with humanity.

I believe that the Catholic Church, as an institution, has tried to remain faithful to support the realization of Church and to respond to our human need for organization, structure and order. Therefore, I call myself a Catholic.

I believe that I will never really die. Nobody is reduced to nothingness by death. When I die, my soul, spirit, ego, or any other definition of the immaterial in me, will persist. Therefore, I do not fear death.

I believe that I am playing a certain part in the life of the universe, how minuscule that part may be. My existence plays a role, in its own way, towards the fullness of all that exists.

I believe that as a member of the People of God, I have the duty to remain a part of the prophetic voice, speaking and acting from within, not from without.

I believe that religion is poetry. The poetic language of the liturgy, the devotions, songs and psalms, express most intimately the mysteries that lie beyond us.

I WOULD LOVE TO SEE A CHURCH...

I love to see a church which recognizes the hierarchy of value: reign of God, Church, church. A church which is subservient to Church.

I love to see a church that lives by Pope John XXIII's ideal: "Unity in essentials, freedom in uncertainties, in all things charity."

I love to see a church where clergy comes down from its pedestals of power and "specialness." Where the hierarchical structures are seen as means to fulfill its mission and as instruments to serve and not to dominate and control.

I love to see a church which reduces the ostentation in the symbols of authority to a more "Franciscan" simplicity: miters, reds, purples, baldachins, elevated platforms and red shoes are only symbols of power and not of service.

I love to see a church "purged of triumphalism, clericalism and legalism." [67]

I love to see a church where justice is not only an integral part of its mission to the world but where justice is fully practiced in its own household, where theologians, missionaries, and even bishops are not threatened with sanctions or even excommunication when they disagree, in conscience, with the hierarchy's opinion.[68]

I love to see a church where bishops rediscover the Vatican II approved collegiality and make it into a reality.

I love to see a church where no member of the People of God is afraid to speak the truth and where unconditional obedience is believed to be due only to God.

I love to see a church where the ministerial priesthood is at the service of the common priesthood of the baptized; where baptism is recognized as the basis instrument which gives the faithful the power to witness God's action in the world; where lay ministries are not seen as a threat to priestly ministries.

I love to see a church where the faith experience of women is taken into account, and where they take their rightful place as full members of the People of God, including being able to answer the call to the ministerial diaconate and priesthood.

I love to see a church which welcomes married men to the priesthood, even if they are not Anglican or Episcopalian, and accepts the service of resigned married priests who are willing to serve.

I love to see a church where non-Catholics and non-Christians feel at home because the church reaches out in dialogue and brotherhood, without denying its own Catholic identity.

I love to see a church which moves from hostility to friendship, from monologue to dialogue, from coercion to conscience, from rivalry to partnership, from suspicion to trust, from threat to persuasion, from law to ideals, from command to invitation, from superiority to humility. [69]

I wish to end my epilogue with a prayer I wrote during a Notre Dame sophomore retreat in 1999. Up to her death, Sister Helen Marie Duffy, SSND, prayed it every day and she shared copies with Notre Dame graduates. I wish that, what I am asking in this prayer, becomes more true in my remaining days.

Dear God,
Father and Mother

I ask you to bless me
and to watch over me this day.

May my feet walk
where my presence will be
a glimpse of you.
May my hands
touch someone in pain.
May my eyes
always see
the good in everyone they meet.
May my ears listen
only to praise
and not to words that tear down.
May my mouth
always speak the truth.
May my mind not judge others
because they are different.
May I just be myself
and a reflection of you.
May my heart be restless
until it rests in you.

I ask this in the name
of your Son
and your Spirit
for today,
tomorrow
and all my days.
Amen!

APPENDICES

APPENDIX A: DOCUMENTS OF VATICAN II

This is a summary of what I deem to be the most important ideas in each of the sixteen Vatican II documents. The date of the promulgation of the document is mentioned at the end of each section.

1. Dogmatic Constitution on the Church
(*Lumen Gentium/Light of the Nations*)

The Church is a mystery and a sacrament called to proclaim the Kingdom of God. It is the pilgrim People of God moving through history and it "subsists" fully in the Catholic Church, though also in other churches. To permit the People of God to operate in history, the Church has a hierarchical structure. The authority is embedded in the whole Episcopal order who guide the Church with the Roman Pontiff. Their authority is seen as a service to be guided by collegiality. The clerics, religious and the lay people are all commissioned to the Church's mission by the Lord himself by reason of their baptism. The Church remains imperfect and is therefore in pilgrimage, in need for continued renewal. (21 November 1964)

2. Dogmatic Constitution on Divine Revelation
(*Dei Verbum/The Word of God*)

The Word of God is communicated through Sacred Scripture, the sacred tradition and the teaching authority of the Church, all linked together. This teaching authority is not above the Bible but must serve it. In Bible research, the Church recognizes genuine science. It also accepts that within doctrine growth in understanding is in principle possible. While Scripture study is advised for all believers, it must be the soul of theology, the liturgy, and preaching.(18 November 1965)

3. Pastoral Constitution on the Church and the Modern World
(*Gaudium et Spes/ The Joy and Hope*)

The Church has the duty to address the whole of humanity and human concerns; hence the pastoral nature of this document. The Church sees itself in solidarity with the world as sent into the world for the service of humankind. It therefore must act as a leaven in society, inspired by Gospel values, without tying itself yo any culture, political, or economic system. The document sees the split between the secular world and religion as among "the more serious errors of our age." The Church has to live within the world without dominating it and contribute toward "making the family of humankind and its history more human." The document recapitulates the teachings of the papal social encyclicals since Leo XIII's *Rerum Novarum* and discusses in detail specific areas like atheism, marriage, economics, politics, and war and peace, with a strong call for the plight of the weak.(7 December 1965)

4. Constitution on the Sacred Liturgy
(*Sacrosanctum Concilium/The Most Sacred Council*)

The Church is called to proclaim God's message in word and sacred signs. The document delineates general principles for restoration and renewal, keeping the fundamental elements while adjusting aspects of the rituals to the requirements of our times(63). Therefore, the signs must be understandable and simplified through, among others, an expanded use of the vernacular, the language of the people. Among the other areas of renewal are the absence of rigid uniformity, the expanded Scripture readings and the restoration of preaching in the liturgy, the liturgical training of ministers, and the revision of the administration of the sacraments and the liturgical year. The constitution was the first to be approved on 4 December 1963. The Liturgical Commission gave concrete form to the suggestions of the Council on 7 March 1965. (4 December 1963)

5. Decree on Ecumenism
(*Unitatis redintegratio/Restoration of Unity*)

The decree on Ecumenism "marks the full entry of the Roman Catholic Church into the ecumenical movement."(Walter M. Abbott, S.J. Vatican II, etc., 339) From a church which considered other Christian communities as a danger and the enemy, the decree calls for a restoration of Christian unity, not a return to the Catholic Church. The Church recognizes other "ecclesial communities" as Churches, with whom it has a common heritage. Recognizing that both sides were to blame for many of the divisions in history, the Church asks for reconciliation and collaboration in theology, dialogue and social action. (21 November 1964)

6. Decree on Eastern Catholic Churches
(*Orientalium Ecclesiarum/Of the Eastern Churches*)

The document is a complement to the Decree on Ecumenism. For a long time the church of the western (or Latin) rite tried to "latinize" the churches of the eastern rite, preventing reunification with non-Catholic eastern churches. The council fathers corrected this approach by recognizing the equality between western and eastern traditions. The Catholic church accepts the validity of priestly ordination in the Orthodox churches. There is also an opening towards the exchange of sacraments between the Catholic and the Orthodox churches. (21 November 1964)

7. Decree on The Ministry and Life of Priests
(*Presbyterorum ordinis/The Order of the Priests*)

The document describes the nature of the priesthood and the special tasks the priest has in building the Kingdom of God in union with the bishop. The emphasis is on the priest, not as member of a 'privileged state,' but as a servant and member of the People of God, in a position of leadership united with the lay people. It also discusses elements of priestly piety. (4 December 1965)

8. Decree on Priestly Formation
(*Optatum totius*)

The decree calls for adaptation and reform of priestly training. This should mainly happen by integrating theology and spirituality with pastoral life. In a unique approach, expressing the 'spirit of Vatican II,' the decree gives this responsibility to the episcopal conferences, because the program should be undertaken by individual countries and reflect local pastoral needs and conditions. The document gives counsel and suggestions to be worked out on the local level: theological studies should be centered on the Bible; all training should include ecumenism, history and should be personally formative. Priestly formation "should always answer the pastoral needs of the area in which the ministry is to be exercised."(1) (28 October 1965)

9. Decree on the Bishops' Pastoral Office
(*Christus Dominus/Christ the Lord*)

The decree further develops the ideas on collegiality in *Lumen Gentium*. The bishops exercise their episcopal office at three levels: on their own dioceses, in episcopal conferences, and as members of the college of bishops in union with the pope, in the universal church. This collegial responsibility is expressed is expressed in the *synod* (college of bishops together with the pope). The bishops is no more just a delegate of the hierarchy (the pope), but "the proper, ordinary and immediate pastor" of his own diocese.(11) They should share this responsibility with pastoral counsels of priests and lay people and even create parish pastoral counsels. The Roman administration should include bishops from dioceses and lay people and reform its procedures. The whole mode of operation should be characterized by a spirit of service. (28 October 1965)

10. Decree on the Appropriate Renewal of Religious Life
(*Perfectae caritatis/Perfect Charity*)

The life based on the practice of the evangelical counsels of poverty, chastity, and obedience must be based entirely on the Gospels. The religious life is not superior to the lay people state; it is just another way to live as part of the People of God. While the decree recognizes traditional ways to live the religious life, it asks the individual orders to renovate themselves by going to the sources of the Sacred Scriptures, the spirit of their founders and make adjustments to the changed conditions of the times. (28 October 1965)

11. Decree of the Apostolate of the Laity
(*Apostolicam actuositatem/Apostolic Activity*)

The decree develops the ideas about the nature of the apostolate of the laity already discussed in *Gaudium et Spes* and *Lumen Gentium*. The document is historical because it is the first conciliar document dedicated to the laity. The theological center is the notion that laypeople are the People of God, co-responsible with bishops, priest, and religious for Christ's mission on earth because of their baptism. The layperson shares in the universal priesthood and as such is assigned by the Lord himself to the apostolate. The layperson is not just the representative of the hierarchy as it was presented in previous times. The layperson has to learn to work *with* rather than *for* the person they serve. The document gives advise how the layperson should work in and outside the church and how he should be trained. (18 November 1965)

12. Decree on the Church's Missionary Activity
(*Ad gentes/To All Nations*)

The decree on missionary activity of the church is based on the mission theology of *Lumen Gentium* and *Gaudium et Spes*, but focuses of the Church's active presence in non-Christian cultures. This presence should not be imposed as an alien culture, but should be imbedded in local cultures and traditions. The document provides biblical and patristic justification for the church's missionary activity. Missionary activity has to be characterized by enculturation and a respect and understanding of non-Christian religions. All members of the People of God are called to participate in missionary activity. (7 December 1965)

13. Decree on the Instruments of Social Communication
(*Inter merifica/Among the Wonderful Things*)

The decree on the media, approved at the end of the second session of Vatican II, recognizes the importance of the media for the evangelization of the world. The document, whose tone looks backward rather than forward, is considered as one of the weakest documents of the council, not yet influenced by the views of the Church in the Modern World and other documents. (4 November 1963)

14. Declaration on Religious Freedom
(*Dignitatis humanae/The Dignity of the Human Person*)

For centuries, the Church has suppressed "errors" and preached that only the truth had rights. Signaling acceptance of the "development of doctrine," the Council declares that every person has the right to free exercise of religion -- a right that "has its foundation in the very nature of the human person."(2) No person should be prevented from practicing his religion; no person should be discriminated because of his religion. This fundamental right is to be protected by both society and the church. (7 December 1965)

15. Declaration on Christian Education
(*Gravissimum educationis/The Paramount Importance of Education*)

The decree on education sketches some basic principles of Christian education to be worked out by the episcopal conferences. Parents are responsible for the education of their children. The schools have to form the whole human person and integrate Christian education into the whole pattern of human life. They have to train students to be personally mature, spiritually adult, and socially responsible for their society. Thus they become as graduates "the leaven of the human family."(2) Teaching is seen as a vocation and a ministry. (28 October 1965)

16. Declaration on Non-Christian Religions
(*Nostra aetate/In Our Times*)

The church has always attempted to "convert" adherents of other world religions. The declaration is the first official council document with an open approach to world religions. "The Catholic Church rejects nothing which is true and holy in these religions....(They) often reflect a ray of that Truth which enlightens all persons."(2). Other religions therefore deserve understanding and respect. The church has to search for dialogue and collaboration. The church has a special link to the other monotheistic religions and a special relationship with the Jews. The Jews are not responsible for the death of Jesus.(28 October 1965)

APPENDIX B: THE SCHEUT FATHERS

The *Congregation of the Immaculate Heart of Mary* is a Belgian missionary congregation founded in 1862 by the priest Théophile Verbiest. Concerned about the abandoned children in China, he founded the *Belgian Mission in China*. The Prefect of the Propaganda Fide commissioned him, however, to begin a seminary in Belgium to supply priests for the mission and in 1863 the seminary opened at the Field of Scheut in Anderlecht, a suburb of Brussels. The missionaries became known as the *Scheut Missionaries* or *Scheutists*. The first four Scheutists arrived in Mongolia in 1865 and expanded their Christian communities. Verbiest died in 1868 of typhoid fever at the age of 48.

Over the next hundred and forty-eight years the congregation grew by 1967 to almost 2,000 members and expanded its missions in Africa: Congo, Cameroun, Zambia, Senegal, Nigeria, Tchad, Mozambique, Angola and South-Africa; in Asia: the Philippines, Indonesia, Japan, Taiwan, Singapore, Mongolia and Hong Kong; the Americas: Guatemala, Haiti, the Dominican Republic, Brazil, Mexico and the United States. Today the congregation has still 892 priests and brothers coming from different nationalities.

Chapter / Chapitre	year / année	Superior General / Supérieur général	country / pays	members / membres
	1862	VERBIST Théophile	Belgium	
	1865		China	
	1869	VRANCKX Frans		11
Gen. Conf.	1887			
	1888	VAN AERTSELAER Jeroom	Congo	112
I	1898	VAN HECKE Adolf		309
	1899		Nederland	
	1904		Roma	
	1907		Philippines	
II	1908	BOTTY Albert		507
	1909	MORTIER Florent		
III	1920	RUTTEN Joseph		649
IV	1930	DAEMS Constant		928
	1931		Singapore	
	1935	VANDEPUTTE Jozef (Vic.g.)		1202
	1937		Indonesia	
	1946		U.S.A.	
V	1947	VANDEPUTTE Jozef	Japan	1479
	1953		Haïti - Chili (+ 1957)	
	1954		Hong Kong - Taiwan	
	1954		Guatemala	
VI	1957	SERCU Frans		1902
	1958		Rep. Dominicana	
	1961	DEGRIJSE Omer		1943
	1963		Brazil	
	1966		Cameroun	
VII	1967	GOOSSENS Wim		1986
VIII	1974	VAN DAELEN Paul		1683
	1976		Zambia - Sénégal	
	1977		Nigeria (+2003)	
	1979		México	
IX	1981	VAN DAELEN Paul (2a)		1556
X	1987	DECRAENE Michel		1441
	1990		France ('89) Tchad ('90)	
	1992		Mongolia	
XI	1993	THOMAS Jacques		1380
	1995		Angola	1359
XII	1999	LAPAUW Jozef	Mozambique (+ 2002)	1247
XIII	2005	TSIMBA Edouard		999
	2006		South Africa	990
	2010			892

History of the Scheut Fathers 1862-2010
(Elenchus Sodalium 2010)

APPENDIX C: THE SCHOOL PHILOSOPHIES OF NOTRE DAME PREPARATORY SCHOOL

1972 PHILOSOPHY

"Notre Dame Preparatory School is a Catholic private school for girls whose goal is primarily the development of the total person and the fostering of spiritual, moral, and intellectual values. It provides a personalized education endeavoring to prepare the student to live as an effective presence in the complicated and conflicting situations of her society.

The development of the person is accomplished most effectively in an intellectual and spiritual atmosphere which presupposes and encourages trust, honesty, and openness on the part of the faculty and students. In this atmosphere, faculty and students share creativity, search for meaning and discover values together.

The discipline which is offered to the Notre Dame student moves her, as she becomes more mature, from external regulation to personal responsibility. It introduces the student to self-directed learning whereby she moves from a concentration upon the requirements of group exercises to the freedom and challenge of personal interest and effort.

Notre Dame believes that learning is not confined to the classroom or text book; therefore it offers activities which promotes spirit, close community, and physical well-being.

Although education is fundamentally the responsibility of the parents, the school shares in this responsibility.

The concrete realization of Notre Dame's philosophy depends upon the concerted effort of the administration, faculty, parents and students."

1982 PHILOSOPHY

"Notre Dame is a Catholic, independent college preparatory school for girls. With dedication to academic excellence, spiritual growth and social consciousness, we emphasize the dignity and the value of each student and the concomitant achievement of her potential. Accordingly, we aspire to graduate young women with a sense of internal strength and confidence to face life, cope with change, and influence the social processes that affect their lives.

We believe that students, faculty, staff, and parents join in the process of building a community in which human culture and knowledge-personal and global, past and present-are shared through reflective and creative study. As we work to maintain uncompromised academic standards, we emphasize purposeful learning as a lifelong process to be enjoyed and applied through critical thought and reason. To this end, each student is encouraged to accept responsibility for the development of her personal and intellectual capabilities. We, in turn, assume the responsibility of preparing our students for admission into colleges consonant with their abilities.

Notre Dame willingly and actively accepts its obligation to provide an education based upon the Gospel. It is, therefore, our urgent concern that the Notre Dame student assimilate the religious and ethical principles inherent in the exercise of the Christian faith: a faith which we believe is genuine when it practices love and justice. As a particular expression of this commitment, the school encourages the student to become aware of her responsibilities to her immediate and distant environment, and to convert this commitment into action, now and in the future.

Correspondent to the advancement of a faith toward justice, we recognize and emphasize the equality of all persons before God. It is grounded in this truth that we educate our students with an awareness of their importance as women in a challenging and changing society. As we build confidence, we hope to foster creative expression, independent thinking, and effective leadership.
Notre Dame recognizes that it is but one of the many formative influences in the life of the student, yet it is with hope that we concede to this reality.
We believe, ultimately, that to learn and to know is to develop a sensitivity that enables one to become loving, just, and wise. It is in this believe that we strive to instilling our students the love for knowledge which leads to wisdom. "

1993 PHILOSOPHY

Notre Dame is a Catholic, independent, college preparatory school committed to the education of young women in the tradition of the School Sisters of Notre Dame. Aware of the advantages of single-sex education, Notre Dame creates an environment that develops and nurtures each student's growing sense of self-confidence. Notre Dame aspires to graduate young women who are ready and eager for leadership and competent to confront the intellectual, ethical, social, and technological challenges of the new millennium.

We, the faculty, students, staff, parents, board members, and alumnae, recognize ourselves as a community with common needs and aspirations. Sustained by faith we seek the goodness and beauty that Christ asks us to see in all people and all things. Notre Dame strives to be a community that is a living realization of God in us and in the world. Our commitment to Gospel values compel us to a social consciousness that inspires us to become women of faith with a real understanding of Church in all its dimensions, and with a commitment to converting their faith to action that will shape the world.

Believing that learning emerges from inquiry, challenge, self-discovery and growth, we are committed to a vigorous academic program. Notre Dame is a dedicated community of learners where students and faculty work to discover productive learning processes, to uncover connections among disciplines, and to practice critical thinking skills that will make us all responsible and caring members of a global community. We believe that this sense of responsibility extends to our earth as well as to all peoples.

Notre Dame's curriculum, emphasizing the dignity of all human beings, seeks to empower the whole person. In addition to endowing our student with knowledge from which she may draw in the future, we encourage her to strive to become spiritually mature, emotionally whole, esthetically aware and physically fit. Moreover, it is our sincere hope that she will also grow to an enduring hunger for knowledge and enthusiasm for learning. Ultimately, our goal is that each Notre Dame student will become a person of integrity seeking to become ever more loving, just and wise.

MISSION STATEMENT 2002

Notre Dame Preparatory School exists to educate and inspire young women. It is a Catholic, independent, college preparatory school in the tradition of the School Sisters of Notre Dame. Its dedicated religious and lay educators are committed to academic excellence, spiritual growth and the practice of justice in the school community, in the Church and in the world. Notre Dame provides a diverse program that emphasizes the dignity and value of each person as it prepares young women of moral integrity to become more loving, just and wise.

MISSION STATEMENT 2012

Notre Dame Preparatory School educates and empowers girls to become women who transform the world. As a Catholic, independent, college preparatory school for girls in grades 6 through 12, Notre Dame Prep inspires students to pursue academic excellence, spiritual growth and the practice of justice. Infused with the spirit of the School Sisters of Notre Dame and rooted in the teachings of the Catholic Church, the NDP community strives to answer God's call"...to act justly, to love tenderly, and to walk humbly with God." (Micah 6:8)

BELIEF STATEMENTS 2012

* We believe that health in mind, body and spirit is witness to the sacred dignity of all persons.
* We believe that education grounded in the Gospel fosters wisdom and spiritual growth.
* We believe that single sex education develops confident women who are independent thinkers.
* We believe that a challenging and nurturing educational program best serves the needs of adolescents.
* We believe that tradition must be balanced by openness and change.
* We believe that demonstrating genuine personal integrity is at the foundation of the authentic self.
* We believe that direct experience of leadership develops courage and fortitude.
* We believe that commitment to experiences beyond the classroom is a critical part of self-discovery.
* We believe that respecting the dignity of all people creates a welcoming, trusting and compassionate community.
* We believe that intentional stewardship affirms the reality that we belong to a global community linked to all creation.
* We believe that our solidarity with the world calls us to serve persons who are marginalized.
* We believe that courageous pursuit of systemic change, wherever needed, will transform the world.

GRADUATE PROFILE 2012

Academic Excellence

A graduate from Notre Dame Preparatory School
* Has a broad foundation of knowledge able to support a lifetime of learning

* *Understands her learning process and has developed effective study skills and habits*
* *Thinks critically and creatively to solve problems*
* *Has both the confidence to lead and the humility to collaborate*
* *As a self-directed learner, sets, goals, evaluates information and realizes objectives*
* *Approaches new situations with an open mind and critical eye*
* *Effectively uses innovative technologies*
* *Speaks and writes effectively*
* *Develops a deep appreciation for the arts*
* *Remains curious and chooses to pursue an intellectual life*

Spiritual Growth

A graduate from Notre Dame Preparatory School

* *Prayerfully develops a personal relationship with God and a deep appreciation for the gift of faith*
* *Explores her God-given talents as she seeks to discover and follow her passion*
* *Understands the teaching of the Catholic Church*
* *Recognizes that genuine success requires harmony in mind, body and spirit*
* *Makes healthy decisions based on ethical principles and demonstrates moral integrity through her behavior*
* *Creates and nurtures quality relationships*
* *Values the dignity and uniqueness of all persons*
* *Seeks to discover the positive contribution she can make to the world*

Practice of Justice

A graduate from Notre Dame Preparatory School

* *Is personally accountable for her actions*
* *Ethically uses information*
* *Intentionally educates herself about local and global issues*
* *Demonstrates a strong sense of teamwork and fair play*
* *Reverences our earth and its resources*
* *Defends the dignity of all persons through empathy, compassion and respect*
* *Engages in acts of direct service and supports charitable causes*
* *Advocates for persons who are marginalized and works to create systemic change*

APPENDIX D: Donna Steichen, *Ungodly Rage, the Hidden Face of Catholic Feminism,* Ignatius Press, San Francisco 1991; 2nd printing 1992. (*This appendix provides important quotes from the work of Steichen*)

Helen Hull Hitchcock, of Women for Faith and Family, states in her foreword that "Steichen documents with chilling accuracy the progressive takeover of a substantial portion of the Church in the United States by an ideology which is not only alien to authentic Catholicism, but inimical to the most essential Christian beliefs."(13) That ideology is Catholic feminism, which was particularly adopted by female religious professionals and many female religious orders of nuns. Catholic feminism's goal is the obliteration of Christianity. "It's 'spirit of Vatican II' is a spirit of dialogue with the world, the flesh and the Devil" The unintended side effects of the Second Vatican Council are seen as catastrophic (Introduction). When the Church "cast away her ancient Tradition, and plunged into chaos." The agents of this catastrophe were middle level professionals, who betrayed the intent of the Council and were inspired by "dissident theologians and leftist politicians." They promoted a new neo-modernism "that eroded traditional theology, liturgy and catechetics that was already in vogue some years prior to the council."

"The post-conciliar metamorphosis has been more profound among female religious professionals" (such as Monika Helwig, Rosemary Ruether and Elisabeth Fiorenza) " than any other group and were instrumental to the misapplication of the 'spirit of Vatican II'"(21) "They internalized the heretical premises of the revived modernizing...and exploited their positions within the Church to subvert trusting innocents."(21,23) Entire religious communities enthusiastically adopted the neo-modernist ideas and "have done incalculable damage within church institutions over the past generation"(25) Steichen ends her introduction with," Until its subversives are removed from the influential post they currently hold, there will be no Catholic restoration in North America."(27)

Seeing the situation as an "internal persecution," Steichen calls for a "restoration of the authentic faith." She lists some signs of a new spring: John Paul II and Cardinal Ratzinger "recognize the need for reform. The Pope is attempting to tilt the balance within the national bishops conferences away from schism by appointing papal loyalists as sees become vacant"; the orthodoxy and piety of a surprising proportion of young priests in seminaries, notwithstanding the teaching of aggressive neo-modernism; organizations who take care of authentic laypeople, such as *Catholics United for the Faith, Opus Dei, Women for Faith and Family*, and orthodox seminaries like the Legionnaires of Christ; colleges known for their Catholicity like Christendom College in Virginia and The Franciscan University of Steubenville, Ohio; conservative publications as *The Wanderer, The Sunday Visitor* and the *National Catholic Register*. (386-389)

Catholics can "no longer depend on parochial schools to educate their children as Catholics...These schools, for twenty-five years have failed in their chief purpose, which is to teach the Catholic Faith."(390) Furthermore, "neo-modernist bias saturates diocesan education offices, religious education offices, catechetical certification programs, Catholic education congresses and textbooks."(ibid)

What can we do about the Feminist Revolution? asks Steichen. Since many Catholic institutions are corrupt and systematically corrupting... American Catholics can no longer look with confidence to Church institutions and agencies" (393) "Unless one knows beyond doubt that the directors, teachers and materials used in parish or diocesan programs are sound, it is prudent to assume they are not." The author then uses Vatican II to suggest that the laypeople come to the rescue. "By dire necessity, this an age for the laity. Perhaps its unseen approach was the otherwise obscure purpose of the Holy Spirit at Vatican II: to prepare us with conciliar documents providing the theological framework and formal authorization for lay responsibilities."(393)

If surrounding parishes are dominated by revolutionaries, the first step is to find the best parish in the area because it is "antithetical to the essence of worship to be affronted constantly by illicit liturgical and homelitic innovations."(393) Once a parish where you can "worship without agony," consider ways to combat the revolution. If your parish, school or diocese presents "feminist or revolutionary speakers... Register your complaint with your bishop and diocesan authorities and encourage other faithful Catholics to object as well... Evidence of any outrage to the Faith should be reported to the bishop...If he does not respond to your letter or dismisses your concerns, you might write a courteous but factual letter to the editor of a secular newspaper." As a remedy to "survive as Catholics until order is restored" Steichen advises parents to be countercultural and consider educating their children at home. (395ff) The book ends with stating that in the end, "feminism, like all religious revolutionaries, will dash themselves to destruction against the rock of the Church." God will restore his Church. "If it seems that we are exiled to the catacombs while we wait for the restoration of the American Church, we can be comforted with the knowledge that it is not an appropriate place for Christians to begin rebuilding." (399)

ENDNOTES

1 Few Americans are aware that Belgium only emerged as an independent nation in 1830. Located between The Netherlands, Germany, France and Luxembourg and approximately the size as the state of Maryland, this small European nation has for centuries been the focal point of international power politics. For 1,000 years before 1830 Flanders was ruled by Flemish and Burgundian Counts, Spanish and Austrian kings, the French Republic and Empire and the United Kingdom of the Netherlands. Belgium is a constitutional monarchy with a population of ca 11 million. King Albert II, the current monarch, is the titular head of state. Brussels, the capital city is currently also the headquarters of the European Union and Nato. The federal government comprises three autonomous regions, namely, Flanders, which is Flemish-speaking; Wallonia, which is French-speaking; and Brabant, the capital region which includes the city of Brussels and which is bilingual in Flemish and French. The three regions are self-governing, comparable to the state system in the United States. Of the three official languages, approximately six million Belgians speak Flemish, four million speak French and ca 70,000 speak German. The regions are made up of nine provinces. Four of these -- West-Flanders, East-Flanders, Antwerpen and Limburg-- are Flemish; four -- Hainaut, Namur, Liège and Luxembourg-- are French, and one, Brabant, is partly Flemish and partly French.

2 In the first half of the twentieth century, Catholics were dominating the politics of Belgium and Catholic schools were practically the only ones in existence. In the 1950s a school war broke out about the plight of public education. This led to the 1952 laws which gave full freedom of choice to parents between free and state education (or what we here would call private and public education), all subsidized by the government. Although many battles continued, the system survived until the present. Today there are subsidized public schools and subsidized free schools (about 70%), mainly organized by an organization affiliated to the Catholic church.

3 The Minor Seminary of Roeselare provided 197 Scheut Fathers by 197

4 Vic De Donder, *Kom eens naar mijn kamer. Een halve eeuw collegeleven in Vlaanderen.* Elsevier/Brussel-Amsterdam,1986. p. 115.

5 Cardinal Joseph Cardijn (1882-1967) was the founder of the Young Christian Workers (YCW) which had started as the Young Trade Unionists in 1919. The YCW are also known as "Jocists." The movement grew fast and by 1938 they numbered 500,000. By the year of Cardijn's death in 1967 it had grown to 2 million in 68 countries. Cardijn's understanding of the role of the laity in the church was incorporated in Vatican II's Gaudium et Spes and the document of the laity. He believed that the Christian vocation was lived out in the ordinary day-to-day life and that the Christian layperson had the power to bear the Gospel

message to the world. The basis of his belief was that he saw no separation between ordinary life and religious life. Furthermore, Cardijn was convinced that faith must be put into action -- a hallmark of Vatican II theology. The method he devised was called *Review of Life* expressed in *Observe, Judge, Act*. These principles have been adopted and practiced by the organizations which emanated from his original ideas: Young Christian Students, the Christian Family Movement, and the International Confederation of Christian Family Movements. I am particularly proud having served as an acolyte at his bishop ordination in Rome on 21 February 1965, by Cardinal Leo-Joseph Suenens and Bishop Emiel Desmedt of Brugge.

[6] In Diksmuide, where the German and allied forces fought each other on the banks of the Yzer River for four years in World War I, the Flemish gather each year to celebrate Flemish nationalist causes. The Yzer Tower commemorates that war with the famous axiom,"No more war."

[7] The official language in Flanders is Flemish or Dutch -- the same language as spoken in The Netherlands. The difference between the two could be compared to the difference between American English and British English. Dialects in Flanders is another matter: dialects are not just different accents, but almost different languages. A native West-Fleming is almost incomprehensible in the Limburg province, and so they use official Flemish to be understood.

[8] In 1969 he published an autobiographical account of his apostolate *They Called Me the Bacon Priest*.

[9] *Aid to Eastern Priests* expanded its activities in the next decade to Hungary, Poland, North Korea and Vietnam and was placed under the direct jurisdiction of the Holy See in 1964. Five years later it adopted the name *Aid to the Church in Need.(ACN)*Website www.churchinneed.org. Today ACN, with headquarters in Königstein, has offices in Europe, the USA and Canada, South America and Australia. Relying on more than 600,000 individual benefactors worldwide, the organization supports construction, theological formation, pastoral care, catechesis and media projects in 140 countries worldwide.

The *Bouworde* grew dramatically. Two years after its foundation more than 3,000 volunteers participated in building camps. National branches were created in Italy, Germany, Spain, Switzerland and elsewhere and were brought together in 1962 in the *International Building Organization (IBO)*. They became member of the Coordinating Committee for International Voluntary Service of the UNESCO. By the 70s the IBO counted 7,000 yearly volunteers. Today the IBO keeps adapting itself to local demands and serves in countries all over the world. The Flemish Bouworde alone still sends 700 volunteers on a yearly basis. Over the 50 years of its existence 153,000 building volunteers have served all over the world, of which about one-third were Flemish.

[10] 11 July is a Flemish national holiday. On that date in 1302, an army of Flemish knights, peasants and guilds defeated an elite army of the French king who tried to annex the Flemish county to France. The Battle of the Golden Spurs is named after the spurs collected from the French knights. 11 July 1302 remains a symbol of Flemish pride and nationalism until the present.

11 See Appendix B. Frans Deroo served as a CICM missionary in Taiwan for several decades. Toon Ramon was assigned with me to study theology at the Gregorian. He later left the congregation, got married and became a professor in Switserland.

12 http://www.sint-rembert.be/college/

13 Het vak R-K godsdienst in de scholen van Vlaanderen (8-7-96): visietekst van de commissie in opdracht van de bisschoppen. (The subject Roman Catholic religion in the schools of Flanders [8-7-96]: vision text of the commission as commissioned by the bishops. *Author's translation*)

14 D. Pollefeyt, et.al. *Godsdienstonderwijs uitgedaagd. Jongeren en (inter) levensbeschouwelijke vorming in gezin en onderwijs. Opzet, methode en resultaten van empirisch onderzoek bij leerkrachten rooms-katholieke godsdienst en leerlingen van de derde graad secondair onderwijs in Vlaanderen.* Leuven, Peeters, 2004.

15 Nieuwsblad, 8 May 2010.

16 Scheut Familie, nr 4, 25 December 1956.

17 The Scheut fathers accept "brothers" in the congregation, i.e. candidates who profess the three religious vows but choose not to be ordained a priest.

18 Elechus 2011, Congregatio Immaculati Cordis Mariae, CICM

19 In 1898 a group of Chinese peasants in Northern China, called "The Boxers," thus called because they believed that practicing boxing would protect them against bullets, intended to purge China from all foreign influence. By late 1898 bands of Boxers massacred scores of Chinese Christians and foreign missionaries. In 1900 the Scheut missionaries were severely hit by the Boxer Rebellion in Mongolia. More than 2,000 Catholics and ten CICM missionaries were killed, a number of churches and institutions were burned or destroyed. Bishop Hamer was one of those martyrs.

20 The encyclical *Aeterni Patris* (Of the eternal father) was issued in August 1879 by Pope Leo XIII.

21 *Aeterni Patris*, 4 Aug 1879, 4.

22 *Philosophy Course for the use of seminarians.* Desclee de Brouwer, 1937.

23 After my retirement in 2001 I dedicated myself to genealogy and research on the Goethals family. I published four books on the subject. More information later in chapter seven.

24 *Holy Office*: Originally a tribunal for final appeals and papal causes established by Pope Paul III in 1542 and reorganized by Pope Sixtus V in 1587. It became the Sacred Congregation for the Doctrine of the Faith (SCDF) under Pope Paul VI in 1967 and retained the title when Pope John Paul II reorganized the Curia in 1988. (Richard McBrien, Encyclopedia of Catholicism, 626.)

25 De Ecclesia I: Quaestiones theologiae fundamentalis.

26 The University of Toronto is publishing the collected works of Lonergan in 25 volumes.

27 The moral theology of *fundamental option* states that each person gradually develops a basic orientation either for or against God. This orientation is said to be for God if one's life is fundamentally devoted to the love and service of others, and against God if one's life is essentially devoted to self-love and self-service. Individual mortal sinful acts only exist when the fundamental option for God is rejected.

28 *De Wet van Christus. Een katholieke moraaltheologie voor priesters en leken.* Spectrum, Standaard, 1959.

29 The name "holy Office" changed to "Sacred Congregation of the Doctrine of the Faith," SCDF, adopted 7 December 1965 at the end of Vatican II. The "sacred" was dropped in 1988 and now it is "Congregation of the Doctrine of the Faith."

30 Three years after the end of the Council in 1968, the Gregorian, under the leadership of Donatien Mollat and Zoltan Alszeghy, with the participation of faculty and students, began a drastic renewal of the theology department. They instituted more rigorous requirements for its baccalaureate (three years instead of two) and created a track for students who were more academically inclined next to a pastoral track for regular seminarians. The framework of all courses became the Church document *Lumen Gentium* with more intense and expanded bible study and they integrated history, canon law, liturgy and moral theology into the theological framework. See: A Report on the Reform of the Faculty of Theology at the Gregorian University. *Gregorianum* 50, nr 3-4, 839-858.

31 Licentiate is an ecclesiastical academic degree granted between bachelor's degree and the doctorate at many European universities.

32 The Curia is the bureaucracy that assists the pope in his responsibilities to govern the universal church. It includes the Secretariat of State, Congregations (such as the Congregation for Causes of Saints, Divine Worship, and Evangelization), tribunals, pontifical Councils, Commissions (such as the Biblical Commission, the Archeology Commission), and other supporting institutions like the Vatican Library and Archives, Academy of Sciences, and Vatican Radio and Television.

33 Pope John's opening Speech to the Council, Oct 11,1962. *The Documents of Vatican II,* Walter Abbott, ed., Geoffrey Chapman, London-Dublin, 1966, 710-719 passim.

34 In the course of church history, churches from the eastern part of the Roman Empire -- who celebrated in their own Eastern liturgical traditions -- separated from the western Latin church because of theological and jurisdictional controversies. (Syrian, Coptic, Ethiopian, Armenian) The largest split happened after 1054 A.D. When the Byzantine church separated. Certain groups within these churches later reunited with the church in Rome and are now the *Eastern Catholic Churches*. Next to the Latin rite of Rome, we have the Armenian, Byzantine, Coptic, Easy and Western Syrian and Maronite rites within the Catholic church. Vatican II improved the relationship with the Eastern Catholics by recognizing them as "churches" not just rites. After Vatican II, the Catholic

church and Eastern churches (who are not in full communion with Rome) recognized each other as "sister churches" in a partial communion. (See *Encyclopedia of Catholicism*, Richard Mc Brien, under 'Eastern Churches' and 'Catholic Eastern church')

35 The Petrine principle states that the pope, bishop of Rome, follows in the line of Saint Peter as vicar of Jesus Christ and has the authority to speak for the church.

36 *Documents of Vatican II*, Walter Abbott, Edit., 13.

37 Calvert Alexander S.J., Introduction to Ad Gentes, *The Documents of Vatican II*, Abbott, p.883.

38 http://cicmworld.niceboard.net

39 Of the 43 confreres who were my study companions in Rome, 22 left the congregation and 21 still are active members, among whom five became bishops and one a cardinal.

40 Edward Dozier, *Mountain Arbiters. The Changing Life of a Philippine Hill People*. University of Arizona Press. Tucson Arizona, 1966

41 This priest happens to be Father Victor Pil, CICM. Author's note.

42 *Mountain Arbiters*, 193, note 3.

43 *Fr. Charles Foubert*, CICM. A few months after I left the Philippines, Charles was summarily dismissed from the Philippine Province and he accepted to finish his doctorate at the Gregoriana in Rome. Disappointed, he wrote me in April 1970 that he really wanted to spend his life there and that "the CICM might well have lost one more man today." An ardent follower of liberation theology, Charles worked with the Philippine Solidarity Movement once he had left the congregation. Supported by the World Council of Churches and the Lutheran World Federation, he founded IDOC (International Documentation and Communication Center) where liberation movements from all over the Third World could gain and exchange information. This center has developed into INTERDOC, which uses the latest computer technology to inform NGO's from all over the world. Charles authored many IDOC documents and several books, including *Les Philippines:Réveil d'un Archipel,* 1980. He married Marilee Karl, founder of Isis International, a communication network for women's rights. Charles lost his life in May 1987 in a car accident in Sierra Leone while on a small farmers mission for the FAO. *Fr. Conrado Aquino,* became rector of Maryhurst. He died at the age of 33 in a car accident in Tinglayan, Mountain Province in 1971. May they rest in peace!

44 It is noteworthy that at the time of this writing most, if not all, of these proposals have been implemented at Maryhurst seminary.

45 On 12 May 1980, another CICM missionary, Fr. Walter Voordeckers, was gunned down and killed in his parish Santa Lucia Cotzumalguapa. They had tried to kidnap him, and when this failed, they shot him. Walter was forty years old and had served thirteen years as a missionary in Guatemala.

⁴⁶ In 1986 the SSND produced a new constitution, expressing their "charism for our times." Between 1970 and 1986, the sisters had indeed adapted to the times. A comparison between the 1978-1979 and 1986-1987 directories of the Baltimore Province, for example, shows a diversification of their community life and apostolic projects. While in the 70s, the majority of the sisters were directly involved in schooling, the 80s shows a series of other apostolic endeavors: pastoral associates in parishes, social workers, home care, ministry for the elderly and addicts, outreach centers, archdiocesan tribunal staff, registered nurses, and many others. Next to their traditional larger communities, they started living in small sister communities among the 'People of God.'

⁴⁷ *Mariology* is a branch of theology on Mary. This theology is integrated today in the theology of Christ and the Church. *Apologetics* is Christian theology that presents a rational basis for the Christian faith and often defends faith against objections.

⁴⁸ Every ten years, the school was evaluated by the Middle States Association's Commission on Secondary Schools. In the year preceding the visiting committee, the school had to go through a self-evaluation and formulate a new philosophy and objectives. At the end of the visit the school receives a report with commendations and recommendations which have to be implemented in the ensuing years.

⁴⁹ Considering what was to come in 1995 -- an attack on the religion department by pre-Vatican II sources -- it is worth noting that the Middle States stated that the religion department was "the most academically trained and qualified department in the entire Middle States region."

⁵⁰ *Not a Love Story. Sexual Violence and the Media* is a 68 minute video produced by the Canadian Film Board. The film is primarily discussion about sexual violence to women, with 8 minutes illustrating the denigration of women through pornography by using disturbing scenes from pornographic films. The video places this in the context of a strong anti-pornographic message. The video was used for NDP seniors for the last ten years on a basis of voluntary attendance and with parental permission slips. Some parents have attended the workshops. Notre Dame has acknowledged that in 1994 the permission slip omitted a description of the video's explicit material and recognized this as a mistake. The school decided not to use the video any more.

⁵¹ *Defend Life* is a pro-life organization founded by Eileen Bolgiano and Jack Ames in 1987. It came out of the Respect Life Group at the Cathedral of Mary Our Queen in Baltimore. The group organizes pro-life lecture series which started in the fall of 1987 at Loyola College in Baltimore. Later they organized pro-life speakers at nearby schools, seminaries and parishes. Their Defend Life Lecture Series continues today. They publish a bimonthly Newsletter in which the leaflet on Notre Dame was published.

⁵² The enneagram is a theory which tries to determine personality types divided over nine (*ennea* in Greek) different types. Claudio Naranja, a psychiatrist, promoted the enneagram in the USA in the 1970s and influenced some Jesuits to use it in Christian spirituality.

⁵³ See Donna Steichen, *Ungodly Rage, the Hidden Face of Catholic Feminism,* Ignatius Press, San Francisco 1991; 2nd printing 1992.

⁵⁴ Dr. Ronald J. Valenti, Superintendent of Catholic Schools, *Final Report on the Visitation to Notre Dame Preparatory School, March 28, 1995.* Submitted May 5, 1995, 6-7 passim.

⁵⁵ Ibid. p.14.

⁵⁶ The mysterious 'hauling of boxes' was on 20 March 1995, when Lucy Strausbaugh placed three or four boxes of supplies in her car to give a retreat at St. Vincent's parish.

⁵⁷ Sr. Mary Irving, SSND, who attended the Steichen presentation at Loyola College, wrote a three-page letter to the Evergreen faculty advisors, objecting to Steichen's presence and presentation. Excerpt: "I have examined feminist theology in my graduate studies at the Catholic University of America and am deeply disturbed to see it so distorted. Mrs. Steichen's interpretations appear to have come from attending a number of feminist conferences and a reading of some feminist works. She has woven a thesis of evil of Catholic feminism and a judgement of its goals as the destruction of the Catholic Church from questionable examples, insufficient understanding, and uncritical thought." The above was published in *The Wanderer* on 30 November 1995. The writer ends his report with: "If any feminist nuns ever find any of Mrs. Steichen's talks distasteful, why don't they just jump on their brooms and fly away?"

For a critical analysis of the Introduction and first chapter of the book, see: *Donna Steichen. How Trustworthy is She?* Elizabeth T. Knuth, June 1995. www.users.csbsju.edu/~eknuth/dsintro.html (College of Saint Benedict and Saint John's University, Minnesota.)

⁵⁸ Defend Life Newsletter, September 1995, p.3.

⁵⁹ The origin of the Goethals family has been claimed to be situated in ninth century Italy. Based partly on legend and oral sources, it is believed that Honorius, a captain in the Roman army, was appointed by Pope John VIII (872-882), to fight the Saracens in the western Italian coast region of Apulia. During a battle in 880, he received a scimitar blow to the neck which was protected by an iron gorget that saved his life. As a consequence he was awarded the Latin nickname *bonus collus* (good neck) and adopted the name *Honorius Bonicollius*. His grandson Pietro, who used the Italian *Bonicolli*, entered the service of the counts of Flanders as a knight and accompanied the count to Flanders. He was awarded a property in Ghent called *de Mude*. Four generations later Gerem Bonicolli translated his name into the Flemish *Goet hals* (good neck).

⁶⁰ *A Forgotten Family. The Flemish Roots of General George Washington Goethals (1858-1928)* Baltimore, MD: Gateway Press, Inc., 2004.

⁶¹ The Family History Library in Salt Lake City, Utah, has taken microfilm records from 110 countries around the world since 1938. The *Church of the Latter Day Saints* (Mormons) believes that deceased family members can be

baptized by proxy into the church when identified. The collection contains 2.4 million microfilms and more than 725,000 microfiche, which can be ordered at local Family History Centers. Recently, the library has initiated the process of digitizing the collection. See their website http://www.familysearch.org.

[62] *Goethals-Tavernier-Vanmaele, The Ancestors of August Goethals and Elza Tavernier. A Family History.* Baltimore MD: Gateway Press, Inc., 2006 (published in English and Flemish) This book was followed by a handbook for Flemish Americans who are searching for their Belgian ancestry. In collaboration with Karel Denys, CICM. *Searching for Flemish (Belgian) Ancestors.* Baltimore: Genealogical Publishing Co., 2007.

[63] *Goethals 880-1900. The Story of the Goethals Story.* Baltimore MD: Gateway Press, Inc., 2008.

[64] Privately printed: *Baptisms, Marriages and Deaths of the Goethals in selected parish records of Ghent*-Belgium(1584-1796), Baltimore, MD 2001; Debrabander. *Drie eeuwen molenaars in Rumbeke en Roeselare. (Three Centuries of Millers in Rumbeke and Roeselare).* Baltimore MD, 2002; *The Ancestors of Cardinal Godfried Danneels,* Baltimore, MD, 2006; *Vanhauwaert in Machelen, Olsene, Oeselgem, Vichte. The ancestors of Josephine Emelie Vanhauwaert* (1898-1985), wife of Firmin Debrabander (1891-1958), Baltimore, MD, 2006; *The Ancestors of Father Jan Baptist Morel, CICM,* Baltimore, MD, 2006; *The Ancestors of Hennie Irma De Zutter. A Report on the De Zutter Family in Moerkerke, Lapscheure and Blankenberge since 1661.* Baltimore MD, 2007. *The Goethals in Aarsele and Ruiselede, 1550-1800. The Ancestors of Margaret Elodia Goethals.* Baltimore, MD 2009. For more information see http://www.goethalsgenealogyusa.com

[65] *50 Years on Hampton Lane. Wisdom Built This House.* 1960-2010. p.47.

[66] Recently, Jürgen Mettepenningen, the former spokesperson for the archbishop of Mechelen, Belgium, and the Belgian Bishops Conference, has published a work in Flemish which happens to reflect my own thinking on this subject. I am summarizing some of his ideas. Jürgen Mettepenningen, *Welke Kerk. Vandaag en Morgen.*(Which Church? Today and Tomorrow) Davidsfonds Uitgeverijj, Leuven, 2011.

[67] Bishop Emiel Desmedt of Bruges, Belgium. Intervention at Vatican II, 1 December 1962.

[68] We are referring here to the recent threat of excommunication of Maryknoll Father Roy Bourgeois because he is defending women priests. Also the forced resignation of Bishop William Morris of Toowoomba, Australia, because he suggested that the church might need women priests in the future.

[69] See John O'Mally S.J., *What Happened at Vatican II*, Cambridge, MA -- Harvard University Press, 2008.

THE JEWELRY BOOK

Suzan St. Maur & Norbert Streep

ST. MARTIN'S PRESS
NEW YORK

Copyright © 1981 by Norbert Streep and Suzan St. Maur
For information, write: St. Martin's Press,
175 Fifth Avenue, New York, N.Y. 10010
Manufactured in the United States of America

Library of Congress Cataloging in Publication Data

St. Maur, Suzan.
    The jewelry book.

      1. Jewelry.   I. Streep, Norbert, joint author.
II. Title.
TS725.S23   688'.2   80-52099
ISBN 0-312-44230-0

Contents

Introduction	9
1. 'You Don't Have to be Rich to Love Jewellery'	13
2. Jewellery – The Most Meaningful Gift	28
3. What Jewellery Means to People – Past, Present and Future	40
4. A Who's What of the Jewellery Business	48
5. Precious Metals and Mountings – Animal, Vegetable or Mineral?	65
6. From Rough Little Pebbles to Sparkling Stones	85
7. So Much for 'Semi-Precious...	105
8. Jewellery and the Way You Look: That Precious Sense of Fashion	119
9. Never Mind the Quality, Feel the Shine	131
10. Keeping a Watch on Timepieces	141
11. Jewellery and the Liberated Male	156
12. Investing Your Money in Jewellery	166
13. Keeping Your Jewellery Safe and Sound	180

Introduction

Anyone who thinks that jewellery is a specialised subject could well be excused for doing so, but in many ways they would be wrong. There really aren't many people in our world who don't own some kind of jewellery. Like cosmetics, jewellery is an almost universal adornment. And jewellery isn't just worn by people in the industrialised nations. If you're willing to accept that feathers, glass beads, carved wood, and other 'non-precious' substances can be considered as jewellery then you can find examples in even the most obscure nooks and crannies of the earth. Remote African tribes and Eskimos, for instance, wear jewellery just as we do. They may not have the money or the opportunity to buy gold and precious stones, but their jewellery is still important to them. Apparent or not, jewellery forms a pleasing and positive part of just about everyone's life.

So, at this level, jewellery can hardly be described as a specialised subject. If you ask an Eskimo lady why she wears moose teeth on a leather thong around her neck, she's not going to tell you about the rarity of moose teeth these days, or the tanning process of the leather. She will tell you she wears her jewellery because she likes it, it keeps the evil spirits away, and her husband thinks it makes her look more attractive. If you ask an African tribesman why he wears a gold hook through his nose, he won't quote the current price of gold in US dollars at you. He'll tell you that he likes wearing it because he thinks it makes him look more alluring, more masculine, and possibly more wealthy.

Aren't those reasons more or less true for us all? Even in our modern societies where status symbols and financial self-betterment play big parts, in reality we still buy and wear jewellery because it pleases us. And that is how it should be.

Of course, lots of books have already been written about jewellery. Many of them are very good ones, too. But we felt it was time someone wrote a book which talks about the jewellery that most of us wear to please ourselves. Not big, priceless pieces, because most of us can't afford them; merely the pieces that the vast majority of people buy and wear during their lifetime.

From our two respective observation posts – Suzan's, as a writer on consumer subjects with the keen interest in jewellery that most women share; and Norbert's, as a qualified gemologist and diamond expert who sells jewellery to thousands of people every year – we believed that a lot of down-to-earth questions about jewellery were as yet unanswered. From our own experience we knew that most people don't really want to know how much the Orloff diamond sold for a hundred years ago. What we discovered was that most people are interested enough in their own jewellery, and the jewellery they'll buy in the future, to want to learn the straightforward facts we have gathered together here.

In *The Jewellery Book* we have attempted to cover as many of those unanswered questions as possible. Like, what sort of engagement ring should I buy, that's going to please me for a long time? What kind of watch is going to tell me the time accurately, even if I only have limited money to spend? What should I do if I inherit a piece of antique jewellery that I can't stand, and want to get rid of? What should I buy my mother for her birthday? And many, many more.

Although highly technical qualifications aren't necessary in order to appreciate jewellery, a good working knowledge of the basic facts makes a lot of difference. If, as we said earlier, the whole point of jewellery is to please ourselves, to make our lives more beautiful and our emotional landmarks more memorable, there are two ways in which you can look at it.

One is to buy and wear jewellery, uninformed, which can mean your jewellery is not worth the money it costs, is likely to get lost or damaged, is not going to do anything for your face or figure, or any of a hundred other problems that could spoil your pleasure.

The other way, we believe, is to become better informed and increase your enjoyment, your satisfaction, and the enhancement of your looks. The truth is, you don't necessarily need to spend more money to get greater pleasure, and greater value, out of your jewellery. Sensible, informed buying can make the difference between wasting money on cheap, inferior pieces on the one hand, and investing wisely in good jewellery on the other.

Because we both love jewellery, we want to help you to enjoy yours more, and also help you to buy wisely. We want you to look upon *The Jewellery Book* as your basic, realistic guide to genuine pleasure from the jewellery you buy, and the jewellery you already own, for a great many years to come.

CHAPTER ONE

'You Don't Have to be Rich to Love Jewellery'

There aren't many women – or men, for that matter – who haven't at one time or another stopped outside a jeweller's window and gazed through the glass. There they are: dozens of twinkling stones and lots of glittering metal, all staring up at you and daring you to walk through the door brandishing a cheque book.

'Oh,' say the thousands of people like you and us, 'if only I/we could afford that!'

Naturally, similar little cameos can be seen outside the glossy shopfronts of motor-car showrooms, fur-coat shops, and travel agents, but beautiful jewellery has a more emotional appeal. It seems to hold more meaning, more charisma, than a superbly luxurious washing-machine or a fast sports car.

Now, let's look on the bright side. Instead of gazing through jewellers' windows and heaving theatrical sighs, go and have a look inside your own jewellery case – even if it is the size of a matchbox – and, with the guidance of this book learn to appreciate what's in there. And when the time comes to give or receive a present, or even when you feel like spoiling yourself with a treat, think jewellery. Good jewellery isn't necessarily out of your reach; buying jewellery is a pleasure you *can* afford.

The first lesson in appreciating jewellery is to forget about cheap imitations. Not that we're knocking good costume jewellery; some of it is beautifully made and lasts well. In fact, some of it is so well made that it actually costs more than the equivalent in real gold or silver. That's the whole point; imitations will break, wear out or tarnish if they're very cheaply made, and will cost plenty if they're of good quality. There are exceptions, of course, and we'll talk abou those in Chapter Nine.

Real jewellery is like nothing else that you wear. It compliments your clothes, of course, and can compliment just about everything else, including your hair, your complexion, your mood, and the occasion. But unlike an attractive scarf or a smart pair of shoes, jewellery is permanent. Properly looked after, real jewellery lasts for good, and as such is a permanent expression of whatever it means to you. If jewellery is given to you – and more often than not it is – all the emotions that led up to its purchase are there, looking you straight in the eye, for a remarkably long time.

Perhaps it is this permanence which has made jewellery such an important part of history, ever since man first stalked the earth as the superior mammal. Gold, that famous precious metal, has been murdered for, fought for, and battled for. Even today, it is regarded as just about the most important single commodity there is. Why? Because it is permanent, constant, always holding its value. Gold has been money, too; before modern times obliged us to use less costly metals and paper money, gold coins were the norm. Similarly, good jewellery is a sensible investment for anyone – whether you're talking about the huge diamonds bought by the likes of Richard Burton and Elizabeth Taylor, or Joe Soap buying a gold bracelet for his wife.

Obviously the average person does not buy jewellery with the mercenary intention of selling it for profit at a later date. But the very fact that you *know* your piece of jewellery is valuable will make you care for it more; rather like a precious oil painting or piece of antique furniture, the financial value goes hand in hand with the emotional value. And don't feel that to cherish a piece of valuable jewellery is being money-minded. It's not. Think of it as the emotional value determining the price, not the financial value determining the level of emotion.

Having said all this, of course you're still going to dislike a piece of jewellery that's ugly whether it's worth a fortune or not. Personal preference must always be the first consideration. There are lots of different jewellery designs on the market, because the jewellery trade is the first to recognise the fact that people have widely varying tastes. All sorts of factors are responsible for this: social, economic, even regional reasons are all valid. Take, for example, the trends of the Northern people, fair-skinned and often fair haired, who tend to buy paler stones and white gold jewellery. Southern countries of Latin origin, where the inhabitants tend to be olive-skinned and dark-haired, go for richer colours and yellow gold. According to the powers that be in the jewellery business, this theory holds true all over the world, except in Japan. Here, the dark-haired, black-eyed people just love light stones and white gold. Perhaps it's because they are an island nation; they're the exception to the rule!

Wherever you live and whatever your particular taste, jewellery is still going to give you more pleasure than any other inanimate substance. On the assumption that there are very few people in the world who don't already own at least one piece of jewellery (even the most un-fussy man will probably still have a watch), let's now take a good look at pieces of jewellery most of us wear.

So What's Jewellery?

There are a great many different types of jewellery items you can buy. For the exotic-minded, there are nose studs, nose rings and lots of other intriguing pieces you can find if you look hard enough. But if that's your pleasure you won't find too much of interest in this book. Here, then, are the basic jewellery items that we average types are more than likely to own during our lifetime.

Rings

Of all jewellery, the ring can be by far the most emotionally charged. Probably because we've become used to engagement rings and wedding rings, their deep romantic significance has spread to virtually any ring. If you want to give someone a casual present of jewellery, it's best to steer clear of rings for this reason. Unless, of course, you don't mind running the risk of having your gift interpreted more deeply.

Rings can, in theory, be worn on any finger or thumb and even on your toes if you fancy. More usually, though, rings are restricted to the second, third and fourth fingers of either hand. In modern society trends have developed about which sort of ring you wear on each finger. The second, or middle, finger is fairly open territory; but the 'ring', or third finger is often exclusively reserved for the wedding ring and engagement or dress ring – a simple band with a stone or several stones mounted on the top. The little, or fourth finger tends to be encircled by plainer rings, or smooth crest or initial rings, and here there could be a logical reason. The little finger, being on the outside of the hand, is far more susceptible to the hard knocks of life. Washing dishes, driving cars, manual work, household chores and other integral parts of day-to-day living might be necessary, but can ruin more exposed jewellery. Elaborate rings on the little finger look lovely for an evening out, but on the whole just aren't practical unless you're surrounded by servants and never get your hands dirty.

People seem far more particular about their rings than other pieces of jewellery – and anyway, rings are the most popular pieces of all, according to buying statistics. Why this is could be to do with the emotional connotations; but if you think about it, your rings are the pieces of jewellery *you* see most of. Earrings, brooches and necklaces you'll only see properly in a mirror. Bracelets and watches may be tucked up your sleeve. But unless you're wearing gloves, you'll see plenty of your rings all day long. So they've really got to please you, to be part of your personality. Because of this it is often very difficult to buy a ring for someone else unless you know them really well. Perhaps that's another good reason for playing safe and avoiding rings as casual gift ideas.

Engagement Rings

Engagement rings are not just emotionally charged, they're positively seething with it; on the purely romantic front, and at the financial end of the scale, too. The romantic side is obvious, of course. And as the lucky young couple look down, enraptured, at the symbol of their love, others look down at it with calculating eyes, judging the ring's worth as a symbol, not of the couple's love for each other so much as the couple's worth in pounds, dollars, francs, rupees, or whatever. Jealous ladies cover up their own left hands and think envious thoughts. Haughty, wealthier friends smile patronisingly. Family members ooh and aah. Does this sound nasty? It can be. But on the other hand, one of the finest ancillary pleasures of getting engaged is the fun of showing off the ring; just ask any engaged or married girl!

The French had a theory in the eighteenth century about diamond rings having the ability to bring good luck to the wearer. Much to the joy of French ladies of the day, the story went on to proclaim that the good luck would only happen when the diamond ring was given to you – not if you bought it for yourself. Like in the case of a lot of these stories, the finger of suspicion could well be pointed at the commercially-minded jewellers of the time. If they were like some jewellers nowadays, one wouldn't put it past them to start a fable along these lines for their own benefit and profit. But, anyway, the French took to this story like ducks to water, and very soon diamond rings were being given to betrothed young ladies by their suitors as a permanent symbol of the promise to marry.

A thriftier idea was started in some other European countries, notably Germany and Sweden, whereby one ring did both jobs – engagement and wedding. All you did was to get engaged and wear the ring on one hand, and then transfer it to the other hand upon marriage; simple and cost-effective. Another tradition in some countries was two matching rings; starting with the first worn on its own when you were engaged, and doubled up with the second, similar, ring when you married.

A lot of modern couples these days forget about engagement rings altogether, especially when there isn't too much money around. They'd rather spend what money they have on a good holiday, a sofa, a deposit on a car or a house, or whatever. It's sad, in a way, because holidays, sofas, cars, even houses, don't last forever. Although we can all sympathise with young people nowadays struggling against inflation and all the other problems everyone is faced with, many couples do regret their decision in later years. The ideal solution, of course, is for young people to wait until there *is* more money available, when their careers have progressed and their earnings have gone up, and then buy a ring. But for the insatiable romantics among us who don't have a lot to spend and still want an engagement ring at the traditional time, take heart; it is not impossible to find a ring you'll both love, and that your bank manager will love too.

When you haven't got much to spend – for whatever reason – what's best to go for? The best bet as far as beauty and value are concerned is still, surprisingly, a diamond. Even if it's tiny. Diamonds hold their value better than any other stone, and carry on twinkling at you for as long as you wear them – cheering you up when you're down, and flashing along with you when you're happy. Coloured stones don't seem to match your moods and your outfit as well as the diamond; it's better to wait until later for the sapphires, rubies or emeralds, because when you've got the money to spend you can buy these stones and wear them only when you're in the mood for them. Don't forget, you'll be wearing your engagement ring the whole time – so you want to be sure it goes with everything. Only the diamond does.

Semi-precious stones are sometimes used for engagement rings, especially when there isn't a lot in the kitty. Again, you're going to tire of a semi-precious stone a lot faster than you'll tire of a diamond, if you wear it every day.

If you're concerned about your ring holding its value, it's far better to go for a single stone of the largest size and best quality you can afford. Cluster rings, with several stones, may cost as much or more to *buy* because there is a lot more work that goes into their making. You're paying for the work, the labour, as well as paying for the gems and the precious metal. If you should decide to sell the ring one day, you'll find that you'll only get back the price of the stones and the metal – not the work. A single stone, on the other hand, represents less work, because cutting one stone takes far less time than cutting half a dozen. This is one of the reasons why one stone weighing, say, one carat, is worth more than six small stones – adding up to one carat in weight – put together, when it comes to re-sale. Here's an example:

Solitaire diamond ring	working=30% of price stone & gold content=70% of price
Diamond cluster ring with six stones adding up to same weight as solitaire stone	working=60% of price stone & gold content=40% of price

Wedding Rings

A wedding ring is certainly a symbolic item. The traditional shape of the ring, which is a continuous band of some description, is particularly relevant because it has no end, just like – hopefully – the relationship between the man and the woman. Normally wedding rings are made out of 9 or 18 carat gold, and sometimes the rarer metals like platinum or palladium. Often, wealthier people will invest in wedding rings which are a continuous band of diamonds – like an eternity ring. These are fine as long as you don't use your hands to do anything too rough, because boring occupations like washing dishes, peeling potatoes, etc., can cause damage to the ring which might eventually mean that a stone drops out. Plain metal rings are far more common. Usually, the reason for this is pure tradition; but there are some religions which insist that the wedding band is made from precious metal because of beliefs that originated in the days when a man 'bought' his wife for a piece of gold. Some Jewish people believe that the wedding band must be valuable so the wife immediately owns something worthwhile, given to her by her husband.

There are some people who still believe the rather strange myths about wedding rings, to the fury and rage of free-thinkers and the women's movement. These run along the lines that the wedding band placed around the woman's finger was akin to a noose around her neck; the ring showed that she 'belonged' to her husband part and parcel. There's even another story that the wedding ring goes on the woman's inferior hand (the left) to remind her that *she's* inferior. Nonsense, of course, particularly if she happens to be left-handed, and also because for many centuries the tradition was actually to wear the ring on the right hand. In some countries, people still do. And in many societies both husband and wife wear wedding rings, so they 'belong' equally to each other.

Another theory about the placing of a wedding ring on the third finger of the right hand is far more romantic. It goes like this: that particular finger – or rather the nerves, veins or arteries near it – go more directly to your heart than those of any other finger. A doctor, when questioned about this, gave his reply in an extremely rude five letter word. So it would seem that there is no medical evidence to support the theory. But it is romantic.

Legally speaking, there is no compulsion to exchange wedding rings at all in most modern societies, although there would be a few raised eyebrows in the majority of churches if no rings were produced on the Big Day. On the whole, the wearing of wedding bands is just a custom, and can be adapted to suit everyone's inclinations, whether worn by the wife alone or by both partners. But it is a charming tradition; and in this modern age when many such traditions are being thrown out of the window in favour of more liberated thinking, it would be a shame to lose this one. Hopefully, as long as marriage survives, so will the wedding ring. It isn't a sign of ownership at all. It's a public declaration of the love and devotion between two people.

Necklaces

The necklace has always played a very prominent part in just about everyone's jewellery wardrobe. It has often been used, and still is, as a mark of high office among important citizens like mayors, kings, priests and so on. Why this is so is fairly obvious. The neck is probably the most convenient place to hang things, and is certainly the place that will most easily support prominent adornments. In a purely decorative sense, things around the neck are seen more for their own face value and have less influence on the overall look of the wearer than, say, a pair of earrings. Your neck is the best place to display your most interesting bits of jewellery; there, they don't have to compete with parts of your body that demand attention - like the ears, fingers and wrists.

This century the really heavy, gemstone encrusted necklace has been restricted to use amongst royalty and dowager types. The fashion nowadays is inclined towards the light and discreet styles, whether they are simple rows of beads, or pendants hanging on a chain, or even a very smart chain on its own.

Chains have been enormously popular for a long time now, and quite deservedly so. There is a huge variety of different types of links and designs, and of different lengths and thicknesses. A great many chains in gold and silver either originate, or are copied, from Italian designs as these people seem to be the most talented in producing them.

Once you've got your chain, you may like to hang a pendant on it. Pendants can be anything from precious gemstones in an attractive mounting to plain gold or silver objects like signs of the zodiac, religious signs, cartoon characters, coins, good luck charms, and many, many more.

Whatever you decide to do - whether to wear your chain on its own, or with a pendant on it - one or two good chains form the basis of any collection of jewellery. Of course, if you like the thicker type of chain, you may find that a pendant is definitely unattractive worn with it; now we're getting into the realms of necklaces proper. Still using chains, only this time as a part of an overall design, you'll find many beautiful necklaces on the market studded with gemstones, or alternating chain sections and gold items like hearts and many other combinations. For the budget-conscious, though, you'll get far more mileage out of a good, medium-length, plain chain with two or three interchangeable pendants – one plain, one fancy for more special occasions, and maybe one with a small stone or two – that you can put together as the mood takes you.

Then there are beaded necklaces, and the most common variety by far is the pearl necklace. This has been teetering on the brink of being

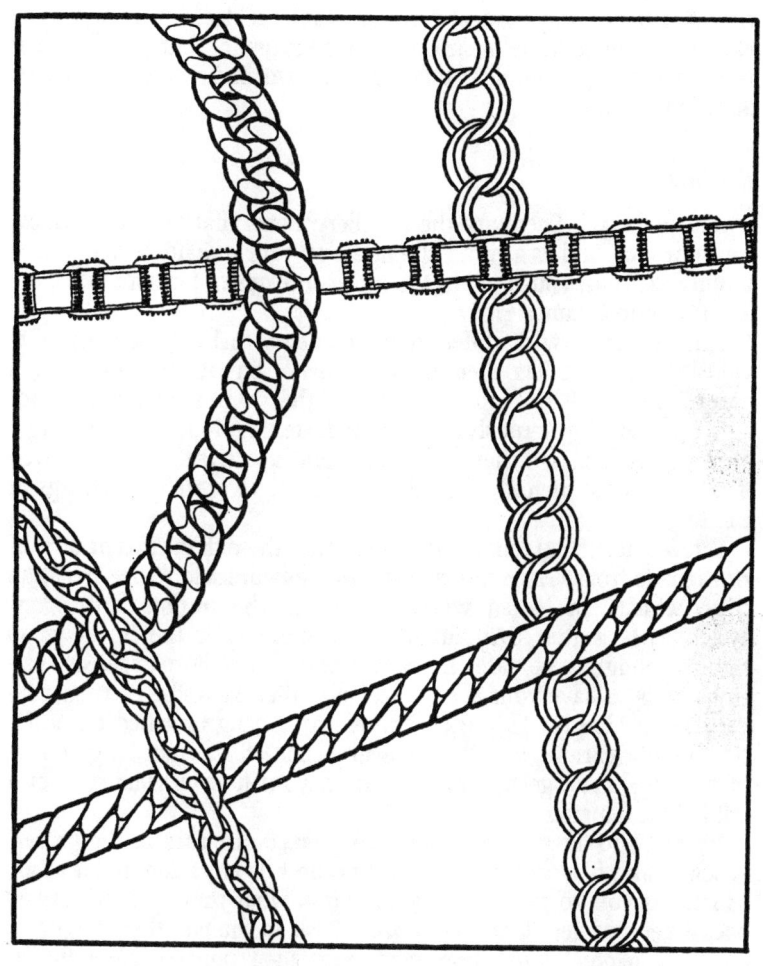

A selection of jewellery chains

fashionable for decades, even centuries. Although only occasionally seen on the glossy pages of fashion magazines, a quick look around any crowded airport building or railway station will usually reveal a few. Whatever way you feel about pearl necklaces, there's a good chance you're going to wear one at some stage in your life. So when the fancy to buy one does take you, it's worth buying a good one. See Chapter Six.

Earrings

Ah, earrings! These are the jewellery items that can do the most for your face, and as a result the most for your morale. When you're buying earrings, you shouldn't just be conscious of fashion. But more about that in Chapter Eight.

Earrings come with different attachments to hold them up. Obviously, everyone has their own favourite, but if you're buying a pair for a friend – and can't remember if they have pierced ears or not – go for a large, generously shaped clip fastening. Make sure the edges are well rounded and that the hinges aren't too tight. This way, even if their ears are pierced, they should be able to wear the earrings in comfort.

Screw attachments aren't seen too often these days, except on earrings made from very expensive stones. They are said to be safer than clips, which can loosen with long wear. The trouble with screw attachments is that they often hurt, especially if they're done up tightly enough to be 'safe'. By far the best way to keep expensive earrings on is to have your ears pierced and then have the earrings converted accordingly. This way, the earrings hang attached on either side of your earlobe, and can't possibly slide off through long periods of wearing them, getting tangled up in your hair or your coat, or a wild bit of dancing.

People who haven't had their ears pierced often think the process is something like torture. In fact, it needn't be anything like it at all, as long as you go to someone who knows what they're doing. Avoid backstreet people; these types are a risk, although they might be cheap. You don't know how many ears their puncher has punched before yours, so the question of hygiene rears its septic head. Good jewellers will do it properly for you; so will some doctors. Once the hole has been made with a special device, you must wear a 'sleeper' – a whole hoop, very fine and small – or a stud; a small knob on the end of a straight wire which has a separate fastening at the back of your ear – day and night for a few weeks to prevent the hole from closing up again, which is its natural inclination. Nowadays, people will often use an automatic device that punches the hole and puts the sleeper in place at the same time. Chances are, the jeweller of doctor will mark the spot on your ear first; do be sure to check that you're happy with the position before the hole is punched. The sleeper or stud must be gold, not silver or other metal as these can cause a reaction with your skin. The people who pierce your ears will tell you all this, but remember to turn the sleeper or stud around in your ear whenever you think of it, to keep the hole open. And a twice-daily bathing in a mild antiseptic lotion is a good idea for the first week or two. Unless you get an infection – which is highly unlikely, provided you take the necessary care – the holes won't hurt. Once the holes have setlled and healed completely, most people find they can still wear screw-backed earrings. And the majority find that well-designed clip earrings are quite comfortable as well. So you win all ways.

Whatever the fastening device, there are still three basic types of earring. There is the stud, which sits close to your ear; the drop, which hangs down up to two or three inches below your ear; and lastly, the hoop, which appears to form a full or almost full circle through your earlobe. The clip is a further style, which can be small like the stud, or outrageously huge, covering most of your ear, if you fancy the design and can stand the weight of it.

Often, the design of a cluster ring, or even a pendant, can be made into an earring shape. And for the really special present, a set of matching cluster ring, pendant and earrings all based on the same design, is truly superb.

Bracelets

Bracelets have been worn by both sexes throughout history for a variety of reasons. Some of those reasons were not purely decorative, either; soldiers in ancient times, for example, found that a tight metal band around their arms helped their tired muscles to cope with all the heavy swords and shields they had to swing about. Bracelets have also been worn as status symbols, your wealth being judged on the number of bands you could cram on between your wrist and your armpit. And in some ancient cultures bracelets were actually used as wedding bands, or even symbols of chastity. Next to rings, bracelets are probably the heaviest in emotional significance. Quite recently, in the United States, it became fashionable for young courting couples to exchange identity bracelets – she wearing his, with his name on it, and vice versa. Identity bracelets have enjoyed long-lived popularity as a sentimental gift. Their convenient shape – either solid metal all round, or a chain with a plaque on it – was perfect for the engraving of names, blood groups, and romantic messages.

Then we have the para-medical bracelet; the copper band. This, strictly speaking, is not jewellery because, although copper fetches a lot of money in some places, this is more likely to be for use in plumbing than in any decorative sense. Copper, some say, has curative properties, especially beneficial to sufferers of rheumatism. And whether or not the medical profession actually believes in it, many millions of bracelets have been sold. Efforts have been made to make them attractive, too; often the plain band is replaced by pretty chains made from copper links. The trouble with copper is that it tarnishes, and can react with your skin so that green or black stains appear. But whatever the drawbacks, many rheumatism sufferers swear by their copper bracelets. The answer is, if it makes you feel better, wear it; but please don't mix it with gold or silver bracelets. Utility doesn't triumph over beauty!

Basically, there are two types of jewellery bracelets. There's the solid type, nowadays often called a bangle, and then there's the flexible type which can be anything from a thin, delicate chain to heavy gold links, or even a huge gemstone flanked by gold, depending on how extravagant you feel.

Bracelets, because they have to be loose – even with clasps – to move freely with you, tend to be lost easily. In a way, they suffer more abuse than other types of jewellery; whether you're actively moving your arms around, taking off a coat, bashing your arm up and down on a table, desk or armrest, bracelets can often get damaged, broken or lost. So when you're buying a bracelet with a clasp, you want to make sure the fastening is pretty strong, and also that it hasn't any protruding bits that could catch on clothing and open the bracelet by accident. Many better-quality bracelets have a tiny little guard chain which fastens separately across the main clasp. So if the big clasp opens the little chain should hold the bracelet in place – as long as your arm doesn't happen to be dangling downwards over a drain or open man-hole cover! Rigid bangle bracelets should be a reasonably tight fit over your hand as you put them on, for the obvious reason that if they go on with a lot of room to spare, they'll come off and get lost just as easily.

Brooches

Ever since the caveman people have been wearing pins of some kind (see Chapter Three). To begin with, these jewellery items played the very practical role of holding clothing together, up, or in one piece – all the way through history, from the caveman's fur to the Roman's toga and, more recently, the Scotsman's kilt. This much-joked-about piece of clothing is pinned in the front with a smart brooch, often made of heavy silver and set with the amber-coloured Cairngorm stone.

Clips, pins and brooches pop in and out of fashion like yo-yos. What type of clip or brooch you wear is very much up to your individual style. If you're thinking about giving a brooch to someone else, you've got to be very careful to match its style to the person concerned. Like all gift buying, it's often tempting to buy something that is in *your* taste; jewellery falls prey to this problem very easily. You mustn't forget that you're not the one who'll be wearing the gift! Brooches do come in many different shapes and sizes, according to fashion and where you look for them. The essential rule of matching the item with the person's personality holds true here in a big way. There is also a superstition about giving someone a sharp object as a gift, which says that a pointed present will puncture the friendship! But fear not; there is an antidote. If the recipient gives the donor a small coin, thereby 'buying' the brooch, the friendship survives.

The only concrete advice we can offer on brooches may seem a trifle obvious, but all the same is a point frequently overlooked by many people. Brooches and any other type of pin are held on with sharp bits of metal that have to puncture the clothing. Similarly, they can also puncture skin; so you want to be careful that the sharp bit at the end is kept out of trouble. Try, if you can, to ensure that the tip is closed in, either by the fastening device itself, or – as in the case of 'stick' pins – that there is a little knob you put on the sharp tip once the pin is in place on your lapel, or wherever. This way, fingers don't get accidentally scratched and clothing doesn't get snagged or torn.

When we think of brooches, we tend to get a mental picture of a smart gold or silver piece, with perhaps a pearl or a semi-precious stone set in it. But brooches can be considerably more elaborate than that, which makes them extremely popular amongst jewellers – who have profit margins in mind. Because the brooch is probably the safest item of jewellery, insofar as it is anchored pretty firmly to your clothes, it can be loaded with lots of heavy precious metal and priceless gemstones. All you have to do is take a look at the British Royal Family's jewels, or at an old oil painting of a rich lady, and you'll see that brooches or pins tend to be more thickly encrusted with treasures than rings, pendants, earrings, and so on. Nowadays, of course, with more casual fashions and – frankly – far better taste amongst the fashion conscious, brooches and pins tend to be more discreet. But for a really formal occasion – even these days – wealthy ladies can often be seen decked out with huge, sparkling brooches on their evening gowns. So if you have, or want to buy, a valuable stone, it is worth considering having it mounted in a brooch rather than anything else – you're far less likely to lose it if it's well secured to your clothes.

Children's Jewellery

Many modern societies feel that children shouldn't wear jewellery, either because it is in bad taste, or because it is wasteful to give kids a piece of valuable jewellery when they're likely to lose it through playing and romping about. However, many other modern societies disagree with this, and start giving their kids tiny pieces of jewellery almost before they're out of the cradle. In Latin countries, for example, where jewellery is considered an investment and a statement of wealth almost as much as it is considered decorative, little girls begin to wear rings at a very early age. Usually it is a gold band around the little finger, often set with a tiny diamond. Another popular adornment for little girls in many countries is a pair of earrings; you'll even see a baby of only a few months old with tiny gold studs. This, of course, involves having the child's ears pierced at a very early age, which is thought by many to be a mistake. Early ear-piercing, especially if it's not done very well, can mean that by the time the girl is twenty her earlobes will be hanging down by her chin ! It is even possible for the earlobe of a growing child to break altogether, and consequently it has to be stitched up again. All this can be very upsetting and even disfiguring for a girl, so it's obviously best avoided. The right age to start thinking about ear-piercing is at around thirteen; from here onwards no damage is likely to occur – provided the piercing is done properly (see p. 21).

Religion has quite a lot to do with children wearing jewellery, too. Although the Jews and the Protestants don't go in for it very much until the child reaches his or her teens, the Roman Catholics will often provide chains and crosses, earrings, rings, small pearl necklaces and other bits of jewellery for a little girl when she takes her first Communion.

Protestants tend to regard a gift of jewellery as suitable for children at the time of their confirmation, although tiny identity bracelets are popular as christening gifts, too. Jewish people will usually give a young boy a gold watch at the time of his Barmitzvah, when he is thirteen.

The first major piece of jewellery most children receive is a watch. This is the gift a proud parent will buy when their little son or daughter has learned to tell the time; it's as well to know which is the best kind of watch for small wrists. Inexpensive watches are probably the best bet, because of the likelihood of damage. And an analogue watch is probably better than a digital one. Half the pleasure of owning your first watch is the independence you feel at being able to tell the time for yourself, and in a way the digital watch takes the pleasure away by doing all the work for you! In a general sense, a watch is not only a good idea for a child of school age, but is an educational present as well. So, in our opinion, watches come at the top of the list of children's jewellery. (See Chapter Ten) for more about watches.

CHAPTER TWO

Jewellery – The Most Meaningful Gift

'With Love, From Me to You'

Cynics often trot out the old line about some poor man on a business trip who, having sampled every available bit of local talent whilst in foreign climes, suffers an enormous guilt complex. So, he races to the nearest branch of a fancy jeweller's and buys his wife a gift of jewellery.

Of course, in fairness to the man, he might also have missed his wife or girlfriend terribly, and want to buy a lovely present of jewellery or perfume to take home to her, just to remind her how much he loves her. All perfectly innocent stuff.

Whatever the wits and comedians say, as an off-the-cuff spur-of-the-moment gift jewellery *is* a natural. For a start, it is usually small and lightweight. Also, jewellery is probably the most emotional, the most romantic of gifts. And spur-of-the-moment giving, or impulse buying, tends to arise out of a warm heart – even if it *is* spurred on by a guilty conscience.

Coming back down to earth a bit, more humble gentlemen will often feel like buying their wife a little treat if their horse comes in at 20 to 1, or they get a wage increase. Often this manifests itself in a piece of jewellery, just like the businessman with the Swiss bank account, only perhaps in a more modest way. It's a combination of warm-hearted, impulsive generosity, plus the desire to let the world know you've had a bit of good luck – perfectly justifiable human behaviour. And really nice, too.

Jewellery is a fairly safe bet to buy for someone else. Unless you've got very weird taste, and as long as you put a bit of thought into your purchase, there's a pretty good chance the person you buy the jewellery for is going to like it. Clothing can easily be the wrong size. Perfume or aftershave can be a brand they don't like. You can only really buy a radio or a camera for them once. But jewellery is universally acceptable; and even if you don't know the person concerned that intimately, a fairly conservative and non-outrageous piece of jewellery is bound to go down well.

Obviously, the giving of jewellery these days is a little one-sided. Purely because it is the fashion for women to wear more jewellery than men, a man buying jewellery for a woman has a lot more scope than does a woman buying for a man. Especially when the man concerned thinks wearing anything but a watch and a key chain is sissy. For these types of male, the only possibility is to buy them a better watch or better key chain than they already have. And this can get pricey, especially when it is a long-standing relationship! So the woman's task of choosing a jewellery item for the man can be tricky. But not impossible! (See Chapter Eleven.)

Giving – and Taking

Like anything else, common sense is the only really important guide to use when you're buying jewellery as a gift for someone. What you buy depends on how much you can afford, for starters, as well as taking careful consideration of the person concerned, what they look like, what suits their style and personality. One very crucial thing to remember is, although you may see a person – especially a loved one – in a certain light, that may be quite different to the light in which they see themselves. Careful observation, and an awareness of their likes and dislikes, will overcome that problem.

It's also important to buy the right piece of jewellery to suit the occasion and the mood of the gift. As we said before, rings have all sorts of involved connotations and can easily be misinterpreted. It might be better to stick to simple earrings or something pretty on a chain.

Another misconception about giving jewellery is that the name on the box is as important as the piece of jewellery itself. This is done all the time, with proud purchasers walking into the fashionably-named shops in modern cities, and quite often paying rather more for an item than they need. Of course, many people do set a lot in store by wearing a Cartier watch or a Van Clef and Arpels ring, or whatever, and if this is the sort of fashion following that you and your friends like, so be it. But when it comes down to it, a few simple mathematics will show you that trendy names, and the equally trendy prices they charge, are a luxury few of us can afford. Read Chapter 4 for details.

A Battle of the Sexes?

As often as not, jewellery is given from one sex to the other. If you think about it, how many pieces of jewellery have you been given by a member of your own sex? Chances are, very few. Most men would rather buy their father, brother or drinking companion a book on wines or a gardening tool. Most women would rather give another woman something pretty for her home or an attractive handbag. Jewellery is a chancy area. Why? Because, like it or not, there is something faintly sexual, or at least romantic, lurking behind every piece of jewellery. And even though there's nothing romantic whatsoever about a woman giving her godfather a key-ring for his birthday, she'll think twice about giving her godmother a bracelet. It's silly, of course; but little prejudices like these do creep up on us and nip us on the ankles all the time. As long as you avoid the sensitive area of rings and all they stand for, jewellery is a lovely, thoughtful and lasting gift, that means to the recipient exactly as much or as little as the donor intends it to.

Graceful Giving

Some special occasions have definite, clear-cut rules about the appropriate gift. Others have few rules, except that a gift is called for. Many of these occasions are just right for a piece of jewellery – whether jewellery is the traditional gift item or not. Here are a few of them.

Coming of age gifts, previously known as twenty-first birthday presents, but now – as in many countries the age of adulthood is eighteen – more loosely named, have to be memorable and long lasting. Jewellery is an obvious one here, and some careful thought and a little imagination can result in a gift that's a little out of the ordinary and consequently appreciated more.

For either a boy or a girl, a watch used to be the traditional gift on coming of age. Nowadays, many youngsters would rather have the money to spend on a car or a holiday. But on the assumption that, up until a young person's late teens, they will have had a functional, school-type watch, this is an ideal opportunity to give a better watch that will last for years and look really smart. A good, plain man's watch is easy to find, and – especially if you go for stainless steel casing rather than gold or gold plate – need not be expensive. For a girl, a simple, feminine gold or gold-plate watch on a plain leather strap, or gold-plated expanding bracelet will always look right, whatever she's wearing.

The gold key, in some countries, is another traditional coming of age present. Mind you, there are places where it holds a quite different meaning; sometimes it is given as a gift from a young man to his sweetheart, symbolising the 'key to his heart'. But in the UK at least, the key means the key to the plain old door, and to the outside world as you step into adulthood. Many such keys can be found in jewellery shops, in the shape of gold pendants to hang from a neck chain, or even as little drop earrings. A development of this idea is to have the real key of the young person's own front door gold plated, and then attached to a gold, or gold-plate key-ring; it makes the point as well, and is far more useful. You can even get keys actually cut from a piece of solid gold, although this is pretty expensive.

For the young man, a money clip is a good idea, especially if he has recently started his first job and is earning a wage for the first time. And cuff links make a good gift if he is beginning to dress up. See Chapter 11 for more ideas.

A gold pen is a superb gift for a young person, particularly if they are about to go to university or college, or if they're in a job that involves some writing. It's as well to avoid giving expensive pens to younger kids, because the rough and tumble of school life can easily mean that the pen gets lost. But once they've reached a more responsible age, a lovely pen in gold (or silver), perhaps even inscribed with a few appropriate words, is a gift they'll cherish for years.

Coming of age is often a good time to give a girl her first really good piece of jewellery. Teenage fashions being what they are, she will probably have been wearing trendy costume jewellery up until this age. But now, with maturity, she'll appreciate a tiny diamond or a pearl, set into a simple ring or pendant. Pearls are very popular in some northern European countries; and most young girls from those nations look forward to their eighteenth birthday, when one of the most traditional gifts is a string of cultured pearls.

A gold or silver heart is a popular piece of jewellery amongst young girls, and can be mounted in many different ways. You can have a pendant, a dangling drop from a bracelet, a ring or earrings, either in the shape of studs or drops. Obviously, the heart has romantic connotations – young men take note! But a little heart pendant is also a lovely thought when given by parent to daughter, or by a favourite aunt or uncle.

Earrings, in themselves, are not popular gifts. There doesn't seem to be much awareness of the reasons for this, even among the people in the jewellery trade, who simply say that earrings tend to be bought rather more for people's own use than as gifts. One reason may, of course, be the fact that there are three different ways of fastening earrings on to your ear; and unless you know the person well, you're likely to buy the wrong sort of fastening. But in the case of a female member of your own family, or a close friend, it's easy enough to observe the sort of fastening she prefers, plus the style she likes. And earrings make a lovely gift. Even some men wear earrings too nowadays; so bear that in mind if you want to buy a present for a trendy male friend!

Further up the age scale, another traditional jewellery-giving time is upon the birth of a child. In America, husbands sometimes buy their wives a diamond watch on the birth of their first child. This is not always that exorbitantly expensive; the gift could simply be a pretty, gold-plated watch with a tiny diamond or two set on or near the dial. In Europe, though, the more favoured item for this emotional landmark in a couple's life is the eternity ring (also given as a wedding aniversary present). This pretty ring is usually a circle, or half circle, of diamonds or other precious stones. It has developed over the years as the classic way for a husband to say 'thank you' to his wife; and even if you don't believe in these types of tradition, an eternity ring is a joy to own.

Some women, once they receive an eternity ring, will change that for their plain metal wedding ring – or put that over on the right hand and wear the eternity ring with their engagement ring. More usually, especially in northern Europe, women will wear all three together on the ring finger, with the wedding band going on first, then the eternity ring, followed by the engagement ring last of all.

Funnily enough, this order seems a bit cockeyed, if you think about it. Assuming your engagement ring is the most valuable of the three, and you got engaged before you got married, a more logical arrangement would be to put your engagement ring on first, secured on top by the wedding ring, or the eternity ring, or both. Some women do wear their rings in this way, but the majority follow the norm and wear wedding band, eternity and engagement rings in that order. Anyway, since when has logical theory looked beautiful?

Another special occasion gift from husband to wife is a replacement for the engagement ring – a bigger one! Although some women feel emotionally attached to their original engagement ring, a lot of couples like to crystallise their upward mobility in life, the success they have created together, with a bigger and better-looking ring. Some would call it mercenary and status seeking, others would call it progress. The real answer is, it's up to you.

When a couple get married, it's very often quite enough that they should exchange wedding bands and spend a lot of money on the trousseau, honeymoon, wedding reception and the rest. But in some countries husband and wife give each other separate, highly personal presents to commemorate their wedding day, and if you can afford it, it seems a lovely idea. Basically, anything goes, but as it is a romantic, emotionally-charged situation, jewellery is a firm favourite. The only common denominator is that the items are usually inscribed with the names and date of the wedding. So the prerequisite is that whatever the jewellery item, it should have a sufficiently large expanse of metal on it to accommodate the inscription!

And Speaking of Inscriptions...

Inscriptions are certainly a very good way of making a gift of jewellery that much more personalised and therefore, hopefully, more important to the recipient. Family crests, initials, dates, little personal phrases, blood groups and other such hieroglyphics are all part of the metal engraver's repertoire. And for the relatively small outlay that engraving involves, it's well worth it. As long as the piece of jewellery has a sufficiently large surface of uninterrupted metal, you should be alright. Your jeweller will advise you on that. Also bear in mind that to engrave something takes a while, even a couple of weeks, so do your shopping in plenty of time. If you go to a jeweller who has engraving facilities on the premises, all well and good; it should only take a few days. But if – as is the case with the majority of jewellers – the article has to be sent away to be engraved, then the process takes longer.

Happy Anniversary

Wedding anniversaries tend to be pretty private things on the whole, celebrated between husband and wife on their own. This is a classic time, though, for a gift of jewellery to change hands – more often than not from the husband to the wife. All the range of jewellery items are appropriate here, according to a couple's taste, but rings – because they are highly romantic – are a good safe bet for any man at a loss to know what to buy his dear lady on that special occasion.

Some wedding anniversaries, notably those in later life, are celebrated by close friends and family as well. And, if you follow tradition, some of those anniversaries are supposed to be feted with jewels or other precious things. The trouble with jewellery, of course, is that it's pretty tricky to give a piece to more than one person! So it's not normally appropriate to give your favourite auntie and uncle a piece of jewellery, even if it is their diamond wedding. But commercialism like this (after all, that's really what started the ball rolling) has spread to other types of anniversaries which involve only one lucky person. Like birthdays, for example. Here, then, is the list of which anniversaries should be presented with what:

Fifth   Wood
Tenth   Tin
Fifteenth   Crystal
Twentieth   China
Twenty-fifth   Silver (here's where it starts to get expensive!)
Fortieth   Ruby
Fiftieth   Gold
Sixtieth   Diamond

What Stone Were You Born Under?

Birthstones have become very popular amongst people from all walks of life, so we must treat these gems with respect. However, it does grate a little bit to hear people swear blind faith in the luck that their birthstone has brought them, when you consider that there is about as much genuine folklore behind birthstones as there is behind vacuum-cleaners. Birthstones were thought up by profit-conscious jewellers, most probably in America, and were cleverly marketed with enormous success. But so what? They're a nice idea, a gimmick, and if they can give someone pleasure, they can't be all bad.

Of course, giving a birthstone to someone who blatantly dislikes that particular stone, or finds it doesn't match their lifestyle, colouring or anything else, is a silly mistake. If you know that person happens to like their birthstone, though, there's no problem. So, if you're interested, here they are; plus a little about how each stone looks best, so your purchase won't be a birthstone, but an attractive piece of jewellery. See Chapters Six and Seven for more information on gemstones.

January: Garnet

This is a dark, red stone, so it should be set in such a way as to let in as much light as possible. It looks best set with yellow gold, in a very light, airy mounting.

February: Amethyst

February is carnival month in many countries, particularly in Brazil where this lovely, lilac/purple stone comes from. Perhaps it is because of this that the amethyst is such a cheerful, happy stone; in any case, it looks pretty in virtually any kind of mounting. On the whole, yellow gold looks better with it than does white gold, as the paler colour of white metal can make the stone look cheap. A heavier mounting will show it off better. It isn't really suitable as a pendant or brooch, because, being a very transparent stone, it will allow the colour of the clothing beneath to show through, taking attention away from its own lovely colour.

March: Aquamarine

Also a pale, transparent stone, the same rules as for the amethyst apply here. You can get aquamarines that are so pale they can pass for diamonds; but on the whole, they are a light, sky blue.

April: Diamond

We don't need to say anything about these sparklers! See Chapter Six for details. If you can't afford a real diamond as a birthstone, one of the diamond substitutes will do – again, see Chapters Six, Seven and Nine.

May: Emerald or Tourmaline

This is an expensive, precious stone. And really, birthstones should all be semi-precious stones, in order to bring them in line with what the majority of people can afford. So, as an alternative to the emerald, we have another green stone, this time semi-precious; the tourmaline. It is slightly darker green than the emerald, but nonetheless very pretty, especially when it's mounted in silver or white gold. As it's a dark stone, rather like the garnet, the mounting should be as fine and airy as possible to let light in. It's especially attractive in a pendant or a ring.

June: Pearl

If you're going for cultured or synthetic pearls (and who doesn't, these days), a piece of jewellery with this particular birthstone is within most people's reach. Apart from the more traditional mountings for pearls, a novel idea is to buy a pearl 'eternity ring'. It's actually a tiny string of pearls that goes around your finger. It looks terrific, but can be a bit bulky and uncomfortable to wear.

July: Ruby

This is also a precious stone, but isn't always as expensive as you think. Small ones don't cost a fortune, and look lovely mounted in white gold as a dress ring or in a pendant. Ear studs are not a good idea with a medium to dark-coloured stone, because you lose a lot of the colour by pressing the stone up against your skin, and partly covering it up with hair. If earrings are what you want, though, try buying rubies in a drop style, swinging clear of the face.

August: Peridot

This is a light green, semi-precious stone, and should be mounted in the same way as amethysts and aquamarines. Yellow or white gold (or silver) look equally attractive with it.

September: Sapphire

The same applies here as applies for the ruby. It's another dark stone, and also expensive – though small ones can be quite effective without costing the earth. They tend to look better mounted in white gold, as the brighter colour of yellow gold tends to fight a bit with the blue of the sapphire. Remember, a light and airy setting will show off the colour far better.

October: Opal

This is an incredible stone, really. It is stunning either in white or yellow gold or silver, and is suitable for mounting in any form. But opals tend to be brittle stones, so avoid buying them in mountings that are particularly susceptible to knocks. Opals are amongst the most valuable of semi-precious gems, so be prepared for a heavyish outlay. Also, bear in mind that they are often found in unusual shapes, which look superb in a simple pendant mounting – a truly original gift.

November: Topaz

This is yet another light-coloured stone, so mountings should be as for amethyst, peridot, aquamarine, and all its other pale, semi-precious stablemates. There are three basic types of topaz: smoky grey-brown, gold, and the 'blood' topaz, which naturally enough has a reddish tint. Very often you'll see a yellow stone being sold as a topaz; in fact, this is likely to be a citrine, which is quite pretty in its own right. As far as mountings are concerned, the paler topazes look better in yellow gold, and the darker ones in white gold or silver. Beware, too, of the giant topazes you see for sale sometimes; they may seem like a huge amount of stone for your money, but they actually look a bit phoney when you wear them.

December: Turquoise

This is an interesting stone. It looks far better mounted in silver or white gold, as this sets off its beautiful colour. Turquoises look great in a really heavy mounting (usually silver) as large bracelets, or even belt buckles, which are good gifts for either men or women. More conventional mountings for turquoises are rings and pendants, but again

– avoid ear studs as the stone's beauty will be wasted. If you've got the money to spend, a turquoise looks beautiful surrounded by small diamonds or pearls. A versatile stone, it can make anything from a very informal item to a piece of fine, expensive formal jewellery.

Wearing Your Jewels on Your Sleeve...

Very often, the jewellery people wear matches their personality. People with gaudy characters tend to wear gaudy jewellery. Big, stout women wear big, heavy jewels; thin, quiet women tend to wear small, discreet jewellery. Men who fancy themselves as being very modern businessmen will often wear ultra-complicated digital watches that tell them everything from the day of the week to the latest news on the Tokyo Stock Exchange. A doctor will wear a classical, elegant unostentatious watch; plain and round, to match his dignified, low-profile profession. People who have recently acquired a lot of money will often show this off by wearing a big showy bracelet or ring. And so on. You can tell a lot about a person by looking at his or her jewellery; about their personality, and about their status in life.

In the past, the jewellery people wore – especially women – was usually a pretty clear indication not only of their preferences, but of their financial status. Nowadays, though, inflation, the tax man and other financial burdens are making us rather more practically-minded. We still like status symbols, of course. But sheer necessity often makes us express our status in more useful things, like cars, washing machines, dishwashers, luxurious kitchens, swimming pools and even larger, better homes or home extensions. A hundred years ago there simply weren't such things, so jewellery was much higher up on the list of so-called luxury purchases. There were far fewer things you could buy to display your wealth or crown your successes. Nowadays, an expensive piece of jewellery is very much of an also-ran, compared with the average family's other priorities. And, as our technological age advances, the creators of status symbols and luxury goods are constantly dreaming up new products for us to aim for. Video cassette TV recorders, TV news services, TV games, ultra-sophisticated hi-fi and kitchen equipment are all examples of recent goodies that no-one would have thought about even as recently as the nineteen-fifties. But now, more and more families buy them. So where does all this leave jewellery?

Jewellery has, in effect, become far less important as a status symbol than it used to be. As a result, it has taken on a more realistic role in people's lives – more personal, more charming. A gift of jewellery these days has more meaning for the individual; it isn't so much a mobile display of your income bracket, as a mobile display of someone's appreciation for you, and your own appreciation of beauty.

CHAPTER THREE

What Jewellery Means to People – Past, Present and Future

There are many theories, quoted by lots of learned experts, about the very early origins of jewellery. Some say the first bits of jewellery were special pins, to hold up the early caveman's fig leaves and bear skins. Certainly, pins made of thorns have been unearthed in prehistoric dressing rooms. And pins of various shapes and sizes, in gold and other metals, as well as earlier versions made from bone splinters, have been found in ancient tombs. It's human nature to make the most of necessities, so here we have the beginnings of jewellery. You needed pins to stop your furs from falling around your ankles? Yes? So you decorated the pins and wore them as status symbols – articles of self-adornment. And why not?

Of course, not all early jewellery was intended for such mundane purposes as holding up your bear skin. Our famous explorers found plenty of it on their travels to the new worlds, worn by natives for a variety of reasons. Self-adornment in primitive cultures was a way not only to attract others and indicate status, but to do just about everything from warding off evil spirits to putting off your enemies.

It's almost as if every element of history that influenced people in any significant way was immortalised by creating a piece of jewellery, reminding you of a good thing or protecting you from a bad one. Ancient gods, sweethearts, astrological powers-that-be, and many other favoured elements have been admired and worshipped. Unsavoury elements have been repelled and driven away by beads, metals, leather, feathers, precious and semi-precious stones and any other bits of hardware that caught people's fancy at the time. Whatever the hardware was, it held some kind of meaning.

Stone age citizens found gemstones extremely useful, as well as beautiful. Most people of that era were well versed in which gemstone was the right one to have handy in case of trouble. Agate, for instance, protected you from thunder, and was also a good precaution against being nipped by a passing tiger. Ferocious fiends would quake at the sight of ringed agate, or tiger's eye, as the cool stare of the gemstone would stop them in their tracks. The rich blue and gold flecks of lapis lazuli would make a poisonous snake change its mind about taking a bite out of your ankle.

As you can see, the purposes of early jewellery were largely functional; in those days one didn't have much time to indulge in luxuries. But even while struggling to survive, early civilisations still had an eye for beauty and some early jewellery was worn for purely decorative reasons. Whether it was a caveman hanging an extra stag's tooth around his neck, or today's modern lady buying herself a pair of earrings, the motivation is much the same. To build on and embellish our own natural beauty, and to feel the actual pleasure of wearing an item which we consider beautiful, is basically what it's all about.

Jewellery as the status symbol has always been popular. Earlier chiefs and kings wore considerably bigger and better baubles than their subjects did, so everyone would know who was boss. Not that this overloading with jewellery was unconnected with beauty; it seemed the more beauty you could wear, the more important you had to be. Nowadays, of course – apart from such traditional ceremonies as coronations, where the monarch usually wears so many precious things they can barely stand up – we've tended to exchange quantity for quality. You don't have to wear a lot of jewellery to emphasise how rich or important you are. One single, very large diamond is often enough to do the trick. But perhaps this is only true because jewellery has become that much more sophisticated, along with technology and civilisation in general. In the old days, life wasn't so subtle.

Take the Egyptians of about 3,000 years ago, although the jewellers of the period were extremely advanced. Their fashion was heavy and ornate, with wide, choker-like collars encrusted with gemstones; 'pectorals', or breast pieces, which you wore hanging from your neck, making it quite a task to hold your head up with the weight of the jewels; and there were even ornate items to cover your wig, which must have been highly uncomfortable on hot Egyptian summer days. Such was the price of looking beautiful. The Egyptians also favoured perfume boxes, lots of different types of rings, some of which were used as seals like the latter-day crest rings, and many more trinkets. It was a rich and opulent era, and the Egyptians' jewellery reflected this well.

Rings were also popular with the Israelites. In fact, this race was so keen on rings they wore them everywhere they could think of – on fingers, in ears, through nostrils, and some say even on their toes. The Israelites also apparently started the fashion for nose studs, which are still common today in certain parts of the world, notably in some Asian and Arab countries.

The ancient Greeks were great innovators as far as jewellery was concerned. They particularly liked brooches in gold and silver, and filigree and enamel work – intricate things to make well, even today. Elegant medallions and pendants were popular, too. Most popular of all were earrings; they became larger and larger as the Greek civilisation progressed, until these ornaments were so heavy they had to be transferred to hang around the neck.

The Romans didn't do as much innovating as they did collecting other people's ideas, bringing back all kinds of beautiful items from their travels. They didn't only bring back the goods, either; they brought back the craftsmen who made all these things, and set them to work under their own supervision. They also sat young Roman apprentices down next to the foreigners to learn the techniques. Their motto must have been 'think big', judging by their lifestyle of conquering nations; and this big thinking showed itself in the jewellery produced. Decorated hairpins became so long they stretched to 25 centimetres or more. Rings could be seen on every finger, including a huge gem-studded specimen on the thumb. Key rings came into being; but these were literally just a ring on your finger to which was attached the key to your house or coffers.

Jewellery became so profuse amongst the Romans that one emperor, Cato the Censor, tried to bring in a law that would limit the amount of jewellery people could wear. His fellow Romans, naturally enough, didn't think very much of this idea, and carried on loading themselves down with precious adornments. The more you were worth, the more jewellery you wore – even if it did mean staggering under the weight of it.

Precious stones in the Romans' favourite colours, blue, red and yellow, were used for other things besides jewellery. They were employed as money for betting on chariot races; and as the Romans' richness grew, so did the size of the stones. Often, when they couldn't find stones big enough, they would substitute fakes made of glass – perhaps a manifestation of that creeping corruption which eventually led to their downfall.

While many races may have suffered downfalls along the line of history, jewellery certainly did not. Gemstones went on to become the greatest status symbol of all time. After the Roman power waned, gems were being worn by the Byzantines all over their bodies – even sewn on to their clothes. But another region of the world was also making some superb jewellery at this time. This was India.

If the Egyptians, Greeks and Romans were thought to be rich, the Indians were positively rolling in it. The leaders of this country, then and onwards into more recent history, had such a huge supply of precious stones and metals that a common birthday gift among the Indian gentry would be someone's body weight in gemstones or gold. So much did they admire their jewels that they even buried their dead surrounded by precious baubles; mausoleums like the Taj Mahal contain waggon-loads of precious and semi-precious gems.

The ancient Chinese, too, made beautiful jewellery. They, unlike many of their contemporaries, used jewellery in comparatively good taste and tended not to overdo the number of jewels worn. Their jewels were status symbols as well, but were allocated in a much more orderly fashion. Mandarins wore different gemstones according to their rank. And of all the materials the Chinese favoured, the first on the list was their beautiful jade. Chinese women, in ancient times, used to grab hold of a piece of jade while they were giving birth. They thought the jade would lessen their pain as it held magic powers. And because of its great status, the women also reckoned it would guarantee great things for the future of the baby. The Chinese love for jade spread across to Western countries and to this day a perfect specimen of jade is truly exquisite.

During the course of English history, a lot of jewellery was made for religious purposes. This was, ostensibly, for reasons of worship and other noble causes and not as a means for displaying wealth. But there was many an ecclesiastic who adorned himself with beautiful jewels and justified them by making sure a crucifix or rosary was attached somewhere. As long as his jewels had a religious connection, however vague, his conscience could be clear. Church books were another item of religious paraphernalia that got the treatment of jewellery in ancient times. Many Russian volumes were studded with precious gems, and often the first word of the text would be encrusted with rose-cut diamonds. Examples of these books are now on display at the Kremlin in Moscow.

The Italians, at the time of the Medicis and Borgias, were experts at the art of making jewellery, and were much better at it than the stalwart, less-inspired British. Rings were great favourites, once again, and pendants dangled from all sorts of places; from ears, around the neck, on the forehead and so on. The accent was still on opulence in those days, but the artistic Italians managed to inject a certain elegance into their designs. This new approach caught on right across Europe during the Renaissance, and soon everyone wanted these smart, graceful jewels. Not everyone could afford them, though, and a few clever craftsmen made surprisingly realistic imitations out of glass. Even King Henry VIII of England was sold a superb set of paste jewellery for a vast sum by a Milanese dealer. It was not until the much-married king got his bargain home that a well-meaning aide told him it was fake.

Everyone who was anyone in Europe at the time was bejewelled to the eyebrows. But along with this increase in adornment came increases in many other things, until society began to suffer something of an indigestion of the good life. Even the Church became concerned about the apparent vogue for high living and low thinking, and as part of its clean-up campaign insisted on a policy of simple clothing and less jewellery. As an indirect result, European jewellers began to make more tasteful jewellery, smaller pieces with more discreet, finer designs. But by the 18th century, greed and opulence had crept back in, and jewellery began to get bigger and flashier once again. Still, people had finally appreciated the point that tastefully designed jewellery looked just as impressive as big, ugly pieces, and a large amount of really attractive jewellery was produced. The superb 'parure' – a set of matching jewels consisting of two or more items like a necklace, bracelets, earrings, diadem or tiara, and others – was the height of fashion for elegant ladies.

Perhaps the biggest step forward that was made in the 18th century, though, was the invention of the brilliant cut for diamonds, and a general shaking up of ideas on cutting all stones to make them really sparkle. Up until then, the way jewellers cut stones hardly did justice to them, not making anywhere near enough use of light and colour. The 18th century changed all that; gem-cutters used the brilliant cut principle of cutting several dozen 'facets', or angled surfaces on a stone, which showed colour and light play to perfection. Present-day cutting of stones has altered comparatively little since the discoveries of that time.

By the 19th century the diamond had really established itself as the darling of society, although this gem had already been around for thousands of years. The bigger the better was the key phrase of the time; huge diamonds were seen on elegant fingers and around graceful throats in the smart drawing rooms all over the Western world.

It is not until the second half of the 19th century that we see jewellery being brought down to the level of the masses. Previously, jewellery of any value had been worn largely by the upper classes, who had the money to buy it and attended the grand social occasions to show it off. Also, machines were now being used on quite a wide scale, so it was possible for some types of jewellery to be almost mass-produced, on a far more economical basis. This was a time when paste and other imitation stones were manufactured in large quantities, and smart people like Mr Pinchbeck began to set the stones in imitation precious metals. In England, Queen Victoria's love of modesty, especially in the latter half of her reign after her beloved husband's death, had a tremendous influence on everyone. Small, simple pieces of jewellery, with lots of semi-precious stones and seed pearls, became widespread, and fine examples still exist today, although they are expensive to buy.

The turn of the century was the heyday of none other than the great Peter Carl Fabergé, whose designs were loved and admired by everyone, including most European royal families. He certainly shook the jewellery world by the tail, breaking away from the age-old traditions and decorating everything he could think of with precious gems and metals. After Fabergé's influence began to fade, jewellery became simpler, following – as it nearly always has – in the footsteps of the fashions people wore. As clothing became less complicated, so did jewellery; as new parts of the body were revealed, like ankles, wrists, forearms and cleavages, new jewellery was developed to match.

The various fashions came and went. Art Nouveau was all the rage for a while, in the early stages of the century, and its influence spread everywhere throughout the arts and crafts of the Western world. Jewellery was an obvious choice for Art Nouveau designers. Although many sceptics say that there was nothing really 'nouveau' about Art Nouveau at all – that it was just a melting pot of design ideas from other cultures and eras – the period produced some very pretty pieces of jewellery. However, the fashion for Art Nouveau came to an abrupt end when the First World War ravaged its way through Europe. After that, in the twenties, we got our first hint of futuristic designs and streamlined modern styles, with Art Deco. Designers of the time got so carried away with all the fun of playing with geometric shapes that they rather forgot to be artistic as well. Not surprisingly, a lot of the jewellery from this epoque turned out to be ugly and meaningless. So Art Deco eventually gave way to the richer, but still clean-cut designs which led to the contemporary jewellery we all know.

Nowadays, jewellery forms more of a compliment to clothing than anything else. In the past, women would have a dress specially designed and made to show off a beautiful 'parure', or set of jewels. Today, fashion seems to dictate a total look, with jewellery forming a part of it, almost as an accessory. Of course, there have been further new developments in the 20th century, most notable of which is probably the increasing use of platinum and palladium as precious metals. They're tougher and lighter than gold, and set off precious stones as well, if not better. We've also gone back to the very early roots of jewellery and made use of materials like glass, feathers, shells, stone and other pretty things – some of which were used by natives hundreds of years ago. Technology has had its say, as well; as soon as the first plastics were being manufactured for industrial and household purposes, some of them found their way into jewellery. The Edwardians, in England, quickly realised that these plastics could be used to copy jet and ivory, amongst other things, and although plastic was still in its infancy at that stage, some of the early imitation jewellery made this way is very realistic indeed.

Further on in the 20th century, we can see the use of perspex in jewellery. Some is used for frankly fake pieces, but the more modern-thinking jewellers have used it to set diamonds and other precious gems.

Other new and exciting techniques are being added to the range of possibilities in jewellery. Laser prints, for example, make stunning pendants – three-dimensional, permanent holograms encased between discs or other shapes of glass and constantly appearing to change colour and depth.

And what of the future? What new things will appear on the horizon, to be incorporated in the jewellery of the 21st century? And what precious things will we find when space travel becomes more common? It is said that there could be diamond deposits on the moon. As we continue to explore our universe, there's no reason to suppose that we won't find a whole new range of precious gems and metals, buried in the mineral deposits of neighbouring planets. It's an exciting prospect, and it is certain, judging from the pattern of history, that whatever happens to our civilisations in the future, jewellery is here to stay. Jewellery will follow us into the space age, and beyond.

CHAPTER FOUR

A Who's What of the Jewellery Business

Behind the Scenes of the Jewellery Business

Most consumers these days don't actually care too much about the whys and wherefores of what goes into the making of goods, just so long as the goods *are* good – so to speak. On the other hand, though, consumers resent paying high prices. Jewellery is a typical example: shelling out a week's salary for one simple gold chain might well make you think that someone, somewhere, is making a great fat profit out of you. Of course, the raw materials are expensive, because they're rare. However, a large proportion of the price you pay is for the labour involved; just like cars, washing machines, calculators, typewriters and lawn mowers, jewellery takes time to be made. And not just anybody's time, either; the people who make jewellery are experts, and most of them have spent years perfecting their craft, so it's only fair that you should pay for that expertise and time.

Some people firmly believe that a lot of extra cost gets piled on to most merchandise because of middle men, as well as the people who physically make it. It's true. But those middle men don't just sit at leather-covered desks juggling telephones; they earn their money like the rest of us. The jewellery business has its fair share of middle men, but far from peddling diamond rings to unsuspecting buyers, they really do perform a necessary job. They work hand in hand with the craftspeople, and with them they are responsible for turning gold bullion and rough stones into the shining, sparkling finished product. It's not an easy task, so let's take a closer look at it. It will help you to understand where your money's going – and take the sting out of the price you pay.

Some people's opinions about jewellers would seem to be a trifle unfair. Those of you who compare a jeweller with a second-hand car salesman would do well to read on carefully; funnily enough, the jewellery business is delightfully straight. It seems almost old-fashioned today, when you think of the cut-throat attitudes many modern businesses thrive on, but the jewellery trade is one of integrity and stout loyalty amongst its members. Naturally enough, there are a few cowboys, most of whom are the types who'll open their raincoats up and show you a neat row of watches pinned to the lining! But as long as you stick to proper sources, you're far less likely to find cause for complaint than you are in the majority of other buying situations.

So first of all, what is a jeweller? That may seem like a silly question. But is a jeweller someone who makes jewellery? Sells it? Works gold? Polishes stones?

The answer is that it can be all, or none. But for the sake of argument, let's refer to a jeweller as someone who sells jewellery to the public. This is the person, or people, with whom you will have contact. They will advise you, help you to select your jewellery, and give you guidance when you're buying for someone else. But before we go any further, let's have a look at the people behind the scenes; the craftspeople who make your jewellery.

First of all, we have the goldsmith. This is a person whose hands are really the only tools that matter. These hands create, from a design that originates in the head, a work of art – possibly one which will never be repeated. The only aids are oxygen torches, to heat up the gold, and a few metal instruments. The goldsmith works quietly, in deep concentration, producing intricate pieces of jewellery that should last for ever. But strange though it may seem, the glamour factor in being a goldsmith is virtually nil; far from working in trendy studios, sitting at luxurious workbenches, the goldsmith's conditions are often cramped and uncomfortable. Sometimes the most beautiful pieces of jewellery will have been made in positively Dickensian surroundings, the goldsmith sitting at a little wooden bench on a low stool, surrounded by priceless pieces of gold, with a leather apron strung underneath the bench to catch the gold filings – which are periodically collected and re-used.

Then, we have the stone manufacturer. Basically, these people start off with the rough stone, pretty well as it comes out of the ground, and through an elaborate series of manoeuvres produce the finished gem. The trick is to judge right from the start the best way to cut the stone, so as it will have as much value as possible, and so there will be as little wastage as there need be. Here's what the diamond cutter does – a suitable example, as diamonds are very popular stones.

Quite often, a cutter will first of all polish a kind of window, or viewing hatch, on one side of a rough stone, just to take a good look inside and work out the best ways of treating it. Then comes the big crunch; cleaving. Beforehand, the cutter will study the stone's formation to work out where it should be split, in order to break it into smaller pieces suitable for making into polished stones. Obviously, any mistakes can be a shade expensive, so the stone cutter has got to know what he or she is doing. Once the decision is made, the cutter whittles away a little bit out of the stone on the spot where the split should be, and then cleaves it, gently but firmly, with a blunt blade. Some stones are sawed, instead, depending on their type.

When that stage is over, the next process is bruting. This means that the rough diamond in question is polished with another rough diamond. The diamond being used as a tool is stuck on the end of a rod, which goes under the cutter's arm. Naturally, all this scraping means that little deposits of diamond powder collect around the workbench. But this is carefully collected up at the end of the day, and used again for other purposes. Waste not, want not; especially with materials as precious as this.

The last stage in diamond cutting (and in the cutting of other precious stones, too) is the actual cutting of the facets on the stone. These, as you probably know, are the many flat surfaces that you'll find on most stones. The reason for making these facets is to get the best light effects on, behind, and through the stone. The diamond cutter uses a grinding wheel, called a 'Schyf', which looks a bit like the old scissor grinding machines that would be brought round to your home by the scissor grinders of the old days. This facet cutting wheel is obviously rather more sophisticated; it is covered first of all in oil, and then with diamond dust – no doubt some that has been collected up from one of the previous stages. The stone to be faceted is put on to a dop, which is a bit like the instrument that holds the stylus in a record player, and the loaded dop goes against the grinding wheel. The cutter keeps a watchful eye on the process, and makes all the necessary adjustments. And when you think that there are several dozen facets on most stones, however tiny, you can imagine just how watchful the stone cutter's eye has got to be.

Knowing how to cut and perfect valuable stones is not a profession you can learn easily. Mistakes are very expensive. So the stone cutter needs to be subjected to intensive training; the apprenticeship usually last between three and five years. The trouble is, a would-be stone cutter can't really practice on anything but the real thing. Other, cheaper materials like glass or crystal have a completely different texture, so it would be pointless to teach an apprentice on these. What happens is that the apprentice sits with an experienced, qualified cutter for some considerable time, and gradually gets more involved. First, the apprentice will be allowed to do a little harmless polishing, which is highly unlikely to give rise to any problems or damage. As his or her confidence and ability increase, more and more tasks are set, until eventually the whole job is being done by the apprentice, still under close supervision. Like many of these intricate crafts, stone cutting is definitely not something you can learn from books or classrooms; you can only learn by watching and doing.

Another important craftsperson in the jewellery trade is the setter. To a large extent, the setter performs the same jobs as the goldsmith, but added to that he or she also has to deal with stones. Not all goldsmiths can set, but most setters know the ins and outs of goldsmith work; there is something of an overlap between the two functions. Anyway, the setter takes, for example, a ring mounting which he may or may not have made himself; the trick is to make sure the stone is correctly grooved or indented, so the mounting will hold it firmly in place. If the setter gets it wrong, the stone may come loose or drop out, to the embarrassment of the jeweller who sells it, and to the annoyance of the owner. If you're wearing a stone-set ring at the moment, have a look at it. Or get one out of your jewellery box. Now, first of all, look at the shank – the rounded piece that actually holds the ring around your finger. This, the setter will make by heating up some gold wire, and wrapping the hot gold around a specially designed tube which has pre-determined settings on it to make rings to specific sizes. This gold hoop will not meet in the middle, at the top. Then, with some more gold wire, the setter makes a little loop which he sticks over the gap between the two ends of the shank of the ring; this forms the base for the claws, which will hold the ring in place. Finally, the setter will get some more, very fine wire, and solder four or six short, straight lengths of this at or near right angles to the shank. These wires are probably the most important bit, because they're the ones that actually hold the stone or stones in place. Once all this has been done, the stone is put into place and the little thin lengths of wire, or 'claws', are carefully bent over until the whole lot is secure. Bear in mind, of course, that this method of making jewellery is very much 'doing it by hand'; often ring mounts such as the one we've been talking about arrive ready-made, having been turned out by machine. But more about that later.

As we said before, there are a few middle men in the jewellery business, as well as craftspeople. These, contrary to popular opinion, are not blood suckers and actually do a very valuable job. Take the stone broker, for instance; he is the go-between for stone manufacturers and jewellery manufacturers. In other words, he has to know what people making the finished jewellery want, plus what the stone manufacturers are producing, and put the two together. This saves a lot of work and effort for both stone manufacturer and jewellery manufacturer; if it weren't for the stone broker, much valuable time would be spent negotiating transactions instead of making jewellery and cutting stones. So the broker's work means that everyone can get on with the job they're good at. And for all this, the broker makes a reasonable profit, which naturally enough goes on to the price of the jewellery. What we tend to forget, of course, is that if the broker weren't around, we'd probably still wind up paying much more for the stone manufacturer or jewellery manufacturer's time instead – as they would be trying to do the same negotiations, possibly not so efficiently!

Leaving stones for a moment, let's take a look at the people involved in dealing with gold. This is a very different kettle of fish, because it's nowhere nearly as straightforward. Conditions vary from country to country, but in the majority of nations, gold is heavily sat upon by governments and authoritative bodies. Pretty well anyone can go to a stone manufacturer or broker and buy a loose stone (other than a diamond – see Chapter 6); but much as everyone has Midas-like dreams of stockpiling gold bars under their mattresses, it's just not on. Not in the UK, anyway. Gold can only be bought through merchant banks in this country. Then it usually goes to a bullion dealer, who will 'found' it – as in the case of most metals – and alloy it with the appropriate other metal, so that it arrives at the jewellery manufacturer's or goldsmith's premises in a large lump, sheet or coil of wire of 9 carat, 18 carat, or whatever type of gold. And before it can be sold, it passes through an incredibly complicated labyrinth, involving big business, the stock market, governments, and all the rest of it. Gold, as any financial expert will tell you, is closely connected with currency and many countries' wealth, so every ounce of it must be accounted for – whether it's hanging as a bracelet around your wrist, or sitting in a pile of gold bars at Fort Knox.

So, now that we have the raw materials of gold (or the other precious metals which arrive at jewellery manufacturers' in much the same way) and stones, plus the individual craftspeople and middle people who deal with them, let's look at the more modern, more streamlined ways in which jewellery is put together. We've already talked about the hand-crafting of jewellery, involving stone cutters, goldsmiths and setters. But much as there is a lot of old-fashioned charm in the idea of diligent artisans slaving away over hot oxygen torches in dingy studios, twentieth century progress has seeped in. Today, much of the jewellery you'll see in the shops has been made in big manufacturing premises, which look more like car factories than artists' studios. Very often, gold is worked not by one person making wire and subsequent one-off jewellery items, but on a much larger scale. Ring mounts can be made by stamping them out of a sheet of gold, rather like using a biscuit cutter. Often, the basic gold lumps are melted down into molten gold, and then poured into moulds. This is called casting, and it gives rise to a certain amount of controversy amongst members of the trade. Although the old-fashioned goldsmiths might well turn red in the face at the idea of casting, provided it is done properly it is every bit as good as hand-made gold jewellery.

As a general rule, large jewellery manufacturers – organisations employing perhaps one or two hundred people – will stick to the less valuable jewellery items. Pieces using semi-precious stones, plus traditional, big-selling types of jewellery, tend to come from these bigger companies. Some expensive jewellery is made this way, too, but on the whole a valuable ring or pendant will probably have been crafted by an individual, working for the more exclusive big-name jeweller with a smart address. Mind you, you mustn't get the notion of diamond engagement rings being churned out of a sausage factory! Although many of the processes hitherto done by hand can now be accomplished with machines, there still has to be a contingent of craftspeople to watch over things, and often to put the machine-made items together.

Like in many other situations, jewellery-making is not purely black or white; there are varying shades of grey. And many of the people involved in making jewellery fall somewhere between the two categories of small hand-crafting studios and large factories. Sometimes, jewellery will be made to order, by hand; other times certain components of a piece will be machine-made, but hand set, and so on. Effectively, the solution lies in the price at the end of the day; hand-made pieces are more expensive than machine-made. If a setter sits down and makes a diamond ring from scratch, or at least from the cut stone and the lump of gold, it's going to take him or her about two days. With a machine-made ring mount – the right size for the stone – the operation will take a couple of hours. The result is that the handmade ring will cost twice or even three times more than the machine-made ring. It's the age-old story; modern technology kicks old-fashioned expertise out of the door, because machines are more economical than human beings.

Of course, the large jewellery manufacturers we've just been discussing deal with the trade – they sell their produce to jewellers. There are some jewellers, though, who have their own manufacturing outfits; they need to be pretty big and well-known in order to afford their own set-up and to keep it profitable, but those in existence work very well. In fact, very big jewellery retailers can find it more economical to have their own manufacturing facility, for a variety of reasons. The obvious advantage is that they can manufacture according to their own needs, to their own market trends, and not run the risk of making stuff that doesn't sell. They know what to make because the customers in their shop or shops tell them what they want – it's very simple. Other, smaller jewellers will often still have a workshop, and make up jewellery from ready-made mounts, do repairs, ring sizing, and so on. But again, their turnover must be sufficiently healthy to sustain the workshop in the first place. The average jeweller will most probably buy in the finished articles from jewellery manufacturers. Or there might be a combination of the two; some pieces are made on the premises, some are bought in. All of this doesn't really have much effect on customers, but it is handy to know that if your jeweller has his or her own workshop, you can get a repair done or a ring sized very quickly because the article doesn't have to be sent away. And for special occasion, when you want to have a piece of jewellery made to order, it will probably be cheaper and quicker to go to a jeweller who has his or her own facilities for making that piece.

We said earlier that jewellery manufacturers sell to jewellery retailers. Not always direct, though; here we go again with a middle man, the jewellery selling agent, or wholesaler. Rather like the stone broker, the wholesaler has got to know his p's and q's extremely well. This is the person who gauges the supply and demand situation very carefully and develops an almost instinctive knowledge of what's going to sell well, where, to whom, and made by whom. Once more, this middle man puts a mark-up on every bit of jewellery, and earns every percent of it. The wholesaler knows just where to go to find every kind of item; he or she will be familiar with everyone who makes jewellery, from the small goldsmith's workshop around the corner to the big jewellery manufacturer a hundred miles away. This person can keep small manufacturing operations going, because he or she can buy their weekly produce of, say, one or two items. This would otherwise be uneconomical to sell. But buying from a dozen different workshops like this, the wholsesaler can then sell the whole lot, as a collection, to a jeweller. The wholesaler also goes to trade shows and exhibitions, and places orders for items that will sell to several of his or her clients. As a result, these orders are bigger than any single jeweller's, so more favourable prices can be negotiated – all of which benefits the customer in the long run.

Some jewellery manufacturers also have their own salespeople who perform much the same function as the wholesaler; only their attitude can be a little more one-sided! Still, they provide a vital contact between the demands of the public and the supply of jewellery, diagnosing the most favoured jewellery items, getting orders from jewellers for goods that people buy most, and instigating the manufacture of the most popular designs.

On Your Side of the Counter

Now that we've had a look at what goes on behind the scenes in the jewellery trade, let's concentrate on the people you deal with; the jewellery retail trade. First of all, we should define what a jeweller did in the old days. He (or she) was someone who had a workshop behind the front shop and sat there making jewellery all day. You went into the shop, rang the bell, the jeweller came out from the workshop wiping his or her hands, and sold you a piece of jewellery made on the premises, personally. That's what jewellers did; everything from start to finish. And there are still the odd few around, although to do business that way nowadays must be a shade unprofitable.

Today, some small jewellery shops operate in a not-too dissimilar fashion. They might well have a workshop in the back, although it will probably be used only for repairs and simple jobs. Most of the jewellery that a small jeweller sells will be bought in from the usual sources; either from large manufacturers or from smaller workshops through wholesalers. The advantage of the small jewellery shop is often the fact that the owner is also the person behind the counter, having built up the business with his or her own two hands. The knowledge and experience of that person will be considerable, greatly enlarged by the fact that he or she is in day to day contact with what the public wants, and what the latest trends in the business are. This is the person who should be able to give you the best, most unbiased advice on buying your jewellery. Also, the jewellery you'll find in a small business – or one of a small chain of shops – is likely to be more interesting and more unusual. Small jewellery businesses don't have such heavy sales quotas to worry about; whereas a big jeweller has to buy pieces in bulk that he knows will sell well, the small jeweller can afford to try out something a bit different. With just one or two shops, say, the small jeweller doesn't have to keep such large crowds coming in; so buying one or two intriguing pieces of jewellery from a wholesaler, pieces that may not sell so quickly, are not as much of a risk. The choice offered to you by a small jeweller may not be so wide, may not offer you so many different ring sizes all in the same design, but within that smaller choice there may well be something unusual and interesting that suits you better.

The medium-sized jeweller who has a small chain of shops is in an excellent position. These people's businesses are small enough that they are free to buy what they like, without too many pressures from the sales targets. And yet, because these jewellers have a certain amount of muscle and a reasonably large buying capacity, they can go directly to manufacturers and lay down the law. This means that wholesalers can be by-passed; and although we've said that wholesalers do a good job, they still cost money. The medium-sized jeweller who is in a strong enough position to by-pass the wholesaler has got it made, because he or she can pass on the saving to the customer without losing any of the retail profit.

From the point of view of the average jewellery purchaser the best bet is to buy from this medium-sized, independent jeweller. Very small operations can mean that you find something unusual, but the choice will be limited. Big chains have their disadvantages, too – more about them later. But the medium-sized jewellery shop or small chain tends to incorporate the best of both. On the one hand they will offer you a wide choice of standardised items like engagement rings and wedding rings. On the other hand, they'll still be small enough to be able to buy in more individual pieces, one-offs, that will appeal to the purchaser in search of something different. And lastly, you'll benefit from the medium-sized jeweller in as much as the person whose name is on the door will not be far away, and will usually be available to offer you sound advice based on his or her own considerable experience.

As far as price goes, it's really a question of swings and roundabouts. Medium-sized jewellers can cut out the middleman and lower their costs; big jewellery chains, because they buy in such huge quantities, can also cut out the middlemen *and* negotiate lower prices from manufacturers. So you'd think that the big jeweller's prices would be best of all, wouldn't you? But that's not necessarily so, because on the other side of the coin, the big jeweller probably has overheads that would make you wince. Huge payrolls, high rents due to the large amount of space his premises occupy, and the need for High Street shops, heavy capital outlay to cover the cost of buying enough jewellery to stock all the shops, etc., more than likely cancel out what the large jeweller saves by clever bulk buying. When all is said and done, jewellery prices don't vary very much from small shop to big shop. The difference between big and small, as far as you're concerned, lies more in the choice and the advice you're likely to get.

While the subject of big chains is being bandied about, let's take a closer look. These marvellous institutions appear on High Street corners just about as regularly as supermarket and clothing chainstores do. Their glittering, if rather crowded window displays stop passers-by in their tracks, to gaze at the rows and rows of engagement rings and watches while they're waiting for the bus or on the way to do their shopping. We've all done it at one time or another. In a sense, these chain shops are appropriately placed, because they're rather like supermarkets in themselves. In a jewellery chain shop, the manager will spend most of his or her time managing – not handling the jewellery and dealing with the customers. So they're not as likely to be in touch with the business as is the smaller jewellery shop owner. On the whole, the chain shop's merchandise will be bought in from wholesalers or from manufacturers direct; many of them do not have their own workshops, except perhaps for a centralised repair and oddjob place which services the whole chain's requirements. The obvious advantage of this sort of retail outlet, like any supermarket, is the huge choice you have – loads and loads of different rings, bracelets, watches and so on, all under one roof. But if it's personal service you're after, forget it. How can a supermarket be personal?

Well, before going any further, we extend a sincere apology to all the hard-working, conscientious salespeople who work in large jewellery chain shops. Wherever you are. You do a fine job, selling the merchandise that the owner has put in your showcases. Your manager comes out of his office occasionally during the day and has a look at what you're doing. He might even ask how you've got on, as he locks up at half past five. But well-intentioned though you are, how much do you know about jewellery?

Many of the salespeople working in jewellery shops all over the world – small shops, as well as big chains – have no real technical knowledge about what they're selling. In many of the larger jewellery shops in the UK there is merely a short training period, while actually doing the job. Some jewellery organisations don't bother with training at all; you just start work under some supervision from more experienced staff members. The amount of formal training, therefore, is relatively limited in Europe – which is quite surprising when you consider the high calibre of expertise and craftsmanship that goes into the making of jewellery. Here again, the smaller jewellery shop or chain is more concerned about their staff, and because they're small some experienced person can devote plenty of time to teaching the new recruit what jewellery's all about. The big, impersonal shop or chain is going to be so busy most of the time that the young trainee may just have to pick up what knowledge he or she can as they go along.

In the United States, where everyone is far more training conscious, the jewellery business does provide courses for trainees run by its own self-governing body. Any member jeweller can send people from his or her staff (for a fee, of course) to one of any of these short courses that cover the basics of jewellery quite well. That training, coupled with the invaluable experience of actually handling jewellery every working day, can make a jewellery salesperson into someone pretty knowledgeable within a few months.

In the UK, official jewellery bodies try diligently to inject some formal training into the sales side of the business, but with comparatively poor response. Young salespeople can attend film shows and lectures, and even embark upon demanding and complicated correspondence courses. But the majority of the information that salespeople can learn is often far removed from the real-life situation in the jewellery shop; knowing the geological composition of a topaz, for example, can be terribly interesting to the gemologist, but our guess is that customers don't really care. What they want to know is which topaz is the best value, which will suit them, which mounting will show it off to its greatest advantage. And that's the sort of thing that isn't always taught. Although people who have studied and passed exams in gemology and jewellery making are highly respected all over the world, the letters after their name aren't going to impress a customer who's looking for the right gift for Auntie Mary and doesn't want to know the difference between quartz and chrysoberyl.

Getting Off the Beaten Track

Up until now, we've been talking about buying jewellery from bona fide jewellers. To a large extent, what we've said rings true of the other main retail outlets where jewellery is sold, like some department stores where there is a jewellery department. This is quite simply because in that situation, although the big boss is the big boss of a department store and not a jewellery shop, the person who runs the jewellery department in that store will almost certainly be well qualified. Costume jewellery is another ball game, and we talk about that in Chapter Nine. Real jewellery, though, is also sold in gift shops and other arty-crafty places; here it's fairly safe to assume that the people who sell it to you probably won't know too much about it, but then again the jewellery they stock is not likely to be anything but lower-value items. So the answer to that one is, if you like it and you believe that the quality is right, go ahead.

One big problem area is that of second-hand jewellery. There are more myths floating about on this subject than the ancient Greeks could ever have dreamed up; there are also lots of pitfalls.

Let's start with the value aspect. A piece of second-hand jewellery should cost less than the same item new, because you only pay for labour and craftsmanship once – in theory. This holds true when you are selling a piece of your own jewellery to a dealer – but does not necessarily follow when that dealer comes to sell it again. Dealers have to earn their living, just like anybody else. The only advantage on your side, in some cases, is that the dealer buys the piece in at a very low price and, not being aware of the item's true value, sells it for only a small profit. Naturally enough, this is *not* a game we would recommend anyone to play unless they know the rules backwards. The second-hand dealer is far more likely to know what the value is than you are, unless you're a real expert. Your chances of making a killing this way are slim.

Another of the many problems of second-hand jewellery is that old-fashioned settings and old-fashioned cuts of stones are worth very little – if you want to sell them again, that is. A diamond, for example, set in a ring some fifty years ago, will have an outdated cut. In order to bring it up to modern standards the stone would have to be re-cut, which would obviously mean that the stone gets smaller – and less valuable. So the original stone, with its old-fashioned cut, is going to be worth less than a stone with modern cut, even if the two are identical in colour, size and clarity.

Metal, too, can be old-fashioned, and can even get 'tired' and break on you. Metal fatigue is a problem that troubles aeroplane manufacturers and other industries; sadly, precious metals suffer the same defects. Metal that has been worn for years can suddenly just give up the ghost, which can mean that stones drop out of settings, or the piece of jewellery drops off you.

What is good about second-hand jewellery is that you can often find designs, mountings and shapes that you no longer see in the shops that sell only new jewellery. If you're buying purely for yourself, there's nothing wrong with an old-fashioned cut for a stone, as long as the mounting is safe. The only trouble is that fifty years ago stone cutting techniques were not as advanced as they are today, so stones cut then were not made to look as attractive as they are these days. But if you like it, buy it. After all, if it pleases you that's what really matters.

Getting back to the value stakes, the second-hand jewellery we've been describing is probably in the 40 to 90 years-old bracket. If the jewellery in question is over 100 years old, we're talking about antique, and that's a magic word that sends prices soaring up into the sky. (See Chapter Twelve about that.) For the best value amongst second-hand jewellery, though, you're best to go for pieces that are under ten years old. That way, you're buying jewellery that has more than likely been made in roughly the same way as it is today. And if you can find a dealer who is not entirely aware of the value of what he or she has sitting in the showcase, you can find the most stunning bargains. Really and truly, though, you should be quite knowledgeable about jewellery before you attempt to find bargains like this, because the not-too-expert dealer can turn the tables on you. What is described as good can easily turn out to be not so good, even if everyone has the most honourable of intentions.

Second-hand gold jewellery is different, when there aren't any stones about. Whereas the price of stones is based largely upon expert's opinions, fashion, cut, which way the wind's blowing, and lots of other reasons, gold has a fixed value no-one but prime ministers and presidents can argue about. The price of gold, in other words what it's worth, will appear every day in the more financially-orientated newspapers. Mind you, to work out how much a 9 carat gold bracelet, weighting six ounces, is worth is not as easy as just doing an addition or two on the back of an envelope. However, it is possible, and if you're determined, you can do it! Let's take, for the sake of argument, a bracelet in 18 carat gold. That means only 75% of it is pure gold, and the rest is an alloy (see Chapter Five). Weigh the bracelet – or ask the dealer to do it – and note down the total. Supposing it weighs 8 ounces in all; that's 6 ounces of pure gold. Now, earlier that same day you've looked up your financial daily paper and found out that pure gold is worth £100 per ounce. Consequently, the bracelet you're holding is worth £600, in terms of pure gold value. Give or take the odd hundred pounds depending on how elaborately the gold is worked, you should allow roughly a 100% mark up, bringing the grand total to £1200 – which is the price you would probably pay for that bracelet new. Yes, there *is* about 100% mark up on jewellery; but think of all the work that's gone into it.

If you're in a second-hand shop, though, you shouldn't expect to pay the new, retail price for the bracelet. Let's just say that if the asking price is £1000, it's fair, and if it's less than £800, you're doing well. If the price is £600 or less, you're on to a winner.

Pawn shops are another source of jewellery, which often arrives there for very sad reasons. However, a pawn broker who has bought in a £1000 piece of jewellery for £100 is perhaps only going to be looking for a profit of 100% or so, so you may be in luck. This is probably the riskiest of all ways to buy jewellery, though; be sure you know what you're doing, otherwise your money could be wasted. There's no way of knowing whether or not the pawn broker is an expert on jewellery, and therefore whether or not he or she is likely to misjudge a value in your favour, unless *you* are an expert and can evaluate the jewellery yourself.

The same story applies to antique shops, which are another source of jewellery. Naturally enough, you're likely to get into the realms of antique jewellery, which has a rather different set of values than those of contemporary stuff.

Antique dealers on the whole tend to be good historians, as you can imagine, so although they may not know too much about the technicalities of making jewellery, they're pretty sure to know about the historical value of the piece. The only time when you might be lucky and get a bargain is if the dealer specialises in small pieces of antiques, like silver snuff boxes, perfume bottles and the like. Many antique dealers buy their stock at auction sales, and a 'lot' at such a sale – one that would interest the dealer in small objets d'art – might include the odd piece of jewellery along with the boxes and bottles. If this were so, then the dealer might well sell off the jewellery at reasonable prices, concentrating his or her more profit-making attentions on the objets d'art.

Auctions, while we're on the subject, are often involved in selling jewellery. In fact, some of the biggest auction businesses, like Sotheby's and Christie's in the UK, have special jewellery departments where you can obtain valuations and opinions. Naturally enough, auctions are places where vendors hope to get the highest possible price for their goods, so these are hardly the places to go for bargains. Again, you might be lucky; it takes perseverance and knowledge. But if you know that a beautiful, valuable piece of jewellery is going up for auction, you can be sure that quite a few others will know about it too. And you may find yourself bidding against very wealthy dealers and individuals who don't care how much they pay as long as they get the item in the end. The moral on this is, auctions can be fun. As long as you're rich.

Duty free shops in foreign airports and ports sell jewellery from time to time. Bear in mind that, whereas they might mark their jewellery as 'duty free', the items won't be 'profit free', and many such duty free dealers work on a swings and roundabouts principle. What they lose on the duty free they make up for on the profit. And anyway, the jewellery you buy from such a place is only duty free until you arrive home, in most countries. There is normally duty to pay on any goods you bring in over a certain value. You should check beforehand how much you're allowed to bring in, and the amount of duty you'll be expected to pay. Obviously, not declaring any goods over and above the value of what you're allowed is an offence. And the law is strictly enforced; so perhaps the answer is to stay away from 'duty free' jewellery in shops, and spend a few hours on your next holiday looking for fun bits of jewellery in local markets. At least the duty on top of what you pay for that might still mean your purchase is a bargain. If you do buy jewellery abroad, be sure to keep a receipt, as your home Customs people may want to see it.

Mail order is an increasingly popular way of buying anything, from kaftans to barbeques. And that includes jewellery, much of which is of good quality and is sold at a fair price. But there is a problem here, and that is quite simply that you can't *see* what you're buying. It is a known fact amongst photographers that jewellery is one of the most difficult things to photograph, because it is extremely hard to light – especially to get the right colour reproduction. If you're going to spend quite a significant sum of money, you're far better off going to a good jeweller and seeing the jewellery in the flesh – feeling it, trying it on, and making sure you're spending your money wisely. Admittedly, mail order laws in the UK are such that a refund on goods you're not satisfied with is usually possible, but all the same, sending merchandise back and forth is a bore. You're better off sticking to the 'try before you buy' principle.

Private individuals will sometimes offer you jewellery for sale. Like we said earlier, the types who do this are often cowboys selling jewellery down at the pub, and anyone who asks where they got it from is answered in a gruff voice and with a black look. This sort of marketplace is best avoided, because at the worst you'll be buying stolen goods, and at best you'll be buying something without having the faintest idea of whether it is worth the money or not. You've also got no comeback – and no consumer protection to speak of.

Your Guarantees of Satisfaction

In many countries nowadays the consumer is quite well protected by law against unscrupulous selling. In the UK, the Sale of Goods Act applies to jewellery as well as it applies to anything else, and states something along the lines of 'goods must be of merchantable quality'. In other words, if you buy a piece of jewellery that falls apart two days later through no fault of your own, you've got a good chance of getting your money back, or at least a replacement. Similarly, the Trades Descriptions Act has made sure that no legitimate jeweller will try to sell you a synthetic stone as a real stone, or any other of the tricks that were sometimes practised in the past by naughty members of the jewellery business. Some jewellers also give guarantees with the items they sell, sometimes even promising to buy back the item for the same amount of money after a specified period. These guarantees are a nice gesture, but basically they do not alter your rights at law very much. However, don't worry; the law tends to be on the side of the consumer in many cases, so any genuine complaint that arises should be properly dealt with as long as the jeweller concerned is a reputable one.

Apart from the law, there are some other safeguards you can abide by, if you want to be sure of getting fair treatment. To start with, if you want to buy a good stone, try to buy it from someone who is a Fellow of the Gemological Association, or of some equivalent body. That way, you're sure that the person who sells you your jewellery is an expert, a real one, and is going to make sure you pay a fair price, as well as making sure you know what that jewellery is like; whether the stone has a flaw, what size it is, and so on.

Also, make a little survey of jewellers before you buy anything. If you find a jeweller who appears to be selling his stock at prices far lower than anyone else, start sniffing for the rat. There's no such thing as being able to sell jewellery at cut prices, because fair mark-ups are always present. In the majority of cases, cut-price jewellery is either phoney, stolen or sub-standard. Beware, too, of certain jewellers and jewellery 'districts' where vast discounts are offered; it's easy enough to offer a 40% discount off retail prices when the retail prices were 100% higher than they should be to begin with! Your best bet is to avoid the cut-price merchants, the non-expert retail outlets, and everything else that isn't a good, qualified, reliable jeweller, until such time as your knowledge is sufficient to help you judge what's good and what isn't. And unless you're going to spend a lot of money and time buying lots of jewellery, it isn't worth taking chances. For the few pieces of jewellery most people buy in their lifetime, the most important things are quality and good value. The safest way to find those is to go to the conservative sources; being adventurous can result in dismal failures. Which way you go depends on whether or not you're a gambler! But can anyone really afford to gamble with something as costly, precious and important as jewellery?

CHAPTER FIVE

Precious Metals and Mountings – Animal, Vegetable or Mineral?

Gold: Does It Glister or Blister?

Gold has been around for the longest time of all the precious metals. Throughout history, gold keeps on cropping up here and there, always as an important commodity. Either as the prize for some swashbuckling pirates on the high seas, or as a form of currency, or whatever. In fact, gold coins are still a form of currency in many places, albeit in a somewhat cosmetic form; imagine the surprise you could create by offering to pay your gas bill with gold sovereigns! In the old days, though, gold coins were just about the only type of material that was considered precious enough to keep its value, and therefore be used as currency. All the stories you hear about 'pieces of eight' and other such folklore were all connected with gold.

As you can imagine, the very fact that gold was valuable gave rise not only to piracy and other naughty escapades, but at attempts to make it – as against digging it out of the ground in the usual way. This was particularly true soon after the Romans had swanked their way into obscurity, because they used so much that existing supplies virtually ran out. In fact, it took something like eight centuries before anyone actually started mining gold in a big way once again. So, the alchemists of the western world began to look around for ways of making gold out of other metals, as well as anything from eggs to horse manure. Others realised that gold was gold, and couldn't be artificially produced, but figured they were on to a good thing anyway and came up with various fakes. The people of the Middle Ages were not quite so suspicious and worldly-minded as we are today, and were often taken in by clever tricksters who persuaded them that it was possible to increase their own gold. One or two cases have been reported of tricksters promising to double people's gold money, as long as the victim handed over the goods for a while. Usually, that was just about long enough for the trickster to disappear into the mists with the loot; the original medieval con-man.

The only good thing that came out of these alchemists' efforts to make gold was that, although gold could never be made, other things could. Many new and important discoveries were made, some by accident, that led to far greater things, many of which benefited the population in other ways. But nobody could get anywhere near real gold; it seems unlikely that anybody ever will. That's one of the reasons why gold is so precious.

Along with all the other uses for gold, jewellery must rate as one of the most popular. And that's true all the way along the line, almost since the days when our old friend the caveman began to stick sharp bits of bone in his furs to hold them in place. Gold was found pretty early on, and even some of the earliest human civilisations are known to have made jewellery out of gold. There's a good reason for this, too; never mind the fact that gold has always been precious, it is also the most suitable of all metals. It is pleasant to wear because it doesn't harm your skin, and it has the right consistency and colour to be made into jewellery that enhances precious stones – plus the fact that it enhances your looks, too.

Although gold is found in relative abundance only in certain parts of the world, you can actually find minute quantities of it in almost any kind of rock, in the sea, in inland waterways, lakes, in sand, and even – believe it or not – in some plants. No-one is too sure about where gold starts out from, but the general belief is that it works its way up from very deep down in the earth's crust.

Several centuries ago, the vast majority of gold that was used for jewellery came from Asia Minor and Egypt. Later, gold was also mined in Spain; and when the Spaniards took to their boats and ultimately settled in South America, they struck gold there, too. Nowadays, though, the country that yields the most gold is South Africa – which also happens to be the home of the world's most significant source of diamonds. Lucky South Africans. The second largest producer of gold is the USSR. But don't imagine that these countries produce gold by the megaton; the total harvest of gold in the world so far only adds up to less than 89,000 metric tonnes.

For those of you who are practically-minded and are interested to know how the gold in your jewellery first saw the light of day, here's a brief resumé. There are basically two kinds of gold deposits. Veins or seams of gold that are worth digging up are usually found in volcanic rock, which more often than not is underground. The other type of gold deposits are 'alluvial', which means that they have either been washed up or 'spat out' by one of the normal geological processes on to the surface. This second type of gold deposit happens when the volcanic rock eventually disintegrates and works its way up to ground level. Have you ever noticed how, when your garden is dug up, you'll often get quite a collection of things appearing on the surface that you've never seen before? Well, this is nature's way of refining the earth, by spewing out the lumps and bumps. It's all connected with gravity and other scientific procedures which don't really have much bearing on jewellery; but in the early days, gold nuggets were spewed out of the earth's surface just like the rocks and old tin cans you find in your vegetable garden.

This fact did not go unnoticed. Early gold prospectors had eyes like X-ray machines, and could spot a gold nugget lying in a river, in a lake, or just lurking about on the ground, with the greatest of ease. But our gold nugget collectors of the good old days neatly cleaned up most of what there was, and today we've had to go underground for our gold supply. Sadly, the era of finding gold nuggets at your feet is well and truly over, apart from in the history books and some old folk songs.

Modern-day gold mining is no romantic, instant-richness matter; it is difficult and very demanding work. It involves the hewing of gold seams, with or without the rock that surrounds them, out of the ground – with all the complications and unpleasant conditions that any kind of mining brings to mind. Once you've got your bits of rocks containing gold up on to the surface, you grind the whole lot up into tiny pebbles and dunk them into a chemical solution. Then, after quite a few more complicated heating and cooling processes, the chemicals sort out the men from the boys and pure gold results. Although perhaps rather flippantly described, this amounts to founding, a process which most metals – including iron, brass, and all the rest – go through. It represents one of the principal parts of today's modern heavy industry.

But pure gold has a problem, precious though it is. For a start, it isn't the bright, vivid gold colour that the prospectors set out to find. It is rather paler. Secondly, pure gold – as described by the Bank of England, which is actually 999 parts of pure gold out of a thousand plus one part of colouring to correct the natural shade – is far too soft a metal to use in jewellery. It would bend and get scratched; go dull and get dented. So gold is normally alloyed with one or more other metals, to give it the extra strength that it needs. Alloying has another advantage, too; depending on the nature of the other metal involved, it changes the colour of the gold. So you get gold that has a red tinge, a yellow tinge, a greenish tinge and, of course, white old.

Alloying basically takes place at the foundry, and in layperson's terms involves melting the two metals together and then cooling them, so they are all nicely blended into one. The metals used for alloying with gold tend to have similar melting points. This helps out both at the foundry, and also when the gold is worked, so you don't get parts of the metal doing different things when you're actually making a ring or whatever. White gold, by far the most common colour after the near-original shade of yellow, is normally gold alloyed with silver. Sometimes nickel is put in with it, too. White gold has been popular for centuries; the Greeks were really the first to start off the fashion, funnily enough. They called it electrum, and used it in quite a lot of their jewellery and precious objets d'art.

Brass and copper are also popular metals for alloying with gold. The resultant yellow or red tinges that appear in the finished product are very distinctive. They also give rise to all sorts of other connotations in some countries; often there is some kind of social stigma attached to one particular colour of gold rather than another. Obviously, to say that one colour of gold is 'better' than another is an absolute fallacy; however, some colours go better with various stones than others. White gold is usually considered the best colour to be set with diamonds, for example, with the actual stones set into a white gold 'head' and the rest of the item often set in another colour of gold. The whiteness of the metal enhances the brilliance of the stone rather better than, say, red gold, because in that case the red could take away some of the attention from the white stone. Personal preference is the only question that really matters at the end of the day. In fact, some people like all three basic gold colours, and mix them up together in, for example, the 'Russian' wedding ring – three plain, intertwined bands, each of a different colour of gold.

Alloying other metals with gold, then, is a way of making the metal stronger. But you're not left with pure gold – you have a mixture. And how do you know just how much of your piece of gold jewellery is gold, and how much is another metal? The answer is in carats. Carats are the form of measurement used to determine just that question. Pure gold is taken to be 24 carats; that figure comes from the old English system where things tended to be measured in dozens, like pence to the shilling and dozens of eggs.

But for reasons stated earlier, no-one in their right mind who leads a normal, active life, would entertain the idea of wearing jewellery made from 24 carat gold. So there are happy mediums. In the UK, the popular carat weights for gold are 22, 18 and 9. Twenty-two carat gold is lovely if you never get your hands dirty and don't move about a great deal, but it is very soft and scratches terribly. Eighteen carat gold is the best compromise, as far as value is concerned. It still contains plenty of gold – 75% – but has enough other, tougher metal to keep it from looking dull and ugly. Nonetheless, it does scratch up to a point, so it's best left for setting with stones, where the gold does not get as much wear. For a large, chunky bracelet, for example, 18 carat gold would not keep its looks too well. Not to mention the fact that, when you're talking about such a large amount of gold as there is in a heavy bracelet, there is a hefty price difference between 18 carat and 9 carat. In small items, like rings, the price difference is not really big enough to worry you too much. Most good stone-set rings are made from 18 carat gold, particularly where a precious stone is involved. Nine carat contains the least amount of gold – only just over one third – but it's the toughest of the lot. As long as the alloying has been well done, 9 carat gold can look as rich and lustrous as 18 carat. If you're very active, and the piece of jewellery in question is of the type that's likely to get bashed around a bit over the years, then go for 9 carat every time. It keeps its shine and good looks for far longer.

Other countries have different ways of describing gold measurements. The Americans started a method whereby pure gold is taken to be 1000 parts, and jewellery is marked with the relevant parts out of a thousand instead of so many carats. Eighteen carat gold, then, is marked as 750 : 9 carat as 375. These figures normally appear on some less visible part of a piece of jewellery, as part of the hallmarks. But more about those later.

The advantage of the American system, whereby carat weights are replaced by parts of a thousand, is largely a question of accuracy. Measuring gold in the American way means you'll get absolutely what it says it is, within a few minute particles. The carat system tends to be less accurate, although the customer is always the winner in most countries, as the people who determine the carat weight of the gold will stamp it according to the nearest carat weight *lower* than the true carat weight. In other words, if you buy a ring in the UK that says 9 carat on the inside, the truth of the matter might well be that the ring is actually 10 or 11 carat gold. In this country, you'll never get an officially marked piece of gold that's of a lower caratage than 9. Modern jewellery in the UK is normally marked with the American system, but older jewellery will have the carat marks, so it helps to know what both systems mean.

Twenty-two, 18, 14 and 9 carat (or the parts of a thousand equivalents) are not the only weights of gold you'll see around. Although these four are the most usual in British jewellery, other countries have other preferences. In continental Europe you'll find 8 carat as well as 9. Some countries also sell 20 and 24 carat jewellery. Fourteen carat is a lovely compromise, actually; it is just over 50% gold, so has value and preciousness more like that of 18 carat gold, but it also has more of the strength you get with 9 carat.

From an Ugly Lump into Beautiful Jewellery

Now we've found the gold, dug it up, founded it, alloyed it with another metal and made it into an ungainly-looking lump, we come to the point where we actually make it into jewellery. There are a variety of ways of doing this. Because gold is such a friendly metal, it lends itself to being worked in whichever way suits the people involved. Basically, there are three ways of making gold jewellery; by hand, by stamping it out of a larger lump, and by melting it down and pouring it into moulds.

Let's start with the hand-made work. The most interesting of hand-made jewellery items are rings, chains and other small intricate pieces; most of these start with what the trade calls gold wire. This can either be bought ready made, or the goldsmith can actually make it him- or herself by feeding the basic lump through a hand-operated machine that's rather like the old-fashioned wringers you used to see on the top of washing machines. This machine has various grooves on it, each of a different size, so you just feed the gold through the right slot and bingo – you have gold wire. Other precious metals can be made into wire this way, and be used for making jewellery. But sticking with gold for the time being, a collection of different-sized bits of gold wire, hand soldered together, can result in the entire setting for, say, a diamond ring. Gold is such a flexible and handy metal that it is possible to make a piece of wire in this way up to 50 miles long, from just one ounce of gold. OK, it will be pretty thin wire, but it just shows you how workable gold is.

A craftperson's time is worth a lot of money in modern times, and if all jewellery were made by hand, prices would be an awful lot higher than they are. The machine age has its part to play in jewellery, and much of the stuff you see in jewellery shops has been machine-made in one way or another. As a general rule, the very expensive designer-made jewellery is done by hand, rather like haute couture clothes. But, just like there are very few of us around who can afford to dress ourselves in Christian Dior originals all the time, there aren't many people who can afford these pricey, hand-made, one-off jewellery creations.

The question of quality rears its ugly head here. Is it true to say that machine-made jewellery may not be as well put together as hand-made items? A lot of jewellers of the old, traditional school will tell you that this is true. Similarly, an haute couture designer will tell you that you should never buy a dress or a suit of clothes off the peg, because it will fall to bits. The truth lies in modern technology; when mass manufacturing first began, quality did suffer enormously. But the fact that a lot of progress has been made in the quality control of manufacturing means that most mass-produced goods – cars, clothes, jewellery – are of reasonable quality, certainly good enough to stand up to average wear and tear. Jewellery is fortunate, too, in that it doesn't suffer from that nasty factor of planned obsolescence, unlike cars and clothes. Manufacturers may want your coat or your motor car to wear out so you'll eventually buy a new one from them. But no-one is going to trade in their engagement ring against a new model every five years, and the jewellery manufacturers know that only too well.

In the jewellery trade, then, there is a certain amount of nit-picking and back-biting over the question of machine-made items. If a ring breaks while it's being sized (altered to a different size), the crafts-person in question may blame the breakage on the fact that the ring was badly made. It may be true, it may not. Breakages happen. Certainly, there is no way of telling in which way a piece of metal jewellery has been made – not unless you're an expert. And to the likes of us, it frankly doesn't matter – as long as we're satisfied that the quality of the item is good enough for us.

So while we're about it, let's look at machine-made gold (and other metal) jewellery, and how it's actually processed. The favourite amongst the manufacturers is casting; this is as it sounds, in other words heating up the gold until it melts and then pouring it into a mould. The disadvantage is that air bubbles can creep into the mixture, and once the gold hardens again – when it cools – these bubbles can cause weak spots which will eventually cause the gold to snap. The problem is overcome by using centrifugal force, swirling the melted gold round and round at incredibly high speeds so that any air bubbles are squeezed out.

Most of the countries that produce cast jewellery in large amounts use this centrifugal force technique, which results in finished items that are as strong, if not stronger, than the hand-made equivalent. However, one or two countries in Europe have acquired a reputation for poor quality in casting, and jewellery coming from these places is not always of as high a quality as it should be. Jewellery casting is being constantly up-dated, though; machinery is becoming more and more sophisticated and those countries which have bad reputations are gradually improving their standards.

Another way of making jewellery is by stamping it out of a large, flattened lump of gold. This can be done by hand, with the jewellery manufacturer whacking a kind of biscuit-cutter tool with a mallet, or it can be done by machine. The disadvantage with this method is rather like the problems you'll get when you're cutting biscuits out of dough; you've got to be careful not to flatten the dough out too much, otherwise your biscuits are going to be rather thin. The same applies to jewellery. If the items being stamped out are ring mounts, for example, the gold may well have been stretched too far, in order to get as many ring mounts as possible out of the original piece of gold. Metal can suffer from stress, and if gold is stretched and pulled about too much it won't be very strong. However, once again quality control is improving every day, so the problems of stamped jewellery are being reduced as technology progresses.

The working of gold in jewellery can be much improved by the right combination of heat and cold, when the gold is actually being made into the finished item. If gold is heated and then cooled slowly, it will be much softer than if it is cooled fast. A good goldsmith, when making a ring mount or whatever, will first of all heat the item up and then let it cool naturally, so he can work it as easily as possible. But before he considers the item finished, he'll heat it up once again, and then chuck it into cold water so that it cools very quickly. This will mean that the finished product is far tougher, and far less likely to scratch and go dull. The only slight disadvantage is that, once the gold becomes this rigid, it is a bit more brittle; a piece of jewellery made like this should not have its size changed or be altered in any way because its brittleness may cause it to break. Jewellery items with stones in them are seldom finished off in this way, though, because if you heat the whole lot up enough for the gold to melt, you might just crack the stone as well.

Fancy it Fancy?

Up until now, we've assumed that the gold we're working with is just the plain, bright gold we know so well. But gold can be finished with different sorts of surfaces, and can have all sorts of fancy work done on it. Again, because it is such an obliging material, it will quite happily lend itself to all kinds of techniques.

For a start, you can press the devil out of it until it's so thin it's like a piece of airmail paper. This is what happens when you're making gold leaf – which isn't jewellery, but is used for gilding priceless antique picture frames, mirrors and so on. These incredibly thin layers of gold are stuck on, one overlapping the other, until a rich sheen is evenly applied all over the surface of the item. Gold leaf work is highly specialised, and to be able to do it properly takes quite a long apprenticeship. Naturally, this process is expensive and is normally reserved for very valuable items. For the less pricey, gold paint is fine.

Another thing you can do to gold is to emboss it; stamp out designs in relief. You can either do this by hammering the design on to the gold, or by applying steady pressure with the gold pressed on to a pre-made form. Because gold is so easy to work, it tolerates the strain of things being stamped on it with little risk of breakage, although a heavy-handed embosser could make mistakes!

Filigree work is another very popular way of working gold (and silver), especially in countries like Spain and Portugal where the art has been truly perfected. The gold is made first of all into metres and metres of terribly fine wire, and then criss-crossed, plaited and otherwise fiddled with into the really stunning, delicate network of gold lines that filigree is. Once all the little wires are in place, they are usually soldered on to a piece of base gold to hold the whole thing together.

Granulated gold has been around for a surprisingly long time, considering the complexity of its making. The ancient Etruscans were dab hands at this, and they were making it many hundreds of years ago. It looks like lots of tiny specks of powdered gold stuck onto a solid base, which is pretty well what it is. In the past, granulated gold was sometimes made by pouring the molten stuff from a height of about half a metre or so onto marble, or some other cold stone, so it would fall down in droplets like rain and, being cooled quickly on the stone, would harden into tiny granules. Another well-known way was to mix small pieces of gold together with powdered charcoal, heat the whole lot up to the melting point of gold, and cool it down again. By this time the gold separated into granules by the interaction with the charcoal. Either way, the finished granules were then carefully soldered on to a plain gold base.

Other, less intricate methods of decorating the surface of gold are done with a variety of tools like knives, files, and even a type of fine sandpaper. Matt gold is rubbed over with this sandpaper very carefully, first in one direction and then at right angles, to give an even, dull finish. The Americans are particularly fond of 'antique finish' gold, which is actually done by applying a chemical solution to the metal.

Engraving is usually done by hand, either with hand-held knives or 'guns', or with a machine that's carefully supervised by a craftsperson. Engraving of metal is an art in itself and learning to do it takes a long while; mistakes can be expensive, as you're actually cutting away tiny bits of gold which are difficult to smooth over or replace if an error occurs.

Hallmarking rules – OK

Most countries around the world now have an official, legal hallmarking system which applies to gold and silver. In the UK, all gold jewellery is marked at an Assay Office (there are three in England, and there's one in Scotland) controlled by the Ministry of Defence. If you look inside a ring, or on any convenient bit of plain gold on another item, you'll see all sorts of strange hieroglyphics. These marks are not as complicated as they seem, and since 1975 the marks have been simplified so you shouldn't have too much trouble reading them. Gold jewellery, British-made and hallmarked before 1975, will have more marks on it, as the American system of measuring gold purity in parts of a thousand was only just being introduced. In most cases, both the carat content and the American symbols are used. Also, British gold jewellery marked pre-1975 will have different 'standard' marks; a thistle and thorns if the piece was marked in Scotland, and a crown if marked in England. From 1975 onwards, though, all British-made gold jewellery has a crown, wherever it was marked, plus the American system of gold measurement only; 916 (22 carat), 750 (18 carat), 585 (14 carat) or 375 (9 carat).

Imported jewellery is marked in a similar way, except there are no crowns or thistles used. (See chart, page 76, for exact details.)

The other marks you'll see on your gold jewellery are usually representing the town in which the hallmarking took place, and the date (which is represented by a different letter for each year – very complicated to decipher unless you work in the Assay Office!)

Foreign jewellery that you see abroad will have different hieroglyphics on it, but will often have either the British or American carat content stamp on it somewhere, so that you know of what purity the gold is. Sometimes, the gold is marked on the outside, or right side up, of the piece – rather ugly, in the case of a plain ring. This is particularly true in France and Holland, as they mark their own gold jewellery on the inside, and imported jewellery on the outside.

Another mark you'll sometimes see on a piece of gold jewellery is a few initials. This usually means that the jeweller concerned has put his or her own stamp on the piece as well, rather like an artist signs a painting. The initials will be those of the jeweller; this is done on silver as well as on gold.

Of course, a lot of gold jewellery you see has no hallmarking on it at all. On the whole, it's a good idea to be a little suspicious if a piece of jewellery is offered to you and you can't find a hallmark, although the absence of hallmarks does not necessarily mean that the item is not gold. What it can mean is that the jewellery has been imported but hasn't been to the Assay Office for hallmarking. Even if the item is gold, it shouldn't be sold to you as gold. There is a ruling in the UK that gold jewellery may be sold to the public without hallmarks, as long as the item is not *called* gold. Some people actually do sell British-made gold jewellery in this way, because of the red tape and sometimes long periods of time involved in getting gold hallmarked. If you find yourself faced with this, the person selling the item to you should say something along the lines of 'this is not gold, but in some countries one would say that it is real gold. . . .' That is all he or she is allowed, by law, to do. You might well buy yourself a bargain this way, but, of course, you've got no guarantee of what carat content the item has, or even if it is real gold or not. If it is a second-hand item, that's a bit worn, like in the case of the shank of a ring, take it into a strong light. If it is gold plate, some of the plating will probably have been worn away somewhere, and you might see another coloured metal showing through. As a rule, though, buying jewellery this way is dubious. Bearing in mind that nearly all countries now have official, legal hallmarking procedures for their own and imported gold jewellery, you're better off sticking to hallmarked pieces.

Beware, too, of the odd-looking hallmarks, ones which look crude and badly done, and also hallmarks where one stamp looks far clearer than the others. If you're buying a piece of jewellery abroad, it may be that their own hallmarking system is not quite so sophisticatedly equipped as it should be. But if you're offered a piece of jewellery in the UK with doubtful hallmarks, and the vendor assures you that it's gold, think twice. And don't be palmed off with remarks that the hallmarks look funny because they're foreign. Even if the piece is imported, if it's being sold to you as gold it should have been to the Assay Office and will have British marks on it as well. Those marks won't look crude. So the funny looking marks are either fake, in which case the jewellery is illegal, or else it is imported jewellery, in which case it shouldn't be sold to you as gold. Either way, your money is at risk.

Silver: Gold's Poor Relation?

You'll see that we haven't written anywhere nearly as much about silver as we have about gold, largely because, when it comes to silver jewellery, much of that is made using precisely the same methods as those used for making gold jewellery.

Stamping, casting and hand-made pieces are all handled in roughly the same way. But silver has a name these days for being an 'also ran' compared with gold and platinum. The obvious reason for this is that silver is cheaper than gold and therefore tends to get relegated to use with semi-precious or imitation stones in less expensive jewellery. There are other reasons, though; more practical ones. Silver is softer

STANDARD HALLMARKS AS USED IN BRITAIN

Prior to 1975	Standard	From 1975
	22 carat gold Marked in England Marked in Scotland	
	18 carat gold Marked in England Marked in Scotland	
	14 carat gold	
	9 carat gold	
	Sterling silver Marked in England Marked in Scotland	
	Britannia silver	
—	Platinum	

These marks just tell you whether a piece was made in Britain or elsewhere, and in the case of gold, how pure it is. If you'd like to study the other marks that are made (i.e. the various different Assay Office marks – in which town a piece was marked – and date symbols) there are several books and leaflets available which should explain it all! Your nearest Assay Office will advise you on the best ones.

than gold, and even when it is alloyed with a small amount of another metal (more often than not, copper) it still scratches, dents, and goes dull very easily. The other problem – one which anyone who owns a piece of silver or silver plate and lives in a city will know only too well – is that silver tarnishes. It requires regular cleaning to keep it as bright as possible – at least with gold, or platinum, this need does not arise.

Mind you, silver hasn't always been seen as such a poor relation of gold. Before anyone had got around to digging platinum and its related metals out of the ground in commercially viable terms, silver was widely used in the setting of precious stones – especially diamonds, as the warm white colour of the metal was ideal. White gold, although it was around as early as ancient Greek days, was not produced in quantity, and at times during the course of history yellow gold wasn't around in large quantities, either. So silver was extremely popular, even as recently as the nineteenth century, for fine jewellery. A great many pieces of the antique jewellery you'll see in shops may well be set in silver, featuring diamonds, rubies, sapphires, emeralds and the other stones which in modern times would almost certainly be set in gold or platinum.

Silver comes out of the ground in virtually the same way as gold does. It is mined, then founded. In the Middle Ages a lot of silver was mined in central Europe and in Spain. These areas produced huge quantities of silver – it would seem there's a lot more of it in the ground than there is gold! As Europeans began to travel across the Atlantic, large amounts of silver were found in North America, which increased the world supply considerably. The greatest source, though, transpired in Mexico. And today, this country still supplies the world with more silver than any other nation does.

In some countries, especially in southern Europe, extremely fine silver wire is used for filigree work. Jewellery made in this way can be relatively inexpensive, and every bit as beautiful as gold filigree, largely because the same techniques are used whatever the metal. Silver filigree jewellery is a worthwhile souvenir, if you happen to be on holiday in Spain or Portugal.

Another advantage of silver's lower cost is that it is a more economical proposition to experiment with. Consequently, it is used quite widely by small businesses in jewellery design, which can produce some very interesting and original-looking pieces. Jewellery designers will often hesitate to create an especially exotic piece out of gold, but will try it out on silver as any mistakes will not cost as much – and can be rectified more easily. So look out for these pieces in your local art and craft shops – they can be good buys.

Recognising silver as against silver plate – or, for that matter, platinum or white gold – is a relatively simple matter. First of all, look for hallmarks; that's the way to tell if the piece is plate or not. If it is plate, it may well have some marks on it, but these will usually be maker's initials and then some more letters. If you see the letters EPNS, this means that the piece is plate – electro-plated nickel silver, in fact. The chances of jewellery being made from EPNS are slim. This process is used more for cutlery, tableware and other large pieces. Because the amount of silver needed in a piece of jewellery is relatively small, most manufacturers can afford to make it out of solid silver, and still sell it at a reasonable price. Solid silver, or sterling, must go to an Assay Office and be hallmarked, just like gold. The thing to watch out for in silver hallmarks is the lion symbol. Since 1975, both English and Scottish silver have used this beast as a symbol for purity. The English lion is walking along and the Scottish one is standing on his hind legs. Before 1975, the English symbol was the same, but the Scots used a thistle and thorn design. Elsewhere, you might find the word 'sterling' actually stamped out somewhere on the piece; the Americans are fond of that way of describing pure silver. On a British-made piece, you'll see other marks as well, which will be stating the town in which the piece was marked, and the date. These are quite interesting, but we'd need about half this book in order to explain them all! If you are interested in silver hallmarks, there are books on the market which you can buy giving you an explicit run-down on what every mark means, stretching back over a period of several centuries. Imported silver won't have any lions or thistles on it, but will show the numbers '925' if it is sterling. If an item of British silver is extremely pure, it is marked as 'Britannia' silver, and will show a symbol of Britannia herself, rather like her colleague that's printed on one corner of paper money. Imported silver of this quality has '9584' (pre-1975) or '958' on it.

To tell silver from the other white metals used in jewellery you'll need a strong light. You'll also need to find a part on the piece you're examining that isn't too worn; very badly worn white gold can look almost identical to a piece of silver in a similar condition. What you need to look for is the colour of the metal; silver is a warm, almost yellowish white, whereas white gold will have a deeper, slightly greyer hue. Platinum is a clear, cold white. Also, even if the pieces are all brand new, you'll find that silver doesn't shine as much as the others do.

Platinum: A Rare Bird?

Platinum is becoming quite popular nowadays as a precious metal, but has only been around in the jewellery business for a very short while, if you compare it with the long histories of gold and silver. It wasn't until the early part of the twentieth century that platinum and its related metals were dug out of the ground in suitable quantities to make jewellery; and even now, it takes something like ten tons of crude ore – which involves rather a lot of mining – to produce just one ounce of platinum. In the 1920's quite a lot of it was discovered lying in the ground in Ontario, Canada, in the vast nickel-copper deposits that exist there. This really started the jewellery boom for platinum, although it had been used very occasionally in the past. Platinum has quite a few members in its family, and for the geologically-minded, here they are: palladium (also used in jewellery), rhodium, iridium, osmium and ruthenium. A fascinating collection of names! One great thing about platinum is that it goes beautifully with diamonds, and this is the area in which it is probably used the most. Its bright, almost blue-white colour sets off these stones really well; even plain platinum jewellery has a quality all of its own. The problem with this metal – another thing that contributes to its expense, as it is possibly the most expensive precious metal of all used in jewellery – is that it has a very high melting point. Now gold and silver obligingly turn into a molten mess at a reasonable degree, which means they can be both cast or worked with oxygen torches in fairly friendly circumstances. But platinum, on the other hand, remains stubbornly solid until it reaches the incredible temperature of around 1770 degrees Centigrade. Which is pretty hot. So, not only is the cost of the raw material high, but the cost of founding and working goes up, because it takes longer. And these extra costs must be passed on to buyers.

Platinum is very strong and as tough as old boots, and although it does cost more many people feel that the extra outlay is worth it. It looks stunning and will keep its looks for a long time. And although you may think it is tough because it is hard, that isn't so; when it comes to working the metal it is often alloyed with a small amount (up to 5%) of another metal to give it the extra hardness it needs. The metals chosen are normally copper, or else one of platinum's relations, like palladium or rhodium. Like gold, platinum jewellery goes to an Assay Office to be hallmarked. This hallmarking of platinum has been in force in Britain since 1975. It has a special symbol of its own, so look out for it; a cross and an orb, surrounded by a five-sided outline. Imported platinum will just show the numbers '950'.

Palladium: The New Face in Jewellery

As we said earlier, palladium is a close cousin of platinum. Like all the others, it is founded and alloyed to give it the necessary qualities for making into jewellery. But it is much rarer than platinum and more difficult to produce, so unless you've got a lot of money to spend, forget it! In looks, it closely resembles platinum, so that only the trained eye can tell the difference

...and the other precious metals

The only other precious metals as such are the further relations of platinum, which we enumerated above. Out of those, the only one that's faintly connected with jewellery is rhodium. This is very like platinum, except if anything it is even tougher and more brilliant – but it costs plenty. It is often used to give a final polish to a piece of white gold or platinum; rhodium plating is quite common, especially on more expensive pieces like diamond rings. This can also be done to silver, to prevent it from tarnishing – until the plating wears off, that is! If you have a piece of white metal jewellery that you're particularly fond of, rhodium plating might cost a bit but it's well worth doing. It will give that piece of jewellery a new lease of life. Your local jeweller will be able to advise on where and how to get this done.

Non-Precious Metals and Materials: Whatever Next?

Here the list is still growing, and the possibilities are endless. Anything like plastic, leather, glass, ribbon, plus some non-precious metals, can be made into jewellery; some of it's hideous and some of it's lovely. The trouble is, it's often very difficult to put a true value on jewellery made from non-precious materials, because although a lot of work may have gone into the making of it, the actual raw materials may be worth very little, which hardly justifies the effort.

Plastic is one of the few non-precious substances which has been elevated to the heights of precious jewellery. In modern designs, the combination of diamonds, gold and perspex have become quite popular. A small diamond, set centrally in a cube of perspex with gold around the edges makes a delightful – and valuable – pendant. Some rings are made entirely of perspex, with a precious stone set inside, appearing to be set in limbo.

Stainless steel is the other well-known non-precious substance, and is very popular for making jewellery – especially in northern Europe, which exports quite a lot to the rest of the world. The advantage of stainless steel is that it is considered inert, a 'non-reactive metal', which isn't likely to argue with your skin secretions and bring you out in a rash, or turn the skin around the piece of jewellery green. The problem with stainless steel is that it has such a high melting point it has to be welded at very high temperatures. This makes it tricky to work with, to say the least, and rather rules out its use with precious stones - as the high temperatures involved could shatter them. Also, it isn't a particularly attractive metal, as it tends to be duller and greyer than silver, white gold or platinum.

Nickel is another metal often used in jewellery, especially that which comes from the Far East. Fortunately, European and American jewellery tends to avoid it, and for good reasons. Nickel, and chrome, can easily start off a nasty allergy if worn next to your skin, and skin allergies like this can take a long time to cure. Of course, even gold can 'cause' a rash, but usually this only happens if you wear, say, a tight, wide wedding band and get soap or moisture trapped between you and the ring. In fact, it is probably the moisture or the soap that causes the rash – not the gold.

Mounting and Dismounting

Mountings in jewellery consist of just about every bit of metal involved, other than plain bands and chains. It's really the metal that holds stones in, or holds jewellery together, that we're talking about here; in principle, these should all be made of a precious metal of some kind. But many of the basics apply to non-precious metals as well, although we hope by now you'll appreciate that non-precious metals are undesirable for anything but a bit of 'fun' jewellery.

Ironically, the prettiest settings and mountings are usually the most vulnerable. That's because the more attractive ones tend to be finer and more delicate, which means that they can break or come adrift easily. Heavy, chunky settings are normally strong, but don't flatter pretty stones anywhere nearly as much. The obvious thing to watch out for in stone settings is that the 'claws', the little prongs that are bent over the stone to hold it in place, don't catch on your clothing or anything else. Quite apart from the damage they can do to you or your clothes, it can also mean that a claw can get caught and bent out of shape – thereby letting a stone fall out. With wear, some settings can work themselves loose, too; a good test is to waggle a piece of stone-set jewellery right by your ear. If you can hear something rattling about, the piece needs to be checked; your jeweller can have a setting strengthened for you for a small cost.

In the old days, stone settings (or mountings; the two words are virtually interchangeable) used to be much lower, much closer in. This was the time when the setting was actually carved out of a solid base, a small hole drilled in the bottom, the stone placed over this, and then the metal edges folded over the stone. On the whole, old-fashioned settings contained more metal than modern ones. And if they were well made, they were very strong. The trouble was that the low, heavy settings of the nineteenth century or so did not allow very much light to get to the stone, which resulted in the stone not being shown off to its greatest advantage. These days, settings are rather higher, letting in plenty of light play. And because the methods of working the metal are better than they were, even high settings can be considered quite strong. Naturally enough, a very high setting can cause its problems, because the stone will stick out and catch on things like gloves and other clothing. These are best avoided.

Old settings can and do wear out. Often, someone who owns a pretty piece of jewellery that's suffering from this problem will think about having the stones remounted. This is a tricky business, and expert advice is essential; for example, the piece concerned could be classed as an antique, which means that the mounting represents a good proportion of the item's value. Re-mounting it would make the value drop. Sometimes wear can be corrected without remounting; in the case of rings where the 'shank', the part that goes around your finger, is worn this is simple. The worn part of the shank is cut out and replaced with new metal. And if you're worried that you might

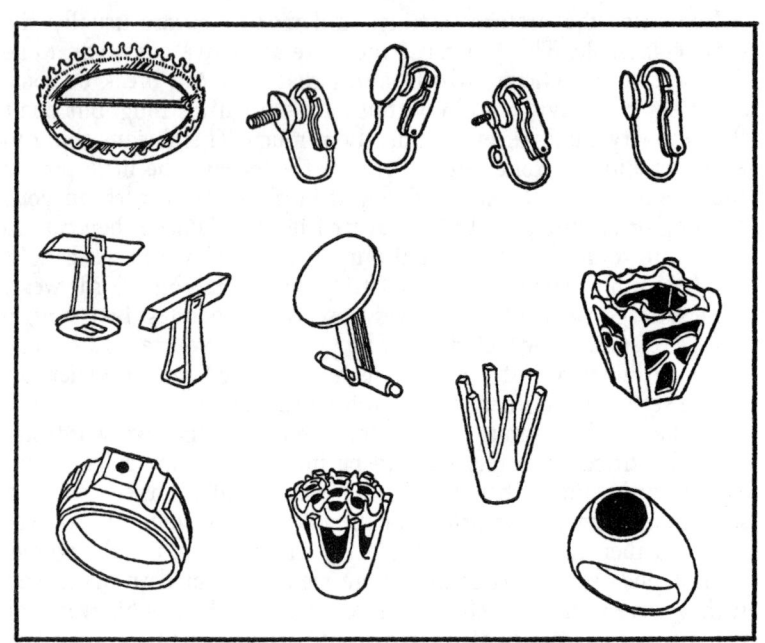

A selection of mountings

lose out when your bit of worn gold is cut out, don't panic. Most reputable jewellers will ensure that the bit they cut out is weighed, and the value of that deducted from the cost of the repair.

Another common problem occurs when an engraved piece of gold or silver has worn so much that the engraving disappears. With, say, a crest or initial ring, there are two ways of going about the repair. If the original ring is still quite thick in gold content, an engraver can simply re-cut the initials or the crest on to the surface. If the ring has worn too thin for this, though, the jewellery repairer will pour a suitable layer of gold on to the surface first, to thicken it to the right dimensions before the engraver carves out the design. All this costs money, of course. But for a special ring, locket or bracelet, a piece which has a lot of sentimental value, these repairs are worth every penny – not from a financial point of view, but from an emotional one.

CHAPTER SIX

From Rough Little Pebbles
to Sparkling Stones

Poets, romantics and song-writers have gone on about beautiful gemstone's until everyone's blue in the face. When Marilyn Monroe crooned how diamonds are a girl's best friend, she was speaking for millions of women – and quite a few men – who cannot fail to be attracted to the sparkle and magic of gemstones, whether they are small and modest or iceberg-sized. Although a lot of people don't wear gemstones every day, there simply can't be too many who actually dislike the look of a beautiful stone; this almost universal love for sparklers has become part of our lives. Indeed, quite a few dreadful deeds have been committed over someone's lust for gemstones; murders, burglaries, and all the rest of it. It's not just the monetary value that creates the attraction, either. It's the depth of quality, the luxury, the charms, the richness of colour, the lustre and sparkle, you name it. Gemstones have got it all; no matter how hard various characters try to imitate gemstones with cheap, non-valuable materials, they just don't come up to scratch. You can't beat the real thing, for a variety of reasons.

But what is a gemstone? What makes these lumps of rock so appealing? You could say that shine and deep sparkle are the answers. But what about the semi-matte lustre of the pearl? Or the opaque richness of turquoise? There are quite a few gemstones that don't sparkle.

But while we are talking about sparkles, let's look at why gemstones do. Many natural stones – those which are dug out of the ground – are crystallised. What this means is that they start off as a piece of wood, or other reasonably solid object, and as time goes on get gradually churned down into the depths of the earth until they become fossils. But gemstones have gone a stage further than a fossil; crystallisation is the next process that occurs, through intense heat and great pressure. Not very exciting, or romantic, you might say. But when you think that this process which we've so glibly described can take as long as five million years, you'll begin to appreciate how gemstones can be so precious and intriguing. If you have a diamond or, say, an aquamarine, lurking in your jewellery case, go and take a look at it. To think that that beautiful stone started life as a rotten chip of wood may not endear you to it; but the thought that it has been sitting underground developing into your stone for millions of years might make you look upon it with a new respect.

Naturally enough, your polished diamond or aquamarine did not leave the ground in its present condition. Rough stones can look like anything from an ugly pebble to almost the finished product, depending on where they come from. Although pearls and amethysts look very attractive straight from their habitat, diamonds and sapphires can look like lumps of stone. The diamond, though ugly in its rough state, can be recognised by beady-eyed experts because of the shape; usually two four-sided pyramids, one upside down, and joined together at the base. But other stones aren't so easy to recognise. A rough emerald, for instance, can look like a greyish pebble with the odd green line running through it. Sapphires and rubies can look more like the real, finished thing, but on the other hand it's terribly easy to make a mistake – just because a rough pebble looks deep blue or blood red does not necessarily mean that it's precious. It can also just be a dark blue or deep red bit of stone. Opals, on the other hand, look almost as fine as the finished product; you just carve them out of their resting place, polish them up, and there you are. There are no hard and fast rules; perhaps that's yet another thing which makes the whole story of gemstones so fascinating. On the whole, though, it's fairly safe to assume that the more valuable the stone, the uglier it looks in its rough state, and the more work that has to be done to it. That assumption, of course, partly explains why some stones are more valuable than others!

Is It All in the Cut?

Having said all this about rough stones, then, how are they cut to become gemstones? We've already mentioned the people and processes involved in Chapter Four, which should give you a good idea of the training and expertise required to do the job. So let's start at the beginning of cutting.

Basically, there are two types of cut; the faceted type and the polished type. In other words, there are stones with lots of flat surfaces

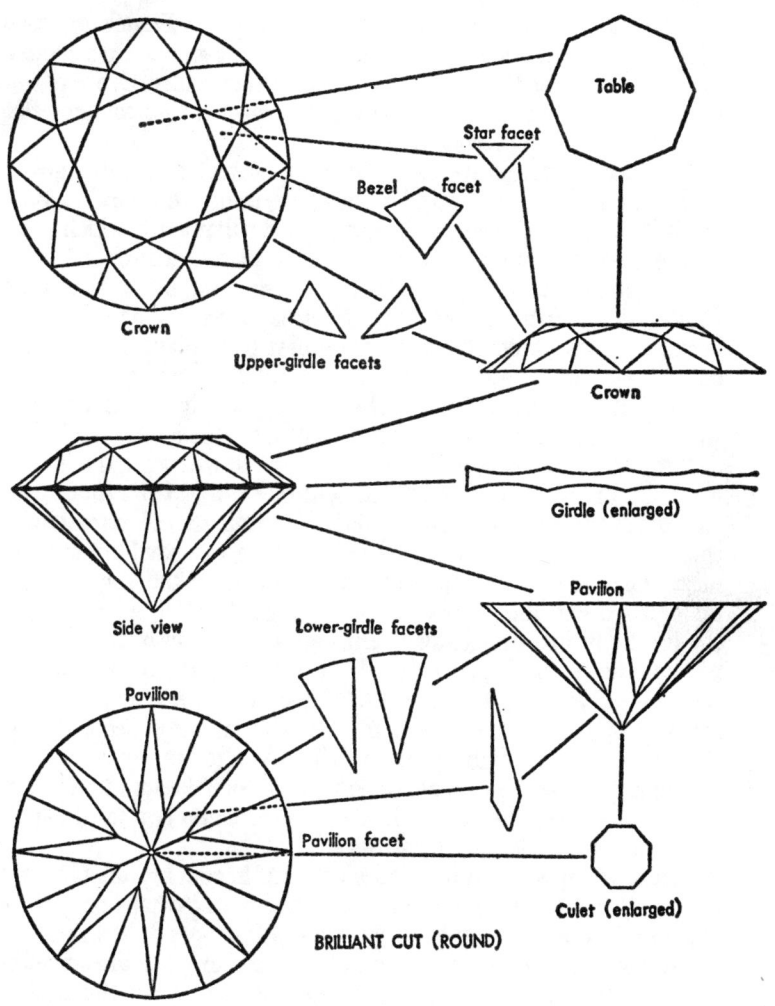

all over them, at different angles; these flat surfaces are called facets. Then there are smooth stones, usually with a flat bottom and a rounded, or domed, top. These are the polished cuts, sometimes referred to as stones cut 'en cabochon', which is a French expression widely used by the jewellery business. Precious stones are seldom cut in this way, other than star sapphires and star rubies. Other polished stones can be in the shape of beads, or flat lozenges – a common shape amongst some semi-precious stones.

The faceted stones are far more complicated, and although each facet design is very precise and geometrical, there are several variations on the theme. Most commonly seen is the brilliant cut, which is done on the basis of a round stone. It has 58 facets, or flat surfaces, all over it and must be carefully proportioned for the best effect. You see, the whole point of cutting stones with facets is so that the light enters and leaves the stone properly, to give the best light play. If the brilliant cut (or many of the others) is not done correctly, you'll get light entering and leaving the stone at cock-eyed angles, which means that the stone is not as valuable or as beautiful. If you take a look at a brilliant cut stone from the side, with the pointed tip downwards, the 'table' or upper bit of the stone should represent one third of the total height, and the 'pavillion' or pointed, conical section should represent two thirds of the height. The actual point where the pavillion and table meet, the edge of the stone, is called the 'girdle'. If the upper part, the table, is too flat, the stone will appear larger but will weigh less, and the light will just dribble away through the bottom of the stone and not be reflected back upwards, which is what it is supposed to do. If the table is too big, it will make the stone appear smaller than it actually is. If the bottom section, or pavillion, is too deep, the light will drift away through the sides. When you're buying a stone, you should always have a look at it sideways on to make sure that the proportions are right; the rule of thumb, one third and two thirds, applies to most types of stone cut in this way.

Often, you'll get semi-precious stones cut in roughly the same way, in a similar shape to the brilliant cut, but with perhaps fewer facets and a shallower pavillion or lower section. In stones of less value, this is not considered a defect; in fact, these types of stone are sometimes cut especially to fit a mounting of unusual design. But this does not happen with precious stones.

Another favourite is the emerald cut, which was specifically innovated for emeralds. This cut also has 58 facets on it (as in brilliant

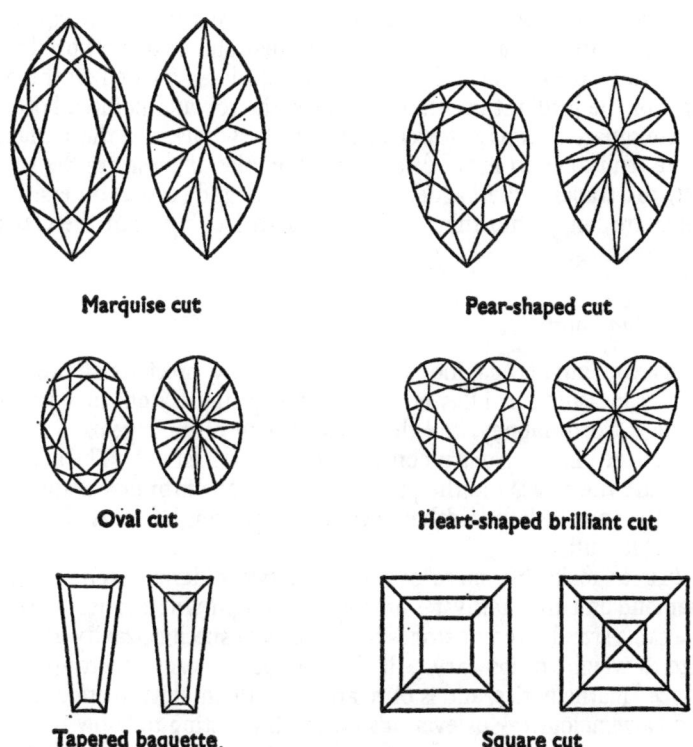

cuts). Emeralds are very delicate stones, so cutting must be done with extreme care. The facets on the emerald cut go in far fewer directions than those of the other cuts; too many different directions of pressure might result in the breakage of the stone. The emerald cut is also used on other stones.

Other cuts are the oval shape, and the marquise or navette, which is an oval shape with two pointed ends – rather like a rowing boat. There is the pear shape, which is an oval with only one sharp point; and then there is the variation of that, with an indentation in the rounded end – the heart shaped cut. This heart shape can only be cut into certain stones, as the incision made can cause damage. The stone cutter must first of all examine the formation of the stone very carefully indeed before deciding whether or not it can stand the extra strain the heart shaped cutting imposes.

Developing from the emerald cut, there are a variety of square or squarish cuts – geometric shapes. Now these shapes don't work by the same rules as the previous lot, which are all loosely based on the principle of the brilliant cut; facets all over the top and pointed bottoms. These square cuts have fewer facets, on the whole, and those that are there tend to go in fewer directions. Examples of these are the square cut, the trapeze, the baguette, the triangle and several others; all of them are fancy, and they're more modern looking than the classical brilliant cuts.

Dangling Carats...

As you might imagine, stones – especially precious stones – are hardly measured in kilos or pounds; every single atom in a precious stone is worth money, and the measurement of these gems is as accurate as the planning of a moon shot from Cape Kennedy. The measures used are the carat, and the point. A carat is one fifth of a gram, and a point is one one-hundredth of a carat. Nit-picking? Not at all – this is valuable stuff.

Just to make life more complicated, two different stones – say a diamond and an amethyst – of identical weight will not necessarily be the same size. Different stones have different specific gravity and their size to weight ratios vary. All this, of course, leads to extremely advanced mathematics, and is of relatively little interest to anyone other than a gemologist. However, it's always interesting to know just what you're wearing on your finger – or what you're about to buy to put on your finger, so for argument's sake, we have included a few little diagrams that will give you a rough idea of what stones of various weights should look like in terms of size.

All the above information, as we've suggested, more or less applies to all stones. So, having talked generally up to now, let us get down to brass tacks and discuss some individual gems. Here are the run-downs on the diamond and the three other precious stones, plus the pearl.

The Diamond

If you put a diamond, and the lead from a pencil next to each other you'd probably find it quite hard to believe that the two substances you're looking at are from the same family. But, hard to believe or not, it's a fact. Diamonds are carbon, and so is the 'lead' in a pencil;

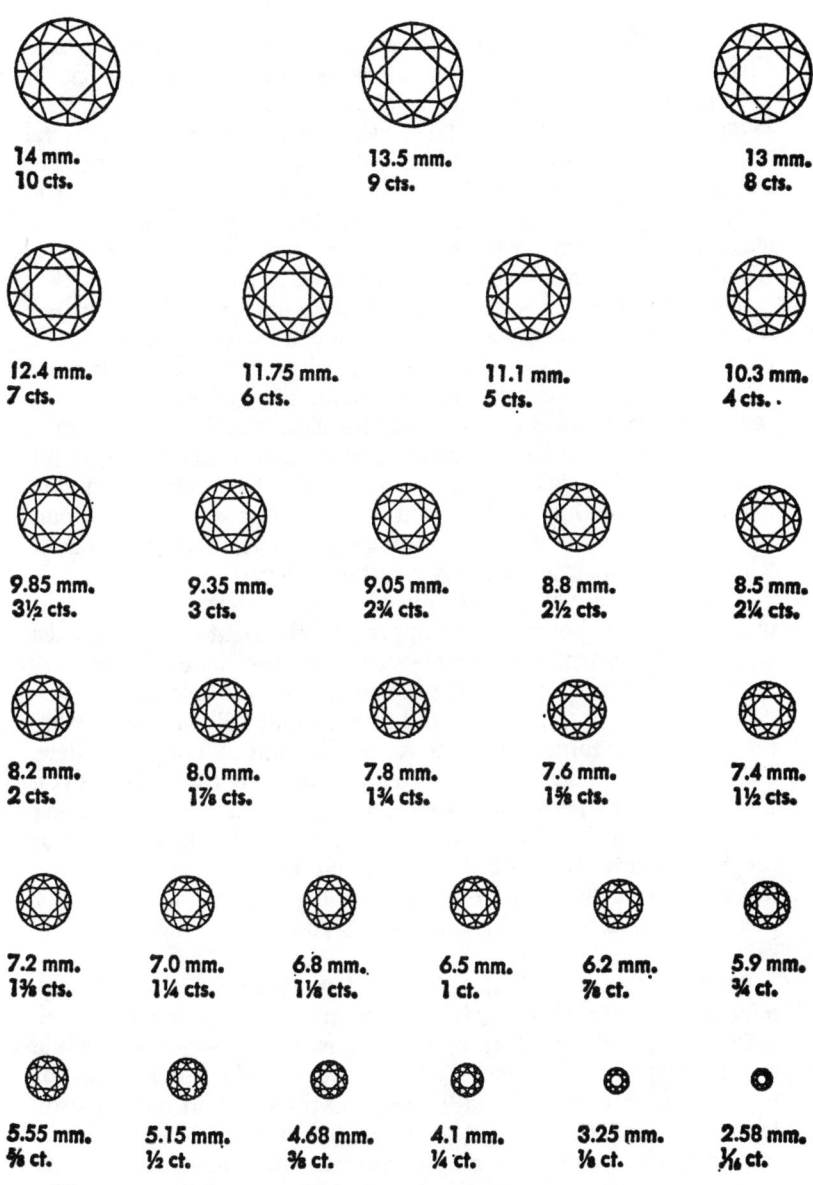

Diameters and Corresponding Weights of Round, Ideally Proportioned, Brilliant-Cut Diamonds

the main difference is around four million years of evolution time. Diamonds have started out in life as pieces of soft carbon on the ground, and through the process of time, plus heat and pressure – being gradually sucked into the bowels of the earth, heated to several thousand degrees Centigrade, and spewed back up again some four million years later – have become the hardest substance known to man. Mind you, most of the diamonds that were spewed out on to the surface of the earth have been picked up now, and other forms of diamond hunting have evolved. But more about that later.

The actual areas in which diamonds are found are wide and varied, but there seems to be some sort of pattern to it. Although it is not a confirmed fact, it appears that the diamonds found in the world come from a belt that runs diagonally around the globe, starting from southern Africa and winding its way up across the Atlantic Ocean to the northern part of South America, and then onwards to parts of the USSR. Naturally, there are exceptions to this; diamonds are found in other places, too. But the large sources of diamonds do seem to come from the 'belt'; whether there is any geological significance to this, or whether it is pure coincidence, is a matter for debate.

Another place where diamonds of the future may well lie is the moon. Unlikely though it may appear, all the right conditions exist on the moon; carbon, heat and pressure. However, there is less gravity there, which simply means that potential diamond sources would lie deeper into the moon's surface, and that the four million years it takes for diamonds to form on earth may well be eight million years there. Unfortunately, it is impossible to confirm the presence of diamonds on the moon, as the people who have been there so far have had rather more important things to worry about on their visits than looking for rough diamonds! But with the small amount of evidence we do have, it does seem likely that once humans have got around to looking for precious substances up there, diamonds could be at the top of the shopping list.

Another question that might be of interest, especially to ecologically-minded readers, is what is going to happen once we've dug out all the existing diamonds out of the earth's depths. The answer is that, while we are digging away, more diamonds are possibly being formed at lower levels. And if we are still around in three or four million years from now, we could still be digging diamonds out of the ground – only from different locations. It's comforting to know that diamonds are unlikely to become an endangered species!

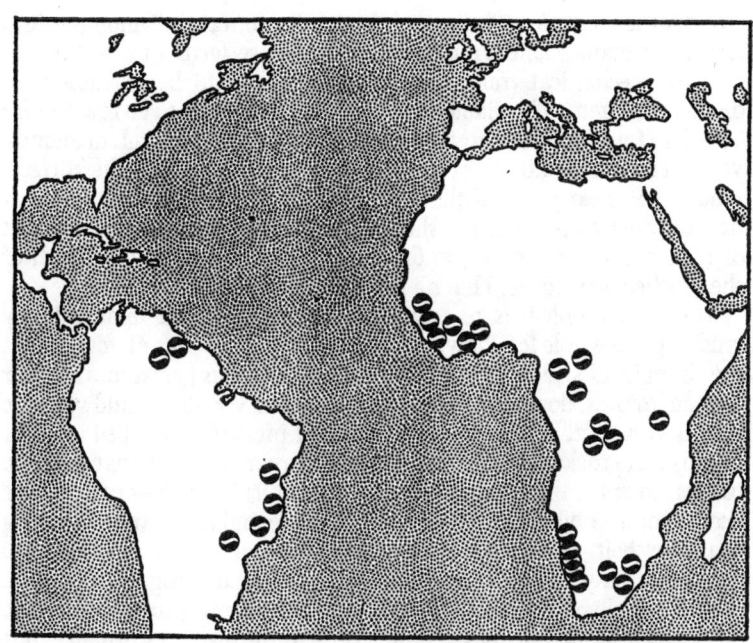
World map showing 'Diamond Belt'

As we said earlier, the rough diamond comes in a fairly recognisable state; in the shape of two four-sided pyramids, one upside down, joined at the base. This shape is called an octahedron. These odd-shaped rough diamonds can be found at anything up to around 2000 feet below the earth's surface, and there are three ways of getting at them. First, you have surface mining; in areas where there are still some rough diamonds floating around near the surface, they can be dug out quite easily from up top. Secondly, there is ground mining, which involves a process rather like coal mining. The third way to find rough diamonds is by sea mining, which is still in its early stages at the time of writing. However, once developed, it could provide a very large source. It involves complicated structures rather like oil rigs, and largely mechanised digging at great depths under the sea bed. Although sea mining and surface mining do happen, by far the most extensively used method is ground mining which, as we said, is run along the lines of coal mining. Rock is hewn out of the ground at depths of up to 2000 feet, using digging apparatus and dynamite; this reduces the volcanic rock – which hopefully contains diamonds – into large, but manageable chunks. The chunks are ferried up to the surface by mechanical transport, and then taken to be examined for diamond content. The diamonds in the rock are likely to be few and far between; for every one carat, or one-fifth of a gram, of rough diamonds, you need to haul up to 250 metric tonnes of rock up to the surface. And if you bear in mind that rough diamonds are reduced by about half in order to produce polished diamonds, you can call the amount of rock necessary nearer 500 tonnes to produce one carat's worth of the finished gemstones. That's a lot of rock.

The next problem is to sort out the rock from the diamonds, by crushing the whole lot. Now, before you leap to the edge of your seat at the thought of steam rollers bashing these precious gemstones in their rock surrounds, don't forget that diamonds are very hard, and volcanic rock is very soft. In this process, sufficient pressure is applied in order to crush the rock only; but you'd need many more times that pressure to even nick the diamonds contained within it. Once the crushing has been done the whole lot goes on to what resembles a large vibrating conveyor belt, which is coated with a viscous substance similar to petroleum jelly. As the rock and rough diamonds progress along the conveyor belt, the vibrating action and a washing process cause the bits of rock to fall off; they will not stick to the viscous substance. But the diamonds, because they are of a different material, do stick to the substance even when vibrated and washed. The rough diamonds go through the cycle several times, to make sure all the rock has been washed and vibrated away.

After this, the rough stones are examined and sorted out into industrial and jewellery groups. Only 15% or so of the total 'catch' will be of the right quality to be used in jewellery.

Actually, the uses to which diamonds are put in industry are very interesting, and rather more far-reaching than most people think. Eye surgery, for example, depends heavily on diamonds for the terribly thin, fine cutting edges required. Steel simply cannot be sharpened adequately when cutting blades are so fine; the only appropriate material is diamond. Dentists, too, use diamonds to drill your teeth, and thank Heavens for that! Old-fashioned drills took an agonisingly long time to do the job that a modern diamond drill can do in just a few minutes. Records are often cut with diamond tools, so that the grooves in the disc are of as high a quality as possible. And although sapphire styluses are cheaper and more common, a diamond stylus will last longer and give a finer sound when you're playing your records at home on your turntable. In more recent times, diamonds have been put to very good use in the precision instruments required for rockets and space craft. Whatever the use, diamond is at the top of its class; both because of its hardness and because of its transmitting qualities (being a crystal, like quartz) this stone does an awful lot of valuable work around the world, as well as adding a great deal of beauty to the jewellery we wear.

Getting back to the diamonds used in jewellery, that mere 15%, the next step after mining and sorting has taken place is distribution. All other stones have very little officialdom attached to their distribution, although some precious gems like emeralds, for example, are in some cases distributed via the national bank of the country in which they are mined. But diamonds are very strictly controlled. Not only the distribution of rough diamonds, but all the mines as well, are controlled by De Beers Consolidated Mines, whose selling organisation is called The Central Selling Organisation. This means that total monitoring of the world-wide diamond market is undertaken by the one concern which keeps a tight watch on price control, as well as quality control. De Beers have a monopoly, yes, but unlike other forms of monopoly within industry, this is one area in which no-one would benefit were prices or quality anything but correct. Diamond values, and increases in those values, are carefully controlled so that everyone gets a fair deal; dealers, jewellers and consumers alike.

With De Beers at the helm of the diamond industry, any diamond you buy is going to hold its value and appreciate gradually in keeping with inflation and all the rest of it, with far less danger of fluctuation than you would find with the majority of other investments you could make. Another, simpler reason why diamonds are a good investment is that, being colourless (there *are* coloured diamonds, but they're a different story) they can be considered as an international currency. They are universally liked, and are not subject to taste, fashion, personal preference, or even superstition, as are coloured stones.

De Beers, once they are satisfied that the quality of the rough diamonds is right, will then sell off specified quantities of these rough stones to selected diamond manufacturers. To buy from De Beers you must be invited by them, and this does not happen easily. Only the top manufacturers are allowed to buy from De Beers; merely a few hundred in the world. In order to receive the invitation, these people or organisations must be extremely well qualified and of the highest reputation. And the goods cannot be chosen by them, either; ten times per year, the invited manufacturers are offered a 'box' of rough diamonds by De Beers, and the stones within those boxes must be accepted as they are. For a manufacturer to turn down or refuse the contents of the box is considered very bad form, although he or she may view the rough stones before purchasing them. To a very small number of people, De Beers will offer a 'dealer's box', which means that the purchaser may sell the contents directly to other manufacturers without processing the stones him or herself. However, these dealer's boxes are only offered by De Beers in very small quantities. The majority of boxes are sold directly to manufacturers, who must then take the rough stones back to their manufacturing organisations and cut and polish the stones to a finished state. Then, they may sell them on to a jewellery manufacturer or whatever. Of course, some manufacturers who buy boxes from De Beers are not in a position to process all the stones themselves. In this case, they can sell some of the rough diamonds to other manufacturers, perhaps through a broker. Now, you may think that as other people get involved, all adding on their percentage of profit, this selling on of rough diamonds is going to result in the stones being more expensive at the end of the day. But this is not necessarily true; the manufacturers to whom the rough stones are sold to may well have different facilities which enable them to cut and polish the stones more cheaply, so that the final price is evened out whichever way the diamonds get sold.

Before we leave the fascinating, but endless, topic of diamonds, we should, of course, talk about what the actual finished stones are like. All the way through we've been referring to diamonds as white, or colourless, but as we mentioned, there are other colours as well. In fact, it is possible to get a diamond in pretty well any colour that you find gemstones; blue, yellow, purple, green, red and so on. However, unless you're very wealthy or a real expert, it is unwise to buy a coloured diamond. You need to know exactly what you're doing, because the values of these stones are extremely capricious. For example, an ordinary yellow diamond will be worth less than a pure white diamond of the same size. But a 'rose' coloured diamond, in other words, a sort of musty pink, will probably be worth rather more than a white diamond. If you buy a diamond that has a total absence of colour and no impurities or flaws (any that a stone does contain should be pointed out to you by your jeweller) you're on to a winner – but at a price!

If you are drawn to coloured diamonds and are that keen that you want to take the risk and buy one anyway, then let us offer you a few tips. Obviously when you're buying from a reputable jeweller you can be sure that, if you're told a stone is a yellow diamond it is a yellow diamond. But other buying situations may not be so safe, and sometimes semi-precious stones might be palmed off as coloured diamonds. When you're talking about dark coloured stones the situation gets really tricky. Even experts are pushed to tell the difference between a dark blue diamond and a sapphire without the aid of instruments. But with the paler coloured versions it is rather easier to say which is which. Take a yellow stone, or a mauve one; they are supposed to be coloured diamonds but you're not entirely convinced. Try this 'skin test'. Lay the stone as close as you can to the skin of your hand – preferably with the stone upside down, pointed tip up. If you can see your skin *through* the stone it is almost certainly a citrine (yellow) or an amethyst (mauve). If you can't see your skin through the stone, then it could well be a diamond. You see, although diamonds are, in theory, transparent stones, they have this way of letting you see into them without letting you see straight the way through to the other side. The great beauty of this is that it means the stone has far greater depth and, of course, more 'life' than any other stone. Your semi-precious look-alike will not only be more transparent than the diamond; it won't sparkle nearly as much either.

So much for diamonds then. You may well think that we're prejudiced in favour of these sparklers. Well, we admit it; we are! But to be fair, diamonds are by far the most popular and well-loved stone of all, wherever you go in the world. And although in some cases other types of precious stone may be more valuable, more rare, there is something about diamonds that puts them up above the rest.

However, we can't ignore the rest. So here they are!

The Ruby

Perhaps the greatest claim to fame the ruby has is in its use in Episcopal rings. These, in case you didn't know, are the rather splendid pieces of jewellery awarded to Bishops when they are consecrated. Other than that, though, rubies have been popular for centuries and centuries, especially in India where a great deal of ruby-set jewellery has been made from comparatively recent times right back to ancient history.

Like all precious stones, rubies had quite a few superstitions attached to them in antiquity. One of the beliefs was that rubies were supposed to bring out the good side of you and were a beneficial omen to have around if you wanted to get on in life; to make money, buy land and property and so on. They were also supposed to stop effervescence in water, whatever use that could have had! On top of those remarkable abilities, the ruby was also thought to soothe a bad temper and protect you from being seduced. There was a proviso, though. If you wore your rubies on the right-hand side of your body, they would have no effect at all.

Sometimes you'll hear rubies referred to as 'oriental' rubies. This expression came about mainly to differentiate between the real thing and other red stones, like garnets or spinels, which are sometimes referred to as rubies as well. The other word you might hear bandied around as a pseudonym for the ruby is 'carbuncle', which sounds more like a foot disease than the name of a precious stone. Actually, it means any red stone and not specifically the ruby.

Rubies are a form of corundum, like their sister stones, sapphires. Both these stones are second hardest of all, after the diamond. The most intriguing thing about the ruby is its incredibly dense, rich colour. Even the name comes from its colour; rubeus, which is a Latin word for red. This colour can range from a deep, blood red to a gentle rose pink; but the most favoured tone for the ruby is the very deepest of reds, verging almost on a purple shade. Rubies can be cut with facets in any of the classic shaped cuts we discussed at the beginning of the chapter. Alternatively, rubies can be cut 'en cabochon', with a flat bottom and a domed top. Although you won't get such interesting light play on the stone when it is cut in this way, the smooth surface can, in some people's opinions, allow you to appreciate the stone's colour rather better. It's really a matter of taste.

Rubies are not found in very many places in the world, hence their rarity. Most of them come from the Mogok mines, which are located in Burma. Some others have also been found in Thailand, Sri Lanka, Afghanistan, Australia, the USSR and the USA. Perfect rubies are very few and far between and on the rare occasion when you will come across the perfect specimen it may well be worth more than a diamond of the same carat weight. Very large rubies are rare, too; most of the stones mined tend to be small compared with other precious stones. So a very large, perfect ruby would be virtually priceless.

The Sapphire

Sapphires, like rubies, are corundum, and are very hard – diamonds are the only stones which are harder. Sapphires and rubies are so closely related that the only real dividing line between the two is their colour. But there are further colours of sapphire, other than the well-known blue; pink, green, yellow and white examples are reasonably common. In fact, it is a bit of a dilemma to say which is a ruby and which is a sapphire, especially when both stones are, say, pink. The general rule of thumb amongst the jewellery trade is that rubies should range from dark red to dark pink, and all other colours of the stone are sapphires.

Sapphires can be cut in the same two ways as rubies; either with facets in one of the classic shapes, or 'en cabochon'. One of this stone's greatest mysteries is its ability to change colour, or offer different colours at the same time. Some say that sapphires change their colour from dark blue to a paler, sea blue, according to whether they're in artificial or natural light. Others say that sapphires can appear blue and greenish at the same time, a quality which you should be able to detect under a strong light.

When it comes to the other colours of sapphire, it is often very difficult to distinguish them from other similar stones. Only a reputable jeweller will be able to help you there. White sapphires can be used as diamond substitutes, and although these are almost as precious as real diamonds, they will not sparkle as much.

Sapphires come from the same areas in which rubies are found. The best sapphires, so some say, are from the Mogok mines in Burma, which is also supposed to be the home of the finest rubies. Thailand and Kashmir also produce good examples. Sri Lanka, or Ceylon as it was, produces quite a lot of sapphires; these tend to be of a cloudier blue. And although gem experts wrangle over which types are the finest sapphires – Sri Lanka's cloudy jobs or the more vivid ones from the Mogok mines and elsewhere – it really boils down to a matter of taste; what the gem experts and the public prefer. Other nations producing quantities of sapphires are Australia, the USA and the USSR.

Old-fashioned beliefs about the sapphire were widespread. Among these were convictions that the stones will protect you from scorpion bites, which must have been pretty useful if you happened to hang around with scorpions. Another of these beliefs was that if you held a sapphire in your mouth, it would get rid of sores, and if you wore one about your person it would make you stay good, chaste, and all the other qualities that were held in esteem at the time. Lastly, sapphires – the kaolin and morphine of antiquity – could cure dysentery, along with internal bleeding. Handy stones to have around!

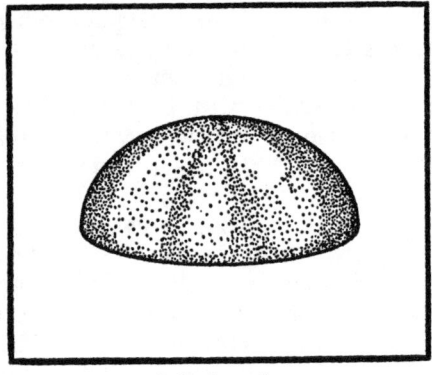

Cabochon Cut

Star Stones

Star rubies and sapphires are fascinating stones. They are always cut 'en cabochon', with a domed top and flat bottom, so you can appreciate the startling star effect. The stone has been formed in such a way that, when light enters the stone it is reflected back in the pale outline of a six-pointed star. Ironically, the most beautiful star stones are synthetic (man-made from precisely the same substances as a natural stone). The main difference is that, with the synthetic stone, it is possible to incorporate the star effect in such a way that it's bang on centre, with a good clear outline. With the natural stone, more often than not the star effect will seem a bit blurred and will be slightly off-centre. So any apparently perfect star stone that you buy is likely to be synthetic; a perfect natural stone is extremely rare and would set you back a not-so-small fortune.

The Emerald

Getting away, now, from the corundum family of stones, we now have the leading member of the beryl family; the emerald. This group takes in other stones, notably the aquamarine, but the emerald is the only family member which is classed as a precious stone.

Almost every emerald has flaws in it. And because these flaws are so widespread, they are acceptable and don't necessarily mean that a stone isn't going to be valuable. In fact, these flaws have become such an important way of life with emeralds, that they're not even called flaws; they're called, rather poetically, 'garden'. Whether that arose because some witty person thought an emerald's flaws resembled shrubs and flowers on a green lawn we don't know. But garden it is, and unless you're extremely lucky, you're unlikely to come across an emerald without it. A pure, flawless emerald of reasonable size is very, very rare, and any such stones in existence are worth a lot of money. Perfect emeralds are just about the most valuable stone money can buy – more valuable than the best diamond.

Emeralds were very popular with the ancient Egyptians, who could always be relied upon to know a good thing when they saw one. Some say that the mining of emeralds was being done as early as 1700 BC. The ancient Greeks were keen on emeralds, too; but it really was the Egyptians who made the best use of these stones. They even carved them, usually with the scarab (beetle) design. Unfortunately, as the Egyptians' days of glory faded away, so did their emerald mines. Since then a few attempts have been made to reopen them, but what with political problems and other drawbacks, the attempts weren't too successful. However, a few of the world's emeralds still do come from Egypt.

In more recent times, many emeralds have been, and still are – mined in South America. These mines were originally started off by the early Spanish settlers, and have expanded and developed along with the mining of many other minerals on that continent. Brazil, Colombia and Peru produce the most. Other emeralds are found in Australia and in South Africa.

Like its fellow precious stones, the emerald had its fair share of superstitions attached to it in ancient times. One of the most interesting of these was that emeralds were supposed to be helpful if your eyesight was poor. If you carried one around with you and held it over your bad eye now and again, or even just gazed at one when your eyes were tired, the stone would work wonders. A theory to explain this superstition has been put forward in more recent times. Emeralds, unlike a great many other stones, do not appear to change colour according to the light; this is why they might have been thought good for the eyes. You see, if the emeralds could look just as good regardless of the light conditions, it may have been possible that they could influence your eyes to perform equally well. Who knows? Anyway, there aren't too many people around who wouldn't find gazing at an emerald easy on the eye...

The Pearl

The pearl is a bit of an outsider amongst gemstones, but we have included it in with precious stones as it is so well known and popular.

Quite a few people hold the superstition that pearls mean tears, and are therefore bad news. The only real truth about that is quipped by the cynics around us; you might shed a few tears if only because you can't afford to buy good pearls. Not that this theory holds true nowadays, mind you; cultured or even simulated pearls can look nearly the same as the real thing and cost a fraction of the price. Without being cynical, though, it is possible that the superstition arises from the appearance of the pearl; it does look a bit like a tear drop, especially when it is a pear-shaped example.

Unlike other gems which mostly come out of the ground, pearls come out of certain mollusc shells. Rather than being precious to the poor old mollusc, they're actually a malformation inside its shell – almost like a wart or a gallstone. A pearl forms when some foreign body gets into the shell by accident (oriental, natural, or 'real' pearls) or when someone puts it there (cultured). The creature who lives inside the shell doesn't like the intrusion and, in trying to isolate it, secretes a liquid around the offending bit. This stuff hardens and the mollusc goes on putting hundreds of very thin layers of secretion on to the foreign object until a pearl is formed. For the average-sized pearl (natural or cultured) the process takes roughly three years.

In the main, pearls come out of certain species of oysters, although freshwater pearls – usually quite small and of less value – are found in mussels and other molluscs as well. Edible oysters species don't normally have the right type of lustrous secretions to produce pearls – so the next time you're eating oysters, don't be too hopeful of finding a treasure inside one.

Colours are pale, ranging from pure white to beige, yellowish, grey and even pink or blue. The only exceptions to the light colours are the very rare and beautiful black pearls, which are actually nearer charcoal grey in colour. The shapes are usually round, or like flattish buttons. Sometimes you'll get a pear-shaped pearl, and if the shape is completely irregular it's rather romantically called 'baroque'. The round pearl occurs when the foreign body (like a grain of sand) has lodged somewhere within the oyster's body. 'Button' pearls are flatter because the foreign body came in near the shell – so the pearl is formed up against the shell and is flat on at least one side. The baroque pearl is formed when an unevenly shaped object, like a tiny piece of wood or a bit of grit, gets into the shell. Lastly, there's the blister pearl. In the natural variety, it's usually caused by a parasite which drills through the oyster's shell from the outside. The oyster stops up the hole by secreting the pearl substance over it, and carries on layer after layer until the blister pearl reaches quite a good size. This can then be cut off. And because it is usually hollow, it will be filled up with Mother-of-Pearl to make it solid. All these pearls can, of course, be initiated by humans, who can insert the right sort of foreign object in the right place and produce cultured versions of each type.

Pearl necklaces have long been the favourite way to make these gems into jewellery. If you're buying one, you want to make sure the string that holds them together is knotted between each pearl. If there aren't any knots the pearls will rub together and eventually could wear each other out. The usual materials used for stringing pearls are string (made of cotton or silk) and plastic or nylon. Silk is best, but the latter two are also good, because they last longer and won't break or wear out as fast as the natural fibres do.

Even now that we have cultured pearls, it still takes a while to assemble a beautifully matched necklace. Matching colour and size is a painstaking process. Although it's possible to produce lots of pearls by inserting grains of sand or grit into thousands of oysters, a well-matched necklace can still cost a lot of money. Graded pearls, in other words a necklace with a big pearl in the middle going down in equal steps to small pearls at either end, are tricky to match as well. These necklaces go through phases of popularity from time to time, and once again a good one will set you back quite a bit.

The most productive oysters, in natural pearls that is, live in the waters of the Persian Gulf and around the coast of Australia. However, natural pearls are seen very rarely nowadays. And those you do see are worth very little; an old string of natural pearls that might have been worth thousands years ago, before cultured pearls were perfected, will now only fetch a few hundred. The bottom has dropped right out of the 'real' pearl market. You see, good cultured pearls look exactly the same. You can only tell the difference between the two varieties by X-raying them, as the central structure differs. But who cares what the core of the pearl looks like? All we are concerned with is the exterior appearance. And in terms of lustre, sheen, colour, richness and depth of tone, there's absolutely no difference at all, because the formation process is exactly the same. It's just that with cultured pearls, nature has been helped along a bit. The most avid producers of cultured pearls are the Japanese. They have got it down to a fine art; implanting foreign objects inside oysters by the million, and putting them back into the sea while the creatures coat the objects into millions of nice, fat pearls.

CHAPTER SEVEN

So Much for 'Semi-Precious...'

The Not-so-Precious Sparklers

The actual expression 'semi-precious' has been known to drive gemologists and jewellers mad, because it is imprecise. For the sake of simplicity, we have lumped the five 'precious' stones together – diamond, ruby, sapphire, emerald, pearl – in Chapter Six, and classed all the others as 'semi-precious'. But very often there is infringement of territory between the two groups. In real terms, there's no way a pearl should rank as a precious stone, especially since cultured pearls have been around. Similarly, some fine examples of semi-precious stones, like tourmaline or alexandrite for example, can be more valuable than mediocre precious stones of the same weight. Hence the jewellery business's rather perfectionist scorn for the terms. The Gemological Institute of America, the powerful ruling body of the jewellery business in that country, has decreed that the whole lot should be called 'gemstones' with no discrimination. However, the distinction is still made almost everywhere, so we have retained it.

Semi-precious stones can be broken down into three categories; transparent, translucent and opaque. Transparent stones are the ones you can actually see your skin through when you place them on your hand, like amethysts, aquamarines, topazes and so on. Translucent stones let some light through, but don't actually let you see what's going on at the other side; in this group are tiger's eye and moonstones. Lastly, you have the opaque stones through which no light or eyesight can pass; here you'll find onyx and turquoise.

On the whole, it's fair to say that semi-precious stones are cheaper to buy than the precious species. The main reason for this is that there are more stones around in the semi-precious categories, and often they are easier to get out of the ground – or otherwise collate. Another reason, though, is that semi-precious gems can usually be cut and polished by machine. Precious gems are too valuable to allow anything but the minimum amount to go to waste in cutting and faceting, so they're cut by hand. Machine cutting and faceting means that several stones can be processed at the same time; but the wastage with machines is greater than if the work were to be done by hand. Machine processing, therefore, saves time and so cuts the cost of making rough semi-precious stones into jewellery; more of each stone is lost through wastage, but this still doesn't affect the cost very much. The actual cuts used are the same as, or at least based on, the classic precious cuts. Obviously, where you get smooth substances like coral, agate, bloodstone and opal (to name a few) the cutting only amounts to thorough polishing. Often the stone's natural shape is left unaltered, as it is attractive in its own right.

Within the jewellery trade, semi-precious stones are bought and sold in much the same way as for precious stones (other than diamonds). But, whereas rubies, sapphires and emeralds tend to be bought and sold in very small quantities, semi-precious stones are often sold by the weight – say, a kilo or two. The market is very open, and the supply – unlike the supply of precious stones – is usually good, so prices remain reasonable.

There are actually several hundred varieties of semi-precious stones, the majority of which you are not likely to see in common use. On top of that, there are sometimes several different colour variations of most individual semi-precious stones which all adds up to a hideously confusing picture. Fortunately, there are only a few dozen such stones used in jewellery in any noticeable quantity, and those are the ones we describe. Here, then, are the most common semi-precious stones and materials arranged according to colour and texture. When it comes to a stone that exists in several different colours, we've placed it according to the colour (or colours) in which it is most often seen. We've also added the precious stones as well, just to give you a better overall picture.

	Transparent	Translucent	Opaque
White (colourless)	Diamond Quartz Zircon White sapphire (precious)	Moonstone Opal	Coral (not a stone) Ivory (not a stone)
Yellow to Orange	Citrine Topaz Cairngorm	Amber	

	Transparent	Translucent	Opaque
Brown	Smoky Quartz Smoky Topaz Smoky Citrine	Cat's Eye Tiger's Eye	Cameo
Light Blue	Aquamarine	Opal	Turquoise
Dark Blue	Sapphire	Opal	Lapis lazuli

Purple	Alexandrite
	  (dark to red)
	Amethyst (pale)
	Rose quartz
	  (pale to pink)
		Jade
		  (greenish)	

Green	Emerald
	Tourmaline
	Peridot
		Emerald (with
		  a lot of
		  garden)
		Jade
			Malachite
			Moss Agate
			Agate (brownish)
			Turquoise
			Bloodstone
			  (very dark)

Black		Hematite	Jet (not a stone) Onyx Coral (not a stone)
Light Red	Ruby		Coral (not a stone)
Red	Ruby Garnet Spinel		
Several colours in common use	Diamond Zircon Quartz Spinel Amethyst Sapphire	Opal	Agate Coral (synthetically coloured; not a stone)

Quartz

A large piece of rough quartz looks rather like an ice-cube, and even when it is cut and polished up it still has a far icier look about it than a diamond ever could. Chances are, on closer examination, you'll find lots of flaws or 'inclusions' in it. Other names for the colourless variety of quartz are Rock Crystal and sometimes Bristol Rock. In ancient times, rock crystal was supposed to signify virginity, chastity and innocence; today, it is sometimes used as a substitute for diamonds. But the quickest way to tell whether or not the 'diamond' is real is to look through the stone. If you can't see anything, it should be a diamond, but if you can see your skin through it very clearly, there's a good chance it's quartz.

Zircon

Colourless zircons seldom occur naturally. What is far more likely is that a coloured zircon has been heated in a special manner which makes it turn colourless. These stones are normally used as diamond substitutes, and will seldom be called zircons – they are usually referred to by a variety of other names. They tend to look a bit more fiery than quartz, which has a truly watery look about it, but they still don't have the incredible sparkle of the diamond. In ancient times, zircons symbolised prudence; sometimes the zircon is said to be a gypsy's stone, as these people seem to have favoured them on and off throughout history.

White Sapphire

These are the albino sisters of the blue sapphire, as we said earlier. Once again, they are common diamond substitutes, although they are precious stones in their own right and should therefore be quite expensive. The colour of the white sapphire is a warm white, with perhaps a slightly greyish or beige sparkle. It will also be more transparent than a diamond. Another stone which is quite wrongly called 'white sapphire', and is often sold as such, is the spinel. Natural spinels are normally coloured and white ones are normally synthetic. White spinels, whether described as white sapphires or not, will have a very glassy look about them, as against the warm, slightly dull glow of the true white sapphire. So beware of any piece of jewellery containing 'white sapphires', if it is being offered for sale at a low price. Although spinels officially qualify as semi-precious stones, they have very little value.

Moonstone

A good moonstone should look like the moon when it's just coming up in a still-light sky. It's a translucent, glowing, milky white stone, and is normally cut en cabochon. You might also hear it referred to as Adularia.

Opal

This is one of the semi-precious stones that comes in several colours, and you will see from the chart on pages 101–102 that we have included it under the headings of white, light blue and dark blue. In fact, opals come in a variety of background colours, white and blue being perhaps the more common. Opals have specks in them, which are called 'fire'; these can be red, blue, gold, green, etc., and are what makes the opal such an interesting stone. We've classed it as a translucent stone, but it is almost opaque; the light seems to burn at you from inside the stone – so vivid is its lustre. In ancient times poisoning your enemies was a popular pastime, and wise types carried an opal around with them as this was supposed to protect them against poisoned food. In more recent times opals have had superstitions attached to them, largely based on the idea that they were unlucky. They *are* unlucky, or at least they can be, but only because they're a delicate stone. If they're damaged or knocked they can drop out of their mounting unnoticed – which certainly is bad luck !

For the technically-minded, opals are formed from hydrated silica, which in its youth would have been a viscous substance before it hardened into the opal stone. As a result, it isn't particularly robust and doesn't always stand up to heat or grease. In fact opals can absorb grease, which makes them go a bit dull; on the other hand, the grease an opal absorbs can also help to make it less brittle. Opals are normally cut en cabochon, and sometimes an unusually-shaped rough stone is simply polished and left in its original shape, which can be quite stunning to set in gold as a pendant.

Coral (white)

All coral (whether white, red or black) is nothing whatever to do with rocks or stones. It comes from the sea and up until the 18th century was thought to be a form of marine vegetation. However, in that century an eagle-eyed Frenchman worked out that coral actually comprises the skeletons of tiny little animals, which cluster together and secrete calcium carbonate. Once the animal itself has passed on, its remains – along with those of millions of others – harden into the coral we know so well. As most conservation-minded people will already know, coral reefs have been fished out of existence all over the world, and in many regions the fishing of this lovely substance has been stopped altogether. However, human nature being what it is, people still swim around looking for coral and mysteriously it appears in the shops! In addition, of course, there has been no ban on existing coral jewellery, so older pieces are quite OK. In any case, if the fishing continues, there soon won't be any new coral left in our seas. Coral is not only used as a gemstone in the strict sense; it is also used to make whole pieces of jewellery like rings and bracelets, and other small objets d'art.

Ivory

Here again, we're up against conservation which is very strict. It may be hard to control the fishing of coral, which goes on under the conveniently murky depths of the sea, but a dead elephant (or rhinoceros) is pretty hard to conceal under your jacket. And ivory hunters have been firmly relegated to the ranks of poachers and pirates. However, existing ivory is still acceptable, and it makes lovely jewellery; either on its own as a ring or a bracelet, or set with yellow gold. Beware of shark bone or plastic imitations, as there are more and more around – especially now that the heavy hand of conservation has fallen upon stocks of the real thing. Shark bone is very difficult to tell from the genuine item, but plastic will have a soapy feel to it and will probably look a bit too shiny. Keep an eye open, too, for telltale mould marks on a suspect piece, and for the absence of a genuine grain – hard to fake on the plastic version.

Citrine

These stones are clear lemon or canary coloured, and are extremely transparent. That's the quickest way to tell whether or not a yellow stone is a diamond; the diamond won't be anywhere near as transparent. Another distinguishing feature of the citrine, as against any other yellow stone, is that it is very brittle. Even set in a ring, sitting in a jeweller's window, the stone may already have acquired a few tiny chips on it, usually around the sharper edges at the middle of the stone or on the edge of the facets. The citrine is seldom cut in any way other than with facets, based on the classic cuts.

Topaz

The topaz is similar in transparency to the citrine, but is of a more goldish yellow. It also appears to reflect light rather better than the citrine; this is because its geological composition is quite different and lends itself better to light play. So the topaz will sparkle rather more than a citrine. Many people become very worried when they feel they might have been sold a citrine rather than a topaz, or vice versa; but even though the stones are two different things, their values are not dissimilar. So the answer is, don't worry. If you like the stone, but you're not sure whether it is a topaz or a citrine, console yourself with the thought that either stone will represent the same sort of investment. Topazes, like citrines, are normally faceted. But the genuine topaz is becoming quite a rare commodity these days.

Cairngorm

This stone is a member of the quartz family, and as the name suggests, comes from the Cairngorm mountains in Scotland. This stone is not seen very often, but it has a charm of its own; it has a rich, glowing brownish-amber colour, although unlike genuine amber, it is quite hard and transparent. It is normally faceted. Probably the most popular use for the cairngorm stone has been in the pins used to hold traditional Scottish kilts together. These pins are usually made of silver, with a cairngorm set in the centre. The stones were also quite popular in Victorian times, and you'll still see the odd ring or brooch with a cairngorm in shops specialising in antique jewellery.

Amber

Amber is a stone, as such, but perhaps hasn't been in the ground for as long as some of the other stones. It is, in effect, fossilised resin. It can be mottled or variegated, and can even include the remains of small animals or plants. By far the most usual colour is the deep amber, reddish-yellow. In Victorian times, amber was made into bracelets, rings and necklaces. The most common use in those days was to make the amber into smooth beads, which were then strung like a pearl necklace and worn round your neck. You can still see old amber necklaces in many antique shops and curio stores, although modern amber jewellery is scarce. It can also be used to make small objets d'art.

Smoky Quartz, Smoky Topaz, Smoky Citrine

These three are very similar, and have few distinguishing features other than those adaptable from the sections on the non-smoky stones, above. Smoky quartz tends to be a brownish colour and doesn't sparkle as much as the other two. The topaz and the citrine will tend towards a yellowish or reddish tint; but effectively, the differences are so small that it would take an expert with fine instruments to tell which is which. Don't worry, however; value wise, all three are similar.

Cat's Eye and Tiger's Eye

These two stones have brownish backgrounds with yellow, gold or orange stripes. They have roughly the same value. They are very similar to look at, but there is one sure way of telling which is which. Often, the stones are set into a ring and are cut en cabochon. If this is the case, pick up the ring so that the stone is facing you, with the stripes or lines running horizontally. Then turn the ring back and forth so that the lines are moving up and down, still keeping the ring towards you with the lines running horizontally. If the stone seems like an eye that is opening and closing – in other words, the lines disappear when the stone is downwards or upwards and only appear when the stone is facing you square in the middle – it's a Cat's Eye. If you can still see the lines or stripes distinctly marked whichever way you turn the ring, it's a Tiger's Eye.

Cameo

These are unusual stones because, although in their uncarved state they are a light orangey brown, carved areas will become a pale yellow or beige. This gives a lovely two-toned effect. A classic mistake to make, especially when buying cameos in Italy – where they are very popular – is to find a flat, uncarved cameo stone with a plastic carving glued to the top. If you examine a suspect cameo carefully, look at the join between the two colours. You may well notice a tiny air bubble, or a minuscule gap between the brown and the white; a genuine carved cameo will not have either of these faults.

Aquamarine

In the good old days, these were useful stones to carry around with you. They were thought to make your marriage happy, and to cure toothache or liver disease! This stone is a close relation of the emerald and is found in roughly the same areas of the world. Unlike the emerald, though, the aquamarine has far fewer flaws and is a lovely, watery, sea-blue. Aquamarines pass the 'skin test' (seeing your skin right through the stone) very well; they are extremely transparent. They are normally faceted.

Turquoise

These stones were originally made popular, as the name suggests, in Turkey. Today, though, a lot of turquoise is mined in Arizona, in the USA, and in some parts of California. The American turquoise can be easily recognised because it has black 'veins', or lines, running through it. The finest turquoise is the plain variety, with just one pure colour. However, it is very easy to fake this, and often so-called pure turquoise is actually a mixture of powdered turquoise stone and glue. You're better to go for turquoise which has even a slight vein running through it, as this almost certainly is the real thing. Of course, if you know your jeweller, and he or she is qualified to identify stones, then go ahead – buy the beautiful, plain variety. Turquoise, though usually blue, can be green.

Lapis Lazuli

This is another smooth stone that's used for making objets d'art, ashtrays, boxes and even watch faces as well as jewellery. Ideally it should be dark, rich blue and it contains tiny little gold flecks. These are not real gold, in fact, but pyrites. Because lapis lazuli is strong, it can be carved and as such is often used to make crest or initial rings.

Alexandrite

This strange but beautiful stone was named after the Russian Tsar, Alexander II. He was the person who first made alexandrites popular in Europe, although the stone had been around for a while even then. The extraordinary thing is that the colour of the stone changes completely, depending on the way the light hits it and your angle of vision. Within seconds, the stone will be dark blue and then purple. The difference is very vidid – utterly fascinating. Most alexandrites you see these days are synthetically made, but have this same composition which creates the colour change. The man-made versions are usually more attractive than the natural stones, and even though they aren't 'real', are fairly valuable. Alexandrites are normally faceted, and look stunnning set in rings, pendants, or long earrings – anywhere where the superb colour changes can be displayed.

Amethyst

A good stone to have handy, if you are an agriculturist and believe in fairy tales! Amethysts of old were thought to protect crops from storms and insects, and also got rid of evil spirits while they were about it. Today, the charms of the amethyst lie largely in its lovely, mauve colour. As far as character goes, the amethyst has a lot in common with the aquamarine; other than the colour difference, they both have that same rather watery, highly transparent look about them. Amethysts are normally faceted.

Rose Quartz

This stone shares all the qualities of other colours of quartz, and is usually faceted. Its colour is a plain, clear pink, as against the colour of an amethyst which may also appear pink. But the amethyst will almost always have a touch of violet in it; the rose quartz stone will not. Also, the strength of colour in rose quartz will not be as great; it will be a pale, baby pink. Rose quartz, like the other quartz colours, is very transparent.

Jade

Although we've classed this type of jade under the heading of purple, this shade of the stone is not a true purple. It will have the more usual tone of green included in it as well. In fact, much jade that is found in the purplish colour is artificially tinted back to the more commercially successful green. The green variety should be a rich, pure green, which is used not only in jewellery but in many beautiful objets d'art, some of which are carved. Tinting does not really lower the value. Jade is almost always cut and polished to a smooth finish.

Tourmaline

The tourmaline is a dark, 'pine tree' green, and in theory is a transparent stone. However, because it is such a deep colour it is often quite hard to see through it. It is also very shiny on the outside, and has a lot of sparkle and light play for such a dark stone. It is normally faceted. You've got to buy tourmalines from a very reputable jeweller, as they can easily be faked. They will either be totally replaced by tinted glass, or else a thin slice of real tourmaline will be sandwiched between two pieces of glass. This second fake is easier to notice, because if you look at the stone sideways in a strong light, you should be able to see the joins. However, expert faking is quite an art and not one which you'll detect easily with any stone – especially a dark one like the tourmaline. The tourmaline is also one of the more valuable semi-precious stones, as it is quite rare. If you see a piece of jewellery for sale with tourmalines in it, expect to pay quite a lot for it; if it is offered to you cheaply, then beware of fakes. The right price to pay is rather more than for an amethyst, or for a topaz.

Pedidot

Another green stone, but this time a lighter green. Like the aquamarine and the amethyst, the peridot has a certain watery look to it, and has about the same amount of colour depth as those other two stones. It is also sometimes referred to as olivine, or chrysolite. It is a difficult colour to describe, but the nearest is probably a pale leaf green with perhaps a small trace of yellow or gold mixed in with it. The peridot is usually faceted, and looks terrific set in yellow gold.

Malachite

This stone is by no means restricted to use in jewellery. It can be used to make all sorts of objets d'art, including ashtrays, lamp stands, desk sets, etc., as it isn't a particularly expensive material and can be worked easily. Malachite is not difficult to recognise, as it is always a rich, darkish green with black streaks or 'veins' running through it. Another common use for malachite is to make entire rings (with no metal included) and bangle bracelets. It is usually cut according to the shape required and then polished until smooth.

Moss Agate

This is just another variety of agate, but with a moss green colour and often deeper green veins running through it. Like malachite, it is popular for use in smaller objects for the home and for the desk, as well as being used in jewellery. The crucial difference between moss agate and malachite, visually speaking, is that whereas most agrate has darker green veins running through it, the veins will never be black.

Agate

Although we've put agate in with the green or greenish stones, in actual fact agate can be of almost any combination of colour. In ancient times, it was supposed to inspire eloquence in the owner; in Victorian times in the UK, it was very popular for use in brooches, mounted in gold or silver. Today, it is still used in some jewellery, but as it is relatively inexpensive, it is more commonly used for objets d'art, and all the various items which that category can include. Agate is almost always a combination of two or more colours, with streaks, spots and lines forming a pattern within it. When small agate stones are polished, they are often not done individually; they are placed in a machine that resembles a tumble dryer, and left in there for a while. The tumbling action causes the stones to rub together and effectively they polish each other.

Bloodstone

This is another smooth polished stone, and although it can be used to make objets d'art, is actually more favoured in jewellery. It is a very dark green, which in a poor light can look black, with small red flecks or veins running through it. Normally, bloodstones are used to make flat beads or flat lozenges for use in necklaces, or else a flat, smooth bloodstone will be used as the centrepiece of a signet or initial ring. Bloodstones can be carved, although they're quite brittle. It takes a real expert to carve an intricate design on a bloodstone, and sadly, there are very few such experts around any more.

Hematite

Hematite is the only black stone that actually contains any natural sparkle and life. In fact, it has so much life in it that its surface, when faceted and polished, reflects light like a mirror. Hematite is not all that common, but you will occasionally see it in jewellers' shops, often advertised as 'black diamond'. Mind you, there are real black diamonds; these are not particularly valuable, compared with white diamonds, but still would fetch rather more than a hematite. However, real black diamonds tend to remain small, whereas it is quite usual to find large hematites. So if you're faced with a 'black diamond' that's quite large, there's a good chance it isn't a black diamond at all, but a hematite.

Jet

Jet is not a stone, as such, but a form of extremely hard coal. Nonetheless, it is still soft enough to carve, and in Victorian times, in the UK, was used to make very pretty beads for necklaces, brooches and so on. This was not for reasons of pure fashion, though. When the much-loved Prince Albert died, Queen Victoria began a whole new trend in jewellery – mourning jewellery. And jet, because of its colour, was an obvious choice. Today, much of it is still around in the antique shops, and if you don't mind the rather sombre colour, it is quite attractive. There have been quite a few imitations, including glass (sometimes called French jet) and plastic, but the real thing is quite easy to distinguish by its warm, soft, velvety feel.

Onyx

In the old days, onyx was supposed to make sure you had a healthy body and spirit, and people believed it could cure epilepsy. Actually, onyx is a variety of agate, and is very similar in texture to that stone, apart from the fact that it is all black with no stripes or veins. Unlike hematite, onyx is pure, dense black with a sheen – but without a sparkle. It is almost matt. Onyx is used in jewellery, especially in watch making as it is strong enough to be sliced very thinly, which makes it ideal for a watch face. In addition, it is used to make the usual objets d'art.

Garnet

Garnets were, once again, very popular in Victorian times in the UK. They are dark red stones, with an almost brownish tint to them; they hold a great deal of sheen and glitter, but can't really be said to sparkle as such. They are very common amongst older jewellery, and although in modern times less garnet jewellery is being made, there is still plenty of the old stuff around. These stones can be cut with facets, or else en cabochon; both ways manage to bring out the rich colour and lustre of the stones. There is no question of a garnet posing as a ruby, as the colours are quite different. Imitations are few and far between, as the garnet is a relatively inexpensive stone and to produce fakes would not have been, or be, worthwhile.

Spinel

Spinels actually come in a variety of colours. The red spinel is perhaps more common than the others, except white. But white spinels are normally man-made, whereas red spinels will more usually be natural. Red spinels are primarily used as imitation rubies, because the colours are similar. However, the spinel is rather more transparent than a ruby; once again, try the 'skin test'. If you can see your skin very clearly through the stone, it's likely to be a spinel. Another distinguishing factor could be that a natural ruby may have slight colour variations, looking at the stone from left to right; the spinel will have even colour throughout, and will also have a rather more glassy look to it. Spinels, because they have many of the properties of more valuable, hard, stones, are nearly always faceted.

CHAPTER EIGHT

Jewellery and the Way You Look: That Precious Sense of Fashion

Telling people what is fashionable and elegant is an arrogant and dictatorial task. It's probably best left to the Christian Diors, Halstons, Puccis, Mary Quants and Pierre Cardins of this world. When you really come down to it, fashion should be whatever makes you feel good – and that applies equally to jewellery as it does to clothing, motor cars, restaurants, night clubs, and everything else.

So having taken a bite out of that humble fashion pie, we still can't get away from fashion. It's a subject we can't brush under the carpet, or gloss over; it must be discussed in any book of this kind! What we've tried to do is to guide rather than dictate, to help you to develop your own taste and style through pointing out a few basics you may have overlooked.

The first things to eliminate from any argument over fashion and jewellery are the wedding ring and, in the case of women, the engagement ring. These two are above fashion; whatever the country, whatever the culture, whatever the social occasion, a wedding ring and an engagement ring are OK. Of course, many women choose not to wear their fancy precious stone-set engagement ring when they're weeding the garden, or going down to the local shop to buy a packet of breakfast cereal. These situations, if they do preclude the wearing of a diamond or other precious ring, arise more out of practicality than out of a fashion sense. A mis-guided snip with the secateurs could miss the rose bush and knock a stone out of a setting; some women might feel they're overdoing things a bit by wearing a large precious stone to do their morning shopping. The answer is, though, that nobody in their right mind could possibly criticise someone who wears the symbols of their love and devotion to their spouse, whatever the circumstances. So even if it makes you happy to wear your engagement ring to dig the garden or service the car, don't give it a second thought. Do it; just bear in mind you may get the stones dirty or even damaged.

In a more general sense, the wearing of jewellery does need to be matched to the occasion up to a point. From a psychological point of view, your jewellery sometimes plays an important part. For example, you could argue that a woman in business – still, sadly, subjected to rather more emotional pressures than men – should select the jewellery that she wears to work with some care. Obviously valuable jewellery can give rise to jealousy amongst smaller-minded female colleagues, and can set off wry remarks from male workmates. No jewellery at all can make a business woman appear too unfeminine and create a dull image that might get projected on to her professional ability. Now, you may be thinking that such nit-picking is so petty it isn't worth considering, and you'd be quite right. But other people can be petty and can be impressed by people's appearances, whether it is conscious or sub-conscious.

A freelance advertising consultant we know, a female, admits quite openly that she dresses the part according to whom she is going to see. In a job like hers, of course, visual images count rather more than they do in other professions. Still, she adapts her clothes and her jewellery to suit the image each particular client expects to see; trendy clothes and junk jewellery when she's working for an advertising agency or creative unit; smart, business-like clothes and classical jewellery when she works for an industrialist or manufacturer; and elegant, fashionable clothes and jewellery when she does a job for the fashion or cosmetics businesses. Needless to say, she spends a lot on her wardrobe, but she believes it's worth it. The wrong image for the type of client concerned can suggest that she's the wrong person for the job. And to a degree a little of that philosophy can be applied to all of us who are active in public or business life; just think how much importance the Queen of England, Margaret Thatcher, American Presidents' wives and other prominent female figures have to attach to the image they project. Jewellery, being an important part of the way we look – and a statement of our status in life – can tell the rest of the world a lot about what we are.

Choosing the right jewellery to wear, then, holds a lot of deep psychological meaning. But in choosing that jewellery, we mustn't lose sight of the fact that the main job it should do is to complement our looks and our clothes. The first thing you need to do is to take a good, long, hard look at yourself, and decide just what type of person you are – not necessarily what you'd like to be. First of all, the question of your size is important; if you have a heavy frame your jewellery should be heavier in setting and design. Similarly, if you have a light frame, your jewellery should be lighter, airier and smaller. Of course, you don't always have to stick to the rules, but it is true to say that big jewellery on a small person can actually make them look smaller, and light jewellery on a large person can underline their size. You can't compensate for a heavy frame by wearing small jewellery; even though that jewellery may make you think you look less heavy, it won't.

The other thing you must decide is your social type. You can be elegant, trendy, arty, classical, or whatever. If you're clever, you can change images according to your mood, but your jewellery will have to change along with you! To mix up one image in clothes with another image in jewellery looks a mess, and totally destroys the effect you're trying to put across.

When you're buying jewellery, always try it on before you hand your money over, even if the salesperson is pressing you to get on with it. No matter how attractive a piece may look in the window or the display case, it may do nothing for you. And if you can persuade the people in the shop that you're not going to do a flit with the goods, take the jewellery over to a door or window and look at it in daylight. You'd be surprised how much the colours of both gold and stones can appear to change. If no daylight is available, or the shop door is a long way away from the counter, hold the piece under a fluorescent light – this is the nearest you'll get to real daylight.

Earrings

Although we've actually gone into some detail already about individual items of jewellery in Chapter One, we felt we ought to take you through some of them again – only this time from the fashion point of view. Earrings seem an obvious place to begin, if only so we start from the head and work downwards. Actually, earrings are also a good place to start because they are possibly the most crucial pieces of jewellery, from the fashion angle. Earrings can influence the way you look in a big way.

Before we look at the hardware, let's take a look at human ears. Unfortunately, these pieces of flesh are not always very attractive; unless you're lucky enough to own a pair of the shell-like variety, ears are ugly appendages to your head. Unlike some other appendages, though, your ears can't be greatly improved by cosmetic surgery or

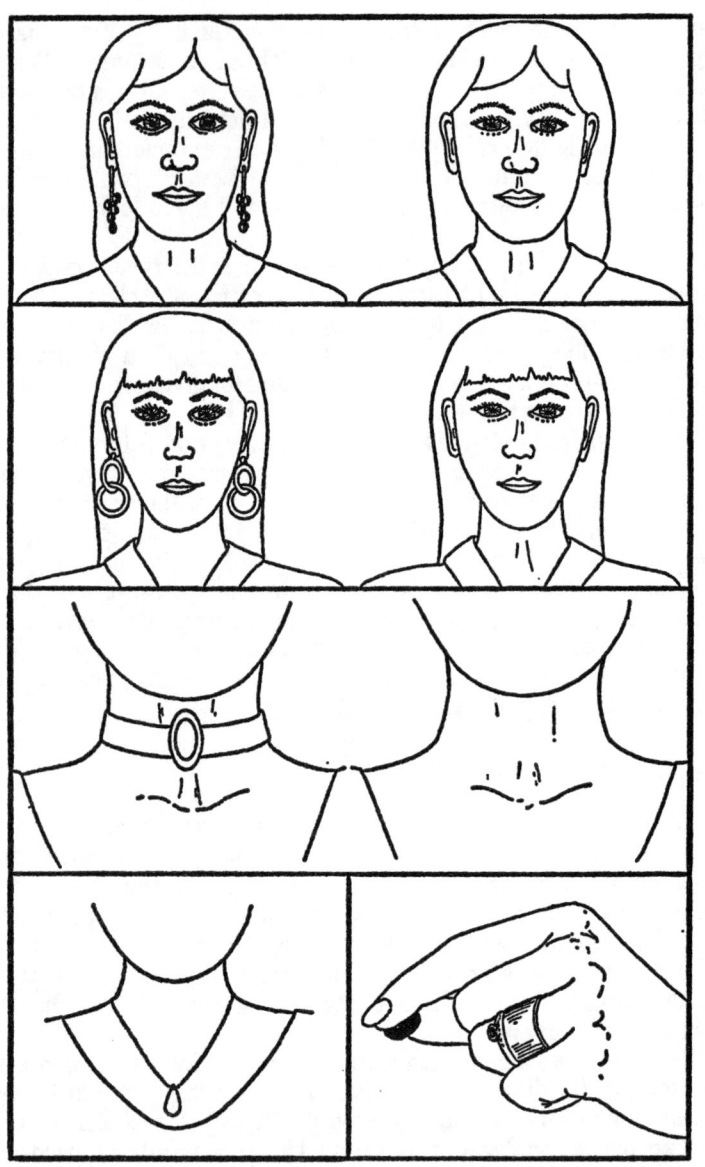

makeup, so you need to brighten them up a bit while they perform the vital and delicate function of allowing you to hear. Although your ears themselves won't do a great deal to correct any imbalances you may have in your face, earrings will, and so the choice of the right earrings becomes even more important. Take your nose, for example; earrings can make it look smaller or larger. They can make a wide face seem narrower, a long face seem shorter, or a round face seem slimmer.

Earrings can also make a noticeable difference in the image you project. Precious or semi-precious stones set in stud earrings, plain gold or silver hoops; grown-up and sophisticated, wild and daring, trendy, or any of the other innumerable styles, can all influence the way you look. The only really important thing to remember is the same thing you must remember when selecting all jewellery – you've got to match the style of your earrings to what you're wearing and to the occasion.

Long, dangling earrings will make your face look longer, and will have the same effect on your neck. So slim-faced, long-necked ladies should avoid these, as they can bring out the giraffe in you! They will also tend to make you look quite dressed up and elegant, which would probably exclude them from being worn with jeans or casual clothes. But remember, rules are made to be broken. Big earrings, like round, flat clips, tend to fill out a slim face, and balance pronounced cheek hollows. If you want to wear big earrings and you haven't got a slim face, it's a good idea to step up the cheek blusher or shader, which will then counteract the widening effect the earrings could have on your face. Big earrings will also minimise a large nose.

Hoop earrings have always been popular, especially since Natalie Wood – that lovely American actress – started to wear them every time she showed her face in public. They look attractive whether you're dressed casually or formally, and although they don't really change the look of your face that much, they do have a certain slimming effect. There's something exotic about hoop earrings – something sensual, even sexy. Perhaps it has something to do with the classic early Hollywood gypsy lady or flamenco dancer, both of whom were always portrayed as daring, vamp-like creatures complete with hoop

---

Wide face, short neck with and without long earrings
Slim face with and without earrings
Short, fat neck with and without choker
Short, fat neck with long chain and pendant
Wide wedding ring with small engagement ring

earrings and low-cut dresses. One thing these earrings really do complement is long hair – often a problem when choosing earrings, as long hair seems to dwarf all but a few styles. The hoops, though, even if they're not in full view, manage to poke through your tresses and gleam suggestively.

Another type of earring that looks superb with long hair is based on the chain idea. It came into fashion in a surprisingly small way in the late 1970's; but because it is not particularly outrageous, and therefore not likely to date, it may well stay around for some time. A length of fine chain, say five centimetres or so, is suspended from your ear by attaching one end to a stud, a tiny clip, or sleeper. The chain is left to hang loose and mingle with your hair, with perhaps a small gold or silver bobble on the far end of it. Another version, more suitable for shorter hair, is to catch the dangling end and tie it up to the back of the clip, stud or sleeper in a way similar to the hoop effect. If you can't find these locally, your jeweller may well be able to have them made for you; the cost shouldn't be too much as the lengths of chain can come from standard chain stock, and can simply be soldered on to the clip or stud. In fact, if you have pierced ears and own a pair of studs or small sleepers, all you require are the lengths of chain, which could even come from an old gold or silver neck chain or bracelet of your own, so the making-up charge wouldn't involve any extra metal.

If you wear glasses, especially ones with quite prominent frames, you really want to stick with the plainer types of earring. Fancy earrings can positively scream at your spectacles, which results in a slanging match going on across your face – hardly the sort of thing that will make you look at your best. Plain gold or silver (unless your frames are gold or silver, in which case you should be sure to match the colour of the metals) are fine. So are pearls and diamonds, or other colourless stones. Coloured stones or enamel work should tone with the colour of your frames, and also with the colour of your lenses if you wear the tinted variety. Of course, if toning the colour of your earrings with your glasses has to be done at the expense of clashing with the colour of your clothes, then all this good advice goes out of the window. The answer is to reach a compromise, so that even if all three elements are of different colours, they should at least harmonise with each other.

Necklaces

There isn't really a great deal of advice we can offer you on the subject of necklaces, other than fairly obvious, facile remarks like you shouldn't wear glass beads on a leather string with a formal outfit. Fashion is a lot more flexible now than it used to be, following on after the progress which has been made in other areas. So even that last piece of information could be wrong for someone who might look stunning at a formal occasion in an ethnic kaftan and leather and beaded jewellery. The only genuine rule is that there are no genuine rules; not any more, anyway.

In physical terms, though, short and/or large necked people should avoid wearing short chains and chokers because these only accentuate the problem areas. Short necklaces are good, though, if your neck is on the long side, or is thin. If your neck isn't long, you should stick to long chains and strings of beads, or better still, chains with pendants. These last types form a deep natural V shape which has a slimming effect on the neck and the face, as does a V neckline in your clothing.

Rings

As we said way back in Chapter One, rings are the most complex – and the most profuse – of all jewellery items. In fact, there are so many different types of rings around that it would be impossible to describe them all. Basically, though, you can divide rings into two groups; stone-set and plain metal. Stone-set rings are, on the whole, more 'dressed up' in appearance than are plain metal rings. Mind you, with fashion trends being so open-ended these days, a highly fashionable lady could probably wear a stone-set ring with a pair of overalls and look terribly elegant.

Some of the basic fashion rules also apply to rings. But these stem, on the whole, from common sense. Small, fine rings only look attractive on slender, small and delicate hands; on bigger digits small rings look tiny and therefore accentuate the size of the hand. On the other side of the fence, large and bulky rings look like knuckle-dusters on small, slim hands, but won't exaggerate large hands. If you have short fingers, you'll find that stones cut in rectangular or marquise shapes will make them appear longer. Generally speaking, only people with long fingers look attractive wearing round or square cut stones, and also rings set with several stones running horizontally across the finger. On short fingers, all of these create a widening effect.

At odd times throughout the last few centuries, the fashion of wearing several rings on one or both hands has cropped up. Again, sadly, it is only the lucky few who possess long, slim hands who can follow this fashion and look elegant. Don't forget, any horizontal line in the design of a ring, or in this case a line created by wearing several rings next to each other, is going to have a widening effect. So if your hand is already wider than you'd like it to be, avoid wearing more than one finger's worth of rings.

Wedding rings are probably the most important of all, aesthetically speaking, as they're the ones that people wear most. And although we've said that a wedding ring goes whatever the occasion and whatever your outfit, brides-to-be should consider the shape and design of their ring very carefully. After all, it's a ring you'll be wearing all the time for a long time – so it needs to suit you really well. Fancy or ornate wedding rings come into fashion now and again, and they can be lovely. But you've got to remember that it is a lot easier to tire of a fancy ring than it is of a plain one. A plain ring will go with everything you wear, and if you want to make the whole ensemble look fancier, simply slip another, more elaborate ring next to the wedding band, either on its own or accompanied by your engagement ring as well. Remember too, that a wedding ring – especially one with an ornate engraved design – should not be too tight when you buy it. Like it or not, there's a good chance that you might put on some weight as you get older, and your ring will have to be made larger. Of course, this is nearly always a feasible alteration, but sometimes the sizing work will show. And because wedding rings have no top or bottom they tend to slip round your finger, revealing a sizing mark for all to see. Fancy wedding rings suffer from sizing even more, because often a continuous design has to be broken into in order to make the ring larger (or smaller). But if your ring is a comfortable – not tight – fit when you buy it, there's a better chance that you can postpone, or even forget, having it made larger.

Wide wedding rings have been popping in and out of fashion regularly throughout history. Choosing one is a question of your own taste and whether or not its style is complimentary to the shape of your hand. The trouble is that if your engagement ring is small, a wide wedding band will make it look even smaller. Another aspect worth considering before you purchase a wide wedding band is the fact that it can trap moisture underneath the metal next to the skin – particularly in hot weather. This is especially true of the barrel-shaped, convex styles. Moisture caught up in this way can lead to rashes and cause havoc if your skin tends to be extra sensitive. Narrower rings avoid this problem, and also don't dwarf a small engagement ring. The other advantage of a narrow wedding band is that, should you feel like wearing what appears to be a wider ring, you can wear another plain ring with it. This could be a simple band, a single or multi 'twisted' gold wire ring, in one or more colours, a 'Russian' wedding ring (three plain intertwined bands, each in a different colour of gold), a coloured ring in enamel, agate, jade, coral or perspex, or even an eternity ring. All of these go very well with the plain lines of a wedding ring, and can be quite happily sandwiched in between the wedding band and the engagement ring, although more than two rings on the same finger can look odd. It is more difficult to wear a combination of rings like this if your wedding ring is wide, as the very bulk of the hardware on your finger can make your skin bulge out at the knuckle – not a pretty sight even on the most beautiful hand.

Wide hands will look wider if you wear a ring on your little or index fingers, as either will serve the purpose of extending the visual line out to the side of your hand. If this is your problem, minimise it by wearing rings on your middle and 'ring' fingers only. If your nails are short or, indeed, your whole hand is short, you'll find that long sleeves and heavy bracelets worn low on the wrist make everything look even shorter. Keep your sleeves to mid-forearm length, and push your bracelets up there too. These two tricks will make your hand seem to merge undisturbed into your wrists so it looks like one long sweep. These tricks are also useful if you have a ring you're particularly proud of and want it to stand out.

The colour of your nail-varnish, vis-à-vis the colour of a plain metal ring, doesn't really make much of a difference. But your choice of varnish can make an enormous difference to coloured or even colourless stones. If you're wearing a stone-set ring that you want to emphasise, a pale shade of nail varnish will set it off better than a dark shade. You should be especially careful in choosing nail colour if the stones you'll be wearing are red, pink or mauve. For example, an orange nail shade worn with an amethyst ring would result in a terrible shouting match between the two colours. The best pale colours to aim for if you want them to harmonise with a coloured stone are the plain, non-iridescent beige tones. Not only do these shades focus all the attention on the stone, they also cover up a multitude of sins if your nails are less than perfect.

Before we leave the subject of nail varnish, though, there *is* one pale colour that does compete with stones, especially diamonds and other colourless gems. This is the white or off-white 'pearlised' iridescent polish, which was very popular in the swinging nineteen sixties, and is still quite often worn – especially in summer. It's a colour that makes your hands look stunning if you're dark skinned or suntanned, but it really does put most gemstones in the shade.

Bracelets

Here again, common sense rules. If your wrist is small and fine, you really want to stick with fine bracelets, as heavy ones can make your wrist appear scrawny. If you have heavier wrists, though, tiny bracelets will look rather lost, and will make your wrist seem heavier than it actually is. Chunky bracelets are for you if this is your problem, as they will balance your overall look far better. Another tip for people with heavy wrists; wear your bracelets higher up on your forearm. This will create a slimming effect.

Lots of bracelets worn together can look attractive if they're all of the same or similar design, like in the case of matching bangles. But several different bracelets, perhaps mixing up bangles and chains, can look messy and unco-ordinated. To break this rule, though, a very fine chain worn with your watch – particularly if you have a plain watch with a dark leather strap – can be stunning. It can also make your watch look more formal; ideal if you've only the one watch which has to do for both every day and special occasion use.

Ankle bracelets go through periods of popularity. But unless your ankle is very slim and sleek, this sort of decoration is best avoided. As with rings, the horizontal line principle applies here; the chain of the bracelet forms a line that goes across and around your ankle at right angles to the direction your leg goes, effectively 'cutting' across it. Thick ankles then look much thicker.

Colours

A lot of jewellery and fashion experts have very set ideas about which colours clash with what, and what you should wear with which. But essentially we believe that your jewellery should be worn so that it pleases you and makes you feel more attractive, more glamorous, more whatever *you* want. So if it grabs you to wear a pair of amethyst earrings next to your flaming red hair, then go right ahead – although many more traditionally-minded fashion people would scream with horror at the thought. If you can't stand the sound of the screams, though, there are a few elementary considerations which can point you in the right direction!

Matching your skin tones, make-up and your hair colour to jewellery is very much a question of taste, although red-heads have to take a little more care. Carrot-coloured hair and red or purple stones are something of a no-no, if only because the colour combinations disagree with each other to the point where neither are noticed in their own right. The whole point of colour choice is to make sure that colours either harmonise, or else contrast effectively. Contrasts that yell abuse at one another cancel each other out; contrasts that give each other a lift look terrific. That's where your own skill, judgement and imagination must decide the issue.

What does really matter is the colour of your clothes. Jewellery and clothes should go hand in hand, but without careful colour matching one can either drown the other, or the two can clash so that the overall look is wrong. If you want to wear several stones at once, say in earrings, a pendant on a chain round your neck and a ring, you ought to make sure that they're the same colour, or at least shades of the same colour. Different colours of stones worn together cause visual confusion. The only exception is a diamond (or other colourless stone), which goes with almost everything; but beware of mixing a real diamond with other colourless gems. The brilliance and fire of the diamond will make the other stones look very dowdy.

Some colours of clothing look better with certain stones and with certain colours of metal jewellery, too. The texture of your clothing makes a difference; a heavy wool jacket will look better with rather chunky jewellery, whereas fine, light summer clothes lend themselves to delicate chains and smaller stones. What is important in selecting the jewellery to match your clothes is time. Trial and error in front of a mirror as you get dressed is the surest way to know your jewellery will go with what you're wearing; but throwing on your jewellery as an afterthought, as you're about to leap out the door, may well result in a disaster. Think out your jewellery beforehand, as you think out your outfit.

There is one famous subject of controversy which should be pushed out of the way here and now; the wearing of white metals with yellow. Some more conservative types feel that they should never be worn together. But more modern jewellery designers cheerfully ignore this dictum and produce some really pretty jewellery using both colours. On the whole, though, the best approach lies somewhere between these two. If you have a piece of jewellery where the two colours are intermingled, like in a twisted wire ring or bangle, fine. The very fact that the colours are intermingled means that they will merge together into one pattern. But a yellow gold watch worn on the same arm as, say, a silver ring –or a white gold necklace worn near yellow and gold earrings look incongruous. Wedding rings and engagement rings of different coloured metals can look awful together; you might think that this is a fairly obvious combination to avoid, but you do see them around. Another thing to watch out for is the jewellery you choose to go with metallic fabrics. By this we mean the rather formal cloth that has metal, shiny threads woven through it; ideally, you want to pick gold or silver jewellery that is of the same colour as the metal threads.

And lastly, men! Women tend to overlook men's jewellery, largely because many men will only wear a watch anyway. But consider the man who wears a yellow gold wedding ring and a stainless steel watch or silver identity bracelet together on the same arm. You may not notice it until his sleeve is rolled up, but it can show – and look wrong. Similarly, a man should try to co-ordinate the colours of the less obvious, but still noticeable items, like belt buckles, shoe ornaments and so on. Although no-one's saying that every single bit of metal a man happens to wear on his person should be of the same colour, white metal and yellow metal really shouldn't come too close together.

CHAPTER NINE

Never Mind the Quality, Feel the Shine

As we suggested in Chapter One, costume or imitation jewellery has its problems. Very good imitations are expensive; cheap stuff will break or lose its looks quickly. And then, where do you draw the line between imitation and real? A man-made, imitation diamond made of YAG, Stronium Titanate or Cubic Zirconium (usually with names beginning with DIA) will cost as much as, or more than, a zircon. Yet the diamond imitation is, strictly speaking, costume jewellery and the zircon – although a diamond substitute in its colourless form – is a semi-precious stone in its own right. Just to confuse the issue even further, both stones will probably be mounted in gold, which is a 'real' metal.

There's no answer to the dilemma, other than saying that costume jewellery is any piece which pretends to be something it isn't. And that can be anything from the rings you get out of Christmas crackers to colourless, semi-precious gemstones set in gold which are imitating diamonds. Having said all this, then, it is still only right that we should discuss imitation jewellery. Because, like it or not, most of us possess some of it. And cleverly worn it *can* fool others; a subtle combination of real and imitation pieces can appear to be all genuine. The thing to remember is that costume jewellery should be bought and worn with the right attitude – low expenditure for a bit of fun. Now, low expenditure means different things to people of different income brackets, and whereas one person's bit of fun jewellery will come out of a cracker, another person will spend the price of a Mediterranean holiday on an imitation diamond. What matters is how much you spend in relation to what you can afford. The moment when spending money on costume jewellery becomes ridiculous, is when you spend more on it than you would normally spend on any other bit of fun.

Of course, there is another aspect of imitation jewellery that is of rather more consequence. This is when someone tries to sell you something as the real thing when in fact it is a fake. And perhaps it is in this context that we should justify our whole chapter on the subject! Naturally, you won't be sold fakes if you buy from a reputable jeweller. But many people do buy from private individuals, both at home and abroad, who are sometimes less than honest. We obviously can't teach you all you need to know about recognising fakes; to do so would not only take years of training and experience, but would involve you in buying expensive machinery that's needed to examine the goods. All we can do is to make you aware of what fakes, imitations, copies or whatever you like to call them are around, so that you at least know what chances there are that a piece of jewellery you want to buy is or isn't genuine.

Faking the Old-Fashioned Way

There's nothing new about imitation jewellery, just as there's nothing new about the faking of great paintings and other works of art. But it wasn't until the eighteenth century, in Europe, that costume jewellery really began to be publicly admitted and made in a big way. This coincided with the emergence of the so-called middle class, or bourgeoisie. These people wanted to appear different to the working population but, on the other hand, couldn't afford to pay for real precious metals and gemstones. This was the time when cut steel, marcasite, paste and imitation gold became popular.

Another reason for the increasing popularity of imitation jewellery at that time, in Britain especially, was the rapidly growing danger to travellers. The notorious highwaymen were enjoying the heyday of their careers, and robbery was quite a common occupational hazard if you travelled by road. As a result, even the rich people of the day had their real, precious jewellery copied in imitation materials and wore the ersatz stuff when they were going anywhere that involved a potentially dangerous journey. That way, if they were robbed, they would at least have the small satisfaction of knowing that they were handing over worthless jewellery to the swash-buckling highwayman.

A certain Mr Christopher Pinchbek made quite a name for himself around this era with his alloy of copper and zinc. This was about the closest imitation of gold anybody of his generation could come up with. Ironically, genuine Pinchbek pieces are worth a lot of money nowadays, in antique value, and also because the workmanship that went into their making was excellent. The crafting and decorating of

Pinchbek was almost as elaborate and carefully done as it would have been for real gold.

Over in France, the Revolution created a certain rethinking of people's attitudes to richness and extravagance, with the result that lavish spending on precious jewellery was no longer considered acceptable to many people. Nor was it possible for many of the newly impoverished 'citoyens'. This sudden austerity encouraged the French to turn to imitation jewellery. They went for gold copies, like Pinchbek, and for paste. Also in sudden demand were the semi-precious stones which were more appealing than plain or coloured glass, and yet came within the reach of many more people's finances.

Electro-plating was innovated in the 19th century, which gave a great deal more scope to manufacturers of imitation jewellery. Plating on to cheap base metals meant that the gold or silver finish looked rather more like the real thing than even the valiant efforts of people like Pinchbek. Plating is still a commonly used technique for costume jewellery today.

Rolled or 'filled' gold also became popular in the 19th century. This was something of a compromise between real gold and gilt, or plated metal, because it involved fusing a thin layer of real solid gold on to a cheap base metal. This layer would result in rather more gold being present than if the article had been plated. The technique is still used today, and although it can never be considered as precious as real, solid gold, it will probably keep its looks rather longer than cheap plate or gilt.

Nowadays, there are several metals and combinations of metals used in imitation jewellery. Nickel is one favourite, and brass is another. These two are usually plated with another metal substance in order to give them a gold colour; very often this plating will wear off after a time, to show the dull base metal underneath. Specially treated aluminium is often used, too; this has the advantage of even colour. But of course, quite apart from the difference in feel between aluminium and gold, it is never possible to reproduce the texture and colour exactly. Aluminium will always feel very light in weight, and will have a shallow, more superficial look about its colour. The main trouble with all of these metals is that – unlike gold and stainless steel – they are not inert. This means that the acids in your skin can react with the metal, and anything from black or green staining to severe skin rashes can occur. Anyone who is prone to skin complaints should avoid non-precious metals, and silver, like the plague. Another problem with many of these metals is that they can rust; so if you wear costume jewellery, you should avoid getting it wet!

You Can't Put Too Much Sparkle Into A Glass Eye
...Imitation Diamonds

As diamonds are the most precious of all stones, it seems logical that people should want to copy them more than they copy other stones. This is quite true. And in recent years, some fairly convincing copies have been produced, including the rather unfortunately named YAG, which stands for Yttrium Aluminium Garnet, Strontium Titanate and CZ, or Cubic Zirconium. All of these are sold – under a variety of names as we said earlier in this chapter. Most names have the prefix of Dia- and are widely advertised, often in the form of mail order. In a dim light, these stones could pass for the real thing. But it only takes a glimpse of the real diamond next to a YAG for you to see which is which; regardless of the fact that many manufacturers say only experts can tell the difference, a keen pair of eyes is all you should need. The YAG, Strontium Titanate, or CZ will look too good to be true; too shiny, with too much of a mirror effect. It won't have the same depth or fire as a diamond. Of course, when seen on their own without any real diamonds in the vicinity, these stones do look quite attractive. They are often used to copy real diamonds, even very large ones, when heavy insurance premiums mean that the genuine article has to spend most of its time in the bank. And fake as they are, stones made from YAG, Strontium Titanate, or CZ do look more like the real thing than does glass, or even quartz or zircons, which are also common diamond substitutes.

The trick is to be able to tell the difference between these stones and the real thing *when there is no genuine diamond around with which to compare the copy*. That's where expertise comes in. If someone is wearing a dia-whatever, and that someone is likely to be able to afford the real thing, and you're sitting round a dinner table in a glamorous place all dressed up for an evening out, you're not likely to suspect that the stone is fake. In that case, it certainly won't jump up and hit you in the face with its falsehood. It's only when someone you know isn't particularly wealthy suddenly turns up wearing a 5 carat 'diamond' that you can begin to suspect it might be a phoney. So perhaps there's a moral in that; if you want to fool people into thinking you're wearing a real diamond, then buy a YAG or Strontium Titanate, or CZ, stone that's roughly the same size as a diamond you could conceivably afford. You shouldn't try to fool people into thinking you can afford a 5 carat diamond, when you're earning a modest income – come to that, you shouldn't try to fool yourself into thinking than an imitation diamond is a good investment !

More recently, other people have been experimenting with diamond copies, and have produced one or two types which contain similar, minuscule flaws, like the real thing. These could actually cause some confusion in most potential buyers' minds; but there is one test you can conduct which will certainly indicate which is the real thing and which isn't. Unfortunately, this test only works properly with loose, cut stones, which may be a trifle inconvenient if the stone in question is mounted in a ring. If you are talking about loose stones, however, and you've got a similar-sized, genuine loose diamond handy, press both stones on to the pad of your thumb. The fake stone should fall off a fraction later than the real one. Another test which is perhaps more suitable for mounted stones – but still requires the real thing alongside the fake – is to blow on both. The fake will clear slightly later than will the genuine diamond.

While we're on the subject of imitation diamonds, we may as well take a look at some of the other substances that are used if not to imitate outright, at least to represent colourless stones.

A great favourite amongst these is marcasite. Once again, we have a misnomer; the marcasite we know in jewellery isn't really marcasite at all, but a similar substance in mineral terms – iron pyrites. These are a bit like small pieces of flint, and are cut with facets – usually in the old-fashioned 'rose' cut. They are normally set in silver or other white metals. The finest marcasite comes from France, which exports it to countries far and wide. Well-made marcasite jewellery is quite attractive, although it really bears no resemblance to precious or semi-precious stones, as light is reflected off the stones rather than through them. Although marcasite itself can be considered an 'imitation', there are imitations of marcasite, too; mostly glass and plastic. Real marcasite looks warm and soft, with a greyish lustre, whereas imitations look hard and too bright; they're easy to detect. Also beware of marcasite jewellery that doesn't appear to have any metal settings around each stone or pyrite. Cheap marcasite 'stones' are likely to have been stuck down with cement, and are not worth much at all. If you want to buy marcasite jewellery, go for examples which feel and look well made, with each little marcasite piece well set with metal. That represents your best value for money.

Give Yourself a Pasting

Many people believe that the manufacturing of totally fake stones has only been a recent achievement. This, of course, isn't true; there were expert gem substitute-makers around in Roman times. In fact, these people were so good at it that they passed their craft on down the line even to modern-day Italians. The stuff they produced – paste, which is glass – was not necessarily cheap and nasty. And pieces of paste jewellery that were made in Europe in the 18th century are now collectors' items, with properly cut and faceted stones, all neatly set in silver or other reasonably good metal. They obviously hold antique value, but because the workmanship that went into these pieces was far superior to that which goes into the making of modern paste jewellery, the items do hold a certain value in their own right.

Paste can be made from one of two different types of glass – flint glass, and bottle glass. Of these, flint glass is supposed to be better, because it is brighter. Sometimes a paste stone is backed with a layer of silvery foil to make it reflect light better. And the glass can be coloured to look like just about any precious or semi-precious stone, particularly those among the transparent category. Of course, copying stones still requires a certain amount of work and effort, so it is only really worth while to copy precious stones. Semi-precious stones, especially the less expensive varieties like citrine and cat's eye, are not worth copying as the real thing doesn't actually cost that much more. The assumption in these cases is that if you're going to go to the trouble of making a reasonable piece of jewellery, it's not going to cost that much more to include a real citrine than it is to mount a piece of yellow glass. So you're fairly safe here; you're far less likely to run into any paste copies of semi-precious stones than you are copies of precious stones.

One way of telling whether or not a stone is made of paste is to give it a little scratch with a metal nail file or other sharp object – preferably in an unobtrusive place, when no one is looking. Paste will scratch very easily, as it is much softer than most natural stones. Also, a paste stone will feel warmer to the touch than will a natural stone. The best place to judge these temperatures is on your tongue, as long as you can persuade the vendor of the stone that you're not about to eat the merchandise.

Coloured paste is sometimes used to give a poor quality natural stone an extra boost. This doesn't happen too often in Western Europe or North America, say, but it does go on in countries where there are fewer controls on trading standards. A layer of the natural stone will be laid on top of coloured paste, and the two stuck together; tourmalines are great favourites for this kind of treatment (see Chapter Seven). Without specialist knowledge and equipment, it is sometimes quite tricky to detect whether or not this has been done. It's another reason why you should only buy your jewellery from a reputable jeweller.

A Pearl of Wisdom

Artificial pearls have been around for some considerable time. And the French, the noted experts on most types of fake jewellery, were once again the first to come up with a method of copying the look of a pearl. Hollow glass beads were filled up with a type of wax, but these looked very phoney and were only effective for trimming the rather elaborate clothes people wore in those days. If you took a good look at them, they stood out a mile. It was only later on, in the 1930's, that Europeans hit on a method that was really effective. Basically, this method involves dipping a glass or plastic bead into a solution of special fish scales that have been suspended in nitro-cellulose. Cheap versions will only have been dipped a minimum of times, so the coating is thin and wears off easily. But higher quality ones will have been dipped many more times, and in a finer solution of fish scales to boot; the coating is therefore thicker and better and will not wear off so easily.

Regardless of how authentic imitation pearls may look there are a couple of tests you can give them which should enable you to tell straight away if they're real or not. One way is to look at the drilled hole in a pearl which has been strung; if it is artificial you're likely to see a bit of plastic or glass showing through, around the edge of the hole. The other way of telling, which is rather easier, is to put the pearl on the edge of one of your front teeth and move it back and forth. If it is a real or cultured pearl you'll find that, no matter how smooth the surface looks, it will feel rough as you move it on the edge of your tooth. An artificial pearl will feel quite smooth. Naturally enough, some shop assistants may take exception if they think you're about to take a bite out of one of their pearls, so do the test discreetly. But it works every time.

Genuine, but Man-Made

Now we've said our piece on fakes, let's take a look at some stones which actually fall in between the categories of fake and real. These are synthetic stones, which are not to be confused with anything else. Synthetics are stones actually made up with the same chemical and mineral composition as the natural variety, so they look and feel just the same, but instead of spending millions of years under the ground they are reproduced in a laboratory. The most common stones that are made synthetically are sapphires, rubies (and their star versions), emeralds and spinels. Sometimes synthetic stones are sold as 'restructured' gems, but these are two different things. Real restructured stones are actually made by sticking together pieces and powder from the natural gem; turquoises are sometimes made this way (see Chapter Seven).

Recently, some significant advances have been made towards synthetically producing diamonds. Forgetting YAG; Strontium Titanate and CZ, which have quite different chemical and mineral compositions, General Electric in America have actually managed to make some synthetic diamonds in a laboratory. Very little information about this is available as the technique is still in its very early stages, but much speculation is going on about it in the jewellery business. Many people feel that the only useful purpose these synthetic diamonds could serve would be in industry, especially were the supply of natural diamonds to dry up one day, for whatever reason. Certain fields of medicine and industry depend heavily on diamonds for precision tools, as we discussed in Chapter Six, so the possibility of manufacturing diamonds synthetically would mean that there will always be a supply. By the same token, synthetic diamonds, as they are now, are not thought to be suitable for use in jewellery as there are likely to be many more inclusions – flaws – in these stones than in the natural ones. If you think about it, humans would be trying to achieve in a few short laboratory hours what nature does in four million years or so. In that long time, all the air bubbles and other flaws will get forced out of the stone, through millenniums of pressure. Can the synthetic process achieve the same? It would seem unlikely. And anyway, the cost of producing synthetic diamonds – certainly during these early stages – would be far more than the cost of the natural stones, so it's hardly a financially viable proposition at this point. Time will tell.

The perfection of a technique to make synthetic rubies and sapphires of the corundum family, was achieved by a Professor Verneuil some time ago. His technique involved the development of a special 'oven', plus rather complicated fiddling about in chemical terms. The end result is very good, resulting in synthetically made corundum of various colours. These synthetic stones are almost impossible to distinguish from the real thing with the naked eye, even if you're a knowledgeable expert. To tell the difference, you've got to use complicated machinery and subject the stone to various tests. Once again, only buy sapphires and rubies from a reputable jeweller. He or she may well stock synthetic stones, but will label them as such so you have a choice.

Star sapphires and rubies are often made synthetically, too (see Chapter Six). The method for doing this was perfected by the Linde Company in America in the late 1940's. And Linde star stones have become a well established part of the jewellery trade; although they are not as valuable as the natural variety, they have a certain value of their own, and can be re-sold without risk of losing your shirt. They also happen to be more attractive, on the whole, than natural star stones – as we said in Chapter Six.

Another great favourite amongst synthetic stones in the spinel. As well as being used in its colourless form to imitate the diamond, it can be coloured to copy many other precious and semi-precious stones. With a special addition of gold it can look like lapis lazuli, and with a particular method of heating it can be made to cloud over and look like a moonstone. Once more, a reputable jeweller is your only precaution against accidentally buying a synthetic spinel; these stones are very hard to identify unless you're an expert. Some versions are easier than others, of course; although you may be fooled by a spinel that looks like a ruby, you won't be fooled – or at least, you shouldn't be fooled – by a colourless spinel posing as a diamond. It simply can't have the same fire and light play. Synthetic spinels are very common amongst cheaper jewellery, so be careful of them. Natural spinels do exist, as we said in Chapter Seven, but there are fewer of these around.

Emeralds were first made synthetically in the late 1930's. Methods were developed both in Europe and in the USA, but at the time it was the American method which proved more successful. The actual method itself was a closely guarded secret, but the results were good – even to the presence of flaw-like inclusions, or 'garden'. In more recent years, a European – Doctor Guilson – developed a method of making synthetic emeralds that don't contain flaws. These are beautiful stones in their own right, and they don't really set out to compete with the natural stone. Again, a reputable jeweller may stock synthetic emeralds, but will sell them to you as synthetic stones. Certainly, you may well be tempted by their beauty and choose to buy them regardless of the fact that they were not mined out of the ground. And if you do, you won't be making a poor investment, although naturally enough you should never be expected to pay as much for a synthetic stone as you do for a natural one. Consequently, you won't sell it again for the price you'd get if the stone was one of nature's products.

Other synthetic (as against fake) stones you might see around are garnets, opals, turquoise and quartz. You won't see many, not because it is difficult to synthesize them – necessarily – but, as we said earlier when referring to paste copies, it's hardly worth the effort and expense when the real, natural thing isn't that valuable anyway. As always, your reputable jeweller will label any synthetic stone as such. On the whole, though, it's as well to avoid synthetic semi-precious stones, because for that little bit more you can buy the natural variety which will inevitably hold more value.

CHAPTER TEN

Keeping a Watch on Timepieces

Whether or not a watch is a jewellery item is quite an arguable question. On the one hand, you couldn't really consider a large, bulky, multi-function wrist watch on a leather strap to be an enhancement of your looks. On the other hand, a gold or jewelled bracelet with a small, delicate watch dial set into it could hardly be considered functional and ugly. Perhaps we can find an answer by looking back through history; at the notorious caveperson, pinning his or her bearskin up with bits of splintered bone, and at the Scotsman attempting to keep at least some of the draughts out by holding his kilt closed with a silver brooch. Now you can't deny that those particular bits of jewellery were functional, but they were - or at least could be - decorative, too.

Much as it may be challenging to argue the toss, it's probably fair to say that the majority of people do look upon their watches as jewellery. And if only because watches can represent a heavy outlay of money for something you wear on your wrist, they are worthy of examination in this book!

The first time a wrist watch really hit the headlines - and we say wrist watch, as against the erstwhile popular pocket watch - was when Queen Elizabeth I of England wore one. True to her own splendid style, this watch was thickly studded with precious stones; the bracelet section held yellow diamonds, and the actual face of the watch was hidden under a profusion of flower shapes that were covered in other precious stones. In fact, Queen Elizabeth was apparently obsessed with watches; she had various types of the portable variety, and even employed a special servant just to keep them all wound up.

Early watches weren't terribly accurate. It wasn't until the late 1600's that the minute hand was introduced. Until then, telling the time was such a hit or miss business that an hour hand on its own was about as near as you could get. However, in those early, opulent days, the fact that you could tell the time by a watch was neither here nor there, really. Watches were status symbols, and their desirability arose from how many precious gems and other goodies you could cram on to them.

The second half of the 20th century has probably seen more advancement in watches than ever before, with new technology kicking out the older, traditional ideas and skills. New ways of powering and displaying the time have been invented. So before we go any further, let's take a look at a few basic definitions, just so we all know what we're talking about.

Analogues Versus Digitals

An analogue watch is one with hands and a conventional watch face. A digital watch is one that displays the time in numbers; you just see the time at that precise moment, e.g. 10 : 37, and nothing else.

Analogue watches can either be powered mechanically (with the traditional spring movement), electrically (with a tiny battery replacing the main spring), or electronically (with a battery and a quartz crystal to power the whole thing, directed by a micro-chip). Electrically powered watches were fashionable for a time, but in the main nowadays the favourites are mechanical and electronic power.

Digital watches are almost always powered electronically or electrically. And whereas an analogue watch can be powered by any of the three methods, a mechanically powered watch will always be an analogue. In certain designs of mechanical watch, figures can actually be shown through little holes in the dial, giving 'digital' readings. But this is not a true digital watch.

In the early days of the digital watch, all that showed was a completely blank face. You had to press a button in order to see anything; then the figures would light up on the dial. This was done with LED – light emitting diodes. The trouble with LED's was that you needed both your hands to tell the time; one with the watch around it and the other to press the button. Not terribly convenient if you were washing up dishes, driving along a motorway, playing tennis, pushing a lawn mower, or whatever. So later versions of the digital watch use LCD – liquid crystal display, which is constant. It is always visible in ordinary light, so you can tell the time just by looking at it.

Mechanical Watches; What Makes Them Tick?

A mechanical watch looks, and is, a very complicated little piece of machinery. First of all, you have the mainspring; this is what you

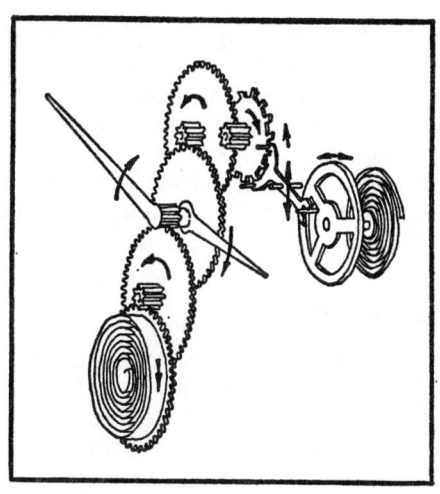

Simplified diagram showing how a mechanical watch works

wind up and by slowly releasing the tension you create by winding it, it drives the watch. Then there are a series of wheels – usually one central and three others. These pass the power from the mainspring on from one to the other, one driving the next one in line, as their little teeth grip into each other. The wheels act as gears, harnessing the power and getting it ready for the next stage. That is when the power reaches the last weel; this one is connected to a 'fork', which clicks along each tooth of the wheel as it turns round. The fork holds the last wheel still for an interval between each click, until the next surge of power is required. This process is also what causes the 'tick tock' noise you hear in any mechanical watch or clock. Each impulse or click that the fork makes is transmitted to a balance wheel, which swings around in an almost complete circle – in one direction after one click, in the other direction after the next click. This swinging of the balance wheel happens very frequently – several thousand times an hour. And if a watch gains or loses time, it is usually because the balance wheel is swinging at the wrong speed. The movement of the balance wheel, through another complicated series of 'gears' – wheels and pinions – causes the hands of the watch to go round the dial.

This, of course, is a very over-simplified version of the full story. Hopefully, it serves to give you a vague idea of how a mechanical watch works. But unless you fancy a long learning period and years of practice, you won't become an expert! You should never attempt to fiddle with the inner workings of a mechanical watch, as untrained fingers can cause untold damage. It's always better to go to a watch expert, no matter how much it may cost. A good mechanical watch should last for years and years, as long as it is expertly maintained, so choosing the foremost expert on watches in your area is a wise investment.

Mechanical Watches: Jewels

Jewel is a word often bandied around when people are talking about watches, particularly when referring to mechanical watches of good quality. What this means is that gemstones – usually synthetic sapphires or rubies – are used inside a watch as bearings for pivots, connected to the various moving parts inside the watch. The reason such precious stones are used is because they are very hard (second hardest after diamonds) and can therefore be polished to a high degree, which means that there is the minimum of friction to interfere with the running of the watch. The more jewels there are, the less friction there is around inside the watch, which is supposed to make for better accuracy and longer wear.

Mechanical Watches: Shockproof/Shock Resistant/Shock Absorbing

If ever anyone tries to sell you a watch as 'shockproof', don't believe them. There's no such thing as a watch that can resist positively all shocks, although they can be made to take some pretty hard knocks without damage. Sometimes, if you're extremely lucky, one of these watches will withstand a very hard blow or heavy fall. But someone, or something, somewhere, somehow, can always find a way to break even the toughest of watches.

The correct way of describing this benefit is as shock resistant, or shock absorbing. All these terms mean is that certain crucial bits of the watch's guts have been padded – almost insulated – with springs. This way, the springs act as shock absorbers and unless the shock is quite a big one, they will protect the important parts. Sometimes another method is used, as well, which involves fitting the watch with a special balance wheel. Shockproof watches are a sensible investment if your work or your hobby is likely to bash your watch around a bit, but you shouldn't expect to pay a great deal of money for the privilege. A great many better quality 'sports' watches have this feature built into them anyway, as a matter of course.

Mechanical Watches: Winding Them Up

Most of us will probably remember our mothers or fathers telling us never to wind up our watches too much as this could break them. Nowadays, fortunately, most watches have a safety device which means you can wind them up as much as you like without risk; a built-in mechanism stops the works from going over the edge. Ideally, you should wind your mechanical watch once every 24 hours. A good time to do this is in the morning; not only so you're sure you won't be late for appointments during the day, but for a less obvious reason, too. A watch which is fully wound is less susceptible to damage from knocks and shocks than one which has wound down quite a way. So if your watch is fully wound during the day, it will be winding down – and therefore more vulnerable – only at night, when it's far less likely to get bashed around. Unless, of course, you work nights ...

Mechanical Watches: Self-Winding

A self-winding mechanism is simply another bit of gadgetry designed to make our lives less difficult, and to avoid the need to remember about winding our watches. What happens is that a weight is added on inside the watch, and as you move your arm around the weight swings about. Via an intricate series of parts, the movement of the weight winds up the mainspring of the watch. The winding up process, rather than happening on a grand scale once every twenty-four hours, occurs little by little over the day's wear. But once it is fully wound up it should run on its own for the same length of time that a manually wound watch would.

If you buy a self-winding watch, make sure it also has a conventional winding knob on it as well. If for some reason you don't wear your watch for a couple of days, you'll probably want to get it going straight away – not hang around for a time while it slowly winds itself.

Mechanical Watches: Anti-Magnetic

Most modern watches – certainly the better quality ones – are anti-magnetic. All this amounts to is that the relevant moving parts of the watch are made from a metal alloy which does not hold any magnetism. Older watches, and sometimes cheaper modern watches, often do have parts in them that could become magnetised. If this happens the parts can malfunction or stick together, which obviously affects the reliability of the watch. Although we're not necessarily aware of it, there is magnetism around in nearly everyone's home. Many kitchen appliances employ magnets to hold doors shut, for example. Close proximity to these can quite easily harm a watch which is not anti-magnetic. So look out, there's a magnet about; and if you're buying a new mechanical watch, an anti-magnetic feature is not just a sales gimmick – it's a good idea.

Mechanical Watches: Waterproof

If a watch is sold to you (by a reputable jeweller or other reliable outlet) as waterproof, you can rest assured that it has passed some fairly stringent tests to prove that it really is waterproof. Bear in mind, of course, that this only applies in countries where there are serious laws about the quality of goods sold. To be waterproof, a watch needs to be well made so that the casing fits properly, and it needs to have special gaskets placed in all gaps or cracks where water could leak in.

While we're on the subject of water, we should mention condensation. No matter how waterproof or apparently watertight a watch may be there's always a certain, tiny amount of air that gets trapped inside the case while the watch is being made. Sometimes there is a small amount of moisture in that air, which can then show itself on the inside of the glass. This usually happens when the air outside is cold; once you move the watch to a warmer atmosphere the condensation will disappear. If this occurs often, you should take your watch to a good watch repair specialist. Even this minute amount of moisture in your watch could eventually cause some vital part of the movement to rust, with resultant breakdown.

Mechanical Watches: Cleaning

You ought to have your watch cleaned and serviced once a year, no matter how much you use it or what sort of treatment it gets.

Quite apart from the fact that some dirt may creep into the watch, there is also friction caused by the moving parts, which can eventually gum up the works a bit. Regular cleaning and checking avoids the problem.

Electronic Watches: Computer Tick-nology

These watches, or to be perfectly accurate, this method of powering a watch (it applies equally to analogue or digital styles) has only been around on the mass market since the early 1970's. With the great electronic age of silicon chips and micro-technology that became widespread around that time, the electronic watch ceased to be an expensive novelty and, through improved techniques and mass manufacturing, was soon seen on trendy wrists everywhere.

There are three main parts to an electronic watch. First, a miniature battery – which can last for up to one year – provides power. This is put through to a crystal, usually made of quartz; the power makes the crystal vibrate like crazy. The vibrations created by the crystal are monitored and geared down by a 'chip', which is a small object covered with micro-circuits. The vibrations are geared to one each second, or part of a second, and that power is then used to drive the watch. Because micro-technology like this has been so thoroughly perfected, the electronic system of powering a watch is extremely accurate. Even the cheapest, lowest 'quality' electronic watches are remarkably reliable.

The only problem with electronic watches occurs when something goes wrong. Unlike a mechanical watch which you can take to any good local watch mender, the electronic watch has to be cared for by someone who is a real expert on the subject of electronics – not just watch mechanics. So far, not many local watch repair people have the knowledge or equipment to deal with these watches, so you'll probably get involved in having the watch sent away. This means you'll wait for quite a while, and it might cost you a fair bit, too – if the guarantee has run out.

Because electronic watches are governed by micro-chip, with a huge number of minute little printed circuits, they can be designed to tell you just about anything. They can even be combined with miniature calculators and tell you the time, the square root of your telephone number, plus the precise hour it is in Kuala Lumpur all within seconds! Mind you, this sort of activity is only possible with the digital type of watch, as analogues have a habit of crowding up the whole face of the watch with hands and numbers. Some versions can also be used as stop watches (although this is possible with very sophisticated mechanical watches, too) and can do several things at once, like recording and storing consecutive lap times. The problem with these computer-like watches is that, micro-technology or not, they often tend to be quite big and bulky. They're fine if you wear loose sleeves and don't mind a lump on your wrist, but if you want elegance, go for an analogue – and mechanical analogues are usually thinner than electronic ones.

The Cheap Watch: What's Good Value?

If you want to buy a watch without spending a lot of money on it, there are two ways you can jump. If you're after reliability and accuracy, pure and simple, you're better off with an electronic watch – probably a digital type. When it comes to electronics, there are very few degrees of quality. A printed circuit and a piece of quartz are much the same no matter what the price tag says; but when you get down to the fine craftsmanship it takes to make a mechanical watch, you get what you pay for. For a small outlay, you won't buy yourself a gold case and a multi-function electronic watch. But if all you want is to tell the time, even the cheapest of electronic digital watches will do that accurately.

Cheap mechanical watches, as we mentioned above, will have cheap movements to them. There will be few, if any jewels – which means that there will be more friction present in the works, leading to potential trouble. Accuracy will be dubious, and reliability may be short-lived. However, the fashions and designs of cheap mechanical watches may be more to your liking. Many of the fine Swiss and French watch makers' styles have been copied in gold plate or other metal with attractive dials. Of course, with a cheap watch the movement won't have been miniaturised to the same degree, so you probably won't be able to buy yourself the lovely flat, thin type of watch that has become so highly sought after in trendy circles. But if you want a watch to look attractive for a comparatively short time, and you're not too worried about its accuracy (or reliability) these cheap fashion mechanical watches will do the job.

The More Expensive Ticks

Up to a point, what we've already said about cheap watches applies to expensive watches, too. Digital watches tend to be functional rather than aesthetically beautiful, even when they are pricey. Although you can get digital watches with gold casing, on the whole you'll find that they tend to be made of other metals, particularly stainless steel. And design wise, they'll usually be bigger and bulkier than analogues.

An expensive analogue may not do so many different things as a digital watch. After all, there is a limit to the number of functions you can cram on to a traditional watch face. So even if the analogue in question is electronically powered – which means that it can, in theory, be made to perform as many functions as its digital brother – all you're likely to get is the time in hours, minutes and seconds, plus a date and a day.

The analogue watch has just one true advantage over the digital: beauty. With the analogue format a watch can be a superb piece of jewellery. And so, your decision is a similar one as for cheap watches; beauty or multi-functional brains? But whereas with cheap watches you're talking about beauty being mechanically powered and brains electronically powered, here the method of driving the watch takes a back seat. Once you get into the realms of expensive watches the real decision you have to make is whether you want a digital or analogue format. Although, no matter how finely tuned a mechanical watch may be, it can never match the accuracy of the microcircuit. However, for the sake of thousands of expert craftspeople all over the world who produce mechanical watches, we must concede that the best mechanical movements are extremely accurate, too!

It's quite interesting to note that even some of the most traditionally-minded watch producing companies are gradually switching over from mechanical to electronic movements in their equally traditional analogue watches. Sad though it is, after years and years have been spent on perfecting the mechanical movement, the technological age has stepped in and taken the glory away. And that's what will probably happen to more and more watchmaking organisations; the microchip will eventually sweep the mechanical movement into history books for good. Whether analogue format watches will go the same way is doubtful, though. The traditional watch face still lends itself to setting in precious metals and gemstones far better than the digital face does. The thought of liquid crystal display numbers staring up from between two diamonds seems incongruous, even in our ultra-modern age.

Ideally, of course, you should have two watches; one digital, for work and hobbies where looks are not as important as performance, and the other a slim, elegant analogue that looks stunning with your formal clothes. But not everyone wants, or can afford, two good watches. So which is better? First of all, you've got to take careful stock of the life you lead, and the functions you require of a watch. After all, what's the point of having a multi-function digital watch if all you're ever going to want it to do is to tell you the time? On the other hand, though, if your work or leisure activity involves careful timing, such a watch is right up your street. A further aspect to look at is the sort of person you are, forgetting about what you do for a living. Do you prefer casual, outdoor-type clothes? Does your social life revolve around sporting activities and drinking down at your local? It that sounds like you, the digital, no-nonsense watch will suit your style. If you have a city centre office job, if you dislike getting your hands dirty, and your leisure time revolves around smart restaurants and night clubs, then an analogue in a fashionable design would be more appropriate.

Whatever you decide on, though, your purchase of a watch of good quality will involve you in spending a fair amount of money. Once again, go to a reputable jeweller or watch expert. That's the only way you can be certain of buying yourself something reliable and of the quality you expect. Watches are very easy to fake, and there are plenty around – especially in countries where standards of merchandise are not too carefully supervised. Under shady circumstances, what appears to be a watch of an excellent name can be a total fake, or else a genuine case with a cheap, nasty movement. Unmarked 'gold' casing can be gold plated – you won't know until you've worn it for a while and the plating wears off. Buying a watch of a good brand name from a reliable source means you have the back-up of two worthwhile organisations, should something go wrong. But things are less likely to go wrong, anyway, if you buy a good brand from a good source.

The Dressed-Up Watch

Fancy, expensive watches with precious metals and gemstones are something you should reserve for the day you're rich and famous. As jewellery items, they can be very beautiful. And if they have been made by a very famous watch manufacturer, the kudos they carry is enormous. But as far as investment value is concerned, it's another story. For a start, the actual watch bit in one of these creations is likely to be an ordinary mechanical type, which, as we hinted earlier, is gradually becoming outdated. That's the least of your problems. Secondly, gemstones used for decorating these creatures are usually small, which means they don't hold their value as well. Thirdly, because of the intricacy of the design and the fact the whole thing revolves around the setting of the watch, a high proportion of the money you pay is for the workmanship – not the raw materials. And by now you should know what that means; if ever you should want to sell the watch, you'll get a comparatively small amount back for it. So if you buy one, you're paying for the name of the manufacturer, the design and work that went into it and the fact that it is a watch not a bracelet. The true, raw material value of the watch – in other words, what it is really worth if ever you want to sell it again – may even be as little as one fifth of the figure written on the price tag. So the only people who should buy fancy gem-encrusted watches are those who've got enough money not to care, or at least those who are never likely to need to sell the watch one day.

If you want to buy yourself a really extravagant watch for a lot of money – but want to know that it keeps some value for a rainy day – then go for a very classical, all-gold electronic analogue. Classic designs may not be as trendy as fancy ones, but they remain constant for long periods of time, without going out of fashion altogether. They also have a wider appeal than wildly individualistic designs. Solid, 18 carat gold will always be solid, 18 carat gold. And an electronic movement is the power of the future. Even so, don't expect to get all your money back; the values of buying and selling watches vary just as much as other jewellery values do. But at least you'll have the best chances of recouping a fair share of your initial investment, if ever you should want to sell your watch. It's a good idea to buy a well-known quality brand name, too, as these will be trusted more readily by any prospective purchaser.

Antique Watches: Old Timers?

Although you're hardly likely to go out and buy an antique pocket watch unless you're particularly interested in antiques in general, you may well have such an old watch that's been left to you. With these, the main thing to remember is that the movement, mechanical though it is, is often the most valuable part of the watch. If you look at an old specimen, you'll often see that many parts of the movement inside the watch have even been engraved and decorated. So it is important that the originality of the watch is preserved both inside and out. Normally speaking, early mechanical watches are not as complicated to work on as modern ones are. In theory, at least, this means that virtually any watch repair specialist should be able to work on an antique watch. But this is not necessarily true; although the movement may be simple in design, the age of the watch may mean that the parts are extremely delicate and require special handling. If you own an antique watch, then, take it to your local watch repair person by all means. But he or she may well refer you to a specialist in antique watches, so be prepared for a little inconvenience and a higher outlay.

It is well worth looking after an antique watch, because it will hold its value well if it is in good condition. Strict accuracy is not one of the first criteria, though, so don't be too upset if it loses or gains time a bit. What is more important, value wise, is for as much of the watch's original movement to be preserved. Most good watch repair people will recommend that you shouldn't get rid of old parts in favour of new ones for the sake of accuracy. Regular servicing and cleaning will go a long way towards maintaining an old watch in working order; leaving it in a drawer for years on end won't necessarily preserve it.

The Swiss Watch

The Swiss have been making consistently good mechanical watches since the 16th century. Today, they're still churning out good, expensive watches which have every bit as much kudos now as they have had for hundreds of years. But unfortunately for the Swiss, their secrets and techniques have leaked out to other nations who – with the aid of machines and other modern technology – are able to produce watch movements of comparable quality. The Swiss are extremely proud of the ancient traditions and strict quality control they have always followed. And if watches still had to be virtually hand-made, the Swiss would undoubtedly be at the top of the tree. Mechanisation has put an end to that, though, and good watch movements are being manufactured in countries a long way from the pretty mountains of Switzerland. No longer do the Swiss have a monopoly on the meticulous, precise and accurate craftsmanship you need to make watch movements. Countries like Japan, plus many of its far-eastern neighbours, the USSR, the USA and several others, are now turning out perfectly respectable watch movements as well. Often, too, the movements are made by, and bought from, one country and fitted into cases made elsewhere.

The rising cost of living and all the other financial problems we know so well have put the Swiss watch, with its years of tradition and expertise behind it, well out of many people's reach. Countries where prices and wages are lower can afford to produce watch movements for far less than can the inflation-riddled Swiss. But there is one factor that no other country can seem to duplicate; snob appeal. A top quality Japanese watch may well possess every bit as much quality and reliability, even style, as a Swiss watch. But the Japanese version will still carry that 'made in Japan' albatross around its neck, in terms of social one-upmanship. Having said that, though, you mustn't think that the Swiss watch is a name alone. Swiss timepieces didn't become the Rolls Royces or Cadillacs of the watch world for nothing; the years of tradition and craftsmanship mean more than a heavy price tag.

Perhaps the most noticeable difference between Swiss watches and the rest is in design. Whereas mass produced watches may work very well, the very fact that they are mass produced means that they won't be too enterprising or individual in looks. Swiss watches, though, always seem to have a very classy look about them. And no-one can dispute the Swiss quality, as these people not only believe in top workmanship, but have several official bodies of watchdogs (sorry!) to make sure that the standards are kept up. If you can afford one, a Swiss watch will last for ages and will keep good time – as well as looking smart, sophisticated and elegant.

Own-Name Watches

Many large shops and jewellery organisations sell watches with their own names on them. Sometimes these can be of very good quality, with precious metal cases and excellent workmanship; but there are times when you'll find watches like these contain movements that don't live up to your expectations. Often, companies will go to a manufacturer and order a large batch of watches to be made up in their name. These can then have simple, inexpensive mechanical movements put in them, in order to keep prices down. But beware; even though the movement of such a watch may be cheap, the casing and the name on the dial may well mean that you pay a fair amount for the whole watch. If all you're after is a cheap, fashion or novelty watch, then you needn't worry – you don't expect long lasting quality or reliability from a cheap mechanical watch anyway. But if the casing is gold, and the price tag quotes a large sum, you could be asking for trouble. If you're going to pay a lot of money for a watch, you're far better off sticking to well-known *watch* brand names (which may well be sold alongside a shop's 'own name' watches). This way you know you're not taking any chances on what's inside the casing.

A Last Word on Watchstraps

Ideally speaking, you really should have several watches with different types of straps and bracelets to suit different occasions. But for those of us who can only afford one watch, we've got to pick a style and a strap or bracelet that suits as many different occasions as

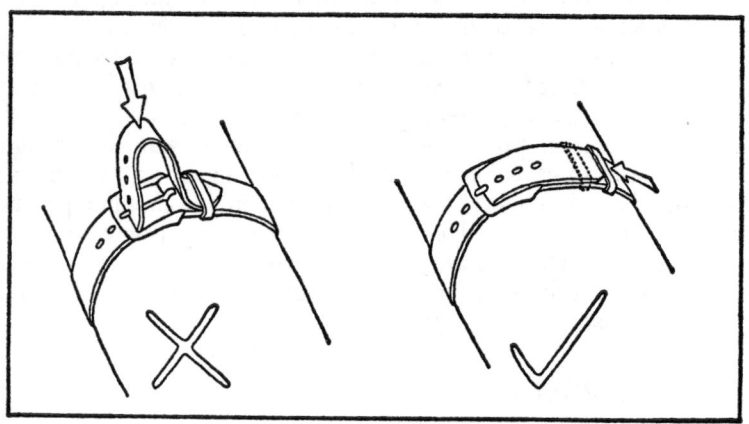

Correct way to wear a leather or crocodile watch strap

possible. In many ways, a plain watch with a leather strap is versatile, because you can simply change the strap. In winter, black or dark brown leather will go with most of the clothes you wear. In summer, a white leather strap will suit your lighter, pastel shades of fabric. But no matter what the colour, leather can still look ordinary.

One way to make your watch look truly elegant, without going to the expense of a gold bracelet, is to have a black or brown crocodile strap fitted. These are shiny and look expensive (they are) and wear out quite quickly – sometimes in less than six months or so. But a croc strap will give even the most modest of watches a whole new lease on life, and will make it look sophisticated and elegant. One thing to remember if you want a croc (or leather, for that matter) strap to last as long as possible, is to do it up and take it off as gently as you can. It is this action of doing up the buckle and bending the end of the strap back and forth that wears it out; you'll probably have noticed that it's nearly always the end of the strap that breaks or splits, sometimes before the rest of the strap shows many signs of wear. Another tip is to thread the end of the strap through the far loop only – assuming there is one fixed loop near the buckle and another, floating loop further down the strap. By doing this you don't have to bend the end of the strap as much.

If you prefer the all-metal look for a watch, you then have a choice between removable metal bracelets, or fixed ones. If you choose a fixed bracelet then you should make sure you really like it! On the whole, a plain bracelet is a better buy than a fancy one; you'll tire of it less easily. For an extra special occasion, you can dress up either a leather strap or a metal one with the addition of a thin chain or bracelet (in the case of all-metal watches, a bracelet of the same colour metal). But you should avoid wearing a particularly heavy bracelet on the same arm as your watch because the banging and clattering it will create could eventually cause some damage to the glass or movement of your timepiece.

CHAPTER ELEVEN

Jewellery and the Liberated Male

It is an undeniable truth that men's jewellery is a subject of some delicacy. Nowadays, the very word 'jewellery' is associated with femininity, which for obvious reasons can put some men off the idea. It hasn't always been like that, though; it was only the rather sobering influences of Napoleon and Queen Victoria that turned the fashion tables back in the early 19th century. Before that, men wore almost as much jewellery as women, and no-one accused them of being sissy. As the 19th century wore on, though, male jewellery began to be associated with effete types who had nothing better to do all day than preen themselves and look smart. Even wealthier men began to roll up their sleeves and get their hands dirty, although more often than not it was just in a metaphorical sense. In those days, the masculine role was extremely clearly defined, and definitely ruled jewellery out as being contrary to the strong, powerful, protective and masterful image. In modern times, with men and women playing equal roles in many societies, you would think that the pressure of looking the masculine part should have been relieved somewhat. But it hasn't been. A lot of men today cheerfully accept women as equals, even agree to role reversal and women in more dominant positions than theirs, yet still steadfastly refuse to wear more than the most butch design of watch they can find.

Presumably, it is a hangover from the days when men had to look like stereotyped conquerors and soldiers, rather than expressing their personalities freely through their clothes and their ornaments. However, modern thinking is creeping into the male way of life, and little by little men are beginning to try out discreet jewellery ornaments that would have been unthinkable fifty years ago.

This chapter is not setting out to judge whether men should wear jewellery or not, all the same. Quite apart from the effects of Napoleon, Queen Victoria, Emily Pankhurst and Women's Lib., we mustn't lose sight of the fact that personality has a lot to do with it, too. Whereas one man might look very smart with fairly flamboyant jewellery, his next door neighbour might look ridiculous wearing the same items. With men's jewellery, as with women's, the only important question is what makes a person feel good, and look good, in that order. In this chapter, all we will do is to put forward suggestions of men's jewellery, discuss them, and then leave the choice up to the wearer and the donor.

We've said in earlier chapters that jewellery makes a fine, thoughtful and personal gift from one person to another, and there's no earthly reason why this should apply to gifts from man to woman only. A gift of jewellery from woman to man, or from man to man, is every bit as meaningful as a gift of jewellery is to a woman. What is vital is for the donor of the piece of jewellery to make sure the gift is appropriate to the style and personality of the recipient, whatever sex that person is. So whether your interest in this chapter is for yourself, or for items which you may wish to give to a man, here is a selection of men's jewellery, plus any information we feel might help you in your selection.

Rings

Although some men dislike rings for whatever reason – they don't look masculine, they are uncomfortable, etc. – it would seem that the majority do wear at least one, unostentatious specimen. Usually this takes the form of a wedding band or a crest/initial ring. Wedding bands are universally accepted, particularly in European countries; some religions decree that both partners should exchange rings in the marriage ceremony, and other religions just go for one ring – the woman's. All sorts of social stigmas have been placed on men's wedding rings in the past, but with the growing trend towards equality all the way down the line, many young couples feel that if the woman is to wear a wedding band, then the man should also. Sometimes, the two wedding bands are of different designs, but a pleasing idea is for two matching rings to be exchanged.

Initial rings are not only popular as gifts for a young man's 21st birthday, 18th birthday, graduation or other similar occasion, but also as substitutes for wedding rings. In many societies, the bride will give her husband a ring with his initials engraved on it as a wedding present, to be worn either on the little finger, the 'ring' finger, or even sometimes the middle finger.

Crest rings, which have the same shape and overall look as initial

Crest Ring

rings make a particularly pleasant gift for a young man (or young woman, for that matter). The trouble is, you must have a crest engraved on them – and not all families have a crest. If there is a crest in existence, though, you can have it engraved on to the plain round, square or oval top of the ring. This must be done by specialist engravers, and may cost quite a lot, as it is a pretty complicated job. Engravers can usually copy the design from another ring, or from a piece of paper that has been printed with the crest. Unfortunately, there isn't such an engraver around every corner, and you may find that to have a crest ring done will take a fair amount of time and money. Your own jeweller will be able to advise you on where to take the ring, or will send it away for you.

Stone set rings for men are not so popular, no doubt because many fellows feel that beautiful stones are too flashy. And on the whole, they're right. Big, coloured stones or diamonds would look very wrong on a man who is otherwise unobtrusively dressed. But many countries favour small diamond set rings for men, worn on the little finger. And as long as these blend in with the overall look, they can be most attractive – especially for a formal evening.

Chains and Pendants

Although a lot of men would be reluctant to admit it, the pendant that hangs from a chain around their neck usually holds some sort of emotional value as well as being decorative. To back up this theory, many fellows wear their chains and pendants underneath their clothing, out of sight except when they put on an open-necked shirt or a swimming costume. Perhaps the reason for this is that they are hesitant about openly displaying an attractive piece of jewellery. Or else they like the idea of keeping a sentimentally valuable item near their hearts! Whatever the thinking behind this, though, it is as well to consider all the pros and cons very carefully if you should ever buy a pendant to be worn by a man.

If you're giving a pendant as a present, don't be put off by the fact that the man in question already has one. It is quite customary for a man to wear more than one pendant on a chain – particularly if the new one is appropriate or is given by someone he holds in high regard.

The real question is what sort of pendant is the right one. There are lots of different types, many of which are suitable for engraving. This is the key to the problem, if you're giving a pendant; a sort, pertinent personal message on the reverse side will make him treasure it for ever. There are a great many different types of pendants to choose from; a huge variety of medallions, shaped pendants and tags. These can have a religious flavour, or they can incorporate some astrological or other symbol like a birthsign or sporting design. Talking of sporting designs, a sensible – if rather pessimistic – engraving for a pendant is the recipient's blood group. For a man involved in dangerous activities like hang-gliding, motor-racing, motor cycling, etc. a dog tag or round medallion with his name and blood group engraved on the back can be a life saver. And you can always couple it with a warm-hearted personal message to make it a bit more sentimental!

Really and truly, there is very little to be said about pendants and their designs, because there is no such thing as a good one or a bad one. Choosing the right style is purely a question of personal preference, although it is always safer to select a plain, simple design if you're not too sure of the person's taste. When you're buying for yourself, you need to be sure that the style you choose will go with your overall look, whatever you're wearing.

Watches

All, or nearly all, that needs to be said about watches we attempted to cover in Chapter Ten. Selecting a watch to give to a man is quite a difficult choice to make on your own, if you want the gift to be a surprise. Mind you, a bit of detective work should help you – for example, a man who only possesses a dressy gold watch might need a plain stainless steel digital watch for sports or hobbies. And vice versa. But watches are very personal things, and choosing one for someone else should never really be left to guesswork alone. After all, if you wear a watch you're going to be looking at it many times each day, so you want it to please you. If you want to give a watch to anyone – male or female – it's best to put in a little groundwork beforehand and find out that person's preferences.

Pens

These are a good, safe bet, if you're giving a present. Everyone, unless they are illiterate, writes. So an elegant gold plate, gold or silver pen set is a gift that is bound to go down well, unless the recipient already owns other pen sets. Always be sure that you're not carried away by the precious wrapping, and see that the pen or pens really do work properly. It's also a good idea to avoid buying someone a fountain pen, because choosing the right nib is something most people like to do for themselves. Go for a ball point pen and pencil set, unless you happen to know what sort of nib His Nibs (ouch!) prefers.

Cigarette and Cigar Cases

Bearing in mind the amount of adverse publicity that has recently been given to smoking, you shouldn't really buy a cigarette or cigar case for a young person. But for an older man who is a confirmed smoker, the moral question isn't so serious. Cigarette cases are seen infrequently in shops selling contemporary jewellery, and those that exist tend to be extremely expensive. Bear in mind that it takes a lot of gold or silver to make a case, and you're paying for every little crumb. However, you often find attractive specimens in antique and second hand jewellery shops, which should be within a more bearable price range. The one thing you must remember if you buy old cigarette cases is that the size of cigarettes has altered over the years. And fifty or more years ago, king-sized cigarettes didn't exist; so the try-before-you-buy principle applies here. Make sure the brand of cigarette you – or the recipient, if it is a gift – smoke fits into the case before you part with your money; there's nothing more infuriating than opening a sophisticated cigarette case to find your cigarettes all crushed and bent inside. Cigar cases, seldom seen in precious metal because the even greater volume of metal required puts them out of most people's reach, are more often made of leather or tortoiseshell. If you see one that you like, take along your favourite brand of cigars (or the recipient's favourite) and try the case for size before you buy it.

Cufflinks

The first question to ask yourself here is, do you (or does the recipient) own any shirts that have the right design of cuffs to take cufflinks? If the answer is yes, there are a great many different types of cufflink to choose from. Selecting a good design is difficult for someone else, as cufflinks are also a very personal choice. Again, stick to plainer styles if you're not sure. The most important criterion, after design, is the fastening device; although men usually curse cufflinks that are difficult to put on, these types are usually the ones which will stay on. Loose, easy-fastening mechanisms are more prone to do a disappearing act – easy come, easy go. The cufflink you must push and prod into position will stay put – but the person concerned must really like cufflinks to persevere with the struggle of getting them on. If you want to personalise a pair of cufflinks as a gift for a man's birthday, coming of age, or other special occasion, a pleasant idea is to buy a pair of plain round, square or oval shapes, and have his initials or family crest engraved on them. Some cufflinks are also set with stones, but beware – this is not every man's cup of tea. The choice of anything but the plainer, simpler styles should really be left to the person who's going to wear them.

Lighters

Once again, we have the moral question. Should you buy a man a lighter and encourage him to damage his health by smoking? Should you buy yourself an expensive lighter and then lose sleep at night because you've invested a lot of money in an unhealthy habit? For those who would answer yes to both questions, think twice about expensive lighters, anyway. Quite apart from the health problem, good lighters can get lost or stolen very easily. And the fact that they may be encased in precious gold or silver does not necessarily mean that they will work well. Lighters with expensive names can be temperamental and can cost a lot to put right when they go wrong. There's a lot to be said for cheap, throwaway jobs; but if you must buy an expensive lighter, at least make sure that it is guaranteed and can be filled with a standard multi-filler gas can. Some brand name lighters can only be filled with their own gas, which tends to be rare and expensive. Petrol lighters are almost obsolete nowadays, but there are still the odd few about. These are best avoided as they are messy and smelly to refill, and they tend to run out of fuel at maddeningly frequent intervals. Many lighters on the market now have side-stepped the need for a flint, which is another element that needs frequent replacement. The new 'electronic' lighters contain a small battery which provides the impetus, and will go on for ages before a replacement becomes necessary.

Bracelets

Various types of bangle, chain and 'identity' bracelets for men go in and out of fashion. As these are considered less conventional male jewellery items, it's best not to buy one for a man unless you're certain he likes the idea. And even if you're buying one for yourself, don't forget that the constant rubbing of the bracelet against the bottom of the sleeve will wear out cuffs in a hurry. For this reason, you shouldn't really wear a bracelet if you dress in a suit every day, unless you can afford new shirt cuffs at regular intervals. If your work and/or leisure activities allow you to roll your sleeves up, or wear short-sleeved shirts, a bracelet can add interest to your arm, and won't cause any damage. Loose bracelets are not recommended for men who work at a desk all day long; the clattering and banging of the bracelet on the desk can drive you mad after a while. Identity bracelets can make a welcome gift for a young man, on a special occasion.

Key rings

These are a classic for giving, either as a romantic present from woman to man, or as an ordinary gift. Naturally enough, anyone who possesses more than one key will already have some sort of key ring;

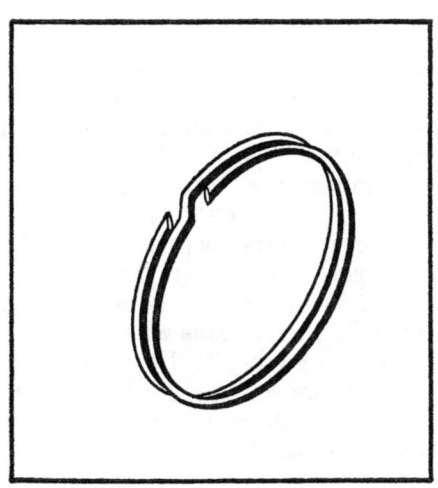

Traditional Key Ring

the gift opportunity arises when you're talking about gold or silver efforts, sometimes even with a gem studded medallion. The choice of the dangling part is entirely up to taste – there are many variations, including initials, birthsigns, religious, and virtually all other styles that can apply equally to neck pendants. Once again, you mustn't get too carried away by the dangling bit; take a long, critical look at the device which holds the keys together. The most beautiful medallion in the world isn't going to compensate for the loss of your keys on a rainy night, through the failure of the fastening device. Sprung clips and screw types tend to be vastly complicated and come undone, especially after lengthy wear. The best type is the old fashioned ring, where you turn the key round two or three times until the entire ring goes through the hole in the key. Although a ring may loosen in time, is it still the most secure way of keeping your keys together. Also bear in mind that there are many pretty key ring designs on the market that will be strong enough to hold two or three keys; but if you or the recipient go about with a great pocketful of keys, these are no good. A large, strong key ring is a necessity. If you're buying a gold key ring, aim for nine carat as higher carat gold will be softer and will wear out quickly. Key rings get bashed around more than any other type of jewellery. Silver is also popular for key rings, but this is quite soft as well and will soon become dull and scratched-looking.

Belt Buckles

Although we mentioned these items in a previous chapter, they bear looking at once again. Belt buckles used to be very fashionable indeed, in the days when belts could be made with interchangeable leather parts. Nowadays, though, the belt buckle seems to be an afterthought, with the leather, fabric or crocodile section taking over the title role. However, perhaps now's the time to revitalise an old fashion! Many larger jewellery shops sell belt buckles, in anything from plain metal to gold with precious gems. And if you buy an expensive belt buckle, a leather or crocodile belt will usually be thrown in with it. As we said earlier, antique silver belt buckles are still seen occasionally, and make a lovely gift. They look most attractive with either casual or formal clothes. Most local shoe repair shops, with a little friendly persuasion, will make a belt to fit. If you have no luck there, try an old-fashioned saddler.

Money Clips

Money clips are an idea which was made popular in the USA, and they are still a great favourite there. Many men prefer not to carry a wallet, and for these types the money clip is ideal. If you (or the recipient of a gift) carry loose bank notes around with you, you will undoubtedly know how annoying it is to find that the odd one has gone astray through a hole in your pocket, or from hiding behind your handkerchief or whatever. A money clip solves the problem without the bulky shape of a wallet in your pocket. Again, the main thing to watch out for with these is that they should be strong and well fastened, otherwise they miss the whole point of holding money together. Designs can be in plain metal, gold or silver, and can vary in shape from the simplest of single fold, sprung clips to complicated patterns. Some even have precious gems set into them. A wide clip could also have initials, a family crest, or a personal message inscribed on it.

Tie Pins and Tie Tacks, plus Tie Clips

Tie pins and tacks seem to drift in and out of fashion. In more recent times they have disappeared from the scene of men's fashion for a very simple reason – who wants to bore a hole through an expensive silk tie? For the elegant gentleman, though, a long tie pin set with a small pearl or diamond can look very smart. A tie tack can also be set with a gem, but has a short pin section with a safety stop that grips the far tip on the other side of the tie. Tie clips, which do not puncture the tie but slide over it and under the buttoning edge of the shirt are not very popular these days. But in plain gold or silver, they can look attractive. And for a man who spends much time in his shirtsleeves, they can protect his tie from flopping on the desk, flying like a flag in the wind and dipping in the soup.

Collar Pins and Clips

These items were extremely popular in the early part of the 20th century, and still look marvellous on the more traditionally-styled man. Unfortunately, the old type of pin means that special holes must be incorporated in the collar, or else a collar on which the pin has been used will bear permanent scars. More modern versions look like pins, but actually have very clever clips which leave the collar free of holes. If you're thinking of giving a collar pin or clip as a present, observe the man in question and see whether he sometimes wears shirts with button-down collars. If he does, there's a good chance that he'll like the idea of a collar pin, as it has a similar effect. A newer variation on the theme of collar jewellery is the kind of collar clip that forms a right-angle, and sits on the point of one side of the collar. These, popularised in the USA, can also have a man's initials incorporated. You won't find them that easily in jewellery shops, but larger shops may carry them. Traditional collar pins, if you can't find them in modern shops, should be fairly easy to find in second-hand shops and antique outlets. All of these can be either silver or gold, although gold looks better.

CHAPTER TWELVE

Investing Your Money in Jewellery

Up to a certain point, any jewellery you buy is an investment. Even when you buy yourself a tiny gold chain, you're not throwing the money away; you can always sell precious metal and precious or semi-precious stones again, and they'll fetch at least a fair portion of what you paid for them. And of course, by buying jewellery you're investing in just about the most important commodity there is – yourself, or someone you care for. That's the sentimentalist's viewpoint. For the more financially minded, though, we've gathered together some information about the investment aspects of jewellery in this chapter. You may not feel inclined to invest large sums of money in precious metals and stones, but for those who would like to buy with at least one eye on the future, we've included a few tips. For those who aren't interested, it may help to read about the background of the investment angle anyway – it's always comforting to know how your jewellery is valued, even if you have no intention of ever selling it.

'There's Gold in Them There Hills...'

Back in the days of the gold prospectors, crawling about on their hands and knees looking for nuggets in California and Australia, people were not too worried about finding lots of gold to make into jewellery for their loved ones; they just knew that gold was a highly desirable commodity. And they were prepared to wear out their knee-caps to find it, purely because of the riches gold stood for. Now, of course, those days are over; most of the gold lying on the surface of the earth has been picked up and either made into jewellery, or more likely into solid gold bars which are now reposing in a vault somewhere. The actual proportion of gold used in jewellery, as against gold used for financial purposes, is smaller than you'd think. The metal's importance in terms of world finances rather eclipses its use as an adornment. So for those of you who aren't already familiar with the part gold plays in the monetary sense, let's take a quick look at how it works.

As far as the financial wizards are concerned, gold is a commodity just like anything else. Other commodities that are lumped together in roughly the same boat are copper, tin, lead and so on. The main thing that makes gold stand out amongst this lot is that it is by far the most precious, and the most rare. Other precious metals, like platinum and palladium, are even rarer and more precious, but there is so little of these metals around in comparison to the amount of gold that they are way down on the list of popular investment commodities.

Gold has another, rather more important reason to stand out in the financial crowd. Many countries, including the UK until the early part of the 20th century, used (and many still use) gold as the only standard by which to set their currency or money. Hence the expression 'gold standard', which you used to hear bandied around quite a lot, and still do hear in certain countries. What this involves is actually fairly simple, although people in the elevated world of finance make it sound complicated. A country's national bank, when it wants to issue brand new, crisp banknotes, can't just print money when it feels like it. It has to have something in the kitty, so to speak, which holds the same, real value as the paper money says – otherwise the money they print is just paper. In other words, before the National Bank of Anywhereland issues out a million dollars or pounds or rupees or francs to circulate in its country, it has to have a million dollars (or whatever) worth of gold back at the ranch in order to back it up.

In recent times, the various governments in the world have been trying to do away with this practice and avoid using gold as a backup to their currencies. But in a few nations, the concept of the gold standard is still used. This is particularly true in the case of nations who have suffered a few hard financial knocks; it would seem that when all the other chips are down, gold is just about the only commodity that keeps on going. Whatever happens, gold can always be relied upon as a stable measure of value.

You would think, after all that, that the value of gold always remains the same. Well, just to confuse the picture, it doesn't. And the National Bank of Anywhereland's currency doesn't always hold the same value either. But just because the value of a currency fluctuates, it doesn't automatically follow that the value of gold should fluctuate in the other direction. In fact, the whole nature of the world's money and other financial markets revolve around these fluctuations; fortunes have been made and lost, countries have become rich or gone broke, because of the rise and fall in values of currency and gold. Why this happens depends on so many things it would take a book merely to describe them; and we're not here to talk extensively about the world of high finance, anyway! Whatever the fluctuations, and whether or not the country bases its currency on gold, a nation's gold reserves and its currency are usually connected very closely. And whether governments happen to like it or not, gold still forms a significant part of the world's currency reserves.

The more gold a country owns, the stronger and more important it tends to be. Countries like America – where billions and billions of dollars worth of gold are enshrined in New York and at Fort Knox – Germany, Switzerland, France and the UK and a few others, always feature at the head of the financial world league tables. As these countries do well, run at a profit if you like, they often buy more gold. And become richer. Obviously, the picture is a thousand times more complicated than this very simplified description. But whatever happens, behind every country's success or failure in monetary terms, gold usually plays an important role, albeit in the background.

There were times in the past, in some countries, where you, as an individual, could not buy gold other than in the form of jewellery. Nowadays, though – in most countries – you can buy gold as an investment if you want, more usually in the form of gold coins. You can't necessarily buy gold bullion or gold bars; your eligibility depends on your nationality, where you live, and where you're buying the gold. The value of your gold will fluctuate, just like any other kind of investment. But bearing in mind the fact that gold looks like remaining the backbone of world currencies for some time to come, it has to be fairly safe. After all, it is still considered *real* money – in any language or currency. In fact, in many countries where the economy tends to be permanently shaky, people still trade in gold as a preferable alternative to money, because gold will usually hold its value whatever happens.

The value of gold goes up and down – again, like other investments – because of the supply and demand for it. For example, in the time it took to write this book, the price of gold went from $160.00 per ounce, up to $420.00 – in the space of a few months! (The price of gold is nearly always quoted in US dollars.) Very often if, say, the US dollar goes down in value a bit, or there is a crisis somewhere in the world that threatens that country's economy, there will be a rush to buy gold because it's safer than money. And if a lot of people want to buy gold, the price goes up. Investment in gold is subject to the dictates of financial fashion, too.

If you feel you'd like to invest some money in gold, you're best to consult an expert like your bank manager or an accountant to find out if that is a good time or a bad time to buy. And don't forget that the gold in your jewellery is subject to the values of financially-used gold as well. The method of determining the value of a gold item, as we described in Chapter Four, is based on the value of gold in the world market. But the gold in a piece of jewellery, as we suggested then, is worth more than the standard world rate because of the work involved in making the jewellery item. It's comforting to know that an investment in gold – in the form of jewellery – can look attractive and give you pleasure, unlike stocks and shares which live in a drawer or in the bank and do nothing for your looks.

People Who Live in Glass Houses...

Most gemstones are not a commodity, as such, and therefore don't really have particularly set standards as to price and value. Diamonds, though, are very popular as an investment because, with the strict controls and the steady increases in value determined by De Beers and the world's diamond organisations, they are quite a safe bet.

If you want to buy a diamond as an investment, this is one of the few occasions when a good, reputable jewellery shop is not necessarily the best place to go. You're better off going to a specialist in diamonds, as this sort of concern will be thinking rather more along your lines.

As we said in the section on diamond engagement rings in Chapter One, when it comes to re-sale you won't recoup much – if anything – of what you've laid out on craftsmanship. You'll only get the value of the raw materials as a rule. Diamond investment specialists will usually deal in loose stones – which you can then have mounted in a simple setting if you want. This way you'll be paying nearer the true value of the stone. The work that's gone into its cutting and polishing will have been taken into account when the price of the stone is being determined; and this will always remain a part of any diamond's value. The four criteria used by dealers when judging a diamond's worth are carat weight, clarity, colour and cut – so the actual manual work on the stone plays an important part.

Settings, if you're buying your diamonds either already made up or with the intention of having them made up into jewellery should be kept very simple. Simple settings are more likely to please, or at least be inoffensive to future buyers. Complicated settings appeal to fewer people, as they are normally a matter of your individual taste. They also date more quickly. And both of these considerations can limit your prospects when the time comes to sell the diamond.

Unfortunately for buyers, the value of diamonds does not work on a pro rata scale. It works on a sliding scale, as we mentioned in Chapter One, whereby the larger the diamond the more valuable it is carat by carat and point by point. (Point is a part of a carat.) A single two carat diamond will be worth far more than four half-carat diamonds put together. One of the reasons for this is that larger diamonds are becoming rare; these bigger stones tend to be found nearer the surface of the earth. As the work of diamond mines continues, the large stones near the top having been collected some time back, the present harvest of gems consists of smaller stones from deeper down. Fewer large ones are found at greater depths. Consequently, the value of bigger stones is going up faster in proportion to the value of smaller stones.

Of course, there is another side to this investment coin as far as the size of the stone is concerned. This is the point that if you are able to afford a really big stone, you may encounter difficulty in selling it; there aren't so many people around these days who *can* afford to buy big stones. Any diamond bigger than, say, two carats, may well appreciate in value quite significantly, in theory. But finding a buyer for it will be more tricky as its price will be way over many people's heads.

The value of diamonds does not increase as rapidly as other forms of investment can; like shares and property, for instance. It is said that diamonds appreciate at a rate of around 10% to 12% a year, but this may increase. So buying one should really be considered as a long term proposition – say, five to ten years before you start to make a healthy profit on its re-sale. Mind you, the rate of increase is normally quite steady, and it's pretty safe to say that whatever happens, your diamond is never likely to go down in value – unlike many other forms of investment including gold. And there aren't many forms of investment that you can wear, either. Like gold, a diamond can give you a great deal of personal pleasure twinkling on your finger (or your spouse's finger) while it appreciates in value. Similarly, there are not many other forms of investment that are so portable, or so convenient to keep – requiring no maintenance or administration.

Putting Your Money Where Your Diamond Is

Many of the diamond investment specialists we mentioned earlier will offer you a 'buy back' agreement when you purchase a stone from them. Be careful if they agree to buy the stone back from you for the same amount you paid for it after a specified time; this may sound like a good deal but in reality you lose. As time goes on, diamonds go up in value, so selling yours back to the dealer at the same price – after a time lapse – will mean you're selling it for less than it's worth. Some will also offer – as an alternative – the chance for you to part exchange your diamond (for the amount you originally paid) against a new, bigger stone. Although these argreements are not strictly speaking essential, they go a bit further in proving that the stone is being sold to you in truly good faith. Whether or not a separate 'buy back' agreement is offered to you, you should insist on a guarantee for your diamond. It's a good idea to check out beforehand just what sort of guarantee the dealer offers. The best ones are those which include a diagram of both the top and the bottom of the stone, showing any inclusions or impurities that the stone might have.

The most important thing to look out for is the guarantee of getting your money back in full if you're not satisfied with the stone. Of course, in many countries there is legislation that covers you anyway, as long as you have a genuine complaint. But bear in mind that diamonds are not like articles of clothing or furniture, which can be seen to be faulty at a glance. Diamonds are rather more the victims of opinion, even amongst experts. So your guarantee should plainly state that, if you are not satisfied with your stone, for whatever the genuine reason, your money will be refunded in full.

If ever you should find yourself in a position where you're not satisfied with a diamond that you've bought, and there is either a dubious guarantee or none at all, you'll need to get a valuation from another expert. Here you must be careful, as a certain amount of professional rivalry may exist. The second expert may value your stone at rather lower than its true price, if he or she knows why you want the valuation. The second expert would do this in the hope that you would abandon the first expert and transfer your custom to his or her establishment. Naturally enough, this sort of thing doesn't happen very often, but it may occur if you're unlucky. To avoid even this small risk, then, it is better not to say why you want a second valuation if you're dissatisfied with your diamond. Tell the second expert a white lie – for example, that you want to buy another, identical stone so you can have the pair made into earrings or cufflinks – and ask how much the identical stone would cost. Then compare the amount you're told with the price you've actually paid for the first stone.

Unfortunately, there can't really be a standard diamond guarantee which is universal in all countries of the world, or even nationally. Because the price of diamonds is always rising, it would be impossible to put a fixed value on any stone. However, don't set too much store by guarantees and 'buy back' agreements. The most important thing is to go, in the first place, to a qualified diamond dealer who is a member of a Diamond Exchange. That way you can be sure of a fair deal which, after all, is the first consideration; rather more to the point than all the guarantees in the world which still can't compensate for a diamond of poor quality. Look upon guarantees as accessories rather than integral parts of the purchase. By buying from a member of a Diamond Exchange, you will be dealing with a qualified expert who is ruled not only by the laws of the country concerned, but by an extremely strict code of ethics determined by his or her Exchange which is virtually a guarantee in itself. As we mentioned in an earlier chapter, the jewellery business – or at least the respected, reliable members of the jewellery business – are old-fashioned types and still believe in the high standards of conduct that many other businesses have let fall by the wayside.

What About Coloured Stones?

Coloured stones, or in the case of investment where we're only really talking in terms of coloured precious stones, have one great problem. That, in a word, is their colour. You see, with diamonds the judging of quality is very simple; the best colour is no colour at all, and the best purity is absolute, with no inclusions. That means that diamonds (the colourless variety, anyway) hold their value anywhere in the world, because there is no argument as to the right criteria by which to judge them. Everyone is in agreement, whether it's in Scotland or Singapore. Coloured stones, on the other hand, are not possessed of such convenient common denominators. A gem expert in Los Angeles may believe an emerald to be the perfect shade of green, whereas some equally qualified expert in Sydney may feel that the stone is too pale or too dark. The introduction of colour into the quality of a stone opens up a whole lot more ifs and buts, and makes the valuation of such stones far more difficult. For this reason we strongly recommend that, unless you become an expert yourself – and that would involve years of study – you should avoid investing your money in coloured stones. No matter how reputable the dealer from whom you buy, and no matter how many guarantees you get, you still have the problems of personal preference, fashion and taste when you come to sell the stones. With diamonds, a good one is a good one by anyone's standards.

If you already own some coloured stones which you would like to sell, the questions of preference and fashion apply just as much. One reputable jeweller may offer you rather more than another, for the same stones. Just to complicate the issue further, there are far fewer pricing standards when it comes to coloured stones than there are regarding diamonds, the price of which is quite closely monitored. So opinions and cash offers will vary enormously according to what a jeweller happens to like and what he or she feels will sell easily, etc. You may get a better price by having your stones valued by a good jeweller and then offering them for sale privately; this way you'll get the full 'retail' price. Don't forget, a jeweller will offer you the going price *minus* what he hopes to make in profit. You know how there are two prices for second hand cars; a lower one at which a dealer buys and a higher one at which the dealer sells, so as to make a fair profit. Well, this in a sense applies to all jewellery too. It particularly applies to coloured stones. So if you aren't in too much of a hurry to sell yours, you might get more favourable results by advertising them in a good local or national newspaper. Just remember, some people feel that to put your address into such an advertisement is inviting burglary – so perhaps a telephone number or a box number would be better!

Made-Up Pieces – A Gem of an Investment?

Made-up jewellery – or any jewellery that is meant to be worn rather than tucked away into a safety deposit box in the bank – isn't a very good investment as such. Up to a point buying jewellery is a hedge against inflation, inasmuch as you'll nearly always get your original stake back when you come to sell it again. But after a period of time inflation will have made that particular sum worth less in real terms; so in a way you'll be losing money. Made-up jewellery won't necessarily appreciate in the same way that raw materials, like gold and diamonds, can gain value. But you'll lose less on investing in jewellery than you will by buying modern cars or electrical appliances that actually depreciate and wear out. If you buy a new car you'll get less than the purchase price once you sell it two or three years later. If you buy a new piece of jewellery, you should get the same price on resale. You see, even though the jewellery you sell will be considered 'second-hand' and therefore worth something less on the retail market, the overall values of the raw materials concerned, in other words the stones and the precious metal, will probably have gone up in value in the meantime. These two factors effectively make the value 'stand still'; but don't forget, to buy the same jewellery item new will cost you more. So if you want to make money, forget about buying made-up jewellery! You should really look upon the purchase of any jewellery as an adornment, primarily, with the added benefit that you won't lose out very much if you should ever decide to sell it.

The Older the Fiddle, the Better the Tune?

We have purposely avoided dwelling on antique jewellery anywhere in this book. This is a highly specialised subject that requires not only a good working knowledge of stones and metals, but a wealth of historical and artistic know-how as well. There are a great many books on the market that discuss the historical and artistic aspects, so for those of you who have a burning desire to learn about the subject, we suggest that you read them!

However, no book on jewellery would be complete without at least a quick look at antique jewellery. And because this chapter centres on the financial and investment angles of jewellery, we felt that the antique variety was best placed here. Not only because knowledgeable buying of antique jewellery is a good investment, but because, apart from a few smaller pieces, it can cost you quite a lot of money.

Let's take a closer look first of all at the artistic and historical value of antique jewellery. This can form a large part of the value of any piece; even an item made from non-precious metal and enamel work can be worth a lot if it happens to be an original Art Nouveau design. In a sense, the raw materials only form about half the value of antique jewellery. It is the artistic content, the rarity of the piece, its historical interest, who designed it, who made it, etc., that gives it the value. We said earlier that old jewellery, with stones cut in the old-fashioned way, will be worth rather less than similar modern jewellery. Old stones have to be recut in order to hold modern-day value – and in recutting any stone you make it smaller and therefore less valuable.

But this is not so with genuine antiques. Where you draw the line between old jewellery and antique is difficult to say unless you are an expert. For the sake of argument, let's take it that any piece of jewellery over 100 years old could be classed as antique. However, an antique piece is only valuable to the right buyer – someone who holds antique jewellery in the esteem it deserves. So here is the first moral, if you get involved with antique jewellery; only deal with experts.

Buying antique jewellery can be advantageous and comparatively straightforward if you're talking about small, low value items. A pretty design in a nineteenth century garnet cluster ring, for example, should be less expensive than a similar ring that's brand new. Naturally, the garnets might be a bit scratched, and the gold mounting may be rather worn. If you're buying purely to please yourself, to wear the ring, that's a good way to get a better deal. This holds true for many antique rings and other smaller pieces of which there are still many about, dating from the late 19th century to the early part of the 20th century. They won't be as expensive as their new equivalents because they're worn, and also because they don't hold any particular artistic value or rarity. Mind you, from the investment point of view, they're not likely to become priceless one day. However, the designs of that period are very pretty – rather soft and romantic – and if you like that sort of thing they make a good buy. And bear in mind that these pieces are still 'second-hand' – and consequently less valuable than modern equivalents.

It's still best to go to an expert when you buy even small pieces of antique jewellery; avoid the junk shops and market stalls, because you and the vendor may not know if the item is genuine or not. Don't forget, faking has been around since Roman times and earlier, and you're just as likely to get a phoney piece of antique jewellery from a non-expert source as you are to get a phoney modern piece from an unreliable vendor. Antique shops and jewellery shops specialising in antique jewellery are the right place to go. And even if the item you buy is only worth a small amount, in most countries you are perfectly within your rights to insist that the person selling you the piece gives you a certificate, in writing, stating what the item is. This we highly recommend, whatever the value of the piece. You may need it for insurance purposes, and it will be comforting for you to know you have a guarantee that the item is what the vendor says it is.

More expensive antique jewellery is best avoided, from an investment point of view, unless you are prepared to study the subject at great length and become an expert. If you want to invest money in jewellery, it is far safer to think in terms of modern items because these are much more readily saleable. Not everyone likes antique jewellery, and not everyone is prepared to offer the right price for it. Modern jewellery has a far greater appeal, and because of this is more likely to command the right price in a wider market.

If you receive a piece of antique jewellery you may – on the other hand – want to realise the capital by selling it. In this case, it's worth your while to take a little trouble; the piece may be more valuable than your local jeweller thinks. Remember, too, that not all modern jewellers know a lot about antique jewellery; and not all antique dealers have the specialised knowledge required to value a precious antique jewellery item.

Although there are jewellers around, mostly in large cities, who specialise in antique jewellery, you're more likely to find satisfaction in an antique dealer who has a particular penchant for the subject. Also, there are probably more suitable antique dealers than there are suitable jewellers – particularly outside the big cities. You may find the right one by asking around, but a safer bet is to approach your country's association of antique dealers (in the UK, BADA – the British Antique Dealers' Association, located in London) and ask them to recommend suitably qualified members in your area. Be sure to mention that you're after members who specialise in antique jewellery. Then take your antique pieces to these people and ask for their opinion and valuation; the opinion may well be free, but expect to pay a charge for a written valuation. Once you know the value of the piece, you have several options open to you. It is possible that the dealer you originally consulted will make you an offer for the piece. Alternatively, take a trip to the nearest large city and approach some well-established, reputable jewellery shops who offer a good selection of antique jewellery for sale. In London there are a few areas where you'll find such jewellers' shops. In any case, the antique dealer you consult will probably be able to recommend a good jewellery shop, if he or she isn't interested in buying the piece.

The other alternative is to take the jewellery to an auction room. Again, avoid the local auction rooms in your nearest market town; these might be perfectly all right for antique furniture, but jewellery is too highly specialised for anywhere but the big, nationally recognised ones. Auction rooms, though, are not always the best places to go in order to get a true picture of the value of your antique jewellery.

A dealer is probably safer because he or she will be buying and selling similar pieces on the open market every day, and will therefore be more conversant with prices on the open market. Auction rooms tend to invite wildly varying prices; how much you get for your piece can depend rather more on luck than on market value alone. So before you accept the auction room's idea of what price your piece should be 'reserved' at (the minimum amount you're willing to take for it), you should already be armed with an expert dealer's valuation as well. Normally, it is your right to say what the reserve price should be; the auction room people will help you if you don't know, but will not ordinarily argue with your own price unless you're being too greedy, or not greedy enough.

The only other bit of advice we can offer you on the subject of antique jewellery is never, ever have a piece broken up to be re-mounted, unless you're absolutely positive that it has no artistic or historical value. And even then, you'll probably wind up paying more for the remounting than the whole piece is actually worth. You wouldn't break up a piece of antique furniture to re-use the wood, would you? The same thinking applies to most antique items – jewellery in particular. The only reason a sane person will break up an antique piece is out of personal choice, provided that they don't mind wasting money. From an investment point of view, though, this is hardly ever worthwhile. If you don't like a piece of antique jewellery, you're far better off – in financial terms – to sell it for the best price you can get and then re-invest the money in a piece you do like. And even if you absolutely hate the piece in question, don't worry; people's tastes vary enormously. Someone else might like it well enough to pay you good money for it, if you're prepared to search around for that person.

The Tax Man Cometh

If you do buy jewellery for investment purposes – in other words, with the intention of selling it one day and making a profit – you must bear in mind that you may be liable to pay tax on that profit.

Of course, anyone who buys new jewellery (in most countries) will be paying a certain amount of tax included in the purchase price. The amount or percentage depends on which country you're talking about; the jeweller who sells you the piece will explain that to you on request. If you buy loose stones, or gold coins, the tax situation may be different – again, ask the person who is selling you the goods to explain, if you're curious! The price of second-hand and antique jewellery may include a lower amount of tax, or none at all, depending on the regulations of the country concerned.

But all that goes for any jewellery, whatever the reasons for buying it. If you buy it for keeps, then the only tax it is likely to incur after that is when you die and leave it to a friend or relation. Then it is likely to be considered as part of your 'estate', and your heirs will be liable to pay the relevant estate duty on the whole lot, jewellery included.

If you sell jewellery worth more than a certain amount, the amount the jewellery has appreciated in value during the time you've had it may be considered as unearned income and taxed as such. In the UK, this would come under the heading of Capital Gains Tax. Roughly speaking, this is calculated on the difference between the jewellery's value when you acquired it and its value when you come to sell it.

Other forms of tax and duty, in particular, are applicable when you buy jewellery abroad. There are no standard international practices in this area, though. The amounts and the differences – if any – between the tax on loose stones and made-up jewellery vary from country to country. If you want to buy valuable jewellery abroad, you should also bear in mind that you may have to pay rather more in tax than you would if you buy it at home. Although you may, as a foreigner, be able to buy the jewellery 'tax free' abroad (not always though!), you will normally have to pay duty on it when you bring it into your own country. That means that unless the purchase price in the foreign country was very low, jewellery bought in this way will not usually turn out to be much of a bargain at the end of the day.

It is unfortunate that we can't be more specific in this section, but tax laws change, and vary a lot from nation to nation. So any information that's correct at the time of going to press could be obsolete by the time you read this book. By far the best advice we can give you on the tax aspect of investment in jewellery is to contact an expert and ask. For jewellery bought and sold in your own country, your bank manager, an accountant, or your local tax office should be able to explain anything you want to know. For jewellery you buy abroad, your Customs and Excise people will tell you how you stand, and how much duty you should expect to pay. And let us say here that if you intend to buy jewellery on your next trip abroad, it is very wise to check up on the rules before you go – otherwise you could be in for a nasty shock when you declare your purchases at Customs on your way home!

Whilst we're on the subject of Customs, here's a small tip that may save you time and embarrassment if ever you're subjected to an inspection on your way into your country. Jewellery and watches, being small and easy to conceal, are extremely popular amongst dishonest types who smuggle goods into the country without paying duty. If a Customs Officer should be suspicious of you for whatever reason, he or she may well ask where you got your jewellery or watch – particularly if they look new. For this reason, you should try to carry the relevant receipts for all the jewellery you've got with you, showing where it was purchased. (This is also a good idea for fur coats and other valuables.) If you can prove straight way that your watch and jewellery were legitimately purchased in your own country, or if purchased abroad at an earlier date, that the correct duty was paid, it should save both you and the Customs Officer a great deal of time.

CHAPTER THIRTEEN

Keeping Your Jewellery Safe and Sound

Cleaning: The Do's and Don'ts

Keeping your jewellery clean and sparkling will enhance its looks and, to a certain extent, prolong its life. Bits of grit, grease and grime can eventually wear away a bit of gold, or scratch a stone. So regular cleaning should become a habit; once every now and then for jewellery you rarely wear, and once weekly for the pieces you wear every day. Don't forget to pay attention to the less obtrusive places as well, like the inside of rings, bracelets, earrings and necklaces. Quite apart from the aesthetic reasons (although the inside of a piece of jewellery doesn't really show) dirt and grime collected over a long period in these areas next to your skin could possibly cause an irritation or rash.

The greatest enemy of faceted, transparent stones is grease. For some strange reason (no doubt explicable in scientific terms) all types of grease and oil from your skin and elsewhere latch on to the backs of stones like a duck takes to water. This results in a film of grease all over the back of the stone, preventing the light from doing its job and so making the stone appear dull and unattractive.

You should, therefore, get rid of this greasy film with a thorough cleaning. Branded jewellery cleaning fluids are available in shops and stores and are quite effective – although they can be expensive. Far simpler, equally efficient materials can be found in your own kitchen and bathroom. Just collect together a litre of boiling water, a teaspoon of salt, an old soft toothbrush and some toothpaste. All you do is put the salt into a kitchen bowl and pour the boiling water over it. Then put in the pieces of jewellery you want to clean (stones and metal only!) and leave them for about ten minutes. A word of warning here; don't ever allow the water to boil while the jewellery is in it. After the time is up, take the jewellery out and rinse it under the tap. Then give it a little scrub with the toothbrush and some toothpaste, remembering to pay particular attention to the backs of the stones that lie closest to your skin. Rinse the jewellery again and then dry it on tissue paper. Easy, isn't it?

Most jewellery can be cleaned in this way, with the exception of turquoise, pearls and to a lesser extent opals. Also non-precious metals and some forms of costume jewellery should be kept away from hot salted water and toothpaste. Turquoise can easily be discoloured by soap, perspiration, cosmetics, perfume or acids, so you need to be very careful of bringing it into contact with any of these. Direct heat – even the heat from hot water – can also cause it damage and sometimes make it break up. So you should never get turquoise wet; just wipe it with a soft damp cloth. And always remember to remove a piece of turquoise jewellery before you wash your hands (if you're not at home, grip the piece in your teeth so you don't forget it) or take a bath.

Pearls can be damaged by all the things that damage turquoise. Oil can damage them, too. Pearls can even get scratched by rough fabric – so it's very important to keep them away from anything hard, both while you're wearing them and when they're stored away in your jewellery box. To clean them, use the same method as you use for turquoise – a soft damp cloth.

Opals absorb grease, as we said in Chapter Seven, and they're also susceptible to knocks and bashes. So you should wash them in tepid water and treat them with respect.

Although a lot of people use tissues (or paper handkerchiefs) for just about every imaginable purpose, you should keep them away from your jewellery. Tissues, as far as most jewellers are concerned, are only useful when you need to blow your nose. They tend to leave little bits of fluff on your jewellery, some of which can get caught in the claws of settings, and this can then be difficult to remove without loosening the claws.

To clean gold, use the same method as described above. Only be careful; over enthusiastic use of the toothbrush can scratch it, especially if it is softer gold (18 or 22 carat, for example), and if there are large expanses of smooth surfaces. Gold that could scratch or dull easily is best cleaned with a bit of toothpaste on a kitchen dishcloth that's first been rinsed in very hot water. But you'll certainly need to use the brush if there are ornate or fancy bits on the piece. And a toothbrush is ideal to clean the links of a chain – simply place the chain, crumpled up, in the palm of one hand and scrub gently with the brush held in the other. You'll be surprised how effective this is;

chains that you wear round your neck and arm get very dirty, and after a good scrub using this method you'll find they look quite different.

Silver jewellery differs from gold or platinum in that it tarnishes. And one of the best ways to keep silver jewellery looking attractive is to wear it a lot; this can actually slow down the tarnishing process. Constant wear will also give silver a rich 'patina' or sheen, all of its own. Tarnishing will occur in time, though, no matter how much you wear the silver. It will happen faster if the silver comes into contact with salt, smoke, gases, egg or rubber. Often a regular wash in hot, soapy water, a thorough rinse and a polish with a soft cloth is enough to keep the tarnishing at bay. But if the piece gets really dirty, you'll need to clean it with one of the branded silver polishes you can buy in most grocery, hardware and other general shops. Follow the manufacturer's instructions carefully. If the piece has a stone or stones set into it, be careful not to get any polish on them as the strong chemicals may cause damage or dullness. A little polish on an old, soft toothbrush will remove tarnish from the nooks and crannies of more ornate pieces. Once you've finished polishing the silver, it's a good idea to give it a wash afterwards in hot, soapy water, followed by a rinse in hot clear water, and a final polish with a soft cloth. If you don't do all this, some bits of silver polish might dry and cling to the jewellery – which can make it look dull and could even cause some sort of skin irritation.

Repairs: The Time for Experts

We have only one word to say about people who feel they can repair their own precious jewellery; don't! Costume jewellery, where the metal is extremely soft and isn't usually soldered (it's just bent into shape) can be repaired using a pair of pliers and a nail file, as long as you're careful. But precious metals like gold, silver and platinum, need to be soldered, in ninety-nine cases out of a hundred. Even if you happen to have a blow torch handy in your kitchen drawer, only an expert can do the job without any risk. And that risk becomes much greater where stones are involved; heating up the jewellery item to the point where the gold melts – so it can be soldered – can result in the stone breaking up. Some stones, of course, are hard enough to stand the strain, but some are not. In fact, we thought you might like to know which stones are harder and which are softer, so we've included a table below that describes each of the more popular gems. This system of measuring hardness was devised by a certain Mr Moh, a household name in jewellery circles, and not surprisingly his method is called 'the Moh scale of hardness'. Here the list has been extended to show metals and other substances as well, just for the sake of comparison. But before you read on, let us repeat; this is for your information only – please don't experiment with repairing your jewellery!

The Moh scale is worked out on the basis of one to ten, with ten being the hardest possible substance (diamond) and one being very soft indeed. Some say that ten, in other words a diamond (there is no comparable substance in terms of hardness) is actually very much harder than nine, and that if the true proportions were quoted, diamond would come out at some figure nearer twenty on the scale. However, this is the way Mr Moh worked it out, and as the method is used as a yardstick pretty well everywhere in the world, who are we to suggest changes?

The Moh Scale of Hardness

Diamond 10	Lapis Lazuli 5–6
Ruby/Sapphire 9	Turquoise 5–6
Synthetic ruby/sapphire 9	Natural glass 5½
Spinel 8	Tooth enamel 5
Synthetic spinel 8	(just for comparison!)
Topaz 8	Palladium 4½
Emerald 7½–8	Iron 4–5
Synthetic emerald 7½–8	Platinum 4–4½
Aquamarine 7½–8	Brass 4
Garnet 7½	Coral 3½
Zircon 7–7½	Jet 3–4
Tourmaline 7–7½	Pearl 2½–4
Quartz 7	Ivory 2½
Peridot 6½–7	Tortoiseshell 2½–3
Jade 6½–7	Silver 2–2½
Marcasite 6–6½	Amber 2–2½
Hematite 5½–6½	Gold 2–2½
Opal 5½–6½	Plastic 1½–3
Glass 5–6¾	Lead 1½
Strontium Titanate 5–6	(as in pencil!)
(imitation diamond)	

Getting back to the question of repairs, you're much better off to go to your local jeweller. He or she may well not have a repair shop on the premises, but will undoubtedly be able to either recommend the best place, or send the jewellery item away to a repairer on your behalf. If you can't achieve success by asking your jeweller, however, you'll find a selection of goldsmiths in your 'yellow pages' or business section of the telephone directory. These are the craftspeople who are trained to make and repair precious metal, and if properly qualified, will do the job safely and well. The only trouble with looking people up in telephone directories, without knowing them, is that you can't be sure how good they are. That's why it is better to get advice from your jeweller, rather than going directly to the goldsmith.

Avoiding Repairs in the First Place

Naturally enough, the best way to avoid damaging your jewellery is quite simply not to wear it. But that's ridiculous, of course. The only way you're going to get real pleasure from your jewellery is by wearing it. On the other hand, though, there are certain things which you should avoid, if you are wearing a particularly precious jewellery item, or perhaps an antique piece with very delicate mountings or settings. One of those things is rough or woolly clothing; if you catch a claw from a stone setting in the fabric, a sharp wrench can be enough to bend the claw. This can eventually cause the stone to fall out.

Most safety precautions in this area are just a question of common sense, really. Active occupations, like driving a car or doing the garden can be very hard on jewellery, even if it is just plain metal. Changing gear, turning the steering wheel, or operating any kind of machinery, are all cases where your jewellery can easily become damaged. You need to use your discretion – and perhaps think twice about wearing valuable jewellery when you're about to do anything that involves heavy physical activity.

Jewellery can even be damaged when it's stored in your jewellery box. If one stone rubs against another stone that's a lot softer, for example, a diamond rubbing up against a pearl, the harder one can do the softer one a mischief. You should keep anything that could be damaging well separated in your jewellery box; refer to the Moh scale of hardness if you want to know what's harder than what! The interior of your box or case should be lined with some soft fabric, like velvet or satin. Man-made fibres tend to be hard and scratchy – so avoid them. The case should be big enough so that items like chains and link bracelets can be laid flat, allowing them to 'rest' – alleviating any strain. Obviously, strain that could be placed on jewellery in a box would take years to show any effect, but it can make a difference, especially if the piece is very delicate.

Valuations: What's Good Value?

Before we go on to talk about where and how to get valuations done, it is worth mentioning the different types of valuation – for those of you who don't already know. The valuation you get depends on what you need the valuation for, and the different types vary quite a lot. This is not 'dishonest', in any way; it's just that different sets of circumstances demand different values.

The first type of valuation is for insurance purposes. This will value your jewellery item at the highest price of all, because for proper insurance cover you have got to take into consideration that not only will you need to replace your item if it gets lost, but you may not have the opportunity to shop around for the cheapest replacement. So, the insurance valuation will be as high as necessary to ensure that your item could be replaced at even the most expensive of jewellery shops. Then you have the straight replacement valuation. This is usually the exact price you paid for the piece, which means that it could be replaced at the same shop, at the same time, but if you don't update your valuation regularly this one could fall behind the times. After that comes the valuation of the resale price – in other words, the amount of money you could expect to get if you were to sell the piece. This will be lower than the replacement value, because of the regrettable fact that you never get as much for a piece of jewellery if you see it as you would pay out when buying the item new. This last form of valuation would be the type you would get were you to approach someone with a view to selling your jewellery; it states what your piece is worth on the seller's market. Lastly, in most countries there is valuation for probate. This happens when someone dies, and the whole of that person's estate must be valued either for estate duty purposes or, if the heirs want to know the deceased's total worth. Obviously, there is a certain amount of overlap amongst all these types of valuation. The important thing to remember when you're having a valuation done is to tell the person who is doing it the exact reasons why you need it. That way they can judge their valuation accordingly.

Where to get your valuation done is quite a tricky problem – in the UK at least. In this country, it is not necessary for a person to have any particular qualifications as a valuer of jewellery (at the time of going to press). Valuations can be undertaken by anyone who is a jeweller, whether or not he or she is even qualified as a gemologist or other connected subject. Obviously, the majority of jewellers who do valuations are experienced and knowledgeable at their jobs and are therefore suitably expert. The trouble is, you don't know for certain. In some European countries – notably Belgium and Holland – valuers actually have to pass an examination set by the government, and be 'sworn in' before they can do valuations on an official basis. Norbert, one of us co-authors, is qualified in this way under Dutch law. But the UK has yet to establish any such formalised qualification.

The other problem concerning valuations is that, in the UK at any rate, you are charged a fee which is a percentage of the total value of your jewellery. This means that if you own a ring worth £100, you'll pay, say, one per cent of its value – £1. But if that ring is worth £1,000, you'll pay £10. And yet it doesn't require any more work on the valuer's part to value one ring than the other. Once again, some other countries have a different practice, which is to charge a standard fee for each item or group of items, regardless of their value; Norbert has introduced this for valuations in his London showroom. At the time of going to press very few other jewellery valuers in the UK have taken up the new way of charging people, but it would seem that it will eventually catch on. Of course, you can understand the thinking behind the old-fashioned method; people who own very valuable jewellery should be able to afford a higher valuation charge than someone with low-value items. But, in this day of increasing fairness to consumers, the new method does seem better. Let's hope that in time it will be adopted everywhere.

Having said all this, then, where do you go to get your valuation done? Well, take your jewellery to the biggest town in your area and preferably to the best and most well-established jeweller. Ask to speak with the manager, or the person who is in charge of valuations, if there is one, and then be sure to tell that person exactly why you need the valuation – whether it is for insurance purposes, for re-sale, or whatever. The valuer will then give you (or possibly send you through the post) a typewritten valuation on their headed notepaper. This is acceptable for most purposes, including insurance.

Insurance: A Question of Values

Hopefully, those of you who own jewellery will already have it insured, and will know exactly how your insurance policies work. But for those of you who aren't clear about the ins and outs of insurance – and Heaven forbid, for those of you who have no insurance at all – we've gathered together a few facts on the subject.

In the UK, jewellery belonging to an individual is normally insured under an 'all risks' policy, that is stuck on to the end of your household insurance. Now, for those amongst you who don't happen to own households, don't worry! A household insurance can be as small as a policy that covers the contents of a rented bed-sit or studio apartment. The important thing to remember, though, is that insurance companies, on the whole, are not wildly keen on insuring a few jewellery items on their own. These are the things that are most likely to go missing, for whatever reason, and as such are a 'bad risk'. Apart from one or two insurance companies, the majority will not be interested in taking on jewellery unless they can have your household business as well. So, to insure jewellery under a separate policy will be difficult to do – and even if you manage to find an insurance company to take it on, it will cost you.

If that sounds threatening, in reality it isn't. There aren't many of us who live out of suitcases in the street. Nearly everyone has a home, somewhere, even if it is modest. And regardless of where you live, it is only common sense to insure not just your jewellery, but your other valuables, like radios, television sets, record players, clothing and personal bits and pieces. Fire or burglary (see later on in this chapter) can happen to anyone. And all those items listed above are just the things that will fall prey to either of the two disasters. Hence, the household policy; it covers the whole lot, and more besides.

An all risks policy takes over where the household policy leaves off. The household policy covers your goods when they are in your home, and all risk covers them when you go out. Something of an oversimplification, as any insurance person will tell you, but basically true! In an all risks policy, you usually have to list and describe individual items over a certain value; like more valuable jewellery, fur coats and so on. This is where valuations come in, as they will be required by the insurance company for items exceeding the specified value. For less valuable things they're normally willing to take your word for it. This is not as generous an attitude as you might think; it you over-value your jewellery, you'll pay a higher premium than you need, and if you under-value it, you won't get as much as you should if you claim for loss, theft, or whatever. Some insurance companies will accept your own personal valuation for anything, regardless of value, but will insist that you substantiate this at the time you make a claim. The answer to that one is, even if your particular insurance company doesn't require a valuation, get one done anyway. It's money well spent, because you then know you're not likely to get caught out if your jewellery is lost or stolen. Once a piece of jewellery is gone – especially when it is a piece of sentimental as well as financial value – you can't normally get it back. But it is always a comfort to know that you'll at least receive enough money from your insurance to buy another, similar item to replace it.

Once your jewellery is properly insured, then, you mustn't just forget all about it and casually ignore precautions. As an insured person, you have a duty to the insurance company to 'behave as if uninsured'. This doesn't mean that you have to carry your jewellery around with you under lock and key the whole time – the severity of the statement is largely jargon! But you must avoid doing things like taking your rings off when you wash your hands (either leave rings on, or else grip them in your teeth – never put them down in a public lavatory because you may forget them), and wearing jewellery you know to be loose or damaged. The insurance companies only expect you to look after your jewellery properly and not take any unreasonable chances, which is fair enough. They expect you to take simple precautions at home, too, like putting your jewellery away in a safe place when you go to bed – not leaving it on the window ledge when the window's open, where a dishonest passer-by could easily grab it.

If you do lose a piece of jewellery, it is normally a condition of your insurance policy that you should report it to the police within 24 hours. Most people will automatically report a burglary to the police, but many don't think of calling the Law when they simply lose something. It isn't just a formality, either; someone may have found the piece of jewellery and turned it in at the nearest police station. It makes sense. Once you're done that, you should telephone your insurance company or broker and tell them what's happened, so they can send you a claims form. When that arrives, you fill it out, and as long as everything's in order you'll get the money in due course.

One thing your insurance company may want to see if you make a claim is a receipt for the item concerned. This will probably be quite separate from a valuation. So keep all receipts for jewellery when you buy it, and unromantic though it is, you should ask for a copy of the receipt even when someone gives you a piece of jewellery. Insurance companies can't afford to be romantic. And if you lose your engagement ring, they'll want to see the receipt even though you'd rather not know how much it cost, or don't attach any significance to the price tag if you do know how much it cost. You see, sometimes the insurance company will want some sort of evidence to prove that you actually owned the lost item. And if it is a piece below a certain value, that doesn't require a valuation, a receipt is just about the only bit of paper you can produce to prove ownership. Although insurance companies would like to be trusting and take your word for it, circumstances have forced them into being more cautious.

If you buy a new piece of jewellery, you should always contact your insurance company or broker and tell them about it. Even if the piece is below the value that requires individual description and valuation, it may be wise to increase the amount you're covered for on your household and/or all risks policy. It is up to your insurer or broker to tell you whether or not this is necessary; but if you don't find out from them in the first place and the piece is lost, you may be at a disadvantage.

One of the most important things to remember about insuring your jewellery is that values go up. A great many people suffer from a disease described by insurance companies as 'under-insurance' – because they don't realise how much the value of their jewellery has increased in a given period, and therefore they find themselves without enough cover. With the price of gold and precious stones going up in leaps and bounds every year, a piece of jewellery that is properly covered when it is bought may be vastly under-valued by the time two years have passed. To say that you should have your jewellery revalued every year is perhaps an exaggeration. But you should have it done every other year, if you want to be correctly insured at all times. And you could even circumnavigate the need for formal valuation if your local jeweller knows you well, and knows your jewellery well too. Because once your jeweller has valued your items initially, he or she can then estimate by how much that value goes up in a year or two – and may well be prepared to tell you to increase cover by X%, rather than go through the whole valuation process once again. As a general rule, though, you really ought to have all your jewellery properly valued once every five years at least. Not only do values go up, but fashions change. An item that was not particularly fashionable – and consequently not so valuable – in year one, might have come back into fashion and be worth a lot by year five.

Although your premiums will go up in proportion to the rise in the value of your jewellery, bear in mind that it is only you who will lose out if something is lost or stolen. Being under-insured may save you a comparatively small amount on your premiums, but will lose you a lot if something goes wrong.

Holidays – Avoiding the Headaches

Holiday insurance is something a lot of people leave to the last minute, or worse still, leave altogether. Very often, too, people will simply take the holiday insurance offered to them by the holiday company or tour operator who is organising the trip. This is fine, but normally the cover you get with these policies is limited to the loss of a fairly small amount per item. If you do not intend to take any valuable jewellery abroad with you, in other words no single item worth more than the limit stated in the small print of the holiday company's policy, then you're OK. But if you want to take a valuable ring or watch to look dazzling with your sun tan, then telephone your insurance company or broker. For a relatively small outlay your household and all risks policies can normally be extended to cover you while you're away. As long as you itemise the pieces of jewellery you'll be taking with you, you're covered as well in Timbuktu as you are in your home town. Some household policies and all risk policies even cover you for a certain amount of time abroad, included in your annual premium. So you may not even have to pay more. But it is sensible to check this out before you go. The only conditions your insurance company might impose are that you 'behave as if uninsured', in other words, take no unnecessary risks; you may be asked to put your jewellery in the hotel safe when you're not wearing it, too. That is, assuming you're staying in an hotel!

If you do lose a piece of jewellery while you're on holiday, the same procedure as you follow at home usually applies. You must report the loss to the local police, and then contact your broker or insurance company when you get home so they can send you a claims form.

Banking on Safety

If you own certain pieces of jewellery that you seldom wear, it would seem silly to keep them in your home and pay comparatively high insurance premiums for the privilege. It's far better to put the jewellery into a safety deposit box at your bank, because that way the premium you'll pay for insuring it while it's in there will be far lower. When you take a piece of jewellery out of the bank, say, for a special occasion you must notify your insurance company or broker. You'll then probably pay a small amount of extra premium for the time the piece is out of the bank. For the items of jewellery that you only wear once a year, or pieces that, say, you've inherited and retain only for sentimental or investment reasons, the bank's a far better, safer and cheaper place to keep them.

Watch Out, There's a Thief About

The classic remark most people make when anyone suggests that they could be burgled is, 'but it could never happen to me'. Wrong. It could. Especially if you live in a city or town, or any urban area, where strange people can walk about unnoticed. In a small village, you might be safer; most strangers are noticed. And someone lurking around your door with evil intent will probably be spotted by a friendly neighbour. But even so, it's never worth taking the chance. A bit of time and effort on your part, and possibly a certain amount of money on good locks and other precautions, can mean that you protect your jewellery and other valuables against disappearing in the hands of a crook. Even if your jewellery isn't worth a lot of money, it is probably worth a lot in sentimental value. So it's still worth protecting. And no matter how insignificant you think your jewellery and other valuables are, remember that to most burglars *anything* is worth stealing.

Before we go any further, let's take a look at an average, run-of-the-mill crook. He (or she, in this age of equal opportunities) is, in about 80% of cases, what the police call the 'opportunist' burglar – someone who just hangs around street corners, waiting for an opportunity to slip into someone's house or flat and whip whatever he can in the shortest possible time. And time is the most important thing in the opportunist burglar's career; the quicker he can get in, grab whatever he can, and get out again, the less chance he stands of getting noticed. So the moral in this story is that the longer it takes for a burglar to get into your house and rob you, the less likely he is to try and steal from you in the first place.

In other words, you must take precautions. Safeguarding your home does not necessarily mean you have to barricade it up like Fort Knox. What you need to do is to make sure it will take your neighbourhood crook quite a lot of time to get into your house or flat. And it's no good installing lots of time-consuming deterrents unless you use them every single time you go out the door. A large percentage of minor burglaries occur during the day, when housewives have gone shopping or to take their children to or from school. These people innocently believe that it will be all right to leave the door unlocked just for five minutes. Or even locked, but not double locked. And yet, five minutes is an eternity to the opportunist burglar. Most of these characters can help themselves to a worthwhile armful of goodies, including your jewellery, in as little as 90 seconds.

As an experiment, come in your own front door and go straight to your bedroom or living room. Time yourself; and see just how much you can pick up and stuff into a plastic bag in a minute and a half. You'll be surprised at the amount you can collect. And that's amateur behaviour, compared to the amount an accomplished burglar can take. Don't be consoled by the fact that you've hidden your valuables, either. You can rest assured, if you've thought of good hiding places for things like money or jewellery, the burglar will have thought of them too. And he'll be attracted to them as quickly as a wasp is attracted to an open jam pot.

Obviously, this little picture we've painted sounds horribly depressing. It is. In 1979 there were over 68,500 private homes burgled in London alone. Out of that number, many took place without forced entry – in other words, the burglar let himself in by slipping the lock with a bit of plastic, opening an unlocked window, or whatever. So the chances of it happening to you are pretty much in favour of the burglars; and there's no way in which you can give yourself 100% protection. Nobody's valuables – and that includes jewellery in particular, because it is easy to carry and easy to sell, which makes it extremely popular amongst thieves – are utterly safe.

To strike a happier note, then, let's get back to the one important precaution you can take. This is to make your home as difficult to get into as possible, so that anyone who tries will have to take a conspicuously long time about it. Fortunately for honest citizens, the time element is so important to opportunist burglars that they will normally avoid trying to get into a house if it looks like taking them too long. They'll just move along the road to another house that's much easier. And until such time as everyone becomes burglary conscious, there will *always* be another house up the road that is easy to get into.

In order to think of the right way in which to protect your home from burglars, you really need to put yourself in a burglar's shoes. Pretend that you wanted to get into your house while it was unoccupied. How would you go about it? Well, obviously you'd try all the doors and windows on the ground floor, if it was a house or ground floor flat. That's the best place to start. You'd try the small ventilation windows in the kitchen or bathroom – even if they're too small to climb through, you could possibly get your arm through and open the catch of a bigger window. Out in your back garden, you'd look around for a ladder so you could climb up to that conveniently open first floor window. Or you'd have a look in an unlocked garden shed, to see if there were any tools with which you could bash a door or window down (after all, in a quiet back garden, who would be suspicious of someone working with a shovel or hammer?). Then you'd look around to see if there was a bathroom window open – often the case – so you could shin up the nearby drain pipe. Bathrooms nearly always have a handy drain pipe very close to the windows – just the job for an agile burglar. After that, you might take a look and see if someone's left a window open near a nice, flat roof that you could easily climb on to. Of course, you'd stick your arm through the letterbox at the front door, to see if you could open the inside latch from there. And you'd look under the dustbins, under the doormat, through the letterbox to see if there's a string behind it, all the places where well-meaning people leave spare keys. Or you could find an upstairs window that just happens to have been left open so pet pussy cat can enter and leave at will.

But before you actually started to check out the possibilities in the house or flat itself, you might have observed the place for a while. You'd have noticed whether or not there were milk bottles collecting on the doorstep. You'd have checked the letterbox to see if there was a lot of mail piled up behind it. You'd have taken a look in the garden to see if the lawn had been mowed, the leaves swept up, or whatever the right horticultural maintenance had been done. All of these things, you see, tell the burglar if there's anyone in the house – or if you are away on holiday. Even if the garage doors are open, revealing that there no cars inside, or the curtains are closed in the middle of the day, or you've heard people chatting in the pub about someone's lovely holidays they've just departed for, you might get the hint that there's no-one at home. If you'd been watching the place at night, you might have noticed dark rooms with the curtains drawn back – and who's going to sit indoors with open curtains and no lights on? Another thing you might do is to check the front and back doors and read a note addressed to someone else, saying that the householder will be back at a certain time. Great, you'd think, that gives me plenty of time to get in and empty the place.

Now these points may seem glaringly obvious to you. They certainly are obvious to the crime prevention officers in the police – because it is just tips like these, left by absent-minded people, that allow so many burglaries to happen. And yet, we are all guilty of letting those very things go by from time to time. We think, 'oh well, it's not going to happen now'. And that's usually when it does happen. Sadly, you've got to think like a burglar in order to anticipate one. And each time you go anywhere, even if it's to the local shop or to post a letter, you must make sure you've taken all the possible precautions. Otherwise, you're a sitting duck every time.

Inside your house, it's a slightly different story. The important thing in all truth is to deter burglars from the outside – so that for them to get in will be as noisy, time-consuming and conspicuous as possible. That involves having correct locks fitted to your doors and windows – which your insurance company or broker, or local police crime prevention officer, will advise on. But getting back to the inside, there is only one safe place to keep your jewellery and other valuables, in the bank. That's right; completely away from your home. Because the trouble is, once a burglar manages to get into your home, he can afford to sit back and relax a bit. He's far less likely to be seen or heard once he's inside. In a sense, it is almost unwise to put things into locked drawers and cupboards, and to lock interior doors, because the burglar is hardly a person who'll care about the looks of your home. He will simply kick, bash, punch and thrash his way through whatever barrier he can, possibly causing you greater expense in damage than you would actually incur through the loss of your possessions.

Naturally, not everyone wants to keep jewellery in the bank, and so the second best alternative is to have a small safe that's either sunk into a solid floor, or in a wall, or else a good, heavy, free-standing type – so the burglar will give himself a hernia if he tries to lift that into his plastic bag. In any case, your insurance company may well insist that you install a safe, especially if you happen to own more valuable jewellery. In many instances, the insurance people will also recommend what type of safe you ought to use; which one is recommended depends on how much jewellery you have, and how secure the insurance people feel it ought to be. But whatever you do, don't put your jewellery in potentially dangerous places – like the woman who bought a huge diamond and took it home with her. Because she had no safe, and couldn't think of a suitable place to put her acquisition, she placed it in her deep freezer. A good security precaution, she thought; no burglar would think of looking there, in amongst the frozen peas and ice cubes. A few days later she decided to take the diamond out of its hiding place and give it a good wash under the hot tap. Not surprisingly, the acute difference in temperature caused it to break. The jeweller to whom she returned it the next day found the stone cracked in several places – and naturally enough didn't feel the need to give her the money back once he'd heard the story! If you don't have a safe, you should still try to keep your jewellery under some sort of lock and key. Remember, the more time consuming barriers you create between the burglar and your valuables – both indoors and out – the more likely he is to lose his nerve and run away without having stolen anything. He may bash a few of the barriers down, but he may not have the courage to continue, if there are more barriers than he feels he has time for.

It's always a good idea to write down the exact details of all your jewellery, and keep the list in a safe place – *away* from your jewellery box! Note down what metal it is, how many carats or parts of a thousand in gold, the hallmarks and what they say – particularly the initials of the maker, if there are any on the piece – where the hallmarks are, and any other distinguishing features, like sizing marks and scratches. In the case of stones, note down the type, colour, and size. With pearl necklaces, count the number of pearls and note the description and any hallmarks that may be on the clasp. All these details will make life a lot easier for the police, if ever you are burgled; your chances of the stolen goods being recovered are always slim, but with detailed descriptions the police stand a better chance of getting your jewellery back. Photographs of each important piece, preferably in colour, are also a good idea for the same reason.

Unfortunately, the golden rule among opportunist burglars is to snatch first and ask questions later. They won't always be selective when they steal your valuables; they'll just grab what they can and look through it at leisure once they're safely away. And they'll never hand in what they don't want at the nearest police station. Even items of jewellery or other precious things that they don't fancy, or don't feel they can sell easily, will just be chucked into the nearest pond, river or rubbish dump. So don't think you can forget about jewellery items that you believe aren't worth stealing; they may not be. But they'll be stolen anyway, and if they're not worth it, they'll be discarded later on when the thief has had time to think about it.

Remember, too, that some burglars are cheeky enough to sneak in when you're at home. So if you're watching television, or working in the garden, make sure that everything's secure – especially doors and windows a long way from where you are. Always lock doors and windows at night, when you go to bed. You may not think you're a sound sleeper, but burglars can work very quietly indeed. Another thing to watch out for is strange callers at your door. When someone like this turns up, ask to see their identification – in most countries, they're obliged to show it to you on demand – and don't let them in unless you're quite happy. Otherwise you could find that the person who is supposed to be reading your electricity meter is actually stuffing your valuables into his briefcase while you're in the kitchen making him a cup of coffee.

If ever you should disturb a burglar in your home, forget about being a hero. It's just not worth it. The majority of burglars are non-violent, as long as they're not interrupted. But remember, someone who is burgling your house or flat – hardened criminal or not – is going to be pretty tense and strung up. So it won't take a great deal of provocation to turn what could be a simple burglary into a full scale assault – and you may get hurt into the bargain, particularly if you corner the burglar. Whatever you do, don't try to prevent the burglar from escaping; that's asking for trouble, as he may panic and lose control completely. Also, in some countries *you* may be prosecuted if you injure or shoot at someone who has illegally entered your home; just because the person steals your possessions doesn't automatically give you the right to blow his brains out. It's far better to stay cool, try to sneak to a telephone without being noticed, and call the police. If you do come face to face with the burglar, try to stay calm and do what he says – don't upset him. That can also cause him to panic and give rise to violence. Whatever the value you place on your jewellery and other personal things, they're never worth risking a scar on your face, or even the loss of your life. Most police forces recommend that you try to keep the crime being committed as uncomplicated as possible – even if it means watching the so-and-so run off down the street with your valuables. That, at least, is better than watching the so-and-so run off with your valuables having thumped you on the nose as well. One thing you must try to do, though, is to get as good a description of the burglar as you can – remember every detail. This will help the police a lot.

As soon as you realise that you've been burgled, phone the police straight away. Minutes count with crime detection, and the sooner the police can get enquiries going the better. They may not succeed in getting your belongings back, but at least they may catch the person concerned – and so prevent him from burgling someone else. Similarly, don't hesitate to call the police if you see someone suspicious lurking around your neighbour's house or flat; the police won't mind even if it does turn out to be the milkman on his rounds. On the contrary; they, and of course your neighbour, will appreciate your concern. And after all, you'd appreciate it if someone stopped a burglary happening at your home in the same way, wouldn't you?

To end on a more cheerful note, by concentrating your efforts on making your home secure, it may never happen. Don't make the mistake of rushing out to buy expensive locks and bolts without seeking professional advice first. If you don't know which locks represent the best value and are the most secure for your type of home, telephone or visit your nearest police station. They will arrange for a crime prevention officer to come round and see you for no charge. He is a trained expert in security and will give you the best possible unbiased advice; he may well save you money, too. For example, you may not need new locks; you may just need to make a few cheap alterations and keep the locks you already have. Although latch locks – the types you can flip back from the outside using a bit of plastic – are next to useless; five lever deadlocking mortices are best for most of your doors. Windows, at least on the ground floor, should have locks on them as well – especially if you live in an urban area. And a chain on your front door is highly recommended, so you can shut the door on unwanted visitors without their being able to push it open first. The crime prevention officer from your local police station will take a look at your whole property – including things like garden gates and fences – and help you to create as many time-consuming burglar deterrents as possible. Your local police station can also give you some useful details which explain in graphic detail how to make your home, your car, your caravan, etc., as secure as you can.